Oracle Press

Oracle Database 11g: A Beginner's Guide

Ian Abramson
Michael Abbey
Michael J. Corey
Michelle Malcher

Mc
Graw
Hill

New York   Chicago   San Francisco
Lisbon   London   Madrid   Mexico City   Milan
New Delhi   San Juan   Seoul   Singapore   Sydney   Toronto

The McGraw·Hill Companies

Cataloging-in-Publication Data is on file with the Library of Congress

Oracle Database 11g: A Beginner's Guide

1234567890 FGR FGR 0198

ISBN 978-0-07-160459-8
MHID   0-07-160459-6

Sponsoring Editor	**Indexer**
Lisa McClain	Jerilyn Sproston
Editorial Supervisor	**Production Supervisor**
Janet Walden	Jean Bodeaux
Project Editor	**Composition**
Laura Stone	Apollo Publishing Services
Acquisitions Coordinators	**Illustration**
Jennifer Housh, Mandy Canales	Kathleen Edwards, Melinda Lytle
Technical Editors	**Art Director, Cover**
Carl Dudley, Ted Falcon	Jeff Weeks
Copy Editor	**Cover Designer**
Julie M. Smith	Pattie Lee
Proofreader	
Paul Tyler	

This book is dedicated to all those who have
helped us learn and become better professionals.
We share this with all of you.

About the Authors

Ian Abramson is the current president for the Independent Oracle Users Group (IOUG). Based in Toronto, Canada, he is an experienced industry and technical consultant, providing expert guidance in implementing solutions for clients in telecommunications, CRM, utilities, and other industries. His focus includes the Oracle product set, as well as other leading technologies and their use in optimizing data warehouse design and deployment. He is also a regular speaker at various technology conferences, including COLLABORATE, Oracle OpenWorld, and other local and regional events.

Michael Abbey is a recognized authority on database administration, installation, development, application migration, performance tuning, and implementation. Working with Ian Abramson and Michael Corey, he has coauthored works in the Oracle Press series for over 14 years. Active in the international Oracle user community, Abbey is a frequent presenter at COLLABORATE, Oracle OpenWorld, and regional user group meetings.

Michael J. Corey is the founder and CEO of Ntirety—The Database Administration Experts. Michael's roots go back to Oracle version 3.0. Michael is a past president of the Independent Oracle Users group (www.ioug.org) and the original Oracle Press author. Michael is a frequent speaker at business and technology events and has presented all over the world. Check out Michael's blog at http://michaelcorey.ntirety.com.

Michelle Malcher is a Senior Database Administrator with over ten years' experience in database development, design, and administration. She has expertise in performance tuning, security, data modeling, and database architecture of very large database environments. She is a contributing author for the IOUG Best Practices Tip Booklet. Michelle is enthusiastically involved with the Independent Oracle User Group and is director of Special Interest Groups. She enjoys presenting and sharing ideas about Oracle Database topics at technology conferences and user group meetings. She can be reached at michelle_malcher@ioug.org.

About the Reviewers

Carl Dudley has worked closely with Oracle for a number of years and presents regularly at international conferences on Oracle database technology. He is currently a consultant database administrator and has research interests in database performance, disaster planning, and security. Carl is a director of the UK Oracle User Group, received *Oracle Magazine*'s Editors' Choice Award for Database Administrator of the Year in 2003 for services to the Oracle community, and achieved Oracle ACE status in 2007.

Ted Falcon, based in Toronto, Canada, is CEO of BDR Business Data Reporting Inc. He has ten years' experience in business intelligence reporting systems, specializing in the Cognos suite of tools.

Contents

Acknowledgments

an Abramson: I would like to thank all of those who are part of my life and who have been part of this great adventure. I would like to thank my family: my wife, Susan, is my true partner who puts up with me being me; and of course my two joys in life, my daughters Baila and Jillian—they have become two wonderful and intelligent women, and I am so proud and expect that their dreams will all be within their reach. To my friends, the people who are part of my everyday journey and whom I am so lucky to have as part of my life: Michael Brown, Chris Clarke, Marc Allaire, Marshall Lucatch, Jim Boutin, Kevin Larose, Al Murphy, Ken Sheppard, Terry Butts, Andrew Allaire, Mark Kerzner, Michael Abbey, Michael Corey, Ted Falcon, Moti Fishman, Tom Tishler, Carol McGury and everyone at the IOUG, and Jack Chadirdjian—you are all an important part of my life, and I am honored to know each of you and call you all friends.

Michael Abbey: Thanks to my wife, Sandy; and my children, Ben, Naomi, Nathan, and Jordan; as well as two new-found wonders of my life—a granddaughter named Annabelle and a daughter-in-law Lindsay.

Michael Corey: Special thanks to my friend, Ian Abramson, whose hard work and efforts made this book happen.

Michelle Malcher: I would like to thank my junior DBAs, Mandy and Emily, for their fun breaks from work to enjoy life. Thanks to my husband for putting up with the long hours I spend sitting in front of a computer. Special thanks to Ian Abramson for getting me involved with this book and his support and encouragement. Thanks to all involved in the IOUG; keep sharing ideas and working with each other to sharpen each others' skills and grow careers.

Ted Falcon: I would like to acknowledge those people whose love and support have allowed me to get to where I am today. First and foremost are my wife, Vanessa; and our 3 children, Mya, Matthew, and Noah. Thank you for everything that you do to enrich and fulfill my life. I love you all more than you know. To my parents, Mel and Tita, thank you for your continued guidance and love. To my brother, Adrian, our battles on the basketball court are legendary. Your quest to one day beat me is inspiring. I love you, little brother. To my huge extended family, thank you for your love and support. To my friends—you are all family, especially Bruha. To my friend Garth Gray, who guided me through the halls of U of T Scarborough and to this crazy world of IT. Thank you for the advice, the support, and the drives down to ITI. Finally, to my friends and colleagues whom I've met throughout my career, especially Ian Abramson; thank you for your friendship, guidance, Raptor tickets, and for allowing me to be a part of this book.

Introduction

he release of Oracle Database 11*g* is one that comes with much anticipation. We are at a time when data is exploding and the cost of operations must be reduced. Oracle 11*g* is a release that addresses many of these concerns and provides a database that can help organizations move forward without boundaries. With the release of *Oracle Database 11g: A Beginner's Guide*, we bring back together the Abramson, Abbey, and Corey team that has been writing these books for over 13 years. That time slice is pale compared to the length of time the Oracle database software has been embracing the information highway. Recently Oracle celebrated its 30th anniversary with the customary hoopla and fanfare…justifiably so.

One cannot rub shoulders with fellow information technologists without experiencing Oracle's technology, and quite a piece of technology it is! In the beginning, there was a database, and then came development tools. The Oracle product line added components at an ever more accelerating rate. This book is all about the foundation underneath just about everything running the Oracle technology stack—the database. Regardless of what corner of the technology you work with, being familiar with the underpinnings of the database technology makes you a better practitioner.

Where has Oracle been, and where is it going? The former question is not that hard to answer, the latter a mystery until it unfolds. In 1979 we saw the first commercial SQL RDBMS offering from a new company in Redwood Shores, California—Software Development Laboratories. Close to two years later, the company morphed into Relational Software, Inc. in Menlo Park, not far from its origin. The VAX hardware platform was the initial home of the database offering. The rest of the story of this company, now known as Oracle Corporation, is revolutionary—all the way from the first read-consistent database (1984), through its first full suite of applications (1992), to the first web database offering (1997). The calendar year 2000 saw the first Internet development suite, followed not long thereafter by the release of Enterprise Grid computing with Database 10*g* in 2003. The acquisitions path emerged strongly in 2004 with the purchase of PeopleSoft, and it did not stop there. Significant technology acquisitions are now common for this software giant, with Stellent Inc., Hyperion Solutions Corporation, and, more recently, BEA Systems. As of the publication date of this book, Oracle has acquired over 40 companies, making their products a significant component of its growth strategy.

The database will always be the backbone of Oracle's product line—hence the fifth release of this successful suite of works: *Oracle Database 11g: A Beginner's Guide*. What many people find so fascinating about the Oracle technology stack is how you can bury yourself in such a small part of the database offering. The part that you are familiar with compared to the complete technology stack can be likened to a little itty-bitty street corner compared to the network of intersections in a thriving urban metropolis. Many of us live and breathe our piece of the database technology, never having the opportunity to experience the features and functionality leveraged elsewhere. That is why we wrote this *Beginner's Guide*. Our main audience is just that, the beginner, but there are also chapters in this book that cater to the information needs of seasoned veterans with the technology.

In the earliest days of the *Beginner's Guide*, we continually heard two dramatically opposing opinions about the same thing. On one hand, some people said "One thing I really like about the Oracle database software is that it's so easy to tune"; on the other hand, some claimed "One thing I really hate the Oracle database software is that it's so hard to tune." Exactly where you align yourself as you get further and further into this book remains to be seen; suffice it to say, the material covered in *Oracle Database 11g: A Beginner's Guide* will help you make more informed decisions and adopt better best practices now and in the future. Oracle Database is a powerful tool, and this book will be your first step toward empowerment and your future of becoming an Oracle expert.

This book features the following elements, which enable you to check your progress and understanding of the concepts and details of the product:

- **Critical Skills** listed at the beginning of each chapter highlight what you will learn by the end of the chapter.

- **Step-by-step Projects** reinforce the concepts and skills learned in each chapter, enabling you to apply your newly acquired knowledge and skills immediately.

- **Ask the Expert** questions and answers appear throughout the chapters to make the subject more interactive and personal.

- **Progress Checks** are quick, numbered self-assessment sections where you can easily check your progress by answering questions and getting immediate feedback with the provided answers.

- **Mastery Checks** at the end of each chapter test proficiency in concepts and technology details covered in the chapter through multiple-choice, fill-in-the blank, true/false, and short-answer questions.

This book introduces you to many aspects of the Oracle database software. Chapter 1 starts with the concept of a database and how Oracle is structured so that you understand the fundamentals. Chapter 2 covers installing the software that you are going to need to try things out. We have provided a step-by-step guide to installing the software on Linux, but if you wish to install it on another platform, this chapter will help you understand the choices that you need to make when installing the database.

Once your database is installed, you will need to communicate with it; in order to do this, you may need to install Oracle client software to access the database. Chapter 3 on connecting to Oracle will guide you through the tasks that can often be complex, but we provide information on how to keep it simple.

Once the database is installed and you can communicate with it, you need to speak the languages that the database understands. We provide you with a solid introduction to Structured Query Language (SQL) in Chapter 4, as well as Oracle's own programming language, PL/SQL, in Chapter 5. These two chapters will help you create robust interactions with the database to get data into and out of your database.

The administration of the Oracle database is largely a function of the people who work closely with Oracle's software. Thus, we provide you with a deep introduction to these functions and features. In Chapter 6 we will show you what database administrators (DBAs) do on a daily, weekly, and other basis. In Chapter 7 we provide guidance on how to do backups and, in case things really go wrong with your database, how to restore your old database.

Oracle 11g has many features that are at the leading edge of technology, and Oracle Rapid Application Clusters (RAC) and Automatic Storage Management (ASM) are important technology in the order to support the high-availability needs of today's applications. Take time in Chapter 8 to become familiar with all of this technology to ensure that you understand how today's databases are deployed and optimized for performance and availability.

Finally, in Chapter 9 we discuss features that apply to large databases. As you will learn or are already aware, databases are growing at an exponential rate. We need to use the facilities of the database that address this growth and ensure that we optimize the investment an organization makes in its Oracle software. This book closes by discussing many of the features that will become everyday necessities in your Oracle job.

There is one thing you must keep in mind as you travel around the pages of this book: Oracle Database 11g is a complex product with many, many more features and facilities than we can discuss here. We have chosen topics based on our own experiences of what Oracle customers use 90% of the time, but realize that this is just the start of a very interesting journey. As we say, "You have to start somewhere."

Oracle Database is an exciting product, and one that will provide you with limitless chances to learn more about it. This book is one of your first steps; we hope you take from it the curiosity to dig deeper into the topics.

CHAPTER
1
Database Fundamentals

CRITICAL SKILLS

his chapter is the start of your Oracle Database 11*g* journey. The Oracle database is a complex product and you will need to learn the basics first. From this point forward, we will walk you through the skills that you'll need to begin working with Oracle Database 11*g*. We'll begin at the core of this product, with the fundamentals of a database. This chapter will also give you an understanding of the contents of your database and prepare you to move into the more complex areas of Oracle Database 11*g* technology.

CRITICAL SKILL 1.1
Define a Database

Oracle Database 11*g* is the latest offering from Oracle. Perhaps you have heard a lot of hype about Oracle Database 11*g*, and perhaps not. Regardless of your experience, 11*g* is a rich, full-featured software intended to revolutionize the way many companies do their database business. Think of a database as the Fort Knox for your information. A database is an electronic collection of information designed to meet a handful of needs:

1. **What is a database?**   Databases provide one-stop shopping for all your data storage requirements, no matter whether the information has to do with human resources, finance, inventory, sales, or something else. The database can contain any amount of data, from very little to very big. Data volumes in excess of many hundreds of gigabytes are commonplace in this day and age, where a gigabyte is 1,073,741,824 bytes.

2. **What must it be able to do?**   Databases must provide mechanisms for retrieving data quickly as applications interact with their contents. It is one thing to store tax information for the 300 million citizens of a country, but it's another kettle of fish to retrieve that data, as required, in a short time period.

3. **How is it suitable for corporate data?**   Databases allow the sharing of corporate data such that personnel data is shared amongst one's payroll, benefits, and pension systems. A familiar adage in the database industry is "write once, read many." Databases are a manifestation of that saying—one's name, address, and other basic personnel information are stored in one place and read by as many systems requiring these details.

Figure 1-1 shows, in a nutshell, the components that come together to deliver the corporate database management solution affectionately called Oracle Database 11*g*.
   There is a great deal of academic interest in the database industry, because the theory of the relational database is founded in relational algebra. As data is entered into and stored in Oracle Database 11*g*, the relationships it has to other data are

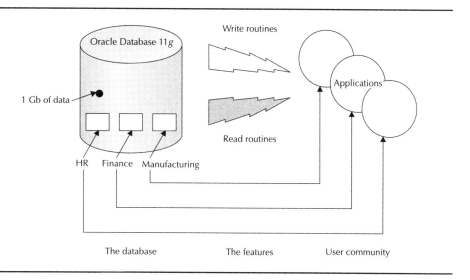

The database   The features   User community

FIGURE 1-1. *The players in the Oracle Database 11g solution*

defined as well. This allows the assembling of required data as applications run. These relationships can be described in plain English for a fictitious computer parts store in the following example:

■ Each geographical location that the store does business in is uniquely identified by a quad_id.

■ Each manufacturer that supplies parts is uniquely identified by a ten-character manufacturer_id. When a new manufacturer is registered with the system, it is assigned a quad_id based on its location.

■ Each item in the store's inventory is uniquely identified by a ten-character part_id and must be associated with a valid manufacturer_id.

Based on these three points, practitioners commonly develop statements similar to the following to describe the relationships between locations, manufacturers, and parts:

■ **A one-to-many relationship**   Locations and manufacturers— more than one manufacturer can reside in a specified location.

■ **A many-to-many relationship**   Manufacturers and computer parts—the store purchases many different parts from each manufacturer.

These two relationships are established as data is captured in the store's database and other relationships can be deduced as a result—for example, one can safely say "parts are manufactured in one or more locations based on the fact that there are many manufacturers supplying many different products." Oracle has always been a relational database product, commanding a significant percentage of market share compared to its major competition. Let's get started and look at the Oracle Database 11*g* architecture.

CRITICAL SKILL 1.2

Learn the Oracle Database 11*g* Architecture

As with many new software experiences, there is some jargon that we should get out of the way before starting this section.

- **Startup** This is the act of issuing the appropriate commands to make an Oracle Database 11*g* accessible to applications. After a startup activity completes, the database is referred to as *opened*. Once opened, the database moves to the next step where it is started. At this point, the database is ready to use.

- **Shutdown** This is the act of stopping Oracle Database 11*g*. When Oracle Database 11*g* is shut down, nobody can access the data in its files.

- **Instance** This is a set of processes that run in a computer's memory and provide access to the many files that come together to define themselves as Oracle Database 11*g*.

- **Background processes** These are processes that support access to an Oracle Database 11*g* that has been started, playing a vital role in Oracle's database implementation. Various background processes are spawned when the database is started and each performs a handful of tasks until a database is shut down.

Let's look at the assortment of files and background processes that support Oracle Database 11*g*.

NOTE
In order to work with the code snippets and the sample schemas we discuss throughout this book, you will need to have the Oracle Database 11g software installed and the first database successfully created. The Database Configuration Assistant (dbca) is the fastest way to set up your first database. Most of the time you simply accept the defaults suggested on the dbca screens. If you have any problems with either the software installation or the dbca, please either consult a more senior colleague or surf MetaLink (http://metalink.oracle.com) to get assistance (after supplying appropriate login credentials).

The Control Files

Oracle's *control files* are binary files containing information about the assortment of files that come together to support Oracle Database 11*g*. They contain information that describes the names, locations, and sizes of the database files. Oracle insists there is only one control file, but knowledgeable technicians have two or three and sometimes more. As Oracle Database 11*g* is started, the control files are read and the files described therein are opened to support the running database.

The Online Redo Logs

As sessions interact with Oracle Database 11*g*, the details of their activities are recorded in the online redo logs. Redo logs may be thought of as transaction logs; these logs collect transactions. A *transaction* is a unit of work, passed to the database for processing. The following listing shows a few activities that can be referred to as two transactions:

```
-- Begin of transaction #1
create some new information
update some existing information
create some more new information
delete some information
save all the work that has been accomplished
-- End of transaction #1
-- Begin transaction #2
update some information
back out the update by not saving the changed data
-- End transaction #2
```

Oracle Database 11*g* insists that there are at least two online redo logs to support the instance. In fact, most databases have two or more redo log groups with each group having the same number of equally sized members.

The System Tablespace

Tablespace is a fancy Oracle Database 11*g* name for a database file. Think of it as a *space* where a *table* resides. As an Oracle Database 11*g* is created, a system tablespace is built that contains Oracle's data dictionary. As Oracle Database 11*g* operates, it continually gets operational information out of its data dictionary. As records are created, this system tablespace defines attributes of the data it stores, such as

- **Data types**   These are the characteristics of data stored in the database. Are they numeric, alphanumeric, or perhaps binary of some video or audio format?

- **Field size**   This is the maximum allowable size for fields as they are populated by the applications. This is where, for example, a country description is defined as from 1 to 30 characters long, containing only letters.

- **Ownership**   Who owns the information as the database data files are populated?

- **Viewing and manipulation rights**   Who is allowed to look at the data and what are the types of activities that each database user can perform on that data?

The system tablespace is a very close cousin of the sysaux tablespace discussed next.

The Sysaux Tablespace

Many of the tools and options that support the Oracle Database 11*g* activities store their objects in this sysaux tablespace. This is mandatory as a database is created. The Oracle Enterprise Manager (OEM) Grid Control repository used to go in its own oem_repository tablespace, but with Oracle Database 11*g* (and its predecessors), its objects now reside in sysaux.

Default Temporary Tablespace

As the dbca does its thing, a tablespace is created that serves as the default location for intermediary objects Oracle Database 11*g* builds as it processes SQL statements. *SQL* stands for structured query language, an industry standard in the database arena, which is used to retrieve, create, change, and update data. Most of the work Oracle does to assemble a result set for a query operation is done in memory. A *result set* is a collection of data that qualifies for inclusion in a query passed to Oracle. If the amount of memory allocated for query processing is insufficient to accommodate all the activities required to assemble data, Oracle uses this default temporary tablespace as its secondary work area for many activities, including sorting.

Undo Tablespace

As sessions interact with Oracle Database 11*g*, they create, change, and delete data. *Undo* is the act of restoring data to a previous state. Suppose one's address is changed from 123 Any Street to 456 New Street via a screen in the personnel application. The user who is making the change has not yet saved the transaction. Until that transaction is saved (referred to as *committed* in the world of Oracle Database 11*g*) or abandoned (referred to as *rolled back* in the same world), Oracle maintains a copy of the changed data in its *undo tablespace*.

The Server Parameter File

Oracle Database 11*g* sometimes calls the server parameter file its *spfile*. This is where its startup parameters are defined and the values in this file determine the environment that database operates in. As one starts an Oracle instance, the spfile is read and various memory structures are allocated based on its contents.

Background Processes

Essentially, background processes facilitate access to Oracle Database 11*g* and support the instance while it is running. These are the main background processes; many of their names haven't changed over the past few releases prior to Oracle Database 11*g*.

■ **The database writer (dbw0) process**   This process (named dbwr in earlier versions of Oracle Database) is responsible for writing the contents of database buffers to disk. As sessions interact with Oracle Database 11*g*, all the information they use passes through Oracle's database buffers, a segment of memory allocated for this activity.

■ **The log writer (lgw0) process**   This process (named lgwr in previous versions of Oracle Database) manages the writing of information to the online redo logs. A log buffer area is set aside in memory where information destined for the online redo logs is staged. The transfer of this information from memory to disk is handled by this process.

■ **The checkpoint process (ckpt)**   This is responsible for updating information in Oracle Database 11*g*'s files during a checkpoint activity. A *checkpoint* is the activity of writing information from memory to the appropriate locations in Oracle Database 11*g*. Think of a checkpoint as a stake in the ground allowing the restoration of a system to a specific point in time. The checkpoint process may trigger lgw0 and dbw0 to do their specialized tasks.

■ **The system monitor (smon) process**   This is the gatekeeper of consistency as Oracle Database 11*g* runs. *Consistency* defines the interrelatedness of the database components with one another. A consistent instance must be established every time Oracle Database 11*g* starts, and it is smon's job to continually enforce and reestablish this consistency. Plainly put: an inconsistent database is trouble!

■ **The process monitor (pmon)**   This is responsible for cleaning up any resources that may have been tied up by aborted sessions interacting with the database. The famous CTRL-ALT-DEL that people tend to use to reboot a personal computer can leave resources tied up in Oracle Database 11*g*. It is pmon's job to free up these resources.

■ **The job queue coordination (cjq0) process**   This is responsible for spawning job processes from Oracle Database 11*g*'s internal job queue. Oracle Database 11*g* does some self-management using its job queue, and users of the database can create jobs and have them submitted to this cjq0 coordinator.

■ **The archiver (arc0) process** This is responsible for copying online redo logs to a secondary storage location before they are reused by the next set of transactions. In the "Online Redo Logs" section of this chapter, we discuss how Oracle Database 11*g* insists there are at least two online redo logs. Suppose we call these groups A and B. Oracle Database 11*g* uses these two groups in a cyclical fashion, moving back and forth from A to B to A to B and so on. The arc0 process, when and if instructed, will make a copy of a file from log group A before allowing it to be reused.

Figure 1-2 illustrates the way the architecture components we have described come together to support Oracle Database 11*g*. Oracle Database 11*g* is opened and then started, and the control files are read to get its bearings. Then the online redo logs and the assortment of tablespaces listed in the control files are acquired. As the instance comes to life, the background processes take over and manage the operations of the database from there.

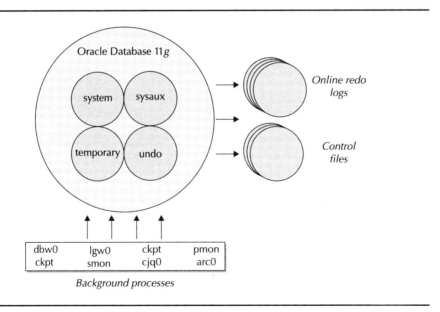

FIGURE 1-2. *Tablespaces, support processes, and infrastructure files*

Project 1-1   Review the Oracle Database 11g Architecture

There are many types of files that come together to support Oracle Database 11g. In this section, we have discussed control files, online redo logs, the system tablespace, and an assortment of datafiles and tablespaces that support the database. As well, we have looked at the series of background processes that allow users to interact with Oracle Database 11g. In this brief project, you will apply what you have learned about the processes that support Oracle Database 11g. As you descend into the land of Oracle Database 11g, you'll find that this information is crucial to your understanding of this remarkable software solution.

Step by Step

1. There are a few pieces missing in the following diagram of the infrastructure of files that support Oracle Database 11g. Fill in the missing text where required.

Where the data dictionary resides	_____ tablespace		A record of transactions against the database
Where intermediary objects are created	__ __ tablespace		
Where information is stored to back out transactions	_____ tablespace		Descriptive information about the files that make up the Oracle Database 11g

2. The second diagram shows a partial makeup of the background processes with Oracle Database 11g. Complete the missing text where indicated by broken lines.

(continued)

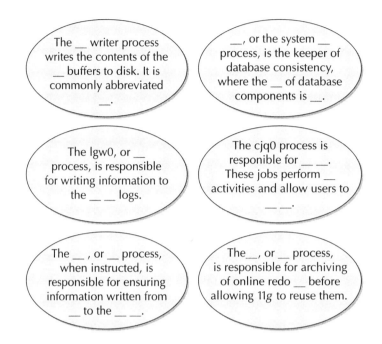

The __ writer process writes the contents of the __ buffers to disk. It is commonly abbreviated __.

__, or the system __ process, is the keeper of database consistency, where the __ of database components is __.

The lgw0, or __ process, is responsible for writing information to the __ __ logs.

The cjq0 process is responible for __ __. These jobs perform __ activities and allow users to __ __.

The __ , or __ process, when instructed, is responsible for ensuring information written from __ to the __ __.

The__, or __ process, is responsible for archiving of online redo __ before allowing 11*g* to reuse them.

Project Summary

You don't need to master Oracle Database 11*g* architecture to become fluent with the software. Just as an electrician needs the assistance of a good set of blueprints, the Oracle Database 11*g* technical person should understand some of the inner workings of the software. A peek under the covers, as brief as it may have been in this section, is a good path to follow while becoming familiar with what Oracle Database 11*g* is all about.

Before moving on to discuss Oracle Database 11*g* data types, let's spend a minute looking at the database administrator, the ultimate director of the operations of the database.

The Database Administrator

This privileged user of Oracle Database 11*g* is commonly the most experienced technician in the shop, with some exceptions. Often, recent adopters of the Oracle technology have little or no in-house experience, and one or more employees may find themselves targets of the familiar directive "So, you're the new Oracle Database 11*g* DBA!" One scrambles to find sources for technical knowledge when thrust into this role. What better place to be than reading *Oracle Database 11g: A Beginner's Guide*? The following list outlines common responsibilities of the Oracle Database 11*g* DBA:

- **Installation and configuration**   The DBA must install and customize the Oracle Database 11*g* software and any assorted programs that will run alongside and access the database.

- **Create datafiles and tablespaces** The DBA decides which application the data will reside in.

- **Create and manage accounts** The DBA sets up the accounts with the usernames and passwords that interact with the database.

- **Tuning** The DBA tweaks the environment that Oracle Database 11*g* operates in by adjusting initialization parameters using the system parameter file.

- **Configure backups** Alongside recovery testing, the DBA performs this activity to ensure the usability and integrity of system backups.

- **Work with developers** This is an ongoing process for DBAs, to ensure that the code they write is optimal and that they use the server's resources as efficiently as possible.

- **Stay current** DBAs keep abreast of the emerging technology and are involved in scoping out future directions based on the enhancements delivered with new software releases.

- **Work with Oracle Support Services** DBAs initiate service requests (SRs) to engage support engineers in problem-solving endeavors. The front-end of the SR creation process is called MetaLink (described earlier in the chapter).

- **Maximize resource efficiency** The DBA must tune Oracle Database 11*g* so that applications can coexist with one another on the same server and share that machine's resources efficiently.

- **Liaise with the system administrators** DBAs must ensure that the appropriate disk space and processor power are available and properly utilized.

As with most lists, after reading the preceding bullet points, you may wonder what else DBAs do with their time. As you work with Oracle Database 11*g*, you'll experience other activities that will plug any loopholes that may exist in the previous list.

CRITICAL SKILL 1.3

Learn the Basic Oracle Database 11*g* Data Types

Very early in one's journey through the world of Oracle Database 11*g*, it becomes time to learn its common data types. Regardless of your past experience in information technology, data types are nothing new. Let's look at the most common type of data that can be stored in Oracle Database 11*g*; keep in mind that the list is much longer than the one presented here.

varchar2

By far the most common data type, varchar2 allows storage of just about any character that can be entered from a computer keyboard. In earlier software solutions, this was commonly referred to as *alphanumeric* data. The maximum length of varchar2 is 4000 bytes or characters, and it possible to store numeric data in this data type. This is a variable length character string, with no storing of trailing insignificant white space:

```
create table ... (
   name        varchar2(30),
   city        varchar2(30),
   ...
   ...
   state       varchar2(2));
```

If a program or SQL statement tries to store a set of characters in a varchar2 field that is longer than the field's specification, an error is returned, and the statement stops running and returns control back to you.

number

The number data type allows the storing of integer as well as integer/decimal digits. When non-integer data is stored, the total number of significant digits of the number is referred to as *precision,* while the portion to the right is called *scale* or *decimal places.* For example, the number 29.1963 has a precision of 6 and a scale of 4. The maximum precision is 38 and the maximum scale is 127. The confusing part of the specification of a number data type comes into play when storing non-integer information. Table 1-1 illustrates this concept.

When defining a number data type with decimal places, it's important to know that the maximum integer portion of the number data type is the difference between the two numbers specified. The specification (6,3) allows for two, not six, integer

Number Specification	Column Length (Precision)	Decimal Digits (Scale)
(3,2)	3	2
(6,3)	6	3
(17,12)	17	12

TABLE 1-1. *Number Data Type Specification*

digits. If more decimal digits are received than the column definition permits, it rounds the value before storage.

date

The *date* data type stores time and date information, with the time component rounded to the nearest full second.

There are many, many functions available to be performed on date fields as they are extracted from an Oracle Database 11*g*.

When date columns are selected from Oracle Database 11*g*, it is common to perform a function on their values to make them more readable. By default, the time component of a date column is not displayed without manipulating its contents using a to_char function, described in Chapter 4. By default the general display format for a date is DD-MON-YY (day, month, and year). This format may be changed via the NLS_DATE_FORMAT parameter or by using a display format function.

timestamp

The *timestamp* data type is a close relative of date. The major advantage is that the timestamp stores information about the second to a much higher accuracy. In this time when every subsecond counts, the timestamp can be a valuable asset. There is a time component in this data type, displayed with the data without the need for the to_char function. This listing illustrates this concept:

```
SQL> create table timestamp_test (ts timestamp);
Table created.
SQL> insert into timestamp_test values (sysdate);
1 row created.
SQL> select * from timestamp_test;
TS
------------------------------------------------------------------------
14-DEC-09 05.25.07.000000 PM
SQL> create table date_test (d date);
Table created.
SQL> insert into date_test values (sysdate);
1 row created.
SQL> select * from date_test;
TS
---------
14-DEC-06
```

clob

The *clob* data type allows storage of very large objects in excess of four gigabytes in size. Since this is a true character data type, it is very similar to the varchar2 data type except for its much larger maximum size.

blob

The *blob* data type permits storage of large unstructured binary objects. Sound and video are examples of blob data.

It's now time to have a look at the most common object in Oracle Database 11*g*: the table. After that, we will have a look at a few types of programming units written using SQL, which a person can store in Oracle Database 11*g*.

CRITICAL SKILL 1.4

Work with Tables

The best way to think of a table in a relational database such as Oracle Database 11*g* is to see it as a spreadsheet with rows and columns. With this in mind, note the following:

- Rows are often referred to as *records*.

- Each column has a name unique to the table that it resides in.

- The intersection of each row and column, referred to as a cell in a spreadsheet, is called a *field* in Oracle Database 11*g*.

Picture the following SQL statement, which creates a table (the line numbers are not part of the code):

```
1- create table part_master (
2-    id                    number(8) not null,
3-    manufacturer_code     number(4) not null,
4-    inception             date not null,
5-    description           varchar2(60) not null,
6-    unit_price            number(6,2) not null,
7-    in_stock              varchar2(1));
```

Let's pick apart the code and highlight the main points in Table 1-2.

Table 1-2 mentions the concept of a relational database. Let's inspect a few other tables and see how they are related to one another.

Tables Related to part_master

The manufacturer_code column in part_master points to a record in manufacturer. Also, some columns in manufacturer may end up being related to column values in other tables. Figure 1-3 illustrates these relationship concepts, the heart of the Oracle Database 11*g* implementation.

Line	Important Points
1	The table has a unique name, from 1 to 30 characters. It is stored in Oracle Database's data dictionary in uppercase.
2	The ID column is numeric with anywhere from one to eight digits. The application that creates and keeps track of parts may insist that the first character of the ID be a digit between 1 and 9. Since the field is defined as numeric, if the leading digit were a 0, the part ID would only be seven digits long.
3	The manufacturer_code is the only manufacturer information stored in part_master. Further information about who made the product is in a related table—hence, the terminology *relational* database.
4	inception, as a date field, contains a date and time specification, though it will display a default month abbreviation and a two-character year unless some manual manipulation is performed (for example, 12-NOV-05).
5	description is a free-form field with a variable length of up to 30 characters.
6	unit_price can accommodate up to four integer and two decimal digits.
7	in_stock is a one-character flag of sorts; thus, the system designers can decide to use an indicator like a "1" or "X" to represent items that are in stock. Notice how this is the only one of seven fields in the PART_MASTER table that can be left blank.

TABLE 1-2. *part_master Table Definitions*

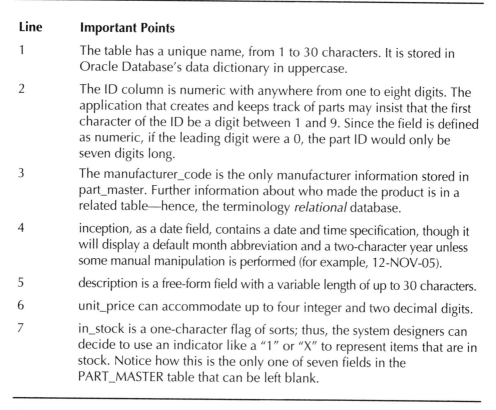

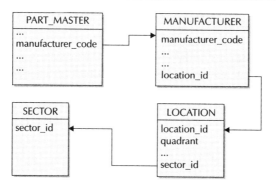

FIGURE 1-3. *Relationships to part_master*

Table	Part Number	Column Value	Related Column Value
part_master	33499909	manufacturer_code	3490
manufacturer	3490	location_id	5
location	5	quadrant	Pacific Northwest

TABLE 1-3. *Following Relationships Between Tables*

Suppose someone wanted to know where in the country a certain part was manufactured. By looking at Figure 1-3, that information is not readily available in part_master. However, part_master has a manufacturer_code. So, a person would traverse to manufacturer using manufacturer_code to get a location_id. Armed with that value, one then proceeds to location to get a quadrant column value. After this navigation is complete, a person would know where a specific part is built. Table 1-3 maps out this journey.

As illustrated in Table 1-3, you can deduce that part 33499909 comes from the Pacific Northwest—a deduction that is made by following the relationships between matching columns in the three tables in question.

CRITICAL SKILL 1.5

Work with Stored Programmed Objects

Oracle Database 11*g* offers the ability to store user-defined programming units in the data dictionary, called *stored objects*. These programming units are written in PL/SQL, the topic of Chapter 5. Without worrying about what goes inside these objects, let's do an overview of what they are all about.

Views

Views are predefined subsets of data from an Oracle Database 11*g* table. The SQL query that builds the view is stored in the data dictionary and need not be reassembled every time the view is used. Suppose a personnel application stores the location of all employees in its EMPLOYEE_MASTER table in the loc_id column. With Oracle Database 11*g*, you can define a view called emp_hq as follows:

```
create or replace view emp_hq
as select * from employee_master
where loc_id = '2';
```

EMP_HQ becomes a valid object of the select statement just as if it were a table of its own.

Ask the Expert

Q: What is the major difference between the clob and blob data types in Oracle Database 11g?

A: The clob stores only alphanumeric data, whereas the blob can accommodate any type of data, including sound and video.

Q: When specifying the number data type, how is the total length of the field determined?

A: The total length of a numeric field is determined by the digit(s) to the left of the comma if the specification includes an integer and decimal component. For example, *number(4,1)* denotes a maximum of four digits, of which one digit can be stored to the right of the decimal point.

Q: Which of the Oracle Database 11g background processes is responsible for writing information from memory into the database files?

A: This is the job of the database writer, or dbw0, process.

Q: Where does Oracle Database 11g read its environment from as it is started?

A: The startup parameters are read from the system parameter file, which can be a binary file stored in Oracle Database 11g.

Q: As sessions interact with the data in Oracle Database 11g, what role does the undo tablespace play in the architecture of the software?

A: When transactions change the contents of information in Oracle Database 11g's tables, this special tablespace keeps a "before image" of the changes in case the operator decides to back out before saving newly entered information.

NOTE
At this point, you should realize that views are generally built based on more than one table. A view provides the perfect environment to predefine join conditions between tables to ensure that they adhere to business rules and perform at an optimal level.

Triggers

Just as their name implies, *triggers* are stored objects that fire based on the execution of certain events. Suppose a payroll application wants to audit salary increases: a trigger is created that fires when the salary column in hr_master is updated. The trigger could do the following:

1. Create a record in sal_audit.

2. Trap the time and date of the transaction.

3. Place the user's login ID in the doer column.

4. Place the old salary value in the old_sal column.

5. Place the new salary value in the new_sal column.

Code in the trigger traps the event by specifying *on update.* While triggers are commonly used for auditing, the types of activities they can initiate are endless.

NOTE
Triggers cannot exist independently of an Oracle Database 11g table. They are associated with one and only one table and, if a table is dropped, so is the trigger.

Triggers, as well as procedures, packages, and functions described next, are most commonly written using PL/SQL. The PL/SQL programming language is the topic of Chapter 5.

Procedures

Procedures perform specific tasks as applications interact with Oracle Database 11*g*. If there are a number of interrelated activities to carry out in one place, a procedure is an ideal way to do this. Procedures can accept parameters when invoked and can interact with objects in Oracle Database 11*g*. They encapsulate related activities into single programming units that simplify logic and share data values as they perform various activities. They offer extremely flexible features, many of which are not available with triggers.

Functions

Functions are very close relatives of procedures, except that they return a value to the code that called them. Oracle Database 11*g* delivers many functions out of the box and developers can create their own functions to augment what is delivered with the software. Suppose you want to strip all the vowels out of a name with a function. You can pass in a name (for instance, Bellissimo) and gets back the text "Bllssm" when the function completes its work. Let's look at the get_age function, which operates based on the following logic:

```
given a date of birth (format DD-MON-YYYY)
using an SQL function
get the months between today's date and the date passed in
divide the number of months by 12
truncate the results (giving the span in years between the 2 dates)
pass integer back
```

Packages

Packages roll functions and procedures together into a cohesive programming unit. Often, developers prefer to bundle like functionality together since it makes logical sense to call one larger unit and have it perform a series of tasks. Let's look at the CREATE_EMPLOYEE package in Table 1-4.

Component Name	Type	Work Accomplished
give_holidays	Procedure	Creates the default holiday quota based on the new person's rank in the company.
notify_benefits	Procedure	Creates a record in the BEN_QUEUE table to alert the benefits people of the new employee.
is_under_25	Function	Returns a "1" if the new employee is under 25 years old as of December 31 of the year they were hired.
is_over_59	Function	Returns a "1" if the new employee is 60 years old or older as of the calendar date of hire.

TABLE 1-4. *Members of the CREATE_EMPLOYEE Package*

Progress Check

1. Oracle Database 11*g* is referred to as a relational database. Why is the word *relational* used?

2. What is the maximum length of a varchar2 data type that can be stored in Oracle Database 11*g*?

3. What is data consistency when referred to as a feature of Oracle Database 11*g*? Give an example.

4. What types of stored objects can be encapsulated into an Oracle Database 11*g* package?

5. What is the fundamental difference between a procedure and a function in Oracle Database 11*g*?

6. Data in the system tablespace is often referred to as *metadata*—or data about data. Name at least two types of metadata in the system tablespace.

7. What is the difference between the timestamp and date data types?

8. What type of information and data ends up being stored in the sysaux tablespace?

Progress Check Answers

1. The word *relational* is used because Oracle Database 11*g* defines the relationships between tables. It is these relationships that allow applications to navigate an assortment of tables and assemble results from more than one table.

2. The varchar2 data type can accommodate up to 4000 characters.

3. Data consistency refers to the ability to ensure that related items of information are manipulated in a similar fashion. Suppose an application assigns a department to a new employee as a two-digit number field. Sometime down the road, due to company growth, the department identifier is changed to three digits. All the data where this used-to-be two-character identifier is stored must be changed to reflect the expansion of the department codes.

4. Packages can contain a mixture of one or more functions and procedures.

5. A procedure receives from zero to many parameters as it is invoked and then goes about its business until the end of its code segment. A function, on the other hand, accepts one or more parameters as it is called and returns a value to the code from where it was invoked. The procedure passes nothing back to its caller.

6. Metadata defines items such as the names of tables in the database, the owners of the tables, the data types of the columns in each table, and who is allowed to look at what data.

7. When columns are displayed, they use the date data type, containing a day/month/year component, whereas, by default, the timestamp data type columns contain a time-of-day component as well.

8. The sysaux tablespace contains tables required to manage Oracle Database, such as the items required to support OEM Grid Control.

CRITICAL SKILL 1.6
Become Familiar with Other Important Items in Oracle Database 11*g*

So far, you've had a brief look at tables, views, tablespaces, and a handful of stored objects, such as views, triggers, procedures, packages, and functions. Let's round out this introduction to Oracle Database 11*g* architecture by covering a few other items commonly encountered. The following discussion is a hodgepodge of things that are necessary for a person's understanding of the Oracle Database 11*g* architecture and operations. Keep in mind that you must also spend a bit of time looking at the role of the database administrator, affectionately called the *DBA,* who is the gatekeeper of the database and the person responsible for its smooth operation.

NOTE
You'll get a more detailed look at the DBA in Chapter 6, with more information on how DBAs go about carrying out their administrative chores.

Indexes

Tables are made up of rows and columns, which are the basis of all objects in Oracle Database 11*g*. As applications interact with the database, they often retrieve vast amounts of data. Suppose MyYP, a fictitious Internet company, provided Yellow Pages listings for North America, and the data was stored primarily in a table called YP_MASTER. Each row in the YP_MASTER table is uniquely identified by a combination of company name, municipality, and geographic location (state or province). As words are retrieved from the database to satisfy online queries, indexes would provide a quick access path to the qualifying data. Specific index characteristics are relevant to the power they deliver in Oracle Database 11*g*. For instance:

- They are built on one or more columns in a table using simple SQL statements.

- They are separate from the tables that they are built on and can be dropped without affecting the data in the table itself. On the contrary, when a table is dropped, any indexes it has disappear with the table.

- The function they perform can be likened to the index in a book. If one were looking for a specific topic in a textbook, the best place to start would be the index—it provides a shortcut to the information being sought. If one imagined that YP_MASTER were a book rather than a table, finding Y&M Plumbing in Pensacola, Florida would be faster using the index than reading the book from the start to the 25th letter of the alphabet. The names on the corner of the pages in a phone book are like an index.

■ Indexes occupy space in the database; even though there are ways to keep their space to a minimum, extra space is required and must be pre-allocated.

Users

Most of us are familiar with usernames and passwords from our experience logging into corporate networks and other secure systems. Oracle Database 11*g* implements the same mechanism with login credentials and privileges given out by the database administrator. Once accounts are created, people initiate connections to Oracle Database 11*g* and work with their own data and other users' data where the appropriate privileges have been given out. We discuss object privileges in the "Work with Object and System Privileges" section immediately following this one.

NOTE
With Oracle Database 11g, the terminology user, account, and schema are used synonymously.

Once an account is created, it is often given the rights to occupy space in one or more Oracle Database 11*g* tablespaces. This is discussed in the next section.

Tablespace Quotas

As additional nonsystem tablespaces are created, the database administrator gives out quotas that allow users to occupy space therein. *Tablespace quotas* are given out using an SQL statement with three parts:

■ The username to whom the quota is being given.

■ The name of the tablespace within which the username is being permitted to create tables.

■ The amount of that quota—whether it's mentioned in absolute bytes (for example, 500,000) or more commonly in quantities of megabytes (500MB, for instance). Unlimited quotas can be allowed using the keyword *unlimited*.

Regardless of how a quota is given out, the SQL statement passed to Oracle Database 11*g* resembles the following:

```
SQL*Plus: Release 11.1.0.1.0 - Production on Sun Mar 11 10:29:42 2009
Copyright (c) 1982, 2007, Oracle.  All rights reserved.
Connected to:
Oracle11g Enterprise Edition Release 11.1.0.1.0 - Production
With the Partitioning, OLAP and Data Mining options
```

```
SQL> alter user hr quota 500m on hr_data;
User altered.
SQL> alter user ap quota unlimited on ap_idx;
User altered.
```

Synonyms

You'll remember that in the "Work with Tables" section we discussed that the key was passing Oracle Database 11*g* the create table keywords. In a nutshell, table creation is undertaken after establishing a successful connection to the database, and then, with appropriate privileges in place, defining a table. One of the key concepts with all database management systems is sharing data. Since it is key to only have one copy of a table and to have its contents shared amongst applications, *synonyms* are a way to reference other people's data.

Suppose you wanted to use the PART_MASTER table in an application owned by a user other than the owner. That owner would permit us to work with the table's data, and then we would create a synonym to reference its contents. The code would resemble the following:

```
SQL*Plus: Release 11.1.0.1.0 - Production on Sun Mar 11 10:29:42 2009
Copyright (c) 1982, 2007, Oracle.  All rights reserved.
Connected to:
Oracle11g Enterprise Edition Release 11.1.0.1.0 - Production
With the Partitioning, OLAP and Data Mining options
SQL> create synonym part_master for inv.part_master;
Synonym created.
SQL> select count(*)
  2  from part_master
  3  where in_stock is not null;
    COUNT(*)
-------------
       13442
```

The preceding SQL statement references an object called part_master. Depending on how your access is defined, the way that you reach the physical table may be different. When you are the owner of the table and you use the table's name in the from clause, Oracle understands that you would like to use your own table. If you do not own a table by that name, Oracle then looks in a list of table synonyms or pointers to a table with that name owned by someone else. This process of using synonyms is a transparent operation. If you do not own the table by the name or no synonym exists, you will receive an error. There are actually two kinds of synonyms:

- *Private synonyms* are created in one account and are only usable by the creator.

- *Public synonyms* are created by a central privileged user and are available to anyone able to connect to Oracle Database 11*g*.

NOTE
One needs the appropriate object privileges to be able to work with someone else's data using a private or public synonym. The synonym itself does not imply that the appropriate privileges can be circumvented.

Roles

Often it makes sense to group similar users together to streamline the organization of people who use Oracle Database 11*g*. Using roles, the DBA can logically lump personnel together and give out object privileges to roles rather than individual users. Roles can be password protected, though in most implementations they do not have this level of complexity.

Default User Environments

As accounts are created by the DBA, users are given a default environment to use unless some specifics are coded as they interact with Oracle Database 11*g*. Users are commonly set up with the following default environment settings:

- The *default tablespace* is where tables are placed unless the *create table* statement explicitly points at a nondefault tablespace that the user has a quota for.

- *Temporary tablespaces* are the tablespaces where users perform sort and merge operations while the Oracle Database 11*g* engine is processing queries.

Users can be given membership in one or more roles and have their default profile changed as well. As users are created, they do not automatically inherit a default tablespace; one must be manually given out during or following the user creation statement. Users do automatically point at a temporary tablespace, as discussed in the "Default Temporary Tablespace" section of this chapter, unless manually pointed elsewhere.

NOTE
With Oracle Database 11g one is now able to set the default tablespace for the entire database instance. This is done via an "ALTER DATABASE DEFAULT TABLESPACE tablespace-name;" command. You will need to have the privileges to be able to perform this operation.

Progress Check

1. Name at least four tasks handled by the Oracle Database 11g administrator.

2. What is the difference between *public* and *private* synonyms?

3. What is meant by a user's default tablespace?

4. What two units of measurement are commonly used to specify a tablespace quota?

5. Where do DBAs go to create *i*TARs, where assistance is requested from Oracle's support organization?

6. Which of the following—*procedures, packages,* or *triggers*—cannot exist independent of a table to which they belong?

CRITICAL SKILL 1.7
Work with Object and System Privileges

It's next to impossible to work with data in Oracle Database 11g without looking at object privileges. In this section, we are going to look at these privileges as well as a suite of system privileges closely related to managing Oracle Database 11g. The four main object privileges are select, insert, update, and delete, all discussed in the next four sections. Oracle Database 11g uses the term *grant* when referring to giving out both object and system privileges.

Select

This is the primary and most commonly used privilege, permitting other users to view your data. There are three parts to grant statements:

- The keywords grant select on.
- The name of the object upon which the privileges are being given out.
- The recipient of the grant.

Progress Check Answers

1. Installation, upgrades, tuning, and environment setup are four of many tasks performed by the DBA.

2. A private synonym can only be referenced in a SQL statement by the user who created and owns the synonym. A public synonym, created by a centralized user such as a DBA, is available to all users.

3. The default tablespace is the one within which users occupy space by default, unless another tablespace is mentioned as a table is created.

4. Quota on tablespaces is usually given out using bytes or megabytes as units of measurement.

5. The DBA goes to MetaLink to request assistance from Oracle's support organization.

6. Triggers cannot exist on their own without association with an Oracle Database 11g table.

Once the select privilege has been given out, the recipients, using a private or public synonym as described earlier in the "Synonyms" section of this chapter, can reference your objects in their SQL statements.

Insert

This privilege allows users to create rows in tables belonging to other users. The creator of new rows in other users' objects is bound by the same rules used if they owned the objects themselves. They must adhere to the boundaries defined by the data types of the columns in the rows they create. For example, when rows are inserted into a table that has a column defined as type DATE, they must ensure that valid date type data is placed in the column so defined. As rows are created in an Oracle Database 11*g* table, the transaction must be committed to the database before the row becomes part of the information available to other users. With Oracle Database 11*g*, we use the term *commit* the same way the word *save* is used with other types of software.

Update

This privilege allows a person to change the contents of columns in rows belonging to other tables. The SQL update statement can change the value of data in one or more columns. As with insert activity, the update transactions need to commit their work to make it permanent in the Oracle Database 11*g* files.

Delete

Delete operations interact with one or more rows in Oracle Database 11*g* tables and must be followed by a commit as well to write the results of the transaction to the database files.

You will see more in Chapter 4 about how SQL statements are constructed using the four keywords in the previous sections. SQL statements are subject to rigorous syntax requirements which, if not followed, return an assortment of Oracle errors. Just as with other programming languages you may be familiar with, the SQL statement processing engine is very strict with reserved words and the placement of the pieces that come together to form an SQL transaction. Let's briefly discuss system privileges that allow certain users of Oracle Database 11*g* to perform secure activities.

System Privileges

We have mentioned the database administrator in a number of places in this introductory chapter. Classically, secure operations are performed by the DBAs; however, one can grant system privileges to specified users so that they can perform selected activities themselves. The following list illustrates a few examples of these secure operations:

- **Alter system** There are a number of modes that Oracle Database 11*g* can operate from. The modes are toggled using alter system. For example, this privilege can be given out to Jane by issuing the command grant alter system to jane.

- **Create user/alter user** Often, the DBA wants to partition some of the user creation activities between a handful of users of Oracle Database 11*g*. This is done by giving out the create user system privilege. Once new users are created, you often don't want to tweak their environment; this can be accomplished by issuing the grant alter user statement to one or more users of the database.

- **Create session/table/trigger** Sometimes when new users are created, they are given the create session system privilege which allows them to connect to Oracle Database 11*g*. In many cases, depending on how new users are created, they are not allowed to build any objects until they receive the create table system privilege. As well, many users are not capable of defining triggers until they receive the create trigger system privilege.

System privileges were introduced with early releases of Oracle7 (circa 1993) and have played a useful role in the division of labor in the database since their inception. Now it's time to get into the meat of the seventh letter of the alphabet, *g*, that throughout this chapter has followed the two-digit version number of this software release—11.

CRITICAL SKILL 1.8
Introduce Yourself to the Grid

As many have heard, the "*g*" in Oracle Database 11*g* stands for *grid*. Grid computing is a technology that allows for seamless and massively scalable access to a distributed network of diverse yet homogenous computer types. Oracle Database 11*g* is the glue permitting different vendors' computers to work together providing a seemingly endless supply of shared computer resources. Oracle sees the grid as revolutionizing the way companies go about doing their business. Grid computing targets the delivery of information as a utility, similar to the way electrical and telephone services are currently delivered to the public—hence the term *grid*. The industry as a whole, but Oracle in particular, sees a delivery method from the grid such that consumers will only pay for what they use. Interlaced computers will allow idle

Ask the Expert

Q: Name the four main object privileges used in Oracle Database 11*g*.

A: The four most common privileges are select, insert, update, and delete.

Q: Placing an Oracle Database 11*g* in a state where it can be accessed by applications is referred to as what activity?

A: Putting an Oracle Database 11*g* in a normal operating mode for day-to-day access by a company's applications is referred to as *startup*.

Q: How many integer and decimal digits can a field defined in the data dictionary as *number(10,2)* accommodate?

A: The field would be able to store up to eight integer digits and two decimal digits.

Q: When Oracle Database 11*g* is passed the value "Beginner   " for storage in a varchar2 column, how does it deal with trailing insignificant spaces?

A: The trailing spaces are trimmed before the information is stored in the database. Though not as common as varchar2, the char data type can be used to store trailing spaces.

Q: What would Oracle Database 11*g* store as a value in a number(6,2) field when passed the value 9.8882?

A: It would store 9.89 in a number(6,2) field when passed 9.8882.

capacity to be leveraged by the grid to provide for a form of parallel processing on steroids. The following are the major players that enable the Oracle grid technology:

- **Real Application Clusters (RAC)**   Involves a suite of networked computers sharing a common Oracle Database 11*g* and running platform-independent clusterware, the glue that makes the interconnect between the clustered nodes so transparent.

- **Automatic Storage Management (ASM)**   A front-end management system that can group disks from an assortment of manufacturers together to form a suite of disks that is available to all computers on the grid. ASM encapsulates the complete life cycle of disk management and allocation into a centralized GUI interface.

■ **Oracle Resource Manager** Provides a framework within which administrators can control the computing resources of nodes on the grid.

■ **Oracle Scheduler** Allows the handing out of jobs to members of the grid to facilitate the execution of business tasks anywhere and everywhere where idle resources exist.

■ **Oracle Streams** Assists the processing requirements whereby copies of data need to be streamed between nodes in the grid, providing the mechanisms to keep data in sync on one database with the database from which the data originated. Oracle Streams' tight integration with the Oracle Database 11*g* engine facilitates this synchronization and delivers a preferred method of replication.

Figure 1-4 illustrates the primary differences between grid computing and traditional approaches to providing computer services.

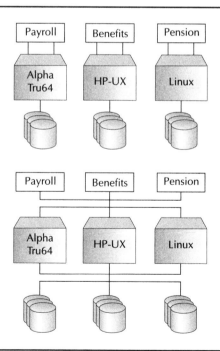

FIGURE 1-4. *Differences between traditional and grid computing*

The following points reinforce the details of the two scenarios depicted in Figure 1-4:

- The three applications at the top of the figure each have a dedicated server, each with its own dedicated disk. If the Linux server were to go out of service, the pension application would grind to a halt. There is no built-in mechanism for pension system processing to carry on another server.

- The three applications at the bottom are interlaced with one another. The benefits application can be hosted on from one to three of the available servers. As well, the database files that support these three applications can reside upon (and be read from) any of the nine disks in the grid's disk farm.

The browser-based OEM Grid Control holds the whole thing together. With the implementation of the ASM component of Oracle Database 11*g*, disks are managed by OEM, database instances are managed by OEM, clusterware is managed through OEM; the list is endless. Figure 1-5 shows the first OEM screen that appears after entering appropriate login credentials.

NOTE
There is an OEM configuration program (called emca) that must be successfully run before you can access the browser-based OEM. The screen shown in your version of Oracle Database 11g may be somewhat different than the one shown in Figure 1-4. The look and feel of the OEM Grid Control screens can change significantly between minor releases of the software.

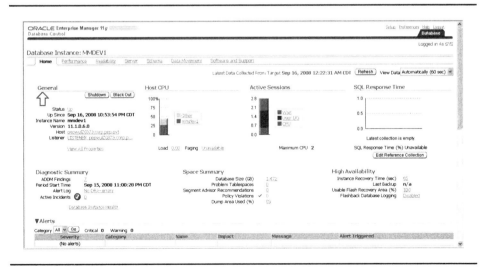

FIGURE 1-5. *OEM startup*

CRITICAL SKILL 1.9

Tie It All Together

Now that was quite a journey! We have covered database fundamentals, with an Oracle Database 11*g* flavor. Relational database management systems have been around for a few decades, and the release of Oracle Database 11*g* is a landmark in the industry. There have been many academic discussions about the grid technology— some claim Oracle Database 11*g* is a grid implementation, while others don't. Regardless of which side of the fence you're on, Oracle Database 11*g* is a big step. Let's pull it all together and spend a bit of time on the big picture.

Oracle Database 11*g* is a collection of special files created using its database configuration assistant and then completing the work using OEM Grid Control. Access to these database files is facilitated by a set of shared memory processes referred to as an *instance*. Many technicians use this term synonymously with *database*. There is nothing wrong with that because, even though they are technically different pieces, they cannot survive without each other.

Relationships between objects in the database are defined in the data dictionary— hence the familiar term *relational database*. It is these relationships that provide the power and allow Oracle Database 11*g* to store vast amounts of data. Storing that data is one thing—retrieving it for applications in a quick and complete fashion is another story. Data retrieval is one of the strengths of the Oracle Database 11*g* engine.

Over the next eight chapters, we will be delving into more details of the Oracle Database 11*g* offering, paying specific attention to the following:

- **Installing Oracle**   In order to become productive with Oracle, it is valuable to learn the steps that are necessary to install and connect to the database. This will help you get started as well as prepare you for the samples within the book.

- **Networking**   The glue that holds many systems together and allows computers to communicate with one another in widely diverse and separated locations.

- **SQL—Structured Query Language**   This is the way we communicate with Oracle Database 11*g*. Whatever the programming language (from C to Java), SQL is all the database engine understands.

- **PL/SQL**   A programming language native to the Oracle Database 11*g* engine, providing more procedural capabilities that can amplify and enhance the functionality of SQL.

- **The Database Administrator**   The person who is the gatekeeper of Oracle Database 11*g* and the one responsible for its smooth operation and optimal performance.

- **Backup and Recovery**   Two areas critical to the smooth operation of Oracle Database 11*g*. Oracle Database 11*g*'s Recovery Manager (referred to as RMAN) is the fundamental building block in its backup and recovery implementation. In addition, your backup and recovery strategy is one that will need to be considered as input to your Disaster Recovery strategy.

- **High Availability**   The need to support databases and applications for extended and uninterrupted times requires Oracle to be able to support these demands. This chapter focuses on Rapid Application Clusters (RAC) and Automatic Storage Management (ASM) to serve as the foundation to your high availability solutions.

- **Large Database Features**   Oracle Database 11*g* expands on an already solid offering in this area. With Oracle9*i*, they boasted the ability to support a database of up to 500 petabytes. Oracle Database 11*g* expands that upper limit to many exabytes, a staggering number, to say the least—where an exabyte is 1,152,921,504,606,846,976 bytes—or about one trillion million!

☑ Chapter 1 Mastery Check

1. The _____ background process is primarily responsible for writing information to the Oracle Database 11*g* files.

2. How many online redo log groups are required to start an Oracle Database 11*g*?

   A. 3

   B. 2

   C. 4

   D. 1

3. Of the following four items of information, which one is not stored in Oracle Database 11*g*'s control files?

   A. The name of the database files

   B. The creator of the database

   C. The location of the database files

   D. The sizes of the database files

4. What is the function of a default temporary tablespace in the support of Oracle Database 11*g*?

5. Differentiate between an Oracle Database 11*g* and an instance.

6. Activities such as allocating space in the database and user management are commonly performed by the DBA. What feature in Oracle Database 11*g* allows some of these secure operations to be carried out by non-DBA users? How are these rights given out?

7. As a user of Oracle Database 11*g* is created, you often specify a default tablespace. In this context, what does *default tablespace* mean?

   A. The system tablespace

   B. A tablespace the user can occupy space in without a private or public synonym

   C. The tablespace within which objects are created if a location (tablespace) is not explicitly mentioned as a table is created

8. The _____ GUI interface is used to create a new database.

9. What happens when one tries to store the text "Madagascar" in a field with a specification of varchar2(8)?

10. What is the most common way one uses triggers in Oracle Database 11*g*? Give an example of this activity.

11. What programming language, native to Oracle Database 11*g*, is used to create stored objects such as triggers and functions?

   A. SQL*Plus

   B. OEM Grid Control

   C. Basic

   D. PL/SQL

12. What is the role of the sysaux tablespace in Oracle Database 11*g*?

13. The clob and blob data types differ in all but one of the following three ways. Which one does not apply to the differences between the two data types?

   A. The clob holds standard alphanumeric data, whereas the blob may store binary information.

   B. The blob contains a time (hour/minute) component, but the clob does not.

   C. The blob contains unstructured free-form data, whereas the rules governing the type of information that can be stored in the clob are more stringent.

14. There are many ways to replicate data from one node to another. What main feature does Oracle Streams provide that is missing from many other methods?

15. What does the acronym SQL stand for?

   A. Structured Query Language

   B. Simple Query Language

   C. Straightforward Question-based Learning

CHAPTER
2

Installing Oracle

CRITICAL SKILLS

2.1 Research and Plan the Installation

2.2 Set Up the Operating System

2.3 Get Familiar with Linux

2.4 Choose Components to Install

2.5 Install the Oracle Software

nowledge of the technology behind Oracle and an understanding its tables and columns are basic skills needed for working with Oracle; however, you need to install the software to take advantage of all of the functionality of the product. There are many product options and features that you will need to select during installation and for this chapter we suggest you consider installing all options for your educational use of the product. Are you ready to install the Oracle software? You are probably not as ready as you think, unless you have already done some research and prepared the environment. Downloading or obtaining the media for the Oracle software is the easy part, but do you know which operating system you are using and have you set up the configurations for Oracle?

Oracle has a proven track record on a variety of operating systems. Oracle 11*g* was first released on the Linux platform (among other Unix-based platforms), then followed closely by a release for Windows, which is the normal pattern in which Oracle develops and releases products. We suggest that you get the latest version of the software from the Oracle Technology Network (otn.oracle.com) for your chosen platform.

It is also critical to be able to configure or verify the operating system configuration for successful installs and, ultimately, well-running and performing systems. We recommend, therefore, that you have administrator access to the server that you plan to install the software on. Being able to tune or discuss the issues regarding the operating system comes in handy when you're looking at configurations for the system as a whole; deciding when the minimum is not enough and starting to understand where the dependencies are is a valuable part of successful implementations. This chapter will walk you through some basic steps for installing the Oracle software on Linux, including gathering the information needed for the system requirements as well as completing a checklist for a Linux installation.

CRITICAL SKILL 2.1
Research and Plan the Installation

Oracle provides some critical information needed for installing the Oracle software, both with the software itself and in the Oracle support site MetaLink notes. These are important documents for successful installs that can help you with the planning and research (for example, the *Quick Installation Guide, Database Readme,* and *Database Release Notes*) and they contain hardware requirements, prerequisites, and the setup to be done before and after installation. Also, information on installation issues for Oracle software can be obtained from most recent release notes, which contain possible workarounds or updated steps for the installs.

Gathering information on what is required to install the software and running it effectively is a very important first step. Neglecting to do this by going straight to the install can mean a lot more work, due to the potential need for uninstalling and reinstalling parts of the software. Important information you'll want to watch for: what is needed for the operating system to be configured for Oracle to run and the fact that the initial settings are minimum values to be adjusted for larger systems.

With Linux and Unix environments, there are kernel parameters and settings that need to be adjusted when the system starts up. The uses for these parameters range from being able to allocate shared memory for Oracle to the number of processes that are allowed to run on the server. Failure to set parameters and verify the needed system requirements may allow the software to be installed, but it could prevent the database from starting up because it is unable to get the system resources that are needed. Each operating system has a particular set of configurations that it needs. There are also patches that need to be in synch with the version of Oracle that is to be installed. So, knowing the requirements that are needed and gathering the needed patches and parameter values for application to the operating system are critical to the install.

Define System Requirements

Hardware minimum requirements are related to processors, memory, and the disk needed to install OS and Oracle software. For Oracle 11g, at least 1GB of RAM is required and the Oracle software requires 3.5 to 5GB of disk space. The processors themselves can be verified in pre-installation checks. Other hardware requirements, such as network adapters or additional disks, all depend on the environment that is being set up: for example, systems with Real Application Clusters or other additional features.

In taking a closer look at how to prepare the operating system for an Oracle install, let's use Linux as an example from installation to configuration. You'll start the Linux installation by obtaining the media and starting up the server with the Linux CDs inserted. Oracle Enterprise Linux has included all the needed packages with the standard install. After a bootup of the server, the install screens will come up and walk you through the simple process of setting up the operating system. The following figures and comments explain the Linux install screens, as well as a basic configuration to get started with Oracle on Linux.

Linux Installation

Most of the beginning screens simply step through and configure the language and very basic server settings. The first install screen that might require additional information is disk partition, which has two options: to leave as is or customize. These include partitions for swap, root, tmp, or other file system mount points. The file system mount points are the disk mounts for the directories where the software will be installed and the databases will eventually be created. Bare minimum partitions are swap and another device for the file mount points. Figure 2-1 shows the install screen with the standard disk partitions, which is definitely enough to get you started with the Oracle install on Linux.

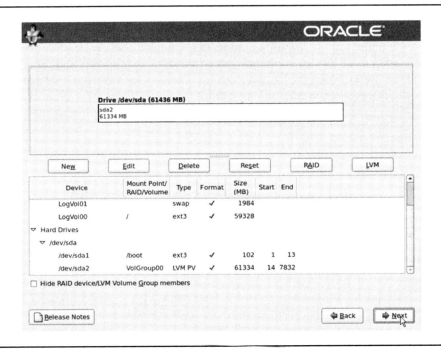

FIGURE 2-1. *Linux install disk partitions*

In Figure 2-1, you can see one logical device for the swap space, which is the memory area on the disk allowing for programs to swap to virtual memory when they need more memory than the physical memory contains. There is another device for the boot area, the initial partition of the disk, and then the rest of the disk under the root directory can be used for creating the directories for tmp, var, home, oracle, and so on. Even if it isn't defined on separate devices, the directories that Linux needs, such as the tmp and var directories, will be created during install. However, you will need to create a directory for the Oracle software before you install it.

As shown in Figure 2-1, the devices are configured based on the disk available to the server, and the values and sizes can be adjusted at this point. The swap space can be adjusted later, but it is just as easy to configure here. Also, new mount points or file systems can be created on the root directory, depending on your needs. After setting the values and mount points, click on Next for the next configuration screen.

After the disk partitions install screen, you need to make a choice about *boot loaders*. In Linux, a boot loader is the piece that loads the operating system into memory (there are usually a couple of them in use). The boot loaders in this case are LILO, Linux Loader, and Grand Unified Bootloader (GRUB). The GRUB boot loader is the default for RedHat and Oracle Linux and can be selected if needed.

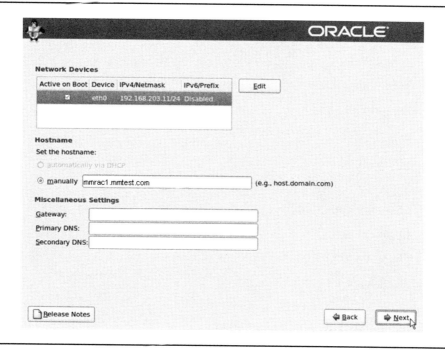

FIGURE 2-2.   *Linux network*

The network configuration and devices are the next step. Plug in the IP address and edit the network device on the installation screen, shown in Figure 2-2. This can also be done after installation, using the network settings. This is where the host name is defined as shown with the domain name; the miscellaneous settings are dependent on the network settings and configurations. Figure 2-2 also shows where to manually enter the server name with the domain and the miscellaneous settings with the Gateway, Primary, and Secondary DNS.

The next couple of installation screens go through the root password and time zone information; the proper time zone for your location just needs to be chosen when going through the installation. Choose and remember the root password carefully. At this point, there is no other way to login to the OS without the root password. The default install will include packages for generic use, but it should also be selected to support software development for this system. The option to customize can be done here or the needed packages can also be installed afterward. During the install, the packages can just be selected and then verified after the install to ensure that they are completed. The required packages for Oracle Enterprise Linux 5.0 (based on the current installation guide) are as follows:

- binutils-2.17.50.0.6-2.e15
- compat-libstdc++-33-3.2.3-61

- elfutils-libelf-0.125-3.e15
- elfutils-libelf-devel-0.125
- glibc-2.5-12
- glibc-common-2.5-12
- glibc-devel-2.5-12
- glibc-headers-2.5-12
- gcc-4.1.1-52
- gcc-c++-4.1.1-52
- libaio-0.3.106
- libaio-devel-0.3.106
- libgcc-4.1.1-52
- libstdc++-4.1.1
- libstdc++-devel-4.1.1-52.e15
- make-3.81-1.1
- sysstat-7.0.0
- unixODBC-2.2.11
- unixODBC-devel-2.2.11

After the installation, the packages should be verified by running the command at the Linux prompt:

```
rpm -q unixODBC-devel-2.2.11
```

If the packages were not installed or if the installation failed, then the following commands can be run to install packages as needed from the Linux source files. Here is an example install command for this package:

```
rpm -ivh unixODBC-devel-2*rpm
```

These steps are seen in Figure 2-3; the rpm –q used to verify the packages shows that the unixODBC package was not installed, so executing the command to install the package completes this step. This step is repeated for each of the packages that are required.

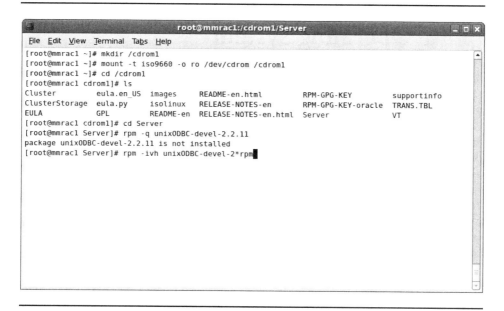

FIGURE 2-3. *Linux package install*

Progress Check

1. What documents are provided for system requirements and installation instructions by Oracle?

2. What is an important first step for installing Oracle software?

3. When installing Linux, which devices are needed when configuring the disk?

4. What is the command for verifying that a package is installed?

5. How much RAM is required for Oracle 11*g*?

Progress Check Answers

1. *Quick Installation Guide, Database Readme, Database Release Notes*

2. Gathering information on system requirements

3. You need two disk devices: swap and / (root) for the file mount points

4. rpm –q package_name

5. 1GB

CRITICAL SKILL 2.2

Set Up the Operating System

After Linux is installed and rebooted, information screens walk you through the license information and an option to create a user. Taking this opportunity to create another user besides root is a recommended practice. This is because the Oracle user is needed along with groups for the Oracle software inventory and dba group. Oracle software should be installed under the Oracle user created here, but additional users can also be created now, as needed, for supporting different pieces of the software or for different options that may be installed.

Figure 2-4 shows the creation of groups using command line in the terminal window that is needed for Oracle installs. The groups are created using the groupadd command and then associated with a user id using usermod with the listed parameters and options. Also seen in this figure are the ways that the passwords for the user can be easily changed with the passwd command. Adding another ID, such as osasm to manage the Automatic Storage Management instance, can be accomplished with the command useradd.

The users and groups can be reviewed and managed using the User Manager in System Tools. This interface is also available for creating new users and for associating the groups to the user instead of using the command line in the terminal window. Any users created using this tool and even the users created by the command line, as in Figure 2-4, also have a home directory that is created for them at the same time they are created. The Add User and Add Group in the User Management Tool do the same task as the useradd and groupadd commands; the tools in Linux make it easy to perform these tasks in a way that is most familiar, with either the command lines or user interfaces.

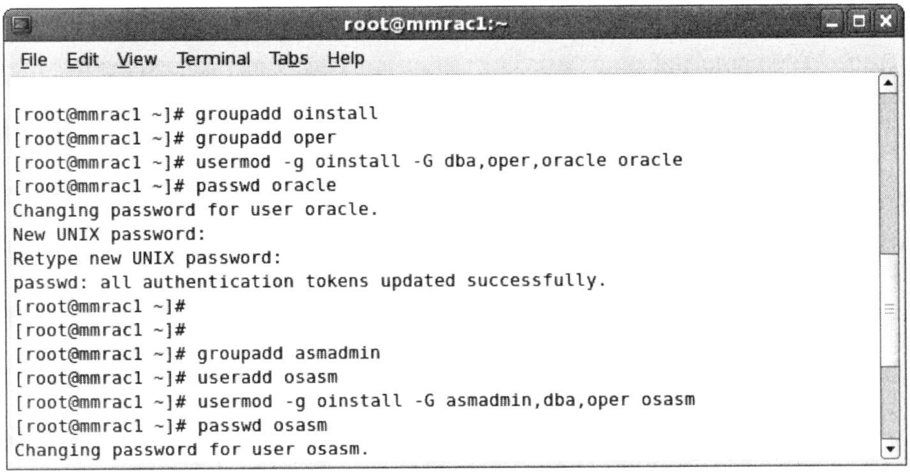

```
root@mmrac1:~
File  Edit  View  Terminal  Tabs  Help

[root@mmrac1 ~]# groupadd oinstall
[root@mmrac1 ~]# groupadd oper
[root@mmrac1 ~]# usermod -g oinstall -G dba,oper,oracle oracle
[root@mmrac1 ~]# passwd oracle
Changing password for user oracle.
New UNIX password:
Retype new UNIX password:
passwd: all authentication tokens updated successfully.
[root@mmrac1 ~]#
[root@mmrac1 ~]#
[root@mmrac1 ~]# groupadd asmadmin
[root@mmrac1 ~]# useradd osasm
[root@mmrac1 ~]# usermod -g oinstall -G asmadmin,dba,oper osasm
[root@mmrac1 ~]# passwd osasm
Changing password for user osasm.
```

FIGURE 2-4.   *Create groups and users*

Ask the Expert

Q: Are there security concerns with adding users? Do you really need any other users besides root and oracle?

A: Security for the operating system is important. Make sure that logins are created for users to install the Oracle software and that additional users are created for the purpose of allowing database administrators to log in and maintain Oracle and the database. Anyone logging into the system should have their own user ID; use of the Oracle login should be limited to installation and patching of the software. Different users should have permissions to access only areas that they should be allowed to access in order to perform tasks as needed. File system permissions should only be granted to the groups and users that need the access, and should be limited where possible. Research best practices for security and don't share logins or root passwords. Keep the environment secure by limiting access to the Oracle software directories; make sure it is not open to just any user who is able to log into the server.

The Oracle user needs certain other permissions along with resource permissions for the software to run well. This is done by adding the Oracle user to the /etc/security/limits.conf and session information to the /etc/pam.d/login file. The file limits.conf, as listed next, shows that the Oracle user has been added with resources to nproc and nofile parameters at the end of the file. These files can be edited with Notepad or a similar editing program when you open the files by using Explorer windows:

```
limits.conf file:
#<domain>            <type>          <item>          <value>
#
oracle              soft            nproc             2047
oracle              hard            nproc            16384
oracle              soft            nofile            1024
oracle              hard            nofile           65536
# End of file

/etc/pam.d/login file:
#%PAM-1.0
auth [user_unknown=ignore success=ok ignore=ignore default=bad]
pam_security.so
auth                include         system-auth
account             required        pam_nologin.so
account             include         system-auth
password            include         system-auth
```

```
# pam_selinux.so close should be the first session rule
session            required        pam_selinux.so close
session            include         system-auth
session            required        pam_loginuid.so
session            optional        pam_console.so
# pam_selinux.so open should only be followed by sessions to be
executed in the  user context
session            required        pam_selinux.so open
session            optional        pam_keyinit.so force revoke
session            required        /lib/security/pam-limits.so
session            required        pam_limits.so
```

Now the operating system is installed and users and groups are created and configured with the needed permissions. You still need to verify (and possibly update) some configurations needed by the kernel parameters so that they match at least the minimum requirements for Oracle. The *Oracle Quick Installation Guide* is the reference for these requirements. We hope that you are starting to see the importance of these documents and why these pieces of information should be gathered before you start the installs.

Project 2-1   Configure Kernel Parameters

The default install of the Linux operating system has values set for the kernel parameters, but the Oracle requirements may need you to adjust these settings. This project will walk you through step by step to change the kernel parameters and show the values of these settings.

Step by Step

1. Get the minimum values from the installation guide. Here is a quick list:

Semmsl	250
Semmns	32000
Semopm	100
Semmni	128
Shmall	2097152
Shmmax	The lesser of the two: either half the size of the physical memory or 4GB
Shmmni	4096
file-max	512*PROCESSES
ip_local_port_range	Min: 1024, max: 650000

rmem_default   4194304

rmem_max   4194304

wmem_default   262144

wmem_max   262144

2. Verify the parameters that are currently set. There may be values already set above the minimum value, so these would not need to be changed. At the command line type the following:

```
# /sbin/sysctl -a | grep <param-name>
```

3. Substitute the parameter name for param-name. For example, shm will show the values for the semaphore parameters:

```
# /sbin/sysctl -a | grep shm
kernel.shmmni = 4096
kernel.shmall = 2097152
kernel.shmmax = 2147483648
```

4. Edit the /etc/sysctl.conf to adjust the kernel parameter values. Use vi or another text editor to add the line as listed under #ORACLE 11gR1 kernel parameters to the end of the file. The other parameter that was changed was kernel.shmmax. Here is the example /etc/sysctl.conf file; the areas that need to change or be added are in bold:

```
sysctl.conf edits:
# Controls the maximum size of a message, in bytes
kernel.msgmnb = 65536
# Controls the default maximum size of a message queue
kernel.msgmax = 65536
# Controls for maximum shared segment size, in bytes
# CHANGED FOR ORACLE 11g # kernel.shmmax = 1073740324
kernel.shmmax = 2147483648
# Controls the maximum number of shared memory segments, in pages
kernel.shmall = 2097152
#ORACLE 11gR1 Kernel Parameters - add the following lines
fs.file-max = 6553600
kernel.shmmni = 4096
kernel.sem = 250 32000 100 128
net.ipv4.ip_local_port_range = 1024 65000
net.core.rmem_default = 4194304
net.core.rmem_max = 4194304
net.core.wmem_default = 262144
net.core.wmem_max = 262144
```

(continued)

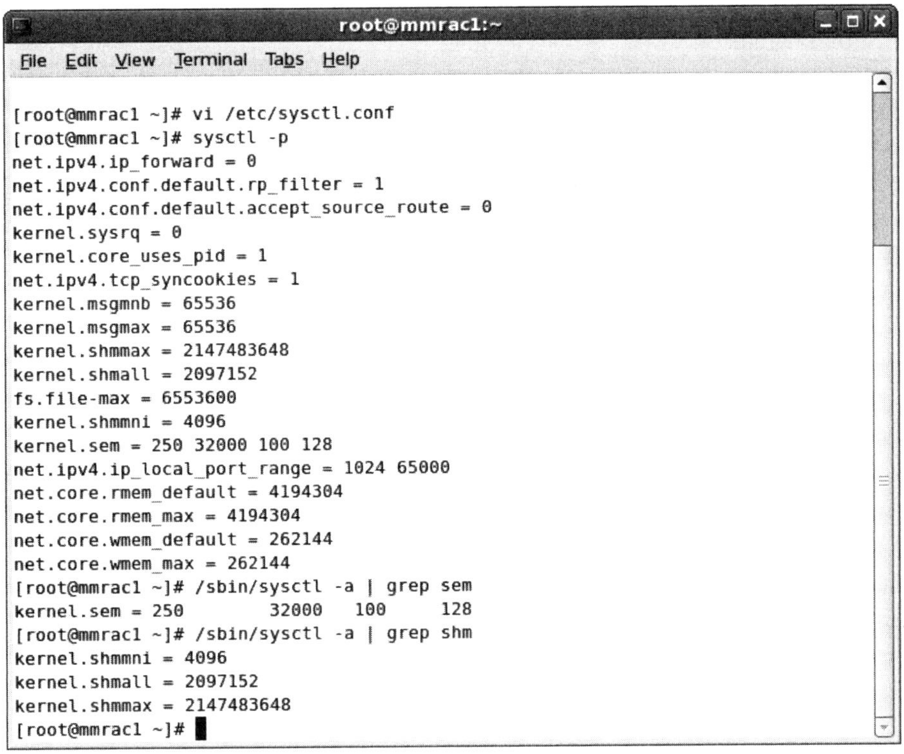

```
root@mmrac1:~                              _ □ ✗
File  Edit  View  Terminal  Tabs  Help

[root@mmrac1 ~]# vi /etc/sysctl.conf
[root@mmrac1 ~]# sysctl -p
net.ipv4.ip_forward = 0
net.ipv4.conf.default.rp_filter = 1
net.ipv4.conf.default.accept_source_route = 0
kernel.sysrq = 0
kernel.core_uses_pid = 1
net.ipv4.tcp_syncookies = 1
kernel.msgmnb = 65536
kernel.msgmax = 65536
kernel.shmmax = 2147483648
kernel.shmall = 2097152
fs.file-max = 6553600
kernel.shmmni = 4096
kernel.sem = 250 32000 100 128
net.ipv4.ip_local_port_range = 1024 65000
net.core.rmem_default = 4194304
net.core.rmem_max = 4194304
net.core.wmem_default = 262144
net.core.wmem_max = 262144
[root@mmrac1 ~]# /sbin/sysctl -a | grep sem
kernel.sem = 250         32000    100      128
[root@mmrac1 ~]# /sbin/sysctl -a | grep shm
kernel.shmmni = 4096
kernel.shmall = 2097152
kernel.shmmax = 2147483648
[root@mmrac1 ~]# ▮
```

FIGURE 2-5.   *Verify the kernel parameters using sysctl –p*

5. Reload the kernel parameters for the new values to take effect. This can be done by restarting the server or by using the following command to reload:

```
# /sbin/syctl -p
```

The execution of this command and its output are shown in Figure 2-5.

Project Summary

In walking through this project, you now know how to see the kernel parameters, make changes to the parameters, and verify those changes. In changing the kernel parameters, you are making the necessary optimizations for the Oracle software to run on the Linux platform.

CRITICAL SKILL 2.3

Get Familiar with Linux

Having the user interface and the terminal window for access to the command line means that there are a couple of ways to navigate through Linux and do what needs to be done. With previous examples of using the command line, files were edited, users were added, and parameters were set up. In managing some of the Oracle files and directories, it is useful to know some of the basic commands or how to look up the option for the commands. Changing directories, copying and moving files, editing, and being able to look at the content of the file are all basic commands in Linux (and almost the same as what is used in Unix, with a couple of possible differences in the parameter options). The following are some useful Linux commands, with a brief definition:

- pwd   This shows the current directory (print working directory).
- more *filename*   This lists the file.
- ls   This lists the files in the directory.
- echo $VAR   This shows value of variables or echoes back the text.
- mv *filename newfilename*   This renames a file.
- cp *filename* /*newdirectory*   This copies a file.
- rm *filename*   This removes (deletes) a file; wildcards can be used but are not recommended for a root directory.

Manual pages are available to provide details for commands as well as available options. There are also examples for how to use the commands in the details. This information can be accessed by typing **man** and then the command. Here is an example of the command, and Figure 2-6 show the results of this command and what can be found in the man pages.

```
$man grep
```

Progress Check

1. How are kernel parameters verified on Linux?

2. What is the Linux command to view the manual pages for grep?

3. What is the command to create a Unix group?

Progress Check Answers

1. sysctl –p

2. man grep

3. group add oinstall

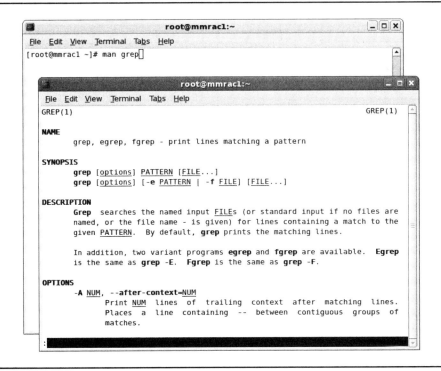

FIGURE 2-6. *OUTPUT of man commands*

Choose Components to Install

Various components of the Oracle software are automatically installed; some are available on the companion CDs or as additional downloads. With Oracle 11*g*, the following products are now installed by default with the database:

- Oracle Database Vault
- Oracle SQL Developer
- Oracle Configuration Manager
- Oracle Application Express
- Oracle Warehouse Builder

This section is not going to turn into a discussion of licensing for standard or enterprise editions and of the different products that are available; however, there are products that provide benefits for different needs. Reviewing the products and versions to match them with business needs before installing is helpful for performing the install of these products at the same time as the initial install. It is possible to add products by running through the install again and choosing the options that have not yet been installed.

The Oracle Universal Installer allows for the Basic install, which is just going to install the default options for Oracle. There is an Advanced option available for deselecting or selecting other available options.

CRITICAL SKILL 2.5
Install the Oracle Software

To begin, run the Oracle Universal Installer as oracle, either from the DVDs or from the downloaded software that has been unzipped on the file system:

```
[oracle@mmrac1 database]$ ./runInstaller
```

If the ORACLE_HOME environment variable is set before running the Installer, information will already be populated with these details. Starting with Figure 2-7, let's walk through some of the screens of the Oracle Universal Installer. Each of the illustrations following provides some detail about what options to select and information to provide while installing the Oracle software.

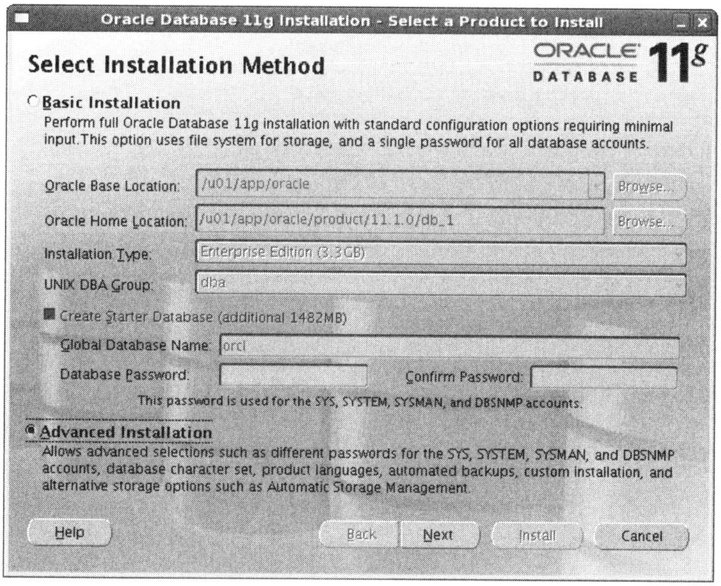

FIGURE 2-7. *Basic vs. advanced install*

The Basic install will start up the database configuration assistant in order to create a database instance after installing the software. Certain configurations are not available, such as Automatic Storage Management (ASM), but the Basic install will install the default components without walking through the options. The Advanced install will allow you to pick and choose from the available options. Advanced install was chosen in Figure 2-7, and the following illustrations for this install will show the options available with the advanced option.

It's a good idea to start to document the options that are chosen for the checklist for the install, so that future installs of the Oracle software will have the same components installed as needed. A checklist will be useful for creating consistent environments and ensuring that the same components are being installed across test to production systems.

The group that was defined on the operating system for the Oracle install is needed for the permissions to the OraInventory directory. This is normally a group such as oinstall, as seen in the following illustration. The OraInventory will contain the information about what was installed and the versions used. OraInventory is used for when the binaries need to be patched and when needing to add or remove components.

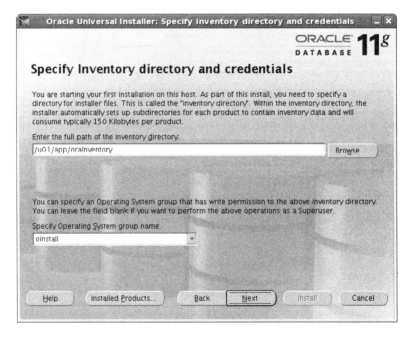

As seen in the next illustration, there are three types of installs: Enterprise, Standard, or Custom. Choosing Enterprise or Standard will install the default products for those versions. Obviously, the Enterprise and Standard versions have different licensing issues, and limitations are set on the Standard edition for CPUs and the options that can be added. There are several product options that come with installing a default type of Standard or Enterprise. Some may argue that you should install only what is needed, while others may suggest that for a development environment, you should install everything to allow developers to test and try out different options. For most systems, we recommend that you use the Custom option to select only options that are needed. Standardize the install so that it can repeated when you are ready for a production environment.

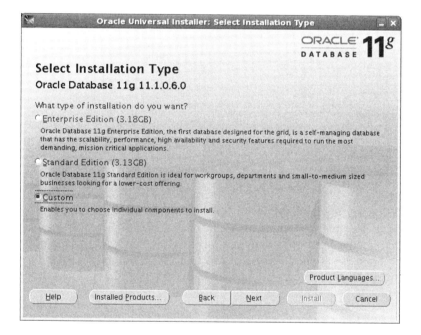

On a server, there can be several home directories with different versions, options, and patch sets installed. The following illustration shows an example of what the base directory and home directory should be set to. If doing a new install and for additional components or patching existing ones, Oracle home directory should be used.

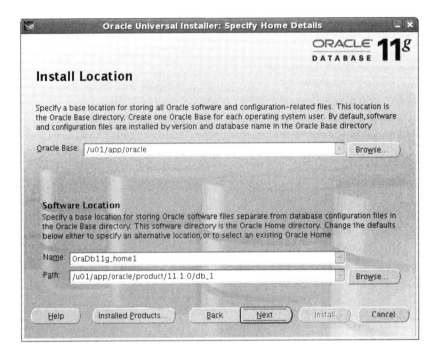

The following illustration shows the install screen running through checks for kernel parameters, memory, and patch sets for the operating system, as well as other requirements that are needed to install and run the Oracle software. If the verification of the operating system was done as part of the planning, these checks should all pass. If there are failures here, they need to be corrected before continuing with the install.

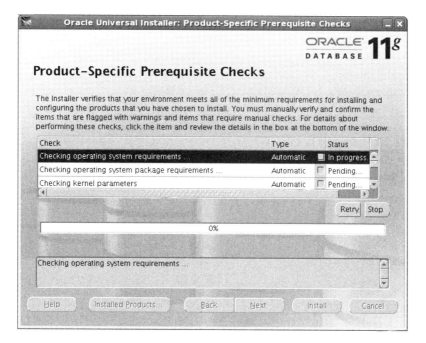

As discussed when using the custom install, there are options for what to install, as shown in the following illustration. Look through the available options and check the components that are desired or uncheck those components not needed.

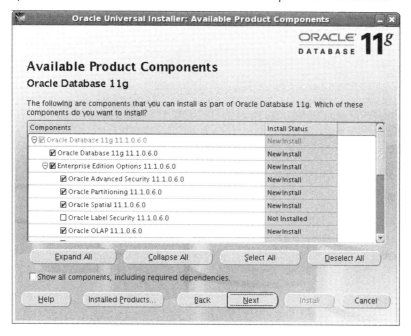

After the software is installed, the installer will open up the database configuration assistant to create a database or to configure ASM. See the following illustration, which shows these choices; in this case, only software has been selected. If you are just installing the software, the database creation assistant can be used at another time for creating databases and ASM instances. The steps for the database configuration assistant are listed in the next section, "Database Configuration Assistant."

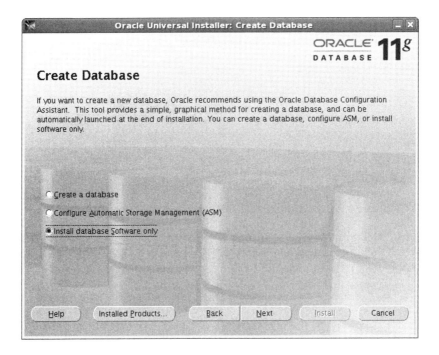

During the last step before the actual install, you still have the opportunity to go back and modify any directories or options for the install. The following illustration shows the screen with this summary information, which has the directories where it is to be installed, installation type, and its space requirements. At this step, take time to review to make sure the information is correct.

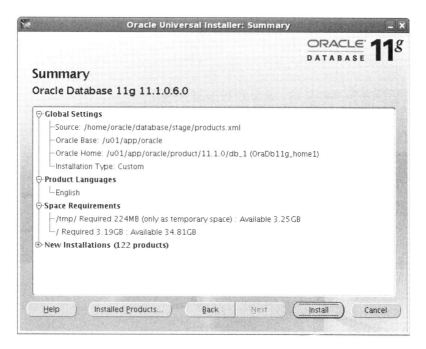

The following illustration shows the files are being copied and installed. Note the location of the log file. If any issues or errors come up, this would be the first place to look for more information.

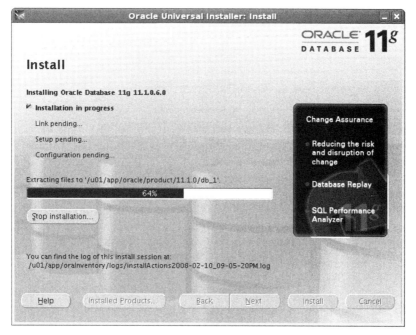

Your last steps are demonstrated in the following illustration. To complete the installation, you will need to make changes regarding permissions and directories that are owned by root. There are two scripts that need to be executed by the root owner to make these changes. Have the operating system administrator log in and run orainstRoot.sh and root.sh (as shown in the illustration).

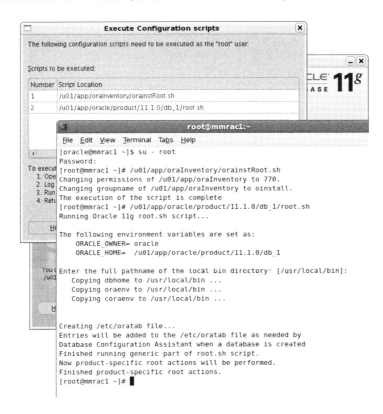

This final illustration is always a good screen to see because it means that the installation of the Oracle software has completed successfully. The installation went through the listener configuration and the instance configuration, so the database is now up and available for use. The listener configuration will be covered in more detail in the next chapter, but for reference here, it is important to have the listener service started to be able to connect to the database instance from another server. This configuration is completed with a default listener name and port as well as starting of the service which will allow the connections to the database.

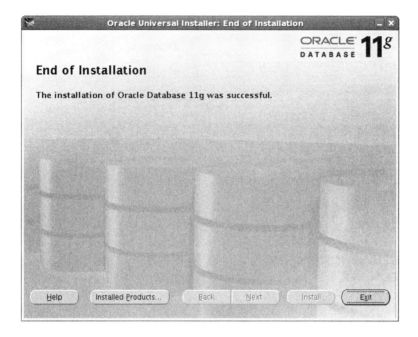

Database Configuration Assistant

As part of the installation, the database configuration assistant (dbca) can be configured to start up after the initial software install. Otherwise, the assistant can be started any time to create a new database instance. The dbca has standard templates to be used for different types of databases; the templates have some parameter settings for memory and others based on the type of instance. The passwords and directories for the tablespaces can use the default values or be customized. As part of the planning process, these configurations should be decided on depending on the directory structures and templates to be used. A checklist needs to be kept to determine which templates, parameter settings, and other choices are to be made within the assistant. The advantage is that even after the database instance is created, parameters and file locations can be adjusted. However, some adjustments are easier than others, and with Oracle 11*g*, there are even more dynamic parameters that can be changed while the database is up and available, instead of having to restart the database instance to make the change in value for the parameter.

As shown in Figure 2-8, the database can be created or an existing database can be dropped. There is also the option to create an Automatic Storage Management (ASM) instance, which will be described in more detail in Chapter 8. Choosing this option for ASM will only install an ASM instance, while running through dbca will be required in order to install a database instance.

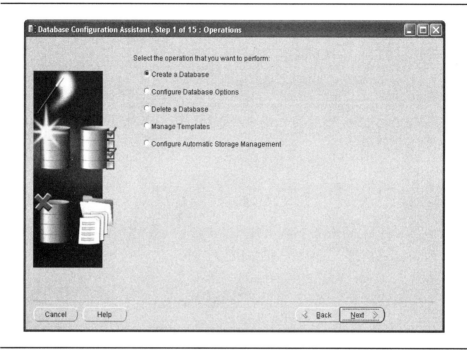

FIGURE 2-8. *Option for install of database*

The next dbac screen has three default options to choose for the databases: General Purpose, Custom Database, and Data Warehouse. For following along with examples that will be used in the rest of the book, it would be useful to install a General Purpose database with the sample schemas. The SH schema that is used for examples is included with other sample schemas.

In stepping through the screens, the next step would be to name the database instance. Passwords should be set for SYS and SYSTEM. All of the system passwords can be the same or they can all be different. The main thing is that these passwords should not be set with a default value as they have in the past. Anyone who knows about installing Oracle and default passwords would be able to log into the database if the default was not changed. For now, the choices to be made with the database install can be kept to defaults or basic choices. As you learn more about what the system is to be used for, you can make more adjustments with parameters and configurations.

For a test database instance with schemas and to work through the examples, check Sample Schemas, as shown here.

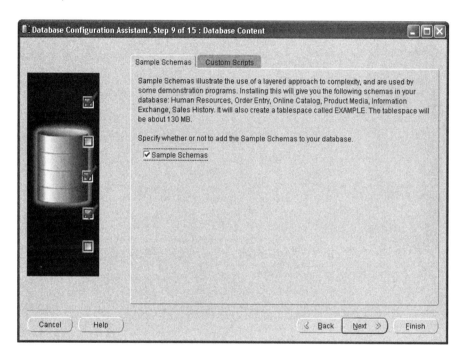

The initialization parameters can be configured as you create the database. The following illustration shows step 10 of the database configuration assistant, where these parameters can be configured. The memory can be customized or default values can be taken, based on a percentage of overall available memory. The character set should also be set up; it is more difficult to change, unlike the memory settings, so verifying the character set for the database is important. The character sets are important for databases with international characters and globalization of the characters. When dealing with international characters, it is suggested to use a character set that allows for these values. Unicode character sets support characters with different sizes and in multiple languages.

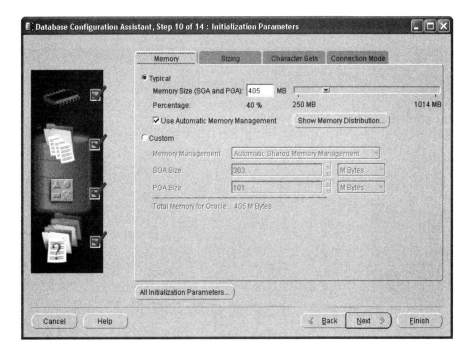

Creating the database, creating the scripts, and developing a template are the final steps before the database is actually created. The following illustration shows the option to save the database as a template and to generate database creation scripts. Having scripts is a valuable tool for creating another similar database, or when needing to create the database again without the assistant. The templates will be added to the creation process of other databases in this Oracle home, again, making it easier to create another database that is similar in nature.

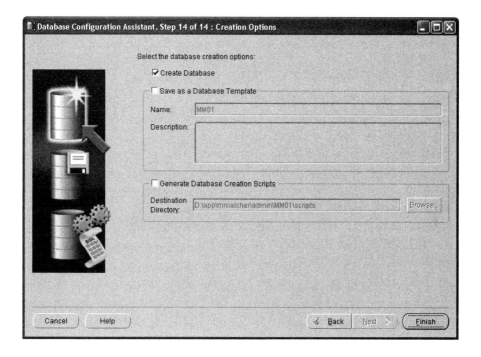

Verify the Installation

The operating system is now configured, the Oracle software is installed, and an initial database has been created. Now the system should be reviewed to confirm that everything is in the right place and that everything is working as expected. Looking through the directories and log directories of the database to verify the install is very useful. Check the install log file, which was the log file that was listed during the install of the software. See Figure 2-9 for example output of the log file.

Review the alert logs of the database and check the logs for any issues with the startup or parameters of the database. The default location for the log files are $ORACLE_BASE\admin\SID. This information can also be retrieved by queries to the database and selecting the value from v$parameter where the name = 'background_dump_dest'. Look at the file systems to make sure that the datafiles

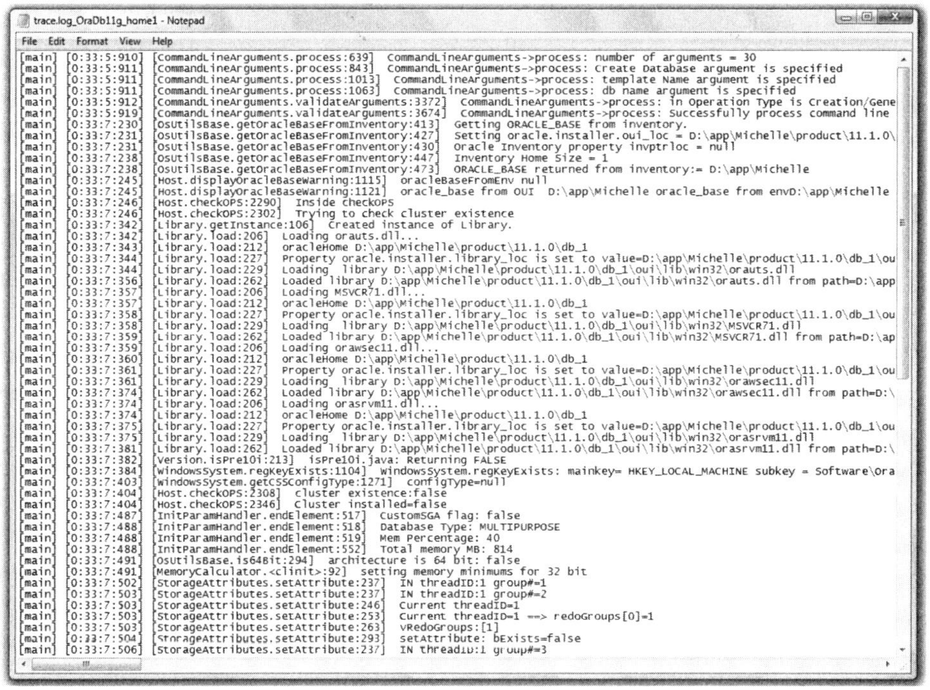

FIGURE 2-9. *Log file details*

are going to the directory that is expected. Again, a quick query against the database, such as select file_name from dba_data_files, will show all of the current data files.

Log into Oracle Enterprise Manager (OEM) and make sure the database can be accessed. Several of these checks are listed in greater detail in later chapters of the book and will show more details about Oracle Enterprise Manager as well as information about tablespaces and data files. Check the memory usage on the operating system level to ensure that the right amount of memory was configured for Oracle and that there is space available for user processes too. Use commands like top to see what the top processes are and to view memory usage for the processes. The file systems should also have enough space; you should verify this after installing Oracle and creating the database.

After these initial checks the system should be ready to use, allowing you to install the front-end application, add users, and set up monitoring and backups. Setting up backups and monitoring help also verify that the system is ready to go and might be a good step to complete before allowing other users to access the database.

Tie It All Together

When doing an Oracle install, the upfront planning and research is important. Gathering business requirements in order to match up database options and versions is also a critical first step to doing the installations. A basic understanding of an operating system is needed to work through the install and to ensure that the user permissions, required system, and hardware components are available. Oracle Enterprise Linux has a standard install, with packages that match up to the database requirements. Gathering documents that provide the latest information about issues and needed prerequisites will make the overall installation go smoothly plus give the added bonus of starting an install process that would be repeatable in the production environment.

☑ Chapter 2 Mastery Check

1. How much disk space is needed for installing Oracle software on Linux?

2. What users and groups are used for installing the Oracle software?

3. True or false: Installing Oracle software will automatically install an Oracle database.

4. What are the prerequisites for installing Oracle software?

5. What are the types of installation options for the Oracle software?

6. What is the Oracle home directory? Can there be more than one?

7. Besides the database, what are some of the other products that are installed by default?

8. What is the tool for creating a database, after the Oracle software install?

9. What is the default password for SYS and SYSTEM users in the database?

10. Which scripts need to be run by root (system administrator) after the install of the software?

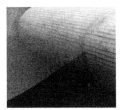

CHAPTER
3

Connecting to Oracle

CRITICAL SKILLS

3.1 Use Oracle Net Services

3.2 Learn the Difference Between Dedicated and Shared Server Architectures

3.3 Define Connections

3.4 Use the Oracle Net Listener

3.5 Learn Naming Methods

3.6 Use Oracle Configuration Files

3.7 Use Administration Tools

3.8 Use Profiles

3.9 Network in a Multi-tiered Environment

3.10 Install the Oracle 11*g* Client Software

his chapter introduces Oracle Net Services, which allows database applications running on remote systems to access an Oracle database. It creates and maintains the network connection, and also exchanges data between the application and the database.

Oracle networking plays a critical role in performance and availability. Each new version of Oracle is designed to support more data and users than the previous release. This increased amount of database activity and network traffic needs to be addressed from an availability and performance perspective and should be managed by the DBA. A DBA also has to be able to determine if a performance issue is due to networking, and if so, then they must be able to resolve any network performance issues from a database configuration perspective.

Throughout this chapter we will refer to DBAs, which in this context means anyone that is performing networking administration operations to make the database connectivity work. These days, more developers are managing their own development databases and performing operations traditionally reserved for DBAs.

NOTE
Oracle Net Services is a large topic. The emphasis in this chapter is to introduce DBAs to Oracle Net Services terminology and concepts, feature/functionality, and key components and tools. Once a beginning DBA reads this section, they should be able to understand the Oracle networking references and be capable of performing simple operations using the Oracle GUI tools and wizards for Oracle Net Services.

CRITICAL SKILL 3.1
Use Oracle Net Services

Oracle Net Services is the software component that allows enterprise connectivity across heterogeneous environments. Oracle Net is the part of Oracle Net Services that manages data communication between a remote application and the Oracle database; it runs on top of a network protocol like TCP/IP. The software used by Oracle Net software resides on the remote system and the Oracle database platform.

A listener process must be running on the database server to receive the network request. (A *listener* is a program that listens on a port for incoming network requests and then hands the request to another program for processing.) The listener then determines the appropriate type of process to handle the request.

The network protocol sends a request to the Oracle Protocol layer, which sends the information to the Oracle Net Foundation layer, which in turn communicates with the database server. The Oracle network communication stack, shown in Figure 3-1, is similar on both the client and server sides.

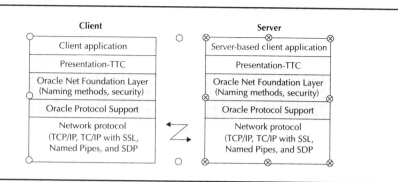

FIGURE 3-1.   *The Oracle network communication stack*

Oracle Net (Oracle Net Foundation Layer and Oracle Protocol Support) fits into the session layer of the Open Systems Interconnect (OSI) model (visit www.ietf.org for more information about the OSI model).

Network Protocols

Oracle supports a number of industry standard protocols. These protocols transport the data between the remote platform and the database server platform. The protocols also display how users need to work with data differently than they did a few years ago. Oracle-supporting protocols like SDP, HTTP, FTP, and WebDAV show that Oracle Database 11*g* enhances network performance and offers increased flexibility for users working with data. In this section, the term *application server* will be used to address both web and application server services available in the middle tier. Table 3-1 lists the supported industry standard protocols.

Optimize Network Bandwidth

Multi-tiered architectures need to maximize the bandwidth between the application server and the database server platforms. Oracle Net Services supports the high-speed networks of InfiniBand, a channel-based, high-speed interconnect technology designed to optimize performance between different platforms. It's used for server clustering and for network interfaces to storage area networks (SANs) and local area networks (LANs). Vendors such as Hewlett-Packard, IBM, Sun Microsystems, Dell, and Microsoft support InfiniBand technology; the SDP protocol, an industry-standard wire protocol, is also used with the InfiniBand network. Highly active multi-tiered environments should consider using high-speed interconnects between the application server and the database server.

Protocol	Description
TCP/IP	The Transmission Control Protocol/Internet Protocol (TCP/IP) is the standard protocol used in client server environments.
TCP/IP with SSL	TCP/IP with Secure Sockets Layer (SSL) provides authentication (certificates and private keys) encryption. The Oracle Advanced Security option is required for this protocol.
SDP	The Sockets Directory Protocol (SDP) is an industry-standard high-speed protocol. SDP is used with an InfiniBand network. The InfiniBand network takes the messaging burden off the CPU and onto the network hardware. This network reduces the overhead of TCP/IP, providing increased bandwidth.
Named pipes	This supports inter-process communication between remote platforms and the database server platform using pipes. A pipe is opened on one end and information is sent down the pipe to allow I/O between the platforms.
HTTP	The Hypertext Transport Protocol (HTTP) is an industry- standard protocol that is primarily used between clients and application servers. Oracle can also start up an HTTP listener to handle a request over HTTP directly.
FTP	File Transfer Protocol (FTP) is a standard method for transferring files across the Internet. It makes it easy to transfer files back and forth between different platforms. A server that can receive an FTP connection is referred to as an FTP server or FTP site. FTP addresses looks similar to HTTP; ftp://ftp.beginner.com is an example of an FTP server address.
WebDAV	The Web-based Distributed Authoring and Versioning (WebDAV) protocol supports collaborative authoring over the Internet. The benefits of WebDAV include locking mechanisms, interoperable publishing with HTTP and XML support, writing over the Web with embedded devices, versioning, and Access Control Lists.

TABLE 3-1. *Standard Industry Network Protocols*

Connections

A *connection* is an Oracle communication path between a user process and the Oracle database server. If this communication path is dropped, a user must establish a new session. The current transaction is rolled back if the connection for its session is lost. A session is a specific connection for a user between the user process and the Oracle database server.

If a connection cannot be made, it is important to be able to troubleshoot these issues and problems. In the Automatic Diagnostic Repository (ADR) for Oracle 11*g*, the network information is also captured. The repository holds trace files and other errors collected into a standard place. This troubleshooting facility for diagnosing network problems is the same as the one you will use to analyze and diagnose database problems. With tools like this it will be easier to find connection issues or avoid problems.

Maintain Connections

The Oracle Net Foundation Layer establishes and maintains connections with the database server. Transparent Network Substrate (TNS) is the common interface between all the industry-standard protocols. Oracle Protocol Support maps the industry-standard protocols (TCP/IP, TCP/IP with SSL, SDP and Named Pipes) used in the connection.

Figure 3-2 shows us how Oracle Net works. Oracle Net software will reside on the database server platform and the platform that is running the Oracle applications. With an application server, HTTP runs on top of a network protocol between the browser platform and the application server platform. Oracle Net then runs on top of a network protocol between the application server and the database server. For a client/server configuration, Oracle Net will reside on the client platform and the database server platform, and will run on top of a network protocol between the client and the database server platforms.

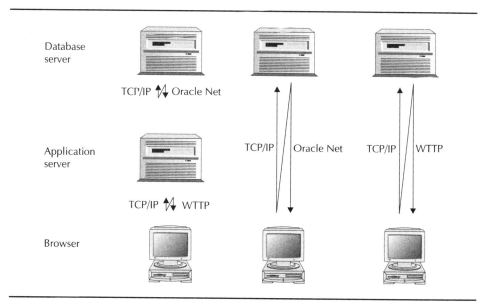

FIGURE 3-2. *An Oracle network overview*

If Java programs are running, a Java Database Connectivity (JDBC) OCI, or Thin driver, will communicate with Oracle Net to process the database request. A JDBC OCI driver requires Oracle Net on the remote platform and the database server. A Thin driver doesn't require a full Oracle Client to be installed and uses network calls to connect to a database. So, a JDBC Thin driver written entirely in Java uses JavaNet to communicate, and requires Oracle Net only on the server platform.

Define a Location

Locations need to be defined so a remote application can find the correct Oracle database server on the network. A service name, such as customer.us.beginner.com, is used to define the unique location of each database server. In the preceding example, customer is the database name and us.beginner.com is the domain name. On the plus side, if the physical location of the database is changed, the service name can stay the same while the definition or settings of the name can change underneath.

A database can support multiple services. The service name, defined with the initialization parameter SERVICE_NAMES, makes the physical location of the database transparent and will default to the global database name (the name of your database), which uses the format database_name.database_domain, as in customer.us.beginner.com.

The database domain name is the domain where the database is located, and is made up of the initialization parameters DB_NAME and DB_DOMAIN. The combination of the DB_NAME and DB_DOMAIN (customer.us.beginner.com) name distinguishes one database from another, as shown in the following examples:

```
DB_NAME=customer
DB_DOMAIN=us.beginner.com
```

Ask the Expert

Q: Why is it important for DBAs to understand the networking setup and configuration for Oracle Database 11*g*?

A: Often as systems interact with the database, networking bottlenecks surface that require attention from DBA personnel in addition to those who manage the applications. Familiarity if not fluency with setting up Oracle Net services and its configuration files arms the DBA with the skills required to intervene.

CRITICAL SKILL 3.2

Learn the Difference Between Dedicated and Shared Server Architectures

An Oracle database server can be configured to run either a dedicated or shared server architecture. This decision determines how the listener processes requests and how server processes work for an Oracle instance. Server processes are the interface between the Oracle database server and user processes, the latter of which must go through a server process that handles the database communication between the user process and the database. Server processes can

- Process database requests, access data, and return the results.

- Perform data translations and conversions between the application and database server environments.

- Protect the database server from illegal operations by the user processes. A server process accesses Oracle database and memory structures on behalf of the user process. This separates user process activity from direct access to Oracle's internal memory.

Dedicated Server

A dedicated server environment uses a "dedicated" server process for each user process. The benefit of this is that each user process has a dedicated server process to handle all of its database requests. If there are a hundred separate sessions, there will be a hundred dedicated server processes running on the same platform as the database server.

The problem is that each dedicated server process is often idle a large percentage of the time. This takes up a lot of operating system resources for server processes that are sitting idle and creates issues when large numbers of users are accessing a system. Oracle databases that allow access from the Internet can have tremendous spikes of activity that generate a large number of dedicated server processes. The dedicated server architecture also does not support FTP, HTTP, or WebDAV clients.

Figure 3-3 illustrates the way that dedicated server processes run on the database server platform. A dedicated server process will be run for each user session.

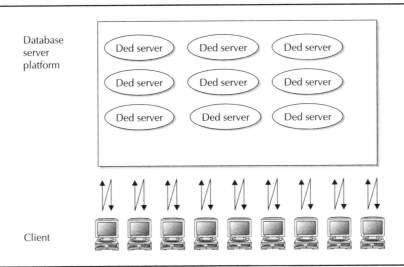

FIGURE 3-3. *The dedicated server architecture*

Shared Server

A shared server architecture offers increased scalability for a large number of users. This is possible because a single server process can be "shared" among a number of user processes, allowing a single server process to be able to support a large number of user processes. If there are 100 separate sessions, there may in turn be 20 shared server processes supporting them. Having a small pool of server processes that can support a large number of sessions increases scalability. This shared server architecture is much more scalable than a dedicated architecture as the number of users for a system increase. The shared server process can also handle large spikes of user activity much better than a dedicated server process configuration.

When a user request arrives, the listener will route the request to a dispatcher, which then processes and routes the request to a common queue. From a pool of shared server processes, an idle shared server will see if there is work in the common queue. Requests are processed on a first-in first-out basis. The shared server then processes the request and puts the results in a response queue (each dispatcher has one) that a dispatcher can return to the user process. Afterward, the dispatcher returns the results from its response queue to the appropriate user process.

A dispatcher supports multiple connections with virtual circuits, which are sections of shared memory that contain the information necessary for client communication. The dispatcher puts the virtual circuit on the common (request) queue accessed by the server process.

There are some administration operations that cannot be performed through a dispatcher, however. To perform these restricted administration operations in a shared server environment, the DBA needs to connect with a dedicated server process instead of a dispatcher process. The restricted operation needs a connect descriptor with a setting of SERVER=DEDICATED, defined in the CONNECT_DATA section of the tnsnames.ora file: (CONNECT_DATA = (SERVER = DEDICATED)(SERVICE_NAME = MMDEV1)). Restricted operations include the following:

- Starting up an instance
- Shutting down an instance
- Media recovery

As Figure 3-4 shows, a shared server process can support multiple user sessions.

Table 3-2 illustrates the initialization parameters that are used to configure the shared server architecture. Possible values for these parameters are dependent on the level of user activity and the types of operations the server processes are executing.

Oracle recommends starting with one shared server process for every ten connections. It then automatically increases the number of shared servers based upon the workload up to the MAX_SHARED_SERVERS that are defined. The PMON process is responsible for adding and removing shared servers; the number of shared servers will never drop below the value contained in the SHARED_SERVERS parameter. You should also note that the parameters that control the minimum and maximum number of these shared servers can be set dynamically; therefore you can always ensure that you can react quickly to shared server issues.

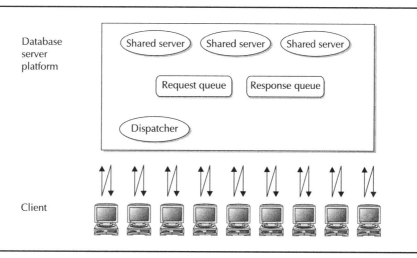

FIGURE 3-4.   *The shared server architecture*

Oracle Initialization Parameter	Definition
DISPATCHERS	This defines the number of dispatcher processes to start in a shared server architecture. The number of dispatchers can be dynamically added or reduced. There must be at least one dispatcher for each network protocol. Additional dispatchers can be defined based upon the workload.
MAX_DISPATCHERS	This defines the maximum number of dispatchers. This is not a fixed limit. In this release, this value can be dynamically exceeded at runtime.
SHARED_SERVERS	This defines the number of shared servers to invoke on database startup in a shared server architecture.
MAX_SHARED_SERVERS	This defines the maximum number of shared server processes.
SESSIONS	This defines the maximum number of sessions that can be active in a system.
SHARED_SERVER__SESSIONS	This defines the maximum number of shared server sessions that can be started in a system. It also allows dedicated sessions to be reserved in a shared server environment. Sessions started above this limit will use dedicated server processes.
CIRCUITS	This defines the maximum number of virtual circuits.
LARGE_POOL_SIZE	This defines the size of the large pool area in the SGA. If a large pool exists, the session information will be stored in the large pool, not the shared pool area.

TABLE 3-2. *Initialization Parameters Used by Shared Servers*

Set Dispatchers

To set the number of dispatchers, determine the maximum number of concurrent sessions and divide this by the number of connections per dispatcher. Then, dependent upon the level of activity, the number of dispatchers may need to be increased or decreased. A single dispatcher can handle a large number of shared server processes, but the number of dispatchers per shared server is dependent upon the activity of the shared server processes.

One of the following attributes—PROTOCOL, ADDRESS, or DESCRIPTION—can be set with dispatchers. PROTOCOL defines the network protocol to use, ADDRESS defines the network protocol address on which the dispatchers listen, and DESCRIPTION is the network description. Default values are used if the attributes are not defined, and additional network options can be defined if the ADDRESS or DESCRIPTION attribute is set.

Additional attributes that can be set with ADDRESS or DESCRIPTION include the following:

- **SESSIONS**   This defines the maximum number of network sessions per dispatcher.

- **CONNECTIONS**   This defines the maximum number of network connections per dispatcher.

- **TICKS**   This defines the length of a network tick (seconds). A tick defines the length of time for a message to get from the client to the database server or from the database server to the client.

- **POOL**   This defines the timeout in ticks for incoming (IN=15) and outgoing (OUT=20) connections, and whether connection pooling is enabled. The number of ticks multiplied by the POOL value determines the total connection pool timeout.

- **MULTIPLEX**   This defines if multiplexing with the Connection Manager is set for incoming and outgoing connections. Multiplexing allows multiple sessions to transport over a single network connection. This is used to increase the network capacity for a large number of sessions.

- **LISTENER**   This defines the network name of an address for the listener.

- **SERVICE**   This defines the server names that dispatchers determine with the listeners.

- **INDEX**   This defines which dispatcher should be modified.

In your init.ora file, you will define the dispatchers. The following are examples of different types of entries that will typically be created to support shared servers.

Define the number of dispatchers to start:

```
DISPATCHERS='(PROTOCOL=TCP)(DISPATCHERS=5)'
```

Define a dispatcher to start on a specific port:

```
DISPATCHERS='(ADDRESS=(PROTOCOL=TCP)(DISPATCHERS=5))'
```

Define a dispatcher with more options:

```
DISPATCHERS=" (DESCRIPTION=(ADDRESS=(PROTOCOL=TCP)
               (HOST=eclipse)(PORT=1521)(QUEUESIZE=20)))
               (DISPATCHERS=2)
               (SERVICE = customer.us.beginner.com)
               (SESSIONS=2000)
               (CONNECTIONS = 2000)
               (MULTIPLEX = ON)
               (POOL = ON)
               (TICK = 5)"
```

As you can see, there are numerous options that may be used, depending on the configuration methods that you select when configuring the dispatcher.

Views to Monitor the Shared Server

The following views can be used to monitor the load on the dispatchers:

- V$DISPATCHER
- V$DISPATCHER_RATE
- V$QUEUE
- V$DISPATCHER_CONFIG

The following views can be used to monitor the load on the shared servers:

- V$SHARED_SERVER
- V$SHARED_SERVER_MONITOR
- V$QUEUE

The V$CIRCUIT view can be used to monitor virtual circuits.

The following views can be used to monitor the SGA memory associated with the shared server environment:

- V$SGA
- V$SGASTAT
- V$SHARED_POOL_RESERVED

These views provide you with the ability to monitor your database and the activity related to your shared servers and database. We encourage you to take a look at the data in these tables before and after you implement shared servers, to see how they change your database and how it functions.

CRITICAL SKILL 3.3

Define Connections

This section will discuss the core components required to handle Oracle connections.

A Connect Descriptor

A *connect descriptor* is used to define the service name and the location of the database. The address component of a connect descriptor defines the protocol, host name, and port number. Though port numbers can be between 1 to 65535, those from 1 to 1024 are usually reserved for special processes. The default port for Oracle Listener is 1521. The connect data component of the description describes the service to which you want to connect. If you do not include the instance_name in your descriptor, it will default to the Oracle SID.

A sample connect descriptor for customer.us.beginner.com looks like the following:

```
(DESCRIPTION =
 (ADDRESS=(PROTOCOL=tcp)(HOST=eclipse)(PORT=1521))
 (CONNECT_DATA=
     (SERVICE_NAME=customer.us.beginner.com)))
```

A specific connect descriptor can be defined for a specific service handler. For example, in a shared server architecture, a dedicated service handler can be chosen, which can be set to dedicated (SERVER=dedicated) or shared (SERVER=shared). If no dispatchers are available, a dedicated server will be used and the default service handler is shared:

```
(DESCRIPTION =
  (ADDRESS=(PROTOCOL=tcp)(HOST=eclipse)(PORT=1521))
 (CONNECT_DATA=
     (SERVICE_NAME=customer.us.beginner.com)
       (SERVER=dedicated)))
```

Define a Connect Descriptor

When establishing a connection, you have two choices: a detailed connect descriptor can be defined or a manual name that maps to a connect descriptor can be used. The following example shows you how to define a manual connect descriptor or name a connection descriptor name:

```
-- Manual definition of a connection descriptor
CONNECT
username/password@(DESCRIPTION = (ADDRESS=(PROTOCOL=tcp) (HOST=eclipse)
  (PORT=1521))  (CONNECT_DATA= (SERVICE_NAME=customer.us.beginner.com)))
-- Connect using a pre-defined descriptor
CONNECT username/password@cust
```

The Oracle Connection Manager

The Oracle Connection Manager processes and filters requests to the database server. It can also optimize network performance for a large number of sessions. Figure 3-5 illustrates the various layers between the users and the database that need to be controlled by the manager.

The Oracle Connection Manager Control utility allows administration of the Oracle Connection Manager. The syntax is

```
cmctl {command} [parameter1 ... parameterN] {-c instance_name}
      {-p password}
```

Connection Manager commands can be executed from within the utility, as shown here:

```
cmctl
CMCTL> startup -c cman0
```

The Oracle Connection Manager can offload network I/O from the application servers.

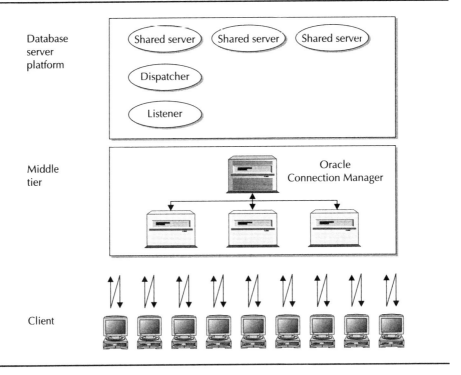

FIGURE 3-5. *The Oracle Connection Manager architecture*

We will now move on and look at the Oracle Connection Manager options to include session multiplexing and firewall access control.

Session Multiplexing

The Oracle Connection Manager allows a number of different client network sessions to be shared (multiplexed) through a single network connection to the database server. Multiplexing sessions increases the number of network sessions that can be supported. Similarly, multiple Connection Managers can be used to handle hundreds or thousands of concurrent users; they run on the application server platform in order to multiplex sessions to the Oracle database server.

Firewall Access Control

The Oracle Connection Manager can define filtering rules to grant or deny access to the database server; this is done via the Oracle Net Firewall Proxy. The Oracle Net Firewall Proxy is software that provides Oracle Connection Manager features through different firewall vendors.

Progress Check

1. The protocol _____ supports collaborative authoring over the Internet.

2. True or False: The SDP protocol adds advanced network security features.

3. True or False: A virtual circuit is a section of shared memory that contains information for client communication.

4. True or False: Port numbers from 1 to 1024 are usually reserved for SSL.

5. The _____ server architecture does not support FTP, HTTP, or WebDAV clients.

6. True or False: The Oracle Connection Manager supports multiplexing sessions.

Progress Check Answers

1. The protocol *WebDAV* supports collaborative authoring over the internet.

2. False. The SDP protocol is used with high-speed networks.

3. True. A virtual circuit is a section of shared memory that contains information for client communication.

4. False. Ports 1 to 1024 are used for special processes. They are not reserved for SSL.

5. The *dedicated* server architecture does not support FTP, HTTP, or WebDAV clients.

6. True. Yes, this is one of the advantages of using the Oracle Connection Manager.

CRITICAL SKILL 3.4

Use the Oracle Net Listener

The Oracle Net Listener (listener) listens on a network port (listening endpoints) for incoming database requests. A listening endpoint defines the protocol addresses the listener is defined to listen on. Listening endpoints include HTTP, FTP, WebDAV, and Oracle XML. Look at the *ORACLE XML DB Developer's Guide* for more detail on registering FTP, HTTP, and WebDAV listening points.

The process is fairly simple. The listener receives a request and hands the request to a service handler, which is a server process that runs on the same platform as the Oracle database server. The service handler can be a dedicated server or a dispatcher, the latter of which works with shared servers.

The PMON background process registers the service information to the listener. During registration, PMON gives the listener information on the database services and instance information. PMON then tries to register with the listener once the listener has been started. Dynamic registration is supported with the alter system register command. If PMON has not registered with the listener, a TNS listener error will occur. View the *Oracle Database 11g Error Messages* reference manual for more details.

The listener will receive the database request and spawn a dedicated server process if the environment is configured for the dedicated server architecture. The listener will hand the request over to a dispatcher if running a shared server architecture. A client application can bypass the listener if it is running on the same platform as the database server. Once the listener hands off the request it will resume listening for additional network requests.

A default listener (named listener) is configured at installation with the Oracle Net Configuration Assistant making it easy to start up the default listener when a system is first built. An additional ICP protocol address is defined for external routes (EXTPROC) during installation.

The following is a sample listener.ora file:

```
LISTENER =
  (DESCRIPTION_LIST =
    (DESCRIPTION =
      (ADDRESS_LIST =
        (ADDRESS = (PROTOCOL = IPC)(KEY = EXTPROC0))
      )
      (ADDRESS_LIST =
        (ADDRESS = (PROTOCOL = TCP)(HOST = eclipse)(PORT = 1521))
      )
    )
  )
```

Parameter	Description
DESCRIPTION	This defines a connect descriptor for a net service name.
DESCRIPTION_LIST	This defines a list of connect descriptors.
LISTENER	This defines the listener alias.
ADDRESS	This defines the listener protocol address.
ADDRESS_LIST	This defines a list of protocol addresses that contain common behavior.

TABLE 3-3. *Listener.ora File Formats*

Table 3-3 illustrates the contents of the listener.ora file.

In the following, host defines the server name, PORT defines the port number, SERVER defines the host server name, PIPE defines the pipe name, and KEY defines a unique name for the service. It is recommended that you use the Oracle SID value for the key.

Table 3-4 defines the components of the protocol definition.

Protocol	Example
TCP	(PROTOCOL=tcp)(host=eclipse)(PORT=1521)
TCP/IP with SSL	(PROTOCOL=tcps)(host=eclipse)(PORT=2484)
IPC	(PROTOCOL=ipc)(KEY=cust)
Named pipes	(PROTOCOL=nmp)(SERVER=eclipse)(PIPE=pipe01)
SDP	(PROTOCOL=sdp)(host=eclipse)(PORT=1521)

TABLE 3-4. *Protocol Examples in the listener.ora File*

After installation, the Oracle Net Manager can be used to modify the listener configuration. Some of the values that can be configured for the listener include the following:

■ If the default port of 1521 is not specified, the LOCAL_LISTENER initialization parameter needs to be defined through a naming method. The LOCAL_LISTENER parameter is dynamic and can be set with the alter system command.

■ Be careful, because the LISTENER parameter overrides the LOCAL_LISTENER parameter. A host system can have multiple IP addresses, and a listener can be configured to listen on them.

■ The I/O buffer size for send and receive operations can be defined.

■ Heterogeneous services can be set to support additional services such as external routines.

■ The QUEUESIZE parameter can be defined for environments that may have a large number of concurrent connection requests for a listener on a listening endpoint.

Password Authentication

In Oracle 11*g*, the listener administration is secure through the operating system authentication. So the administration is then restricted to the account that started the listener. Another option is to set a password for the listener. Also for remote administration of the listener a password is required. The change_password command can be used to change a password or set a new password. If a password is not set, someone can accidentally impact the availability of the database—for example, accidentally shutting down the listener. If you don't have a listener, new sessions cannot be established. It is important that a DBA protect access to listener management.

Using the listener utility, lsnrctl, listener configurations can be managed. The following example sets the listener password:

```
> lsnrctl
lsnrctl> change_password
Old password: <enter>
New password: newpassword
Reenter new password: newpassword
lsnrctl> save_config
```

Multiple Listeners

Multiple listeners can be defined for a service and can offer a number of advantages for more complex environments. These advantages include the following:

- Failover

- Transparent application failover

- Load balancing

The following is a sample connect descriptor for a listener:

```
(DESCRIPTION =
 (ADDRESS_LIST=
   (ADDRESS=(PROTOCOL=tcp)(HOST=eclipse)(PORT=1521))
 (CONNECT_DATA=
    (SERVICE_NAME=customer.us.beginner.com)))
```

Connection Pooling

A shared server architecture is used to improve user scalability. So, it is assumed that if this architecture is being used, there is a potential for a large number of users. As mentioned previously, at any point in time there can be a large percentage of idle processes. Connection pooling allows the database server to time out sessions that are idle and then use the connection to support an active session. These sessions remain open but in an idle state. When they become active again, a connection is reestablished.

CRITICAL SKILL 3.5

Learn Naming Methods

A *naming method* defines the type of repository used to configure Oracle network information. This repository is accessed to define where the Oracle database server is located.

Oracle supports various types of naming methods, such as:

- Directory naming (centralized configuration)

- Local naming (client configuration)

- External naming (external configuration)

- Easy naming (manual configuration)

Directory Naming Method

For centralized network management, Oracle Net Services uses a Lightweight Directory Access Protocol (LDAP) directory server as the repository. LDAP uses hierarchical structures (directories) that contain different components of a communication path. The LDAP directory stores all database network information, policies, security, and authentication information in this centralized repository. Remote applications will go to the centralized repository to find network configuration information. The results are then returned containing the communication path to the Oracle database server.

Different vendors provide their own LDAP directory server. The Oracle LDAP directory, for instance, is named the Oracle Internet Directory (OID). (The Microsoft version of this is named Microsoft Active Directory.)

You should note that there are some restrictions when using the Microsoft Active Directory. The Oracle Net Configuration Assistant may be used with the Microsoft Active Directory; however, the Oracle Internet Directory Configuration tool cannot be used with the Microsoft Active Directory.

Security has been a focus of Oracle 11*g*, and with directories such as the LDAP directory, there are areas that need to be more secure than others. The method of authentication of lookups through parameters in the directory users can be validated and authorized first, which would protect sensitive Net Services information. A simple authenticated user is defined by just a login and a password; in comparison, strong authentication includes encryption. Modification of the directory via Oracle Net Manager or lookups in the directory can be configured securely through simple or strong authentication.

Storing network information in a centralized location is much more efficient from an administration perspective. Make a change in one place, and it is reflected everywhere. It's also better from a security perspective because the database location is stored in a centralized repository instead of a file on a local machine.

Directory Information Trees

LDAP directory servers store information in a hierarchical tree structure called a Directory Information Tree (DIT). DITs are typically organized in a Domain Name Space (DNS) structure (usually along corporate or geographical lines), and are defined by the Oracle Internet Directory Configuration Assistant. Every node in the tree is referred to as an entry, each of which can be modified with the Oracle Enterprise Manager or the Oracle Net Manager. The following example shows how a connect descriptor maps to a DIT:

```
(DESCRIPTION =
 (ADDRESS=(PROTOCOL=tcp)(HOST=eclipse)(PORT=1521))
(CONNECT_DATA=
     (SERVICE_NAME=customer.us.beginner.com)))
```

Figure 3-6 illustrates how the directories are organized and may be navigated when using the Oracle Internet Directory Configuration Assistant. It is important to know your directory trees to ensure that you correctly move through your hierarchy.

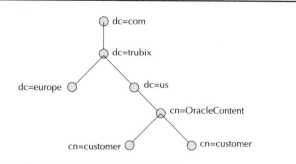

FIGURE 3-6. *A directory information tree*

Distinguished Names

A distinguished name (DN) defines where an entry resides in the directory path, and begins at the lowest entry. The DN for the customer distinguished name is dn:cn=customer, cn=OracleContext, dc=us, dc=beginner, and dc=com. Relative distinguished names (RDNs), on the other hand, define the sequences within the path. An RDN contains an attribute that defines the RDN. An important RDN is the Oracle Context, which defines the default location for connect identifiers. An identity management realm, meanwhile, defines a set of identities that share the same administration policies.

How to Find the Directory Naming Information

With this naming method, a client needs to find the centralized information that is stored in the LDAP repository to be able to connect to the database server. There are two ways to find the centralized directory naming information stored on a separate system:

- The *static method*, which works via a local ldap.ora file.

- The *dynamic method*, which works via a domain name server (DNS).

An ldap.ora file is a statically configured file containing the location of the LDAP server. DNS uses name servers to map names and IP addresses for systems. If the latter changes, the next time the name is looked for on the domain name server, it will map to the new IP address.

Ask the Expert:

Q: Should I be prepared to implement non-TCP/IP-based network transports with my Database 11g installations?

A: Most sites leverage the TCP/IP protocol for network services from Oracle and other vendors that play a role in getting information from the client to the database back end. In most of your travels around the Oracle technology, you too will use the TCP/IP standard almost all the time. Familiarity with other protocols is wise if and when called upon to administer non-TCP/IP networks.

Net Service Alias Entries

A *net service alias entry* is another name for a net service name. A net service alias references the directory location and the name cust in the directory information tree is a net service alias. Aliases simplify management by using a short alias instead of having to specify the full path.

The Local Naming Method

The *local naming method* uses a local configuration file called tnsnames.ora. The tnsnames.ora file stores net service names and connect descriptors and it resides on the platform running the database application. It also contains the information required to find and connect to the Oracle database server. The following definition defines the address (protocol, host, port number) along with the dedicated server environment and which service to connect to:

```
CUST =
  (DESCRIPTION =
    (ADDRESS_LIST =
      (ADDRESS = (PROTOCOL = TCP)(HOST = eclipse)(PORT = 1521))
    )
    (CONNECT_DATA =
      (SERVER = DEDICATED)
      (SERVICE_NAME = CUST)
    )
  )
```

This is a simple file to configure. The problem is that if you have 1000 users, you need to make sure the tnsnames.ora file has been updated for all of the client machines. From a security perspective, it is not ideal to allow clients access to a server location and the connection information.

The Easy Naming Method

The *easy naming method* explicitly defines the connect information. The connect information contains the host, port, service name, and instance name. This allows someone to connect in a specific way without going through the configuration effort. The format is

```
CONNECT username/password@eclipse:1521/customer.us.beginner.com/cust
```

An advantage of the easy naming method is that it is easy to configure. The user need only provide minimal information to get a connection. As a result, no other naming methods need to be configured. This method cannot be used if more advanced features are required.

The External Naming Method

The *external naming method* uses net service names that are defined in a non-Oracle environment. This naming method works well for administrators that want to use their native naming service and allows them to use native tools and utilities with which they have experience. The disadvantage of this approach is that Oracle Net tools cannot be used for these native naming methods. Supported non-Oracle services include the Network Information Service (NIS) or Cell Directory Services (CDS). CDS is part of a Distributed Computing Environment (DCE). DCE is an integrated distributed environment designed to resolve interoperability issues with heterogeneous environments. DCE is maintained by the Open Systems Foundation (OSF).

Which Naming Method to Use

The local naming method (tnsnames.ora) has traditionally been the most popular method. However, there are a number of administration and security issues in stored local configuration with a tnsnames.ora file. The directory (centralized) naming method is more scalable and has less administration than the local naming method. For large systems, the directory method is becoming more popular.

CRITICAL SKILL 3.6
Use Oracle Configuration Files

Remote applications will look for Oracle Net configuration files to determine how to access the Oracle database server. Configuration files can be found in the ORACLE_HOME/network/admin directory location. Table 3-5 defines the primary configuration files.

Network Configuration Filename	Description
listener.ora	The listener.ora file defines how the listeners are configured on the database server.
sqlnet.ora	The sqlnet.ora file resides on the database server and the local platform. Profile information is stored in the sqlnet.ora file. This file defines information on service names, naming methods, external naming information, Advanced Security parameters, and database access information. The TNS_ADMIN environmental variable can override the default location of these files.
tnsnames.ora	Resides on the local system and is used with the local naming method. This defines net service names and connect descriptor information.
cman.ora	The configuration file for the Oracle Connection Manager. This file resides on the same platform where the Oracle Connection Manager runs.
ldap.ora	The directory usage file is created by the Oracle Internet Directory Configuration Assistant.

TABLE 3-5. *Primary Configuration Files for Oracle Net Services*

DBAs can use the management tools to modify Oracle Net Services configurations. However, since the configuration files have a simple syntax, it is easy to modify the configuration files directly. The following is an example of the listener.ora file:

```
# LISTENER.ORA Date: 04/25/2009
LISTENER =
  (DESCRIPTION_LIST =
    (DESCRIPTION =
      (ADDRESS_LIST =
        (ADDRESS = (PROTOCOL = IPC)(KEY = EXTPROC0))
      )
      (ADDRESS_LIST =
        (ADDRESS = (PROTOCOL = TCP)(HOST = eclipse)(PORT = 1521))
      )
    )
  )
```

Should a DBA want to modify the files directly, the following syntax rules must be followed:

■ Comments must begin with a pound sign (#). Anything following the pound sign is treated as a comment.

■ Keywords are not case sensitive and cannot contain spaces.

■ Spaces are optional around equal (=) signs.

■ Values can only contain spaces if they are surrounded by quotes. The values may be case sensitive depending on the operating system and protocol.

■ A connect descriptor can be no more than 4KB in length.

■ All characters must be part of the network set.

■ Care must be taken with parentheses when editing. Troubleshooting a connection problem might be necessary because a simple edit was made to the file and close or open parenthesis was dropped.

CRITICAL SKILL 3.7
Use Administration Tools

Oracle Net Services contains a number of user interfaces and tools that simplify the management of the Oracle network, including the following:

■ Oracle Enterprise Manager (OEM) / Grid Control

■ The OEM console

■ Oracle Net Manager

■ Oracle Net Configuration Assistant

■ Oracle Connection Manager

■ Oracle Internet Directory Configuration Assistant

■ Command-line utilities

■ Oracle Advanced Security

The Oracle Enterprise Manager/Grid Control

Along with database administration, OEM allows configuration of Oracle Net Services. OEM can be used to perform the following administration features:

■ The configuration of listeners

■ The configuration of naming definitions such as connect descriptors

The Oracle Net Manager

The Oracle Net Manager allows the configuration of Oracle Net Services and can be started from the OEM console, by choosing Tools | Service Management | Oracle Net Manager.

The Oracle Net Manager provides the following administration support:

- **Listeners**   This supports creating and configuring listeners.

- **Naming**   This supports defining simple names. Simple names specify information for connect descriptors and service location information.

- **Naming methods**   This supports the definition of naming methods.

Some of the functionality in OEM is also available in the Oracle Net Manager. Table 3-6 shows the overlapping functionality and the differences between the two tools.

The following can be used to start Oracle Net Manager manually through UNIX:

```
$   $ORACLE_HOME/bin/netmgr
```

Oracle Net Manager can also be started manually through Windows by selecting Start | Programs | Oracle—OraHome11 | Configuration and Migration Tools | Net Manager.

Oracle Enterprise Manager	Oracle Net Manager
Local naming (tnsnames.ora)	Local naming (tnsnames.ora)
Directory naming	Directory naming
Listeners	Listeners
Oracle home support for multiple hosts	Oracle home support for a single host
Search capability on local and directory names	Profiles
Export directory entries to tnsnames.ora file	
Changing tracing and logging settings	

TABLE 3-6.   *Common Features and Differences Between OEM and Oracle Net Manager*

The OEM Console

The Oracle Enterprise Manager Central Console is a web-based interface for managing the entire enterprise from the console. It offers a lot more functionality than the standard Oracle Enterprise Manager that comes with a typical database install. The default ports for running in a nonsecure mode are 7777-7877; default ports for running in a secure mode are 4443-4533.

You can access the OEM Central Console from the following URLs: http://<oms hostname>.<domain>.<port>/em and https://<oms hostname>.<domain>.<port>/em. The OEM Central Console requires the Oracle Management Service unless the Oracle Management Agent is installed separately.

The OEM Components

The OEM console uses the following components installed with the Oracle application server:

- **The Oracle Management Service** This is a web-based application that runs on the Oracle application server. It provides the user interface for the OEM console, and interfaces with the management agents to process and monitor information.

- **The Oracle Management Agent** This monitors information from sites that need to be managed and that are loaded into the management service.

- **The Oracle Management Repository** This contains all the information managed by the Oracle Enterprise Manager.

Before installing the Complete Enterprise Manager, make sure to read the requirements for the complete installation that includes the Oracle Application Server 11*g*, Web Cache, and the Management Service application as well as verifying additional licensing requirements.

The Oracle Net Configuration Assistant

The Oracle Net Configuration Assistant is used during installation to configure the basic network components. The Oracle Net Configuration Assistant can also be run standalone to modify the same values configured during installation. Configurable components include the following:

- Naming methods

- Net service names (tnsnames.ora)

- Listener names and protocol addresses

- Directory server usage

The following can be used to start the Oracle Net Configuration Assistant manually through UNIX:

```
$   $ORACLE_HOME/bin/netca
```

The Oracle Net Configuration Assistant can also be started manually through Windows by selecting Start | Programs | Oracle—OraHome11 | Configuration and Migration Tools | Net Configuration Assistant.

The Oracle Internet Directory Configuration Assistant

The Oracle Internet Directory Configuration Assistant can be used to configure the Oracle Internet Directory. The directory configuration file ldap.ora can be configured with the Oracle Internet Directory Configuration Assistant or the Oracle Net Configuration Assistant. The ldap.ora file can reside in different locations depending on which tool created the ldap.ora file:

- If created by the OID Configuration Assistant, the ldap.ora file is stored in the ORACLE_HOME/ldap/admin directory.

- If created by the Oracle Net Configuration Assistant, the ldap.ora file is stored in the ORACLE_HOME/network/admin directory.

- The ldap.ora file location can be manually specified with the LDAP_ADMIN or TNS_ADMIN environmental variables.

Command-Line Utilities

The Listener Control utility can be used to start and stop listeners, check their status, and perform tracing and other management operations. The syntax is

```
lsnrctl  command [listener_name]
```

Listener commands can also be executed from within the Listener Control utility. The listener name is the one defined in the listener.ora file, but a default listener named LISTENER can be used instead. If LISTENER is used, a listener name does not need to be specified.

The following shows how to stop the listener. Here, executing the lsnrctl command generates an LSNRCTL prompt:

```
$ lsnrctl
LSNRCTL> stop
Connecting to (DESCRIPTION=(ADDRESS=(PROTOCOL=IPC)(KEY=EXTPROC0)))
The command completed successfully
```

The next example shows a sample of the type of information displayed when starting the listener:

```
LSNRCTL> start

starting tnslsnr: please wait...
 TNSLSNR for 32-bit Windows: Version 11.1.0.6.0 -
System parameter file is C:\oracle\ora11\network\admin\listener.ora
Log messages written to C:\oracle\ora11\network\log\listener.log
Listening on: (DESCRIPTION=(ADDRESS=(PROTOCOL=tcp)(HOST=eclipse)
          (PORT=1521)))
Connecting to (DESCRIPTION=(ADDRESS=(PROTOCOL=IPC)(KEY=EXTPROC0)))
STATUS of the LISTENER
------------------------
Alias                    LISTENER
Version                  TNSLSNR for 32-bit Windows:Version 11.1.0.6.0
Start Date               03-FEB-2009 21:26:56
Uptime                   0 days 0 hr. 0 min. 2 sec
Trace Level              off
Security                 OFF
SNMP                     OFF
Listener Parameter File  C:\oracle\ora11\network\admin\listener.ora
Listener Log File        C:\oracle\ora11\network\log\listener.log
Listening Endpoints Summary...
  (DESCRIPTION=(ADDRESS=(PROTOCOL=tcp)(HOST=eclipse)(PORT=1521)))
Services Summary...
Service "cust" has 1 instance(s).
  Instance "cust", status UNKNOWN, has 1 handler(s) for this service...
The command completed successfully
```

The status command displays detailed information on the status of the listener. Information includes the start time of the listener, the location of log and configuration files, and so on.

```
LSNRCTL> status
```

The services command lists dispatchers in a shared server environment and dedicated servers in a dedicated server environment:

```
LSNRCTL> services
```

Here is a list of listener commands:

- change_password

- exit

- help

- quit

- reload

- save_config

- services

- set

- show

- spawn

- start

- status

- stop

- trace

- version

The set command can be used to modify different parameter values for a listener. The set command, by itself, will display the parameter values that can be modified:

```
LSNRCTL> set
password                        rawmode
displaymode                     trc_file
trc_directory                   trc_level
log_file                        log_directory
log_status                      current_listener
inbound_connect_timeout         startup_waittime
save_config_on_stop
```

The Oracle Advanced Security Option

The Oracle Advanced Security option supports data encryption, enhanced authentication, integrity checking, single sign-on, and the Distributed Computing Environment (DCE). The Oracle Net Manager is used to configure Oracle Advanced Security options.

Dispatchers

The DISPATCHERS parameter can be set to define how dispatchers will work with the shared server architecture. Dispatchers must be defined to work with different protocols, as shown in the following:

```
DISPATCHERS="(PROTOCOL=tcp)(DISPATCHERS=6)(CONNECTIONS=1000)"
DISPATCHERS="(PROTOCOL=tcps)(DISPATCHERS=6)(CONNECTIONS=1000)"
```

Connection pooling can also be defined as shown next:

```
DISPATCHERS="(PROTOCOL=tcp)(DISPATCHERS=6)(POOL=on)  (TICK=1)
            (CONNECTIONS=1000)(SESSIONS=5000)"
DISPATCHERS="(PROTOCOL=tcps)(DISPATCHERS=6)(POOL=on)  (TICK=1)
            (CONNECTIONS=1000)(SESSIONS=5000)"
```

NOTE
*TICK is the amount of time for a message to be sent
from the server to the client; for fast networks,
recommended value is 1, but default is 15.*

Project 3-1   Test a Connection

The following project will walk you through the steps of testing a connection to an
Oracle database server.

Step by Step

The first step is to test the network connectivity between the remote system and the
Oracle database server. The ping command will verify network access. If ping is
successful, the remote system can resolve the name of the host server name. The
host server name should be defined in the hosts file for the operating system.

The hosts file in UNIX is in the /etc directory; the hosts file in Windows is in
the\winnt directory. The following is an example hosts file entry:

```
eclipse      customer.us.beginner.com
```

1. Ping the host server name:

   ```
   ping eclipse
   ```

2. If the ping is not successful using the host server name then use the IP
   address to verify that the remote system can access the host server through
   the network:

   ```
   ping 122.23.20.24
   ```

3. Start the listener. If the listener does not start, check the listener.ora file for
   the proper entries. The listener.ora file can be found in the ORACLE_
   HOME/ network/ admin directory:

   ```
   lsnrctl start listener_name
   ```

(continued)

4. Verify that the service registration has been completed and that the listener is ready to handle requests:

```
lsnrctl services listener_name
```

5. Service registration is impacted by a number of initialization parameters. They include SERVICE_NAMES (cust.us.acme.com) and INSTANCE_NAME (cust). The SERVICE_NAMES parameter defaults to the global database name. The global database name is made up of the DB_NAME and DB_DOMAIN parameters.

6. The remote system now needs to be configured. The Oracle Net Configuration Assistant can be used for configuration. Start the Oracle Net Configuration Assistant.

7. Of the four configuration options on the Welcome page, select the Local Net Service Name configuration.

8. Select Add and then click Next.

9. Enter the service name (cust) and click Next.

10. Select the protocol (TCP/IP) and click Next.

11. Select the host name and port number and then click Next.

12. Select Yes, perform a test, and then click Next. If the test fails, check whether the instance and listener are running. If they are, check the protocol information, and if it still fails, double-check the username and password used for the test.

13. Enter the net service name and click Next.

14. Select No when asked if you would like to configure another net service name, and then click Next.

15. At the Congratulations screen, select Next, and then click Finish.

16. The local naming method will create a connect descriptor in the tnsnames.ora file similar to this one:

```
cust=
(DESCRIPTION =
  (ADDRESS=(PROTOCOL=tcp)(HOST=eclipse)(PORT=1521))
  (CONNECT_DATA=
      (SERVICE_NAME=customer.us.beginner.com)))
```

17. For the final test, log into Oracle and see if you can connect using the new net service name:

```
SQL> CONNECT username/password@cust
```

18. The tnsping utility can also be used to test a service. If unsuccessful, it will return the error that occurred. tnsping requires the net service name found in the tnsnames.ora file. The count parameter defines how many attempts are made to reach the server.

```
tnsping net_service_name  [count]
```

19. If unable to connect, the trcroute utility can be used to get more detailed error information. The trcroute utility tracks the TNS address of every node it accesses in the path.

```
trcroute net_service_name
```

Project Summary

This project walked you through the steps a DBA will go through to test a simple connection for an Oracle database server using the local naming method.

CRITICAL SKILL 3.8

Use Profiles

A profile contains a set of parameters that define Oracle Net options on the remote or database server. Profiles are stored in the sqlnet.ora file and can be used to

- Route connections to specific processes
- Control access through protocol-specific parameters
- Prioritize naming methods
- Control logging and tracing features
- Configure for external naming
- Define how the client domain should append to unqualified names

During installation, the priority order for the naming methods will be defined. If the first naming method cannot resolve the connect identifier, the next naming method will be checked. The results will then be stored in the sqlnet.ora file, as shown in the following example:

```
NAMES.DIRECTORY_PATH=(ezconnect, tnsnames)
```

After installation, Oracle Net Manager can be used to modify the sqlnet.ora configuration file.

The sqlnet.ora file can be used to grant or deny access to the Oracle database server. Table 3-7 displays sqlnet.ora parameters that control access.

sqlnet.ora Parameter Name	Description
TCP.VALIDNODE_CHECKING	Determines where to control access to the database. If this parameter is set, the following parameters will be used to define the access.
TCP.EXCLUDED_NODES	Defines which systems are denied access to the database.
TCP.INVITED_NODES	Defines which systems are granted access to the database.

TABLE 3-7. *sqlnet.ora Parameters*

The Oracle Net Manager is used to define database access control. To define database access control, perform the following steps using Oracle Net Manager:

1. After starting Net Manager, select Local | Profile.

2. Choose General.

3. Select Access Rights.

4. Choose Check TCP/IP Client Access Rights.

5. In the Clients Excluded From Access and the Clients Allowed To Access fields, access control can now be defined.

CRITICAL SKILL 3.9
Network in a Multi-tiered Environment

Although the Oracle Database 11*g* has additional features that simplify database administration, the environment the database server runs in is becoming more complex. The following areas continue to increase the complexity of Oracle networking environments:

■ Oracle Database 11*g*–supporting HTTP, FTP, and WebDAV protocols are changing how data is used and accessed.

■ The OEM Central Console is changing how Oracle DBAs perform administration across multiple databases.

■ Multi-tiered architectures are placing increasing demands on network performance and security.

Traditionally, most Oracle networks have been set with the local naming method. In the future, more Oracle networking environments will work with multi-tiered architectures, the Oracle OEM Central Console, encryption, and the directory naming method. Companies are going to need people with skills to manage these complex environments. This chapter introduced you to the main components of Oracle Net Services. To begin working with Oracle Net Services, you may want to look at the following areas in the following order in terms of developing your skills:

■ Strengthen your understanding of the Oracle Net Services architecture.

■ Obtain a solid understanding of configuring dedicated and shared server environments.

■ Become comfortable working with listeners and the local naming method.

■ Get comfortable working with the directory naming method.

■ Be able to work with the OEM Central Console and the environment required to support it.

This list should be able to keep you busy for a few days. After that, developing skill in tuning and troubleshooting the Oracle Net Services environment will be important. Not included in these discussions, but also very important, is the ability to troubleshoot and tune the network from an operating system perspective.

CRITICAL SKILL 3.10

Install the Oracle 11*g* Client Software

Before moving on from Oracle's networking offering, you are going to get a quick look at the Oracle 11*g* client software. Classically, this piece of the puzzle goes on a desktop computer, but in a 3-tier client-server model, it is often put on the middle tier. This architecture makes it accessible to multiple client computers and often eases management and maintenance tasks for the administrator. The journey begins at technet.oracle.com in the download area of the site, as shown in the following illustration.

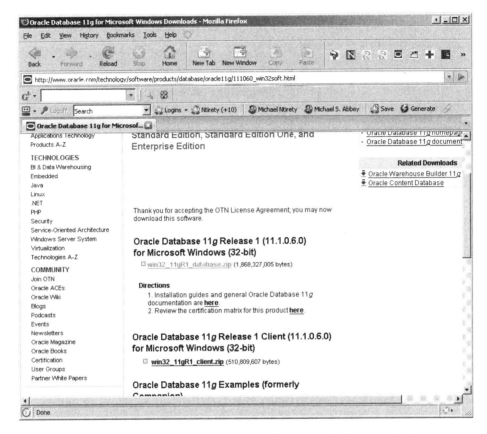

Click on the name of the client software and choose the Save to Disk option as your web browser prepares to download the file for you, as shown next.

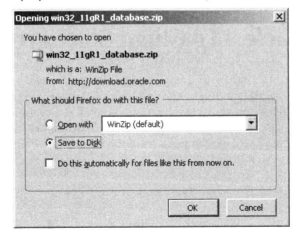

NOTE
You will need a valid username and password to download the Oracle software discussed in the next few sections. The Oracle software contains several components that can be installed, and along with these components, several more options are available as part of the downloaded software. The material we discuss here is an overview of a simple client install; a mere tip-of-the-iceberg so to speak.

With the file downloaded, using WinZIP or the Windows compressed folders feature, uncompress the file in preparation for the client install. Proceed to the location where the media was unzipped and double-click the setup.exe program. A DOS window appears as soon as the setup is invoked, as shown in the following illustration.

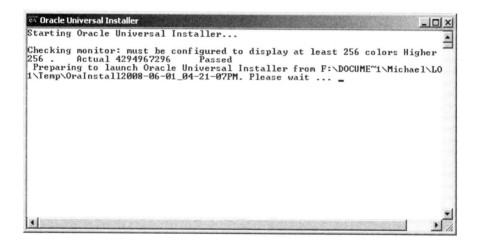

As the first screen appears, click the Advanced Installation radio button as shown in the following illustration, and then click Next. When asked for an Installation type on the next screen, choose Custom, and then click Next. On the Installation location screen, you can overwrite the suggested Oracle Base or leave the default as suggested by the installer. Once you're happy with the Oracle Base location, click Next.

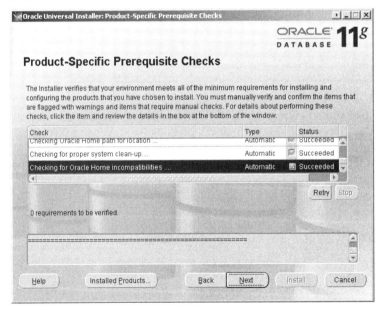

The next screen to appear, as shown in the following illustration, does a quick series of Product-Specific Prerequisite Checks. This ensures that the environment where the 11*g* client is to be installed can support the software. Once the installer completes its checks, click Next to continue.

You will then be positioned on the Available Product Components screen. This tree lists the products that can be installed from the download. All of the products in the tree should be de-selected, except for Oracle Net Services (including the Oracle Net Listener and Oracle Connection Manager). Click Next to display the installation summary screen before the process commences. A progress screen appears with messages about what is being installed and a progress indicator as shown here.

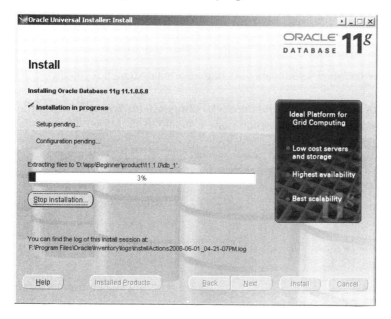

Once the installer completes its work, it will bring up a Configuration Assistant notification screen followed by starting the Oracle Net Configuration Assistant, as shown in the following illustration.

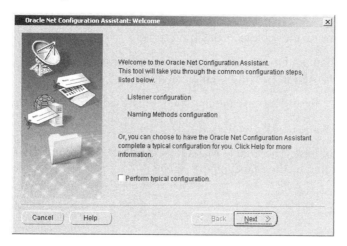

Proceed as follows with the next few screens and the questions they ask, clicking Next to move from one screen to the next:

- When a listener name is suggested, accept the default LISTENER.

- In the Available Protocols/Selected Protocols, ensure TCP-IP is in the Selected Protocols list.

- Allow it to use the standard port 1521 for the listener.

- When asked about configuring another listener, say No.

- When asked if you want to configure additional naming methods, answer No.

You are then done with the network configuration. You will be returned to the setup completion screen, at which point it is safe to shut down the installer.

☑ Chapter 3 Mastery Check

1. The _____ background process registers the service information to the listener.

2. True or false: The LOCAL_LISTENER parameter should be set to work with port 1521.

3. The _____ is used during installation to configure Oracle Net Services.

4. The _____ file can be used to define, grant, or deny access to the Oracle database server.

5. The _____ utility can also be used to test a service.

6. A _____ contains a set of parameters that define Oracle Net options on the remote or database server.

7. The ldap.ora file location can be manually specified with the _____ or TNS_ADMIN environmental variables.

8. True or false: The easy naming method is a valid naming method.

9. The Oracle LDAP directory is called the _____.

10. True or false: The Oracle Management Service is a repository of information generated by the Management Agent.

CHAPTER
4

SQL: Structured Query Language

CRITICAL SKILLS

QL is the fundamental access tool of Oracle Database; in fact, it is the fundamental access tool of all relational databases. SQL is used to build database objects and it is also used to query and manipulate both these objects and the data they may contain. You cannot insert a row of data into an Oracle database unless you have first issued some basic SQL statements to create the underlying tables. While Oracle provides SQL*Plus, a SQL tool that enables you to interact with the database, there are also many GUI tools that can be used, which can then issue SQL statements on your behalf behind the scenes. However you decide to access the database, you will need to understand the fundamentals of SQL. SQL will become your connection to your data and it is an important starting point for all Oracle professionals to master.

CRITICAL SKILL 4.1

Learn the SQL Statement Components

Before you learn the many SQL commands that you will use frequently, you should take a look at the two different categories that SQL statements are classified into. They are DDL, or *data definition language,* and DML, or *data manipulation language.* The majority of this chapter will deal with the latter.

DDL

DDL is the set of SQL statements that define or delete database objects such as tables or views. For the purposes of this chapter, you will concentrate on dealing with tables. Examples of DDL are any SQL statements that begin with create, alter, and drop: all of these commands would act upon a database object like a table, view, or trigger, among many others. Table 4-1 is a sample list of some DDL statements. It does not completely represent the many varied statements that all have a unique purpose and value.

The following SQL statements are examples of DDL create and drop statements in action:

```
SQL> create table b
  2  (colb char(1));

SQL> drop table b;
Table dropped.

SQL> create table state
  2    (state_cd   char(2) not null,
  3     state_name varchar2(30));
Table created.
```

After you have created your table, you should confirm that it was created as you expected. To display a description of a table, the describe command is used. Our

SQL Command	Purpose
create table	Creates a table
create index	Creates an index
alter table	Adds a column, redefines an existing column, changes storage allocation
drop table	Drops a table
grant	Grants privileges or roles to a user or another role
truncate	Removes all rows from a table
revoke	Removes privileges from a user or a role
analyze	Gathers performance statistics on database objects for use by the cost-based optimizer (although we recommend that you use the Oracle built-in package named DBMS_STATS for the most robust statistic collection)

TABLE 4-1. *Common Formats for Date Type Data*

experience suggests that you will find it very useful to be able to describe tables within the database after you create them or any time you need to know the exact nature of the table. You should take a closer look at the state table that you created in the previous example:

```
SQL> desc state;

Name                                        Null?     Type
------------------------------------------- --------  -------------------
STATE_CD                                    NOT NULL  CHAR(2)
STATE_NAME                                            VARCHAR2(30)
```

DML

DML is any SQL statement that begins with select, insert, update, or delete. The remainder of this chapter will deal primarily with DML. Every DML SQL statement consists of a few basic components. The following three items form the basic foundation of most DML statements:

- Each DML statement begins with either a select, insert, update, or delete command:

  - select is used when you want to retrieve data from an Oracle database. It is the most common SQL statement you will see.

- insert is used when you want to add rows into an Oracle table.

- update commands are used to change one or more records in a table.

- delete commands are issued when you want to remove one or more records from a table.

- All DML commands require reference to an object that will be manipulated. More often than not, the object being referenced is a table.

- A conditional statement can be added to any select, update, or delete command. Absence of a conditional statement means that the command will be performed against every record in the object. A conditional statement is used when the DML command is intended to only act upon a group of records that meet a specific condition. The where clause will be discussed a little later in this chapter.

More optional DML statements will be described later in this chapter. For now, you should concentrate on understanding the fundamental structure of each DML statement starting with the insert and select statements.

Use Basic Insert and Select Statements

Getting data into and out of a database are two of the most important features of a database. Oracle provides two basic features that help you do just that. To get data into the database, use the insert command; to get it back out, use the select command. You must master these commands because they form the basics for most data access to your Oracle database. In this section you'll first learn how to get data into your database and then how to get data out.

Insert

Using the state table created in the DDL example, the following is an illustration of using the insert statement in its simplest form:

```
SQL> insert into state values ('AZ','Arizona');
1 row created.
```

Each time you execute an insert command, you receive the message "1 row created." Thus, you get immediate feedback that you are populating the given table with data. When you load data into a table, you may also specify the column to load it into. This ensures that there is no mistaking where you want the data to be placed. In the next example, the columns are specified after the insert command:

```
SQL> insert into state (state_cd, state_name)
2> values ('NJ','New Jersey');
1 row created.

SQL> insert into state (state_cd, state_name)
2> values ('CA','California');
1 row created.

SQL> insert into state (state_cd, state_name)
2> values ('TX','Texas');
1 row created.

SQL> insert into state (state_cd, state_name)
2> values ('FL','Florida');
1 row created.

SQL> insert into state (state_cd, state_name)
2> values ('ME','Maine');
1 row created.
```

Select

As mentioned earlier, the select statement is used to retrieve data from the database. This is the commonest SQL statement you will use. The five basic parts of the SQL statement are as follows:

- First is the keyword select, followed by what you want to retrieve from the database. The names of the columns to be retrieved are listed here. The select clause is mandatory.

- The word from is the next part of the SQL statement. Reference to the object that the data is being retrieved from is made here. This is usually a table name. The from clause is mandatory.

- As mentioned before, a conditional statement is optional for select statements. The word where, followed by the conditions, would be the next part of the SQL statement. (See Critical Skill 4.3 for more details on the where clause.)

- A group by clause is another optional component of the select statement. This topic will be covered in more detail in Critical Skill 4.9, once we have had the opportunity to discuss functions.

- The final component of a select statement is the order by clause. This will also be discussed in more detail later on in this chapter. This is an optional component, which will sort the results of the query before they are presented back to you.

You should now issue your first select statement against the state table you just populated in the insert statement examples:

```
SQL> select *
  2  from    state;

ST STATE_NAME
-- ----------------------------
AZ Arizona
NJ New Jersey
CA California
TX Texas
FL Florida
MN Maine

6 rows selected.
```

Notice the use of the asterisk in the select statement. The asterisk means "retrieve data from all the columns" of the state table. (select * from emp,dept retrieves all columns from the table.)

Rather than using the asterisk as you did in the previous example, you can specify one or more columns after the select command in a comma-separated list. You should rewrite the previous query and only select the state_name column this time:

```
SQL> select state_name
  2  from    state;

STATE_NAME
----------------------------
Arizona
New Jersey
California
Texas
Florida
Maine

6 rows selected.
```

The semicolons in the two SQL examples force the immediate execution of the SQL statement within SQL*Plus. There are two ways to signify you have finished and that the SQL statement can be executed in SQL*Plus:

- The semicolon at the end of a line
- The slash on a separate line

Until SQL*Plus encounters either of these characters, it assumes you need an additional line. The following example highlights this point. Notice the use of the slash and semicolon.

```
SQL> select *
  2  from   a;

SQL> select *
  2  from   a
  3  /
```

The absence of the semicolon in the second example resulted in a new line. In these cases, the semicolon and slash on a separate line would force the execution of the statement.

CRITICAL SKILL 4.3

Use Simple Where Clauses

Up to now, you have seen how the select command can be used to retrieve records from a table. However, our basic examples have all retrieved every record from the table. If you want to see only certain rows, you must add a where clause.

Since the previous examples returned every record in the table, you created a simple table with a few rows in it for illustration purposes. Had you chosen to illustrate the select command against the large sample tables provided by Oracle, you would have returned thousands of rows—far too many for listing in this chapter. Now that you are introducing the where clause, you will be able to control the output. As a result, the remaining examples in this chapter will now use the customers, products, sales, and costs tables that are part of the Oracle sample database; they can be found in the SH schema that is included when you install the sample databases with a default installation. Let's describe each of these tables in the SH schema. This may be done in SQL*Plus or in a GUI that provides this type of table interface:

```
SQL> desc customers;
 Name                                      Null?    Type
 ----------------------------------------- -------- -------------------
 CUST_ID                                   NOT NULL NUMBER
 CUST_FIRST_NAME                           NOT NULL VARCHAR2(20)
 CUST_LAST_NAME                            NOT NULL VARCHAR2(40)
 CUST_GENDER                               NOT NULL CHAR(1)
 CUST_YEAR_OF_BIRTH                        NOT NULL NUMBER(4)
 CUST_MARITAL_STATUS                                VARCHAR2(20)
 CUST_STREET_ADDRESS                       NOT NULL VARCHAR2(40)
 CUST_POSTAL_CODE                          NOT NULL VARCHAR2(10)
 CUST_CITY                                 NOT NULL VARCHAR2(30)
 CUST_CITY_ID                              NOT NULL NUMBER
 CUST_STATE_PROVINCE                       NOT NULL VARCHAR2(40)
 CUST_STATE_PROVINCE_ID                    NOT NULL NUMBER
 COUNTRY_ID                                NOT NULL NUMBER
```

```
CUST_MAIN_PHONE_NUMBER                        NOT NULL VARCHAR2(25)
CUST_INCOME_LEVEL                                      VARCHAR2(30)
CUST_CREDIT_LIMIT                                      NUMBER
CUST_EMAIL                                             VARCHAR2(30)
CUST_TOTAL                                    NOT NULL VARCHAR2(14)
CUST_TOTAL_ID                                 NOT NULL NUMBER
CUST_SRC_ID                                            NUMBER
CUST_EFF_FROM                                          DATE
CUST_EFF_TO                                            DATE
CUST_VALID                                             VARCHAR2(1)

SQL> desc products;
 Name                                         Null?    Type
 -------------------------------------------- -------- -------------------
 PROD_ID                                      NOT NULL NUMBER(6)
 PROD_NAME                                    NOT NULL VARCHAR2(50)
 PROD_DESC                                    NOT NULL VARCHAR2(4000)
 PROD_SUBCATEGORY                             NOT NULL VARCHAR2(50)
 PROD_SUBCATEGORY_ID                          NOT NULL NUMBER
 PROD_SUBCATEGORY_DESC                        NOT NULL VARCHAR2(2000)
 PROD_CATEGORY                                NOT NULL VARCHAR2(50)
 PROD_CATEGORY_ID                             NOT NULL NUMBER
 PROD_CATEGORY_DESC                           NOT NULL VARCHAR2(2000)
 PROD_WEIGHT_CLASS                            NOT NULL NUMBER(3)
 PROD_UNIT_OF_MEASURE                                  VARCHAR2(20)
 PROD_PACK_SIZE                               NOT NULL VARCHAR2(30)
 SUPPLIER_ID                                  NOT NULL NUMBER(6)
 PROD_STATUS                                  NOT NULL VARCHAR2(20)
 PROD_LIST_PRICE                              NOT NULL NUMBER(8,2)
 PROD_MIN_PRICE                               NOT NULL NUMBER(8,2)
 PROD_TOTAL                                   NOT NULL VARCHAR2(13)
 PROD_TOTAL_ID                                NOT NULL NUMBER
 PROD_SRC_ID                                           NUMBER
 PROD_EFF_FROM                                         DATE
 PROD_EFF_TO                                           DATE
 PROD_VALID                                            VARCHAR2(1)

SQL> desc sales;
 Name                                         Null?    Type
 -------------------------------------------- -------- -------------------
 PROD_ID                                      NOT NULL NUMBER
 CUST_ID                                      NOT NULL NUMBER
 TIME_ID                                      NOT NULL DATE
 CHANNEL_ID                                   NOT NULL NUMBER
 PROMO_ID                                     NOT NULL NUMBER
 QUANTITY_SOLD                                NOT NULL NUMBER(10,2)
 AMOUNT_SOLD                                  NOT NULL NUMBER(10,2)
```

```
SQL> desc costs;
 Name                                      Null?    Type
 ----------------------------------------- -------- -----------------------
 PROD_ID                                   NOT NULL NUMBER
 TIME_ID                                   NOT NULL DATE
 PROMO_ID                                  NOT NULL NUMBER
 CHANNEL_ID                                NOT NULL NUMBER
 UNIT_COST                                 NOT NULL NUMBER(10,2)
 UNIT_PRICE                                NOT NULL NUMBER(10,2)

SQL> desc promotions
 Name                                      Null?    Type
 ----------------------------------------- -------- -----------------------
 PROMO_ID                                  NOT NULL NUMBER(6)
 PROMO_NAME                                NOT NULL VARCHAR2(30)
 PROMO_SUBCATEGORY                         NOT NULL VARCHAR2(30)
 PROMO_SUBCATEGORY_ID                      NOT NULL NUMBER
 PROMO_CATEGORY                            NOT NULL VARCHAR2(30)
 PROMO_CATEGORY_ID                         NOT NULL NUMBER
 PROMO_COST                                NOT NULL NUMBER(10,2)
 PROMO_BEGIN_DATE                          NOT NULL DATE
 PROMO_END_DATE                            NOT NULL DATE
 PROMO_TOTAL                               NOT NULL VARCHAR2(15)
 PROMO_TOTAL_ID                            NOT NULL NUMBER
```

The PRODUCTS table contains more than 70 products for sale. The following select statement will retrieve only one record for product ID (prod_id) 117, which is the use of the simplest of where clauses. In this case, you will perform an exact query to find product ID number 117, which is the product ID for a pack of CD-Rs:

```
SQL> select prod_id, prod_name, prod_category, prod_list_price PRC
  2  from    products
  3  where   prod_id = 117;

   PROD_ID PROD_NAME                          PROD_CATEGORY       PRC
---------- ---------------------------------- ----------------    ------
       117 CD-R, Profess. Grade, Pack of 10   Software/Other      8.99
```

A Where Clause with and/or

A where clause instructs Oracle to search the data in a table and then return only those rows that meet the criteria that you have defined. In the preceding example, you searched the products table for one specific record with a product ID equal to 117. This was accomplished with where prod_id = 117;.

You will often be interested in retrieving rows that meet multiple criteria—for example, if you want to retrieve a list of customers from Utah who also have a credit limit greater than $10,000. The SQL statement would produce the following output:

```
SQL> select cust_id, cust_state_province, cust_credit_limit
  2  from   customers
  3  where  cust_state_province = 'UT'
  4  and    cust_credit_limit > 10000;

   CUST_ID CUST_STATE_PROVINCE                             CUST_CREDIT_LIMIT
---------- ------------------------------------------- -----------------
     50601 UT                                                      11000
     24830 UT                                                      15000
     28983 UT                                                      15000
    100267 UT                                                      11000
    100207 UT                                                      11000
    103007 UT                                                      15000

6 rows selected.
```

In the previous example, you retrieved records that met all the criteria. You may be interested in retrieving records that meet one criterion or another. For example, if you wanted to find all the product IDs in the products table that are either in the Hardware product category or have a weight class of 4, you would generate the following SQL statement and output:

```
SQL> select prod_id, prod_category, prod_weight_class WGT
  2  from   products
  3  where  prod_category = 'Hardware'
  4  or     prod_weight_class = 4;

   PROD_ID PROD_CATEGORY                                        WGT
---------- ------------------------------------------------- ---------
        15 Hardware                                             1
        18 Hardware                                             1
       139 Electronics                                          4
```

Ask the Expert

Q: Why is *hardware* in quotes in the sample statement?

A: When a character column is used in a where clause, it is necessary to use the single quotes around the value to be compared.

The and condition and the or condition are known as logical operators. They are used to tell the query how the multiple criteria affect each other. Compound conditions connected by the and keyword all have to evaluate to true for records to be retrieved. Records are returned by compound conditions connected by the or keyword when either one of the conditions is true. If you mix your *and* and *or* conditions, you must carefully evaluate how the these two types will interact.

The Where Clause with NOT

The ability also exists within Oracle to retrieve records with negative criteria. The "not equals" operator is != or may also use <>. For example, you might want to see all the products that are not in weight class 1. The following query and its output illustrate this example:

```
SQL> select prod_id, prod_category, prod_weight_class WGT
  2  from    products
  3  where   prod_weight_class != 1;

  PROD_ID PROD_CATEGORY                                              WGT
--------- ------------------------------------------------------ ---------
      139 Electronics                                                  4
```

The Where Clause with a Range Search

Oracle also supports range searches so you can query for records that are between two values. If you want to find all male customers in Connecticut who were born between 1936 and 1939, you would write a query with three conditions joined by the *and* keyword (all three need to evaluate to true), and one of the conditions would use the range search *between* keyword. The following example illustrates the query and resulting output:

```
SQL> select cust_id, cust_gender, cust_year_of_birth
  2  from    customers
  3  where   cust_state_province = 'CT'
  4  and     cust_gender = 'M'
  5  and     cust_year_of_birth between 1936 and 1939;

  CUST_ID C CUST_YEAR_OF_BIRTH
--------- - ------------------
    20058 M               1937
    17139 M               1936
     1218 M               1938
     3985 M               1939
```

The Where Clause with a Search List

Oracle also supports searching for records that meet criteria within a list. If you wanted to find all customers in Utah and Connecticut with a credit limit of $15,000, this can be done with a search list. The following query represents a search list condition:

```
SQL> select cust_id, cust_state_province, cust_credit_limit
  2  from    customers
  3  where   cust_credit_limit = 15000
  4  and     cust_state_province in ('UT','CT');

   CUST_ID CUST_STATE_PROVINCE                        CUST_CREDIT_LIMIT
---------- ------------------------------------------ -----------------
     24830 UT                                                     15000
     28983 UT                                                     15000
    101798 CT                                                     15000
    103171 CT                                                     15000
    102579 CT                                                     15000
    102238 CT                                                     15000
    101515 CT                                                     15000
    103007 UT                                                     15000
    104381 CT                                                     15000

9 rows selected.
```

The Where Clause with a Pattern Search

The like command exists within Oracle to search for records that match a pattern. The wildcard operator for pattern searches is the % sign. To search for all customers whose last name begins with the letter Q, the following query would produce these results:

```
SQL> select cust_last_name, cust_credit_limit
  2  from    customers
  3  where   cust_last_name like 'Q%';

CUST_LAST_NAME                           CUST_CREDIT_LIMIT
---------------------------------------- -----------------
Quinlan                                               9000
Quinn                                               11000
```

Ask the Expert

Q: Are character searches case-sensitive?

A: Yes. Character columns can contain upper- or lowercase alphas. If you searched the CUSTOMERS table for all instances of "INL" in the last names, you would not have retrieved any records.

Q: The percent (%) sign appears to be a multicharacter wildcard. Is there a single character wildcard available for pattern searches?

A: Yes. The underscore (_) symbol serves as the single character wildcard.

You could also ask Oracle to retrieve customers whose last names contain "inl" by using the wildcard at the beginning and end of the pattern search. The query and output would resemble the following:

```
SQL> select cust_last_name
  2  from    customers
  3  where   cust_last_name like '%inl%';

CUST_LAST_NAME
----------------------------------------
Quinlan
```

The Where Clause: Common Operators

As you can see from the preceding examples, Oracle has a very powerful set of operators when it comes to restricting the rows retrieved. Table 4-2 is a partial list of operators you can use in the where clause.

Operator	Purpose	Example
=	Tests for equality.	select * from customers where cust_state_province = 'UT';
!=	Tests for inequality.	select * from customers where cust_state_province != 'UT';
^=	Same as !=.	select * from customers where cust_state_province ^= 'UT';
<>	Same as !=.	select * from customers where cust_state_province <> 'UT';
<	Less than.	select * from sales where amount_sold < 100;
>	Greater than.	select * from sales where amount_sold > 100;
<=	Less than or equal to.	select * from sales where amount_sold <= 500;
>=	Greater than or equal to.	select * from sales where amount_sold >= 600;
In	Equal to any member in parentheses.	select * from customers where cust_state_ province is in ('UT','CA','TX');
not in	Not equal to any member in parentheses.	select * from customers where cust_state_ province is not in ('UT','CA','TX');
between A and B	Greater than or equal to A and less than or equal to B.	select * from sales where amount_sold is between 100 and 500;
not between A and B	Not greater than or equal to A, and not less than or equal to B.	select * from sales where amount_sold is not between 100 and 500;
like '%tin%'	Contains given text (for example, 'tin').	select * from customer where cust_last_name is like '%tin%';

TABLE 4-2. *Common Comparison Operators*

CRITICAL SKILL 4.4

Use Basic Update and Delete Statements

While select will likely be the command you use the most; you'll use the update and delete commands regularly, too. As you will see in Chapter 5, your programs will have a mixture of DML statements. In this section, you'll take a closer look at the update and delete commands.

Update

It is often necessary to change data already stored within a table. This is done using the update command. There are three parts to this command:

1. The word update followed by the table to which you want to apply the change. This part is mandatory.

2. The word set followed by one or more columns in which you want to change the values. This part is also mandatory.

3. A where clause followed by selection criteria. This is optional.

Imagine that one of our customers has requested an increase in their credit limit and our accounting department has approved it. An update statement will have to be executed to alter the credit limit. For illustration purposes, a customer record will be displayed before and after the update. The following example illustrates a simple update for one customer:

```
SQL> select cust_id, cust_credit_limit
  2  from    customers
  3  where   cust_id = 28983;

  CUST_ID CUST_CREDIT_LIMIT
---------- -----------------
    28983             15000

SQL> update customers
  2  set     cust_credit_limit = 20000
  3  where   cust_id = 28983;

1 row updated.

SQL> select cust_id, cust_credit_limit
  2  from    customers
  3  where cust_id = 28983;

  CUST_ID CUST_CREDIT_LIMIT
---------- -----------------
    28983             20000
```

This example reveals that customer 28983 had a $15,000 credit limit before the update statement was executed. The update statement is written against the CUSTOMERS table with a set clause issued against the column to be changed, cust_credit_limit, and a where clause to make the change only for customer 28983. After the command is executed, a select statement reveals that the customer now has a credit limit of $20,000. The update statement is a very powerful tool. It can be used against one record, multiple records meeting simple or complex criteria, or all records in a table.

Delete

Use the delete statement when you want to remove one or more rows of data from a table. The command has two parts:

1. The keywords delete from followed by the table name you want to remove records from. This is mandatory.

2. A where clause followed by the record selection criteria. This is optional. As with the update, absence of a where clause will remove every record from the table.

If you want to remove all the customers from the CUSTOMERS table, you would issue the SQL statement delete from customer;. As you become more familiar with Oracle, you will learn that the truncate customer; command will also remove every record, but this doesn't allow you to roll back the changes if you make a mistake. It's very easy to accidentally drop all the records in a table. As with the update statement, be very careful when issuing the delete or truncate commands.

Ask the Expert

Q: Can you use a where clause with every type of DML statement?

A: The where clause can be used only with select, update, and delete statements. The insert statement can never have a where clause.

Q: You mentioned that a where clause is optional for update statements. What would happen if one isn't used during an update?

A: If a where clause isn't used with an update statement, every record in the table will be updated.

Let us now illustrate a deletion of all customers in the province of Delhi. The code listing will first show a count of customers in Delhi, introducing count(*) for the first time. This is being used to illustrate the number of records you expect to delete when you issue the command. The second SQL statement issues the delete from command, which confirms the number of records deleted. The final SQL statement is a repeat of the first one to illustrate that there are no records remaining for the province of Delhi. In order to continue to use these records for later examples, you will rollback the changes so that they never get permanently committed to the database and re-run the first SQL statement one more time to confirm that the records have been restored:

```
SQL> select count(*)
  2  from    customers
  3  where   cust_state_province = 'Delhi';

  COUNT(*)
----------
        34

SQL> delete from customers
  2  where cust_state_province = 'Delhi';

34 rows deleted.

SQL> select count(*)
  2  from    customers
  3  where   cust_state_province = 'Delhi';

  COUNT(*)
----------
         0

SQL> rollback;

Rollback complete.

SQL> select count(*)
  2  from    customers
  3  where   cust_state_province = 'Delhi';

  COUNT(*)
----------
        34
```

Progress Check ⏱

1. Of the following four items, which one is not a DML keyword?

   A. select

   B. insert

   C. create

   D. update

2. How can the current column definitions of the CUSTOMERS table be displayed?

3. In order to retrieve data from the database, there are two keywords that are mandatory. Name them.

4. Write a SQL statement to select the customer last name and city for all customers in Florida (FL) with a credit limit less than $5000.

CRITICAL SKILL 4.5

Order Data

So far, all of your select queries have returned records in random order. Earlier, you selected records from the customer table, where the customer was located in either Connecticut or Utah and had a credit limit of $15,000. The results came back in no apparent order. It is often desirable to order the result set on one or more of the selected columns. This ordering of data is known as *sorting*. Sorting will provide guidance to the reader on how they can direct and manage their data review and analysis. In this case, it probably would have been easier to interpret the results if

---

Progress Check Answers

1. C. The four DML keywords are select, insert, update, and delete.

2. The following code listing displays the defined columns for the CUSTOMERS table:

```
desc customers;
```

3. Every SQL statement that retrieves data from the database will have both the select and from keywords.

4. The following SQL statement is a correct answer:

```
SQL> select cust_last_name, cust_city
  2  from    customers
  3  where   cust_state_province = 'UT'
  4  and     cust_credit_limit < 5000;
```

they were sorted by state, and within that state were then sorted by customer ID. You should take a look at the query syntax and resulting output:

```
SQL> select cust_id, cust          ovince, cust_credit_limit
  2   from    cus*
  ?                               00
                                  ('UT','CT')
                                  ust_id;


                                              CUST_CREDIT_LIMIT
             -------------- ------------------
                                                          15000
                                                          15000
                                                          15000
                                                          15000
                                                          15000
                                                          15000
                                                          15000
                                                          15000
```

could be sorted either in ascending ... sort each column in ascending order. In ...cending order, the use of desc following the order by ...complish this. You should look at the previous example one more ...ne with the customer IDs sorted in descending order:

```
SQL> select cust_id, cust_state_province, cust_credit_limit
  2   from    customers
  3   where   cust_credit_limit = 15000
  4   and     cust_state_province in ('UT','CT')
  5   order by cust_state_province, cust_id desc;

   CUST_ID CUST_STATE_PROVINCE                         CUST_CREDIT_LIMIT
---------- ------------------------------------------- ------------------
    104381 CT                                                      15000
    103171 CT                                                      15000
    102579 CT                                                      15000
    102238 CT                                                      15000
    101798 CT                                                      15000
    101515 CT                                                      15000
    103007 UT                                                      15000
     24830 UT                                                      15000

8 rows selected.
```

Employ Functions: String, Numeric, Aggregate (No Grouping)

Up to now, you have illustrated a number of fairly simplistic DML statements. You've selected some records from different tables using criteria, you've updated existing rows, and you've even inserted and deleted some records.

Oracle provides us with many functions that allow us to analyze and aggregate the data, returning results that differ greatly from the result sets you've seen so far. A function manipulates the contents of a column in a SQL statement. You can find what the largest credit limit is in the CUSTOMERS table and you can round numbers or pad results with characters. In fact, when you ran a count of customers that were in the province of Delhi before and after deleting these records, you took a sneak peek ahead at functions.

This section will introduce you to three different types of functions: string (or character), numeric, and aggregate.

String Functions

String functions, also known as character functions, can be categorized in two types: those that return character values and those that return numeric values.

Table 4-3 represents the most common functions you will perform with the character data type; it's only a partial list. The examples that follow all use the *dual* table. The dual table is an internal Oracle table and is useful in SQL and PL/SQL for performing functions that return a single row. It can be used to return the current system date and time, to perform arithmetic functions, or to obtain a generated sequential number (more on this later in the chapter).

Numeric Functions

Table 4-4 illustrates some common numeric functions, their syntax, and the results they produce. These are only a few of the many functions available.

Aggregate Functions

Unlike the character or numeric functions, which act on a single row, aggregate functions act on an entire column of data. Aggregate functions save the developer from having to write a lot of code to determine the maximum column value in a set of records or an average, for example. A single result row is returned by aggregate functions based on the group of rows. Table 4-5 illustrates the more commonly used aggregate functions but is only a partial list. As simple as these are, we're sure you'll agree that they are indeed quite powerful.

Function	Action	Example	Displays
lower(*char*)	Converts the entire string to lowercase.	select lower('DAliA') from dual;	dalia
replace(*char,str1,str2*)	Replaces every occurrence of *str1* in *char* with *str2*.	select replace('Scott', 'S', 'Boy') from dual;	Boycott
substr(*char,m,n*)	Extracts the characters from *char* starting in position *m* for *n* characters.	select substr('ABCDEF',4,2) from dual;	DE
length(*char*)	Returns the length of *char*.	select length('Marissa') from dual;	7
rpad(*expr1,n,expr2*)	Pads *expr1* with *expr2* to the right for *n* characters. Often used for space padding in the creation of a fixed-length record.	select rpad('Amanda', 10, '1') from dual;	Amanda1111
initcap(*char*)	Changes the first character of each element in *char* to uppercase.	select initcap('shane k.') from dual;	Shane K.

TABLE 4-3.   *Common String Functions*

Function	Action	Example	Displays
ceil(*n*)	Returns nearest whole number greater than or equal to *n*.	select ceil(12.3) from dual;	13
floor(*n*)	Returns nearest whole number less than or equal to *n*.	select floor(127.6) from dual;	127
round(*n,m*)	Rounds *n* to *m* places to the right of the decimal point.	select round(579.34886,3) from dual;	579.349
power(*m,n*)	Multiplies *m* to the power *n*.	select power(5,3) from dual;	125
mod(*m,n*)	Returns the remainder of the division of *m* by *n*. If *n=0*, then 0 is returned. If *n>m*, then *m* is returned.	select mod(9,5) from dual; select mod(10,5) from dual; select mod(6,7) from dual;	4 0 6
sqrt(*n*)	Returns the square root of *n*.	select sqrt(9) from dual;	3

TABLE 4-4.   *Common Numeric Functions*

Function	Action	Example	Displays
count(*expr*)	Returns a count of non-null column values for each row retrieved.	select count(cust_id) from customers where cust_state_ province = 'NY';	694
avg(*expr*)	Returns the average for the column values and rows selected.	select avg(amount_sold) from sales where prod_id = 117;	9.92712978
sum(*expr*)	Returns the sum of the column values for all the retrieved rows.	select sum(amount_sold) from sales where prod_id = 117;	170270.13
min(*expr*)	Returns the minimum value for the column and rows retrieved.	select min(prod_list_price) from products;	6.99
max(*expr*)	Returns the maximum value for the column and rows retrieved.	select max(prod_list_price) from products;	1299.99

TABLE 4-5. *Common Aggregate Functions*

CRITICAL SKILL 4.7

Use Dates and Data Functions (Formatting and Chronological)

Date is the next commonest type of data you'll find in an Oracle database after character and numeric data. The date data type consists of two principal elements: date and time. It's important to keep in mind that the date data type includes time when comparing two dates with each other for equality.

The default date format in many Oracle databases is DD-MON-YY, where DD represents the day, MON is the month, and YY is the two-digit year. A date can be inserted into a table without specifying either the four-digit year or a value for the time element. Oracle will default the century to 20 for years 00–49 and 19 for years 50–99. Without a specific time being specified during an insert, the time will default to midnight, which is represented as 00:00:00.

Date Functions

As with the numeric and character data types, Oracle has provided many date functions to help with the manipulation of date data. If you were to routinely print customized letters to your best customers offering them a special deal that expires on the last day of the month, the last_day function could be used to automatically generate the expiration date for the offer. Table 4-6 shows the commonest date functions.

Special Formats with the Date Data Type

Date formats are used to change the display format of a date. This is done using the to_char conversion function along with the date and format mask. Table 4-7 shows a sample of the commoner date formats and their output.

Function	Action	Example	Displays
Sysdate	Returns current system date. Time could also be retrieved using the to_char function, which is discussed in the next section.	select sysdate from dual;	17-MAR-08 on March 17, 2008
last_day(*date*)	Returns last day of the month for *date*.	select last_day('17-MAR-08') from dual;	31-MAR-08
add_months(*d,n*)	Adds *n* or subtracts -*n* months from date d.	select add_months('21-APR-08', 2) from dual;	21-JUN-08
months_between(*d1,d2*)	Returns difference in months between date *d1* and date *d2*.	select months_between('17-MAR-61', '21-APR-62') from dual;	-13.129032
next_day(*d,day*)	Returns the date that corresponds with the day of the week after date *d*.	select next_day('01-FEB-08', 'Saturday') from dual;	07-FEB-08
current_timestamp	Returns the current timestamp along with the time zone offset.	select sessiontimezone, current_timestamp from dual;	01-NOV-08 01.17.56.917550 PM -05:00

TABLE 4-6.   *Common Date Functions*

Format Mask	Returns	Example	Displays
Y or YY or YYY	Last one, two, or three digits of year	select to_char(sysdate,'YYY') from dual;	004 for all dates in 2004
YEAR	Year spelled out	select to_char(sysdate,'YEAR') from dual;	TWO THOUSAND FOUR in 2004
Q	Quarter of year	select to_char(sysdate,'Q') from dual;	3 for all dates in August
MM	Month	select to_char(sysdate,'MM') from dual;	12 for all dates in December
Month	Name of month as a nine-character name	select to_char(sysdate,'Month') from dual;	March followed by 4 spaces for all dates in March
WW	Week of year	select to_char(sysdate,'WW') from dual;	29 on July 15, 2004
W	Week of the month	select to_char(sysdate,'W') from dual;	3 on May 15, 2004
DDD	Day of the year	select to_char(sysdate,'DDD') from dual;	359 on December 25 in non-leap years
DD	Day of the month	select to_char(sysdate,'DD') from dual;	09 on September 9 in any year
D	Day of the week (1 through 7)	select to_char(sysdate,'D') from dual;	5 on January 29, 2004

TABLE 4-7. *Common Formats of Date Type Data*

Nested Functions

It is also common to nest functions within functions. Using the months_between example from Table 4-7, it would be possible to round the number of months between the two dates. The following statement and output illustrates this example.

```
SQL> select round(months_between('17-MAR-61','21-APR-62'))
  2  from dual;

ROUND(MONTHS_BETWEEN('17-MAR-61','21-APR-62'))
---------------------------------------------
                                          -13
```

The inner function is evaluated first, and then the outer function is evaluated second. This is true for all nested functions and as this example illustrates, different function types can be combined. Pay special notice to the parentheses for the outer and inner functions. For illustration purposes, this example nests only one function within another. However, it is possible to nest many functions within each other. Just be careful; the order of the functions is important, and the complexity of debugging nested functions increases with each additional nested function.

CRITICAL SKILL 4.8

Employ Joins (ANSI vs. Oracle): Inner, Outer, Self

Up until now, all of the examples in this chapter have selected data from only one table. In actual fact, much of the data that you need is in two or more tables. The true power of a relational database (and the source of its name) comes from the ability to relate different tables and their data together. Understanding this concept is critical to harvesting the information held within the database. This is more commonly known as *joining* two or more tables.

With Oracle Database 11*g*, queries can be written using either Oracle's SQL syntax or ANSI syntax. While Oracle hasn't made ANSI syntax available until recently, it has been used in non-Oracle environments for some time. Many third-party tools accept ANSI SQL and, as you'll see shortly, the joins are quite different.

Inner Joins

An inner join, also known simply as join, occurs when records are selected from two tables and the values in one column from the first table are also found in a similar column in the second table. In effect, two or more tables are joined together based on common fields. These common fields are known as *keys.* There are two types of keys:

- A *primary key* is what makes a row of data unique within a table. In the CUSTOMERS table, CUST_ID is the primary key.

- A *foreign key* is the primary key of one table that is stored inside another table. The foreign key connects the two tables together. The SALES table also contains CUST_ID, which in the case of the SALES table, is a foreign key back to the CUSTOMERS table.

Oracle Inner Joins

The tables to be joined are listed in the from clause and then related together in the where clause. Whenever two or more tables are found in the from clause, a join happens. Additional conditions can still be specified in the where clause to limit which rows will be returned by the join. For example, when you queried the SALES table on its own, the only customer information available to us was the CUST_ID. However, if you join each record, you retrieve from the SALES table by the CUST_ID to the same column in the CUSTOMERS table, and all the customer information becomes available to you instantly.

This first join example displays both the city and state details for each customer who has purchased a particular product under a specific promotion. The product ID and quantity sold are also displayed:

```
SQL> select prod_id, quantity_sold, cust_city, cust_state_province
  2  from   sales, customers
  3  where  sales.cust_id = customers.cust_id
  4  and    prod_id = 117;

  PROD_ID QUANTITY_SOLD CUST_CITY       CUST_STATE_PROVINCE
---------- ------------- --------------- -------------------
      117             1 Fort Klamath    OR

      117             1 San Mateo       CA

      117             1 Frederick       CO

 .   .   .
```

The from clause identified two tables and the where clause joins them with table_name.column_name syntax. Later on in this chapter, you'll take a brief look at the report formatting capabilities of SQL*Plus, which will allow you to control the look of the output.

NOTE
The reason you must adopt the table_name.column_name construct is to tell Oracle exactly which tables and columns to join. This is to avoid any ambiguity when different tables have columns that are named the same.

SQL statements can become quite confusing once you start joining tables, especially when you're joining more than two. Oracle also allows you to give the tables an alternate name known as a table alias. You should present this query again using "s" as the table alias for the SALES table and "c" as the table alias for the CUSTOMERS table:

```
select prod_id, quantity_sold, cust_city, cust_state_province
from   sales s, customers c
where  s.cust_id = c.cust_id
and    prod_id = 117
```

You should take this join example one step further. cust_id is the column you are using to join the two tables, and therefore it is found in both the SALES and CUSTOMERS tables. If you want to display cust_id as part of the select list, you would need to prefix it with the table alias:

```
select s.prod_id, s.quantity_sold, c.cust_id, c.cust_city,
       c.cust_state_province
from   sales s, customers c
where  s.cust_id = c.cust_id
and    s.prod_id = 117
```

All the column names in this example were prefixed with the table alias qualifier. While it's only necessary for columns that appear in more than one table, it enhances the readability of the SQL statement as the statements become more complex and include more than one table join.

This leads you into the final example, which presents the concept of joining more than two tables. In addition to joining the CUSTOMERS table to the SALES table as you have in all of the preceding examples, you are also joining the CUSTOMERS table to the PRODUCTS and PROMOTIONS tables so you can pull in columns from those tables, as well:

```
select c.country_id, p1.promo_name, p2.prod_category, s.quantity_sold,
from   sales s,
       customers c,
       promotions p1,
       products p2
where  s.cust_id = c.cust_id
and    s.promo_id = p1.promo_id
and    s.prod_id = p2.prod_id
and    s.prod_id = 117
```

It's that simple to join a bunch of tables together. Name each of the tables in the from clause, alias them, and then join them to each other in your where clause using the foreign key relationships.

ANSI Inner Joins

With ANSI joins, the join criteria is found in the from portion of the SQL statement. The where clause only lists the selection criteria for the rows. There are a couple of different ways to join the tables together with ANSI syntax.

ANSI on/using   A simple join can be specified with an on or using statement. The columns to be joined on will be listed, while the where clause can list additional selection criteria. The following two examples illustrate the on syntax followed by the using syntax:

```
select c.cust_id, c.cust_state_province,
       s.quantity_sold, s.prod_category
from sales s join customers c
  on s.cust_id = c.cust_id
where prod_id = 117;

select cust_id, c.cust_state_province,
       s.quantity_sold, s.prod_category
from sales s join customers c
  using (cust_id)
where prod_id = 117;
```

The ANSI syntax also allows for two or more tables to be joined. This can be accomplished with multiple *join on* or multiple *join using* statements in the from section of the SQL statement. The following are two examples:

```
select c.cust_id, c.cust_state_province,
       s.quantity_sold, p.prod_name
from    sales s
  join customers c
    on s.cust_id = c.cust_id
  join products
    on s.prod_id = p.prod_id
where p.prod_id = 117
and c.country_id = 52790;

select cust_id, c.cust_state_province,
       s.quantity_sold, p.prod_name
from    sales s
  join customers c using (cust_id)
  join products p using (prod_id)
where p.prod_id = 117
and c.country_id = 52790;
```

Ask the Expert

Q: Why does the cust_id column in the ANSI on join have a table prefix qualifier while the cust_id column in the ANSI using join does not?

A: The on join syntax tells Oracle which columns to use in the table join. Like the Oracle inner join examples, the table prefix is required for cust_id within both the select list of columns and the table join. The using syntax declares only the column name and allows Oracle to resolve the join. The table qualifiers for the cust_id column are absent from the join portion of the SQL statement and need to be kept out of the select list as well. If you forget, don't worry, Oracle will return an "ORA-25154: column part of USING clause cannot have a qualifier" error message.

ANSI Natural Join ANSI SQL also gives us a third join alternative: the natural join. In this case, the columns to be joined are not specified but rather are resolved by Oracle. They must be similarly named in the tables to be joined. As always, additional selection criteria can be specified in the where clause:

```
select cust_id, c.cust_state_province,
       s.quantity_sold, p.prod_name
from sales s
   natural join customers c
   natural join products p
where prod_id = 117;
```

As you found out with the using syntax, you couldn't use the table alias qualifier on the cust_id column. If you did, you would get an "ORA-25155: column used in NATURAL join cannot have qualifier" error message.

Although it would be very poor database design, it's entirely possible that a similarly named column could exist in different tables but have no relationship to each other. Be careful while naturally joining tables to make sure that it makes sense to join them. While this could just as easily happen with a regular Oracle join, the simple act of having to specify which columns to join could force you to go through this thought process. It's an important fact to know your tables and what you want to accomplish with the joins.

Outer Joins

Unlike an inner join, which only returned records that had matching values for a specific column in both tables, an outer join can return results from one table where the corresponding table did not have a matching value.

In our sample set of data, there are a number of customers that haven't recorded any sales. There are also a number of products that haven't been sold either. These examples will be used in the following explanation of Oracle and ANSI outer joins.

Oracle Outer Joins

In order to find rows from one table that don't match rows in another, known as an outer join, Oracle presents you with the "(+)" notation. The "(+)" is used in the where clause on either of the tables where nonmatching rows are to be returned.

You have found that cust_id = 1 does not have any sales, while cust_id = 80 has exactly two. Now take a look at what happens when you select these two customers from the CUSTOMERS table and request some SALES table details if they exist:

```
SQL> select c.cust_id, c.cust_last_name, s.prod_id, s.quantity_sold
  2  from    customers c, sales s
  3  where   c.cust_id = s.cust_id(+)
  4  and     c.cust_id in (1,80);

   CUST_ID CUST_LAST_NAME                          PROD_ID QUANTITY_SOLD
---------- ----------------------------------- ---------- -------------
         1 Kessel
        80 Carpenter                               127             1
        80 Carpenter                                36             1
```

The *outer join* allows you to display the CUSTOMERS columns alongside the nulls for the nonmatched rows' SALES records. A simple join would have only returned the two records for cust_id 80.

Project 4-1   Join Data Using Inner and Outer Joins

With the sample tables Oracle has provided, there are no *outer join* examples. When you learn about referential integrity and constraints later in this chapter, this will become a little clearer. Suffice it to say that the customers, products, and promotions in the sales table all exist in their respective tables. In this project, you're going to create your own simple tables where you can better demonstrate *outer joins.* Once you discuss the ANSI version of joins, you'll revisit this project and introduce a new concept available only with the ANSI syntax.

Step by Step

You should start by creating and populating two very simple tables that will join on a common column. Open up a SQL*Plus session and issue the following commands:

   1. create table temp1 (id number(3), desc1 char(5));

2. create table temp2 (id number(3), desc2 char(5));

3. insert into temp1 values (123, 'ABCDE');

4. insert into temp1 values (456, 'FGHIJ');

5. insert into temp2 values (456, 'ZZZZZ');

6. insert into temp2 values (789, 'MMMMM');

Table temp1 and temp2 each have two records. The two tables join with each other on the "ID" column, and they have one ID in common: 456. You should continue now by displaying all the records from temp1 and temp2 followed by writing an *inner, right outer,* and *left outer join.* In SQL*Plus, enter the code from the following code listings and check that you get the same output.

1. Display the records from temp1 (remember to use select * when doing so):

```
       ID DESC1
---------- -----
      123 ABCDE
      456 FGHIJ
```

2. Next, display the records from temp2:

```
       ID DESC2
---------- -----
      456 ZZZZZ
      789 MMMMM
```

3. Use an inner join to join the two:

```
SQL> select a.id, a.desc1, b.desc2
  2  from   temp1 a, temp2 b
  3  where  a.id = b.id;

       ID DESC1 DESC2
---------- ----- -----
      456 FGHIJ ZZZZZ
```

4. Create an outer join table called temp2, as in the following:

```
SQL> select a.id, a.desc1, b.id, b.desc2
  2  from   temp1 a, temp2  b
  3  where  a.id = b.id(+);

       ID DESC1         ID DESC2
---------- ----- ---------- -----
      123 ABCDE
      456 FGHIJ        456 ZZZZZ
```

(continued)

5. Generate outer join table temp1:

```
SQL> select a.id, a.desc1, b.id, b.desc2
  2  from   temp1 a, temp2  b
  3  where  a.id(+) = b.id;

        ID DESC1         ID DESC2
---------- ----- ---------- -----
       456 FGHIJ        456 ZZZZZ
                        789 MMMMM
```

6. Now, outer join both sides, as in the following:

```
SQL> select a.id, a.desc1, b.id, b.desc2
  2  from   temp1 a, temp2  b
  3  where  a.id(+) = b.id(+);
where  a.id(+) = b.id(+)
                   *
ERROR at line 3:
ORA-01468: a predicate may reference only one outer-joined table
```

Project Summary

The *outer join* of table temp2 returned all records from temp1 even if they had nonmatching rows in temp2. The *outer join* of table temp1 returned all records from temp2 whether or not they had matching rows in temp1. Lastly, you tried an outer join on both sides to see what would happen. This syntax would not work, and Oracle gave us a helpful error message (that's not always the case!). When you learn the union critical point later on in this chapter, you'll see that there's a way to do this with Oracle's syntax. However, you should move on to the ANSI outer join examples now, where you'll see that it is possible without writing a lot of code (that's a good thing!).

ANSI Outer Joins

With Oracle9*i*, Oracle began down the journey to fully support ANSI SQL standards. To meet this goal, Oracle started the support of ANSI joins as discussed previously. You are now presented with ANSI outer joins. As was just alluded to in Project 4-1, the ANSI outer join syntax allows you to perform right outer joins, left outer joins, and full outer joins.

ANSI Right Outer Joins   As with the ANSI inner joins, the ANSI outer joins have moved the join to the from clause. A right outer join can be written with keywords right outer join or right join since outer is redundant. Rewriting our SALES and CUSTOMERS example from before with the ANSI syntax would produce the following:

```
SQL> select c.cust_id, c.cust_last_name, s.prod_id, s.quantity_sold
  2  from sales s right join customers c
  3       on c.cust_id = s.cust_id
  4  where c.cust_id in (1,80);

   CUST_ID CUST_LAST_NAME                                  PROD_ID QUANTITY_SOLD
---------- -------------------------------------------- ---------- -------------
         1 Kessel
        80 Carpenter                                        127              1
        80 Carpenter                                         36              1
```

As with the Oracle example, the SALES table nonmatched rows are returned. The main difference was that s.cust_id had the (+) notation before; now you state that SALES will be right joined to CUSTOMERS. The join syntax is in the from clause, while the where clause contains only the selection criteria (in this case, only customer 1's and 80's records). This query can also be written with using or natural right join ANSI syntax. Go ahead and try that on your own. Make sure you get the exact same results as you did with the on example from the preceding example.

ANSI Left Outer Joins   The ANSI left outer join works exactly the same as the right outer join and can be written using either left outer join or left join. As with the right outer join, the join on, join using, or natural left join styles are all available. Any of the combinations will produce exactly the same results. Hold off on the left outer join example until you revisit the outer join idea later in Project 4-4.

ANSI Full Outer Joins   A full outer join is possible when using the ANSI syntax without having to write too much code. With a full outer join, you will be able to return both the right outer join and left outer join results from the same query.

The full outer join queries can be written as full outer join or full join and once again, the on, using, or natural joins are all possible. You should revisit the Outer Joins Project and try the ANSI syntax out.

Project 4-2   Join Data Using ANSI SQL Joins

Using the temp1 and temp2 tables you created and populated, try out the ANSI right, left, and full outer joins.

Step by Step

You've just learned that you can write the ANSI outer joins with or without the outer keyword in each of the ANSI right, left, and full outer joins. You also learned that the ANSI on, using, and natural join syntax is available as well. The following step-by-step instructions use a combination of these for illustration purposes. Feel

(continued)

free to try alternate syntax, but we encourage you to adopt a consistent style to allow your code to be self-documenting and traceable by other developers.

1. Use the ANSI right outer join:

```
SQL> select id, desc1, desc2
  2  from   temp2 right outer join temp1
  3            using (id);


        ID DESC1 DESC2
---------- ----- -----
       456 EFGH  ZZZZ
       123 ABCD
```

2. Use the ANSI left outer join, shown in the following:

```
SQL> select id, desc1, desc2
  2  from   temp2 b natural left join temp1 a;


        ID DESC1 DESC2
---------- ----- -----
       456 EFGH  ZZZZ
       789       MMMM
```

3. Use the ANSI full outer join to complete the syntax:

```
SQL> select a.id, a.desc1, b.id, b.desc2
  2  from   temp1 a full join temp2 b
  3            on a.id = b.id;


        ID DESC1         ID DESC2
---------- ----- ---------- -----
       456 EFGH         456 ZZZZ
       123 ABCD
                        789 MMMM
```

Project Summary

The three examples in this project show an alternate way of performing outer joins using ANSI SQL. Our first join, the right outer join, returns all of the rows from the table listed on the right side of the from clause, temp1, regardless of whether or not they match to a row from the other table, temp2.

The second example switches the logic. The table on the left, temp2, returns all rows with a left outer join specified as natural left join.

The final example introduces the full outer join concept available with ANSI SQL. In this case, all rows are returned from each table regardless of whether or not a match was made.

Self-Joins

A self-join is used for a relationship within a single table. Rows are joined back to the same table instead of joining them to a related second table as you have seen with the many CUSTOMERS and SALES tables examples throughout this chapter.

A common example involves hierarchical relationships where all of the records and related records are stored within the same table. A family tree is one such hierarchy that best illustrates the self-join. You should take a look at the FAMILY table that you have defined for this concept:

```
SQL> desc family
 Name                                     Null?    Type
 ---------------------------------------- -------- --------------
 NAME                                     NOT NULL CHAR(10)
 BIRTH_YEAR                               NOT NULL NUMBER(4)
 FATHER                                            CHAR(10)
```

The table contains columns for a person's name and birth year as well as their father's name. The fathers each have their own row in the table with their respective birth years and names. This table could be filled out with every known relationship in the family tree. For this example, Moishe, born in 1894, has a son, Joseph, who was born in 1930. Joseph has three children: Michael, born in 1957; David, born in 1959; and Ian, born in 1963. You can see that Ian then had two children. The example first takes a look at all of the records in the table followed by your hierarchical self-join example. In the first record, we show you all of the data we created. You can simulate this example by creating your own insert statements into the family table:

```
SQL> select * from family;

NAME       BIRTH_YEAR FATHER
---------- ---------- ----------
Moishe           1894
Joseph           1930 Moishe
Michael          1957 Joseph
Davi             1959 Joseph
Ian              1963 Joseph
Baila            1989 Ian
Jillian          1991 Ian

SQL> select a.name, a.birth_year,
  2         a.father, b.birth_year
  3  from   family a, family b, family c
  4  where  a.father = b.name;

NAME       BIRTH_YEAR FATHER     BIRTH_YEAR
---------- ---------- ---------- ----------
Joseph           1930 Moishe           1894
```

```
Michael          1957 Joseph        1930
David            1959 Joseph        1930
Ian              1963 Joseph        1930
Baila            1989 Ian           1963
Jillian          1991 Ian           1963
```

The FAMILY table is found in the from clause twice with table aliases of a and b. The table is joined back to itself to retrieve the father's details. In order to accomplish this, the value found in the father column for each retrieved record (a.father) is joined back to the table to obtain a match on the name column (b.name), which will return the father's details—in this case, his year of birth (b.birth_year). Although this appears complex on the surface, you will find that connecting information together whether from multiple tables or one table back to itself is a regular way for you to view your data in a more meaningful manner.

CRITICAL SKILL 4.9
Learn the Group By and Having Clauses

Earlier, you learned about functions that can work on sets of rows. You can also group sets of rows to lump similar types of information together and return summary information, also referred to as aggregated information. A large number of queries you write will perform group functions as the data is retrieved from the database. Mastering the use of functions and grouping is fundamental to understanding the full power of SQL.

Group By

You can use many of the functions you were presented with earlier with or without the group by clause; but, when you use them without it, Oracle treats all of the selected rows as one group. For example, the following query, when written without a group by clause, returns the average amount sold for products within the Electronics category:

```
SQL> select  avg(amount_sold)
  2  from    sales s, products p
  3  where   s.prod_id = p.prod_id
  4  and     prod_category = 'Electronics';

AVG(AMOUNT_SOLD)
----------------
     125.551667
```

The entire Electronics category was treated as one group. If you wanted to see the average amount sold for each subcategory within the Electronics category, you will need to use a group by clause in your query, lumping each of the Electronics subcategories together before calculating the average. Each group by clause is accomplished by putting the column or columns to group by in the select list followed by one or more functions. A group by statement follows the where clause, and it must include each of the select list columns that are not acted upon by a group function. You should take a look at an example:

```
SQL> select prod_subcategory, avg(amount_sold)
  2  from    sales s, products p
  3  where   s.prod_id = p.prod_id
  4  and     prod_category = 'Electronics'
  5  group by prod_subcategory;
```

PROD_SUBCATEGORY	AVG(AMOUNT_SOLD)
Game Consoles	300.523928
Y Box Accessories	18.7803303
Home Audio	582.175922
Y Box Games	22.640670

This group by example illustrates a column and function in the select list and the repetition of the column again in the group by clause.

Having

Just as you have used selection criteria to reduce the result set, you can apply the having clause to summarized data from a group by operation to restrict the groups returned. Using the previous example, suppose you only wanted to see the Product Subcategory groups that had an average amount sold greater than 300. The following is a having clause executed against the avg(amount_sold) aggregation example:

```
SQL> select prod_subcategory, avg(amount_sold)
  2  from    sales s, products p
  3  where   s.prod_id = p.prod_id
  4  and     prod_category = 'Electronics'
  5  group by prod_subcategory
  6  having avg(amount_sold) > 300;
```

PROD_SUBCATEGORY	AVG(AMOUNT_SOLD)
Game Consoles	300.523928
Home Audio	582.175922

Project 4-3   Group Data in Your Select Statements

One final example will demonstrate the grouping of multiple columns and more than one function being performed for each group. As you build on this example, you will be introduced to column aliases, the round function combined with an avg

(continued)

function, and the use of a substr function, which will serve to select only a specified number of characters for the product subcategories and names results.

Step by Step

Start with the preceding group by example and build on it as you introduce some formatting and intermediate concepts. Look at the output each time and see how you are transforming it along the way. A final output listing has been provided at the end for you to compare against:

1. Start SQL*Plus and re-execute the preceding group by example:

```
select prod_subcategory, avg(amount_sold)
from    sales s, products p
where   s.prod_id = p.prod_id
and     prod_category = 'Electronics'
group by prod_subcategory;
```

2. Add the product name to the select list. Don't forget to add it to the group by also:

```
select prod_subcategory, prod_name, avg(amount_sold)
from    sales s, products p
where   s.prod_id = p.prod_id
and     prod_category = 'Electronics'
group by prod_subcategory, prod_name;
```

3. Rewrite the query to use a natural join, remove the table aliases, and exclude the 'Home Audio' subcategory from the selection:

```
select prod_subcategory, prod_name, avg(amount_sold)
from    sales natural join products
where   prod_category = 'Electronics'
and     prod_subcategory != 'Home Audio'
group by prod_subcategory, prod_name;
```

4. Add a max function calculation on the amount_sold to the query:

```
select prod_subcategory, prod_name, max(amount_sold), avg(amount_sold)
from    sales natural join products
where   prod_category = 'Electronics'
and     prod_subcategory != 'Home Audio'
group by prod_subcategory, prod_name;
```

5. Add a substr function to both the prod_subcategory and prod_name, selecting the first 18 and 25 characters, respectively, to shorten the displayed results. Don't forget to change the group by at the same time:

```
select substr(prod_subcategory,1,18),
       substr(prod_name,1,25),
       max(amount_sold),
       avg(amount_sold)
```

```
from    sales natural join products
where   prod_category = 'Electronics'
and     prod_subcategory != 'Home Audio'
group by substr(prod_subcategory,1,18),
         substr(prod_name,1,25);
```

6. Add a round function to the avg(amount_sold) function. In this step, you should also give the column names aliases to make the results more readable:

```
select substr(prod_subcategory,1,18) Subcategory,
       substr(prod_name,1,25) Product_Name,
       max(amount_sold) Max_Amt_Sold,
       round(avg(amount_sold),2) AvgAmt
from    sales natural join products
where   prod_category = 'Electronics'
and     prod_subcategory != 'Home Audio'
group by substr(prod_subcategory,1,18),
         substr(prod_name,1,25);
```

7. Add a having clause to return aggregated rows that have both a maximum amount sold and an average amount sold greater than 10. As one final measure, you should also add an order by:

```
select substr(prod_subcategory,1,18) Subcategory,
       substr(prod_name,1,25) Product_Name,
       max(amount_sold) Max_Amt_Sold,
       round(avg(amount_sold),2) AvgAmt
from    sales natural join products
where   prod_category = 'Electronics'
and     prod_subcategory != 'Home Audio'
group by substr(prod_subcategory,1,18),
         substr(prod_name,1,25)
having max(amount_sold) > 10
and     avg(amount_sold) > 10
order by substr(prod_subcategory,1,18),
         substr(prod_name,1,25);
```

8. Your final output should look like this:

```
SUBCATEGORY          PRODUCT_NAME              MAX_AMT_SOLD AVGAMT
-----------------    ------------------------- ------------ ------
Game Consoles        Y Box                           326.39 300.52
Y Box Accessories    Xtend Memory                      29.8  24.15
Y Box Games          Adventures with Numbers          17.03  13.78
Y Box Games          Bounce                           25.55  21.13
Y Box Games          Comic Book Heroes                25.76  22.14
Y Box Games          Endurance Racing                 42.58  34.29
Y Box Games          Finding Fido                      16.6  12.79
```

(continued)

```
        Y Box Games          Martial Arts Champions          25.76  22.14
        Y Box Games          Smash up Boxing                 38.64   33.2

        9 rows selected.
```

Project Summary

While the final example, and a few transformations along the way, could be considered more along the lines of intermediate SQL, take some time to study each of the steps and the resulting changes to the output. Once you understand the different components of the SQL statement that evolved in this project, you'll be well on your way to unleashing the power of SQL.

Progress Check

1. Retrieve a list of all product categories, subcategories, names, and list prices where the list price is greater than $100. Order this query by product category, subcategory, and name.

2. List the aggregate total sales for every product category and subcategory group using the ANSI natural join syntax.

3. Retrieve a list of all customers IDs and last names where the customer only has one entry in the SALES table.

Progress Check Answers

1. An ordered list of all product categories, subcategories, names, and list prices greater than $100 is returned by the following query:

```
SQL> select prod_category, prod_subcategory, prod_name, prod_list_price
  2  from    products
  3  where   prod_list_price > 100
  4  order by prod_category, prod_subcategory, prod_name;
```

2. The SQL statement that will return the aggregate amount sold for every product category and subcategory using the ANSI SQL natural join is shown here:

```
SQL> select prod_category, prod_subcategory, sum(amount_sold)
  2  from    products natural join sales
  3  group by prod_category, prod_subcategory;
```

3. The list of all customer IDs and last names for customers that only had one sale is returned by the following SQL statement:

```
SQL> select c.cust_id, cust_last_name, count(*)
  2  from    customers c, sales s
  3  where   c.cust_id = s.cust_id
  4  group by c.cust_id, cust_last_name
  5  having count(*) = 1;
```

CRITICAL SKILL 4.10

Learn Subqueries: Simple and Correlated Comparison with Joins

Within SQL, functionality exists to create subqueries, which are essentially queries within queries. This power capability makes it possible to produce results based on another result or set of results. You should explore this concept a little further.

Simple Subquery

Without the functionality of subqueries, it would take a couple SQL queries to retrieve product information for the product with the maximum list price. The first query would have to find the value of max(prod_list_price). A subsequent query would have to use the value resolved for max(prod_list_price) to find the product details. You should take a look at how you can resolve this with a subquery embedded in the where clause of the main query:

```
select prod_id, prod_name, prod_category
from    products
where   prod_list_price = (select max(prod_list_price)
                           from    products);
```

The subquery is enclosed in parentheses and is part of the where clause. The main query is resolved based on the results of the subquery; in this case, the maximum product list price. As you can see, the ability to have a query within a query is very powerful.

Running SQL queries with embedded subqueries can affect performance. As your experience with subqueries increases, you will find that you will need to work closely with your database administrator, more commonly referred to as a DBA, to optimize statements with subquery processing.

Ask the Expert

Q: What would happen if the subquery returned multiple values?

A: Since the subquery in the example could return only a single value, it was acceptable for it to be written with the equals (=) operand. If multiple values are expected from the subquery, the *in* list operand should be used.

Correlated Subqueries with Joins

A correlated subquery is a query that references a column from the main query. In the example that follows, you are able to first retrieve the average list price for each product category and then join it back (correlate it) to the product category in the outer query. You should take a look at the example and its output:

```
SQL> select substr(prod_category,1,22) Category,
  2         substr(prod_name,1,39) Product,
  3         prod_list_price List
  4  from   products p
  5  where  prod_list_price > (select avg(prod_list_price)
  6                            from    products
  7                            where   p.prod_category = prod_category)
  8  order by substr(prod_category,1,22), prod_list_price desc;
```

CATEGORY	PRODUCT	LIST
Electronics	Home Theatre Package with DVD-Audio/Vid	599.99
Electronics	8.3 Minitower Speaker	499.99
Electronics	Y Box	299.99
Hardware	Envoy Ambassador	1299.99
Peripherals and Access	17" LCD w/built-in HDTV Tuner	999.99
Peripherals and Access	18" Flat Panel Graphics Monitor	899.99
Peripherals and Access	Model NM500X High Yield Toner Cartridge	192.99
Peripherals and Access	SIMM- 16MB PCMCIAII card	149.99
Photo	Mini DV Camcorder with 3.5" Swivel LCD	1099.99
Photo	5MP Telephoto Digital Camera	899.99
Software/Other	Unix/Windows 1-user pack	199.99
Software/Other	Laptop carrying case	55.99
Software/Other	DVD-R Discs, 4.7GB, Pack of 5	49.99
Software/Other	O/S Documentation Set - English	44.99
Software/Other	O/S Documentation Set - German	44.99
Software/Other	O/S Documentation Set - French	44.99
Software/Other	O/S Documentation Set - Spanish	44.99
Software/Other	O/S Documentation Set - Italian	44.99
Software/Other	O/S Documentation Set - Kanji	44.99

```
19 rows selected.
```

The main query retrieves the Category, Product, and List Price details for each product that is greater than the average list price of all products within its category. This wouldn't be possible without the subquery. Data from the subquery's product category is joined with the main query's product category and referenced by the main query's table alias.

Notice as well that the order by exists on the outer query. If it were placed in the subquery, it wouldn't work. The displayed results are what you want to order, not the subquery results.

CRITICAL SKILL 4.11

Use Set Operators: Union, Intersect, Minus

One of the nice things about a relational database is that SQL queries act upon sets of data versus a single row of data. Oracle provides us with a series of set functions that can be used to bring data sets together. The set functions will be discussed in the next few sections using two single column tables: table x and table y. Before proceeding to the discussion on the set functions, you should first take a look at the contents of these tables.

Table x:

```
SQL> select * from x;

COL
---
1
2
3
4
5
6

6 rows selected.
```

Table y:

```
SQL> select * from y;

COL
---
5
6
7

3 rows selected.
```

Union

When you use this operator in SQL*Plus, it returns all the rows in both tables without any duplicates. This is done by Oracle with a sort operation. In the preceding table listings, both tables have columns with values of 5 and 6. A closer look at the union query and resulting output is shown here:

```
SQL> select * from x
  2  union
  3  select * from y;
```

```
COL
---
1
2
3
4
5
6
7

7 rows selected.
```

Union All

The union all set function is similar to the union query with the exception that it returns all rows from both tables with duplicates. The following example is a rewrite of the preceding union example using union all:

```
SQL> select * from x
  2  union all
  3  select * from y;

COL
---
1
2
3
4
5
6
5
6
7

9 rows selected.
```

Intersect

The intersect operator will return all the rows in one table that also reside in the other. Column values 5 and 6 exist in both the tables. The following example demonstrates the intersect set function:

```
SQL> select * from x
  2  intersect
  3  select * from y;

COL
---
5
6
```

NOTE
Please be aware that the intersect set operator can introduce major performance problems. If you are venturing down this path, weigh the alternatives first.

Minus

The minus set function returns all the rows in the first table minus the rows in the first table that are also in the second table. The order of the tables is important. Pay close attention to the order of the tables and the different results in these two query examples:

```
SQL> select * from x
  2  minus
  3  select * from y;

COL
---
1
2
3
4

SQL> select * from y
  2  minus
  3  select * from x;

COL
---
7
```

Project 4-4   Use the Union Function in Your SQL

During the discussion of Oracle outer joins and the associated Project 4-1, you learned that a full outer join wasn't readily available using the Oracle syntax. You also learned about the union set function, and you took a moment to revisit creating an outer join without using ANSI SQL syntax.

Step by Step

You should first recall the Oracle right outer join and left outer join examples you were working on in Project 4-1.

1. Start by using the right outer join example from Project 4-1:

```
SQL> select a.id, a.desc1, b.id, b.desc2
  2  from   temp1 a, temp2  b
```

(continued)

```
3   where   a.id = b.id(+);

       ID DESC1          ID DESC2
---------- ----- ---------- -----
      123 ABCDE
      456 FGHIJ          456 ZZZZZ
```

2. Now, use the left outer join example from Project 4-1:

```
SQL> select a.id, a.desc1, b.id, b.desc2
  2   from    temp1 a, temp2  b
  3   where   a.id(+) = b.id;

       ID DESC1          ID DESC2
---------- ----- ---------- -----
      456 FGHIJ          456 ZZZZZ
                         789 MMMMM
```

3. Now, put the two together with a full outer join using union. ANSI SQL outer join syntax provided you with a full outer join option that wasn't available with Oracle's standard SQL. With the union set function in your Oracle tool belt, you have another way to solve this problem. So now, take the two queries from the recalled examples and union them together:

```
SQL> select a.id, a.desc1, b.id, b.desc2
  2   from temp1 a, temp2 b
  3   where a.id = b.id(+)
  4   union
  5   select a.id, a.desc1, b.id, b.desc2
  6   from temp1 a, temp2 b
  7   where a.id(+) = b.id;

       ID DESC1          ID DESC2
---------- ----- ---------- -----
      123 ABCDE
      456 FGHIJ          456 ZZZZZ
                         789 MMMMM
```

Project Summary

In this project, by combining the right and left outer join Oracle statements together with a union set operator, you were able to mimic the ANSI SQL full outer join functionality.

CRITICAL SKILL 4.12

Use Views

Views are database objects that are based on one or more tables. They allow the user to create a pseudo-table that has no data. The view consists solely of a SQL query that retrieves specific columns and rows. The data that is retrieved by a view is presented like a table.

Views can provide a level of security, making only certain rows and columns from one or more tables available to the end user. You could hide the underlying tables, CUSTOMERS and SALES, from all the users in our organization and only make available the data for states they are entitled to see. In the following example, you are creating a view to show only specific details about Utah-based customer sales:

```
SQL> create view utah_sales
  2   as
  3   select c.cust_id ID,
  4          substr(cust_last_name,1,20) Name,
  5          substr(cust_city,1,20) City,
  6          substr(cust_state_province,1,5) State,
  7          sum(amount_sold) Total
  8   from    customers c, sales s
  9   where   c.cust_id = s.cust_id
 10   and     cust_state_province = 'UT'
 11   group by c.cust_id,
 12           substr(cust_last_name,1,20),
 13           substr(cust_city,1,20),
 14           substr(cust_state_province,1,5);

View created.
```

The create view statement names the view and then uses keywords as select to define the select list, tables, and selection criteria that the view will be based upon. The following code listing issues a desc statement to demonstrate that the view looks just like a table. Notice that the column names have been changed from their original ones and were instead created using the column aliases from the select statement in the preceding view creation DDL:

```
SQL> desc utah_sales
 Name                                      Null?    Type
 ----------------------------------------- -------- -------------------
 ID                                        NOT NULL NUMBER
 NAME                                               VARCHAR2(20)
 CITY                                               VARCHAR2(20)
 STATE                                              VARCHAR2(5)
 TOTAL                                              NUMBER
```

The view looks like a table as demonstrated by the preceding code listing, so you should now issue a couple of queries against it. The first one that follows selects all rows and columns from this view. The second example selects only the name and total columns for customers whose sales are greater than 20,000. Keep in mind, this is still only for Utah customers:

```
SQL> select *
  2   from    utah_sales;
```

```
        ID NAME                  CITY                  STATE      TOTAL
---------- --------------------  --------------------  -----  ----------
       118 Kuehler               Farmington            UT        23258.4
       392 Eubank                Farmington            UT       21297.49
       411 Vankirk               Farmington            UT       19279.94
       462 Nielley               Farmington            UT       64509.91
       599 Robbinette            Farmington            UT       11167.65
      7003 Bane                  Farmington            UT       62605.42
    100207 Campbell              Farmington            UT          11.99
    100267 Desai                 Farmington            UT         240.95
    100308 Wilbur                Farmington            UT         190.96

9 rows selected.

SQL> select name, total
  2  from   utah_sales
  3  where  total > 20000;

NAME                     TOTAL
--------------------  ----------
Kuehler                 23258.4
Eubank                 21297.49
Nielley                64509.91
Bane                   62605.42
```

It's easy to see how you could keep certain users in our company from accessing sales information from more than the states they are granted access to. If this sample database had sale representatives with assigned territories, one could imagine how the use of territory-based views could keep one salesperson from viewing the sales and commissions of another territory representative.

You have demonstrated here that views contain no data. All the data for the view example in this section resides in the underlying tables. In Chapter 9, we will introduce you to materialized views: a physical implementation of a view that is used to improve performance when you have a significant amount of data.

CRITICAL SKILL 4.13

Learn Sequences: Just Simple Stuff

Quite often, primary keys in tables are simply generated numeric values that are sequential. In the sample database that you've used throughout this chapter, cust_id and prod_id in the CUSTOMERS and PRODUCTS tables are likely candidates for creation using a sequence.

Sequences are objects in the database that can be used to provide sequentially generated integers. Without these valuable objects available to users, generating values sequentially would only be possible through the use of programs.

Sequences are generally created and named by a DBA. Among the attributes that can be defined when creating a sequence are a minimum value, a maximum value, a number to increment by, and a number to start with. They are then made available to the systems applications and users that would need to generate them.

For the following example, you will have established a cust_id_seq sequence, which increments by one each time it's called. When you created the sequence, you specified that 104501 should be the number to start with. For demonstration purposes, you'll use the DUAL table to select the next two sequence numbers. More often than not, an application will retrieve and assign the sequence numbers as records are inserted into the associated table:

```
SQL> create sequence cust_id_seq
  2   start with 104501;

  Sequence created
SQL> select cust_id_seq.nextval
  2   from dual;


  NEXTVAL
----------
    104501


SQL> select cust_id_seq.nextval
  2   from dual;


  NEXTVAL
----------
    104502
```

CRITICAL SKILL 4.14

Employ Constraints: Linkage to Entity Models, Types, Deferred, Enforced, Gathering Exceptions

In the section on joins in this chapter, you were introduced to the concept of primary and foreign keys. These were, in fact, constraints on the tables. Constraints preserve the integrity of the database by enforcing business rules.

The primary key for the PROMOTIONS table in the sample schema is an integrity constraint. It requires that each value in promo_id be unique. You should see what would happen if you tried to insert a row in this table with a promo_id value that already exists:

```
SQL> insert into promotions
  2    (promo_id,
  3     promo_name,
  4     promo_subcategory,
  5     promo_subcategory_id,
```

```
 6      promo_category,
 7      promo_category_id,
 8      promo_cost,
 9      promo_begin_date,
10      promo_end_date,
11      promo_total,
12      promo_total_id)
13   values
14      (36,
15       'Thanksgiving Sale',
16       'Newspaper',
17       28,
18       'ad news',
19       4,
20       250,
21       '23-NOV-03',
22       '27-NOV-03',
23       'Promotion Total',
24       5);
insert into promotions
*
ERROR at line 1:
ORA-00001: unique constraint (SH.PROMO_PK) violated
```

Since the value 36 already existed for promo_id, the unique constraint was violated when you tried to insert another row in the table with the same value. This constraint preserved the integrity of the data by enforcing the business rule that every promotion must be identified uniquely.

Linkage to Entity Models

Many organizations have complex databases and, as a result, they use entity models to document each system's database objects and constraints. These models of the organizations' database schemas graphically represent the relationships between objects.

The function of database design could be the responsibility of the developer, DBA, or a database designer. Among other uses, entity-modeling software allows the database designer to graphically define and link tables to each other. The result is a data model with tables, columns, primary keys, and foreign keys. Throughout this chapter, you have issued DDL to create tables. Typically, entity-modeling software will generate the DDL in a script that can be executed against the database. This makes the job of defining and maintaining database objects (and their associated constraints and relationships with each other) a lot easier.

Types

There are a number of different types of integrity constraints. The following is a list of the integrity constraints that are available in Oracle Database:

■ **NULL** constraints are defined on a single column and dictate whether or not the column must contain a value. If a column is defined as NOT NULL, it must contain values in each and every record.

■ **UNIQUE** constraints allow a value in a column to be inserted or updated providing it contains a unique value.

■ **PRIMARY KEY** constraints require that the key uniquely identifies each row in the table. The key may consist of one column or a combination of columns.

■ **FOREIGN KEY** constraints define the relationships between tables. This is commonly referred to as referential integrity. These are rules that are based on a key in one table that assure that the values exist in the key of the referenced table.

■ **CHECK** constraints enable users to define and enforce rules on columns. Acceptable values are defined for a column and insert, update, and delete commands are interrogated and are then accepted or rejected based on whether or not the values are specifically allowed. A separate check constraint definition is required if the requirement exists to perform either similar or different checks on more than one column. The following example illustrates the creation of a table with a single check constraint, followed by an insert with an acceptable value and an attempted insert with a disallowed value:

```
SQL> create table check_constraint_example
  2        (col1 char(1)
  3             constraint check_col1
  4             check (col1 in ('B','G','N')));

Table created.

SQL> insert into check_constraint_example values ('B');

1 row created.

SQL> insert into check_constraint_example values ('C');
insert into check_constraint_example values ('C')
*
ERROR at line 1:
ORA-02290: check constraint (SH.CHECK_COL1) violated
```

Ask the Expert

Q: Is a single space an acceptable entry into a NOT NULL constrained column?

A: Yes. Oracle will allow you to enter a space as the sole character in a NOT NULL constrained column. Be careful though. The single space will look like a NULL value when a select statement retrieves and displays this row. The space is very different than a NULL.

Deferred

When constraints are created, they can be created either as deferrable or not deferrable. A constraint that is not deferred is checked immediately upon execution of each statement and, if the constraint is violated, it is immediately rolled back. A constraint that is deferred will not be checked until a commit statement is issued. This is useful when inserting rows or updating values that reference other values that do not exist but are part of the overall batch of statements. By deferring the constraint checking until the commit is issued, you can complete the entire batch of entries before determining if there are any constraint violations.

CRITICAL SKILL 4.15

Format Your Output with SQL*Plus

Throughout this chapter, you've seen the results of many SQL queries. In some, you added functions like substr to reduce the size of the columns and keep the results confined within one line. In SQL*Plus, there are many parameters that can be set to control how the output is displayed. A list of all of the available settings is easily obtained by issuing the show all command within SQL*Plus. Alternatively, if

Ask the Expert

Q: Once I set parameters, do I ever have to set them again?

A: Yes. Parameters are good only for the current setting. The parameters always reset to their default settings when you start up a new SQL*Plus session. However, the parameter defaults can be overwritten at the start of each SQL*Plus session by entering and saving them in the login.sql file.

you know the parameter and want to see its current value, the command show parameter_name will give you the answer. Before we close out this chapter, you should visit a number of the more useful SQL*Plus parameters.

Page and Line Size

The set linesize command tells Oracle how wide the line output is before wrapping the results to the next line. To set the line size to 100, enter the command set linesize 100. There is no semicolon required to end set commands.

The set pagesize command determines the length of the page. The default page size is 14 lines. If you don't want to repeat the result headings every 14 lines, use this command. If you want your page to be 50 lines long, issue the command set pagesize 50.

Page Titles

The ttitle (for top title) command includes a number of options. The default settings return the date and page number on every page followed by the title text centered on the next line. Multiple headings can also be produced by separating the text with the vertical bar character. The command ttitle 'Customer List | Utah' centers the text "Customer List" on the first line followed by "Utah" on the second line.

Page Footers

The btitle command will center text at the bottom of the page. The command btitle 'sample.sql' places the text "sample.sql" at the bottom center of the output listing. The command btitle left 'sample.sql' results in the footer text "sample.sql" being placed at the left edge of the footer.

Formatting Columns

Quite often, you'll need to format the actual column data. The column command is used to accomplish this. Suppose you are going to select the last name from the CUSTOMERS table along with a number of other columns. You know that, by default, the last name data will take up more space than it needs. The command column cust_last_name format a12 wrap heading 'Last | Name' tells SQL*Plus that there should be only 12 characters of the last name displayed and that the column title "Last Name" should be displayed on two separate lines.

Project 4-5   Format Your SQL Output

Now put these SQL*Plus concepts together and format the output of a SQL query. The following step-by-step instructions will lead you through a few of these basic formatting commands.

(continued)

Step by Step

In this project, you're going to select some customer and sales information for the customers from Utah. Now first take a look at our sample SQL query and output before any formatting kicks in:

```
SQL> select cust_last_name, cust_city, sum(amount_sold)
  2  from    customers natural join sales
  3  where   cust_state_province = 'UT'
  4  group by cust_last_name, cust_city;

CUST_LAST_NAME      CUST_CITY        SUM(AMOUNT_SOLD)

----------------    ---------------  ----------------
Bane                Farmington             62605.42
Desai               Farmington               240.95
Eubank              Farmington             21297.49
Wilbur              Farmington               190.96
Kuehler             Farmington             23258.40
Nielley             Farmington             64509.91
Vankirk             Farmington             19279.94
Campbell            Farmington                11.99
Robbinette          Farmington             11167.65
9 rows selected.
```

The following steps correspond to the set commands in the code listing that follows them. The original SQL query will also be executed a second time with much nicer formatting results.

1. Set the page size to 15. (You'll probably never have such a small page size, but you're doing this to illustrate multiple pages with this small result set.)

2. Set the line size to 70.

3. Add a title at the top of the page with "Customer Sales Report" and "Utah Region" in the first and second lines, respectively.

4. Add a footer with "CONFIDENTIAL REPORT" displayed.

5. Format the last name to be exactly 12 characters long and with a title "Last Name" listed on two separate lines.

6. Format the city with "City" as the title and the data fixed at 15 characters long.

7. Format the summed amount sold with a two-line title "Total Sales." Format the data to include a dollar sign, two digits following the decimal point, and a comma to denote thousands.

```
SQL> set pagesize 15
SQL> set linesize 64
SQL> ttitle 'Customer Sales Report | Utah Region'
SQL> btitle 'CONFIDENTIAL REPORT'
SQL> column cust_last_name format a12 wrap heading 'Last | Name'
SQL> column cust_city format a15 heading 'City'
SQL> column sum(amount_sold) format $999,999.99 wrap
SQL> column sum(amount_sold) heading 'Total | Sales'
SQL> select cust_last_name, cust_city, sum(amount_sold)
  2  from    customers natural join sales
  3  where   cust_state_province = 'UT'
  4  group by cust_last_name, cust_city;
```

```
Mon Jan 12                                          page    1
                     Customer Sales Report
                         Utah Region


Last                             Total
  Name          City             Sales
------------  ---------------  ------------
Bane          Farmington         $62,605.42
Desai         Farmington            $240.95
Eubank        Farmington         $21,297.49
Wilbur        Farmington            $190.96
Kuehler       Farmington         $23,258.40
Nielley       Farmington         $64,509.91
                     CONFIDENTIAL REPORT


Mon Jan 12                                          page    2
                     Customer Sales Report
                         Utah Region


Last                             Total
  Name          City             Sales
------------  ---------------  ------------
Vankirk       Farmington         $19,279.94
Campbell      Farmington             $11.99
Robbinette    Farmington         $11,167.65




                     CONFIDENTIAL REPORT

9 rows selected.
```

(continued)

Project Summary

With some simple formatting commands available within SQL*Plus, you were able to transform the unformatted, difficult-to-read output into a simple and effective report. SQL*Plus has many formatting options available above and beyond the few you have seen demonstrated here. As you become more familiar with SQL and SQL*Plus, take the time to research and try more of the available formatting options. We think you'll agree that SQL*Plus is an effective query tool and report formatter.

Writing SQL*Plus Output to a File

The spool command will save the output to a data file. If your database is on a Windows operating system, the command spool c:\reports\output.dat would capture the output of the query execution in the "output.dat" file.

☑ Chapter 4 Mastery Check

1. DDL and DML translate to _____ and _____, respectively.

2. Which of the following descriptions is true about insert statements?

   A. Insert statements must always have a where clause.

   B. Insert statements can never have a where clause.

   C. Insert statements can optionally include a where clause.

3. In addition to the two mandatory keywords required to retrieve data from the database, there are three optional keywords. Name them.

4. Write a SQL statement to select the customer last name, city, state, and amount sold for the customer represented by customer ID 100895.

5. Retrieve a list of all product categories, subcategories, names, and list prices where the list price is greater than $100 while displaying the results for the product category all in uppercase.

6. Rewrite the query from the previous question and round the amount sold so that there are no cents in the display of the list prices.

7. Retrieve a list of all customer IDs and last names where the customer has more than 200 entries in the SALES table in SH schema.

8. Display the product name of all products that have the lowest list price.

9. Create a view that contains all products in the Electronics category.

10. Sequences provide _____ generated integers.

11. This referential integrity constraint defines the relationship between two tables. Name it.

12. Check constraints enable users to define and enforce rules for:

   A. One or more tables

   B. No more than one column

   C. One or more columns

   D. Only one table

13. Deferred constraints are not checked until the _____ statement is issued.

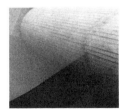

CHAPTER
5

PL/SQL

CRITICAL SKILLS

he basic way we access data with Oracle is via SQL. It provides us with the ability to manage both the database and the information. However, you generally will find that SQL cannot do everything that the programmer needs to do. SQL has an inherent lack of procedural control of the output; it has no array handling, looping constructs, and other programming language features. PL/SQL can be regarded as an extension to SQL for fine control of database data processing. To address this need, Oracle developed Procedural Language for Structured Query Language (PL/SQL), Oracle's proprietary programming language.

PL/SQL, Oracle's contribution to the programming world, is a programming environment that resides directly in the database. You'll learn about its architecture later in this chapter. First, some background about this powerful programming environment.

PL/SQL first appeared in Oracle Version 6 in 1985. It was primarily used within Oracle's user interface product SQL*Forms to allow for the inclusion of complex logic within the forms; it replaced an odd step-method for logical control. It also provided a reasonably simple block-structured programming language that resembles ADA and C. You can use PL/SQL to read your data, perform logical tasks, populate your database, create stored objects, move data within the database, and even to create and display web pages. PL/SQL has certainly developed into a mature technology, and Oracle has shown a very strong dedication to the language, as illustrated by its use of PL/SQL in many of its products (such as Oracle Applications). Oracle also uses the web extensions of PL/SQL quite extensively in many other applications and products. Even products like Oracle Warehouse Builder produce PL/SQL code to move data from one Oracle data source to another. PL/SQL is indeed a powerful language that serves all Oracle professionals who need to interact with the database and the data.

In this chapter, we'll discuss the basic concepts and constructs of PL/SQL so that you'll understand how to create your own PL/SQL programs. There is a lot to cover, but as important as it is to learn SQL, you will need to know PL/SQL as well; if you're looking to become a DBA or an Oracle database developer, you must have knowledge of PL/SQL in your database toolkit.

CRITICAL SKILL 5.1

Define PL/SQL and Learn Why We Use It

Oracle Database 11*g* is more than just a database management system—it's also an engine for many programming languages. Not only does it serve as a Java engine with the built-in Java Virtual Machine (JVM), it's a PL/SQL engine as well. This means that the code you write may be stored in a database and then run as required.

The PL/SQL engine is bundled together with the database, and is an integral part of the Oracle server, providing you with a powerful language to empower your logic and data. Let's look at how PL/SQL fits into the Oracle server. Figure 5-1 shows you how PL/SQL works from both within and without the database.

At the center of the Oracle Database 11*g* server in Figure 5-1 is the primary engine for the database, which serves as the coordinator for all calls to and from the database. This means that when a call is made from a program to the server to run a PL/SQL program, the Oracle server loads the compiled program into memory and then the PL/SQL engine and SQL engine execute the program. The PL/SQL engine will handle the program's memory structures and logical program flow and then the SQL engine issues data requests to the database. It is a closed system and one that allows for very efficient programming.

PL/SQL is used in numerous Oracle products, including the following:

■ Oracle Database Server

■ Application Express

■ Oracle Data Miner

■ Oracle Warehouse Builder

■ Oracle eBusiness Suite

■ Oracle Portal

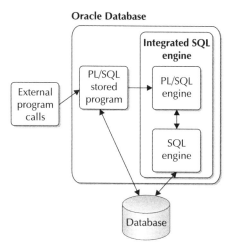

FIGURE 5-1.   *PL/SQL architecture*

All of these programs use PL/SQL to some extent. If you look at the internals of Oracle applications, you'll see that there can be as many as five million lines of PL/SQL code contained within it. PL/SQL interfaces can be developed and utilized from these Oracle development environments:

- SQL*Plus
- Oracle Grid Control/Oracle Enterprise Manager
- Oracle Pre-compilers (such as Pro*C, Pro*COBOL, and so on)
- Oracle Call Interface (OCI)
- Server Manager
- Oracle Application Server 11*g*
- jDeveloper

As you can see, PL/SQL is well established within Oracle's line of products. The reasons for using PL/SQL are primarily its tight integration with the database server and its ease of use. You will find that there are few tasks that PL/SQL cannot handle.

TIP
Use PL/SQL to program complex tasks or for program elements that may be used over and over again.

CRITICAL SKILL 5.2
Describe the Basic PL/SQL Program Structure

The structure you use in PL/SQL is the foundation for the language as a whole. Once you've mastered it, you will then be able to move forward; however, if you do not take the time to get this first step right, your journey will be difficult. Thankfully, it's quite simple.

The structure is quite basic. You will have areas for your program parameters (these are used to pass values from outside a program to the program itself), your internal variables, the main program code and logic, and various ways to deal with problem situations. Let's look at the basic form of a PL/SQL block:

```
[DECLARE]
    -- Put Variables Here
BEGIN
    -- Put Program Here
[EXCEPTION]
```

```
      -- Put exception handlers here
END;
/
```

That's it: the basic structure of every PL/SQL program. When we talk about PL/SQL programs, they are referred to as PL/SQL blocks. *PL/SQL blocks* are simply programs that are complete and that are programmed to run successfully. A PL/SQL program is comprised of one or more of these blocks, which you can think of as *routines*. So at the basic level, you only need one block for a valid PL/SQL program, but as you consider writing a more complex program, you will find it easiest if each block addresses a particular task or subtask; it is these structures that you will use in all of your PL/SQL programs to create the most robust code possible. The PL/SQL block structures form the basis for any program you shall be writing in PL/SQL. This chapter builds upon that fundamental form, each section helping you move toward more complex programs.

In its basic form, you will usually need to declare variables in your PL/SQL program. It is these variables used in the PL/SQL that hold the declarative or working storage area (including constants, local program variables, select statements, data arrays, and such) within your program. These variables are then available for use in your program. So if you need a counter, a data array, data variables, or even Boolean variables, you will declare them here.

Next is the program body or executable section. It is the only section you really need to include in your PL/SQL block, since you could write a program without variables or exception handling. It is in this section that you build your program logic and database access. That is why you must always remember BEGIN and END; these are your PL/SQL bookends. It is between these two lines that your program logic is contained.

The final section is the exception section. It is within this section that you will find all the error handling needed for your program. This section is an optional portion of the PL/SQL block. However, it is recommended that all programs include the use of exception handling to ensure a controlled run of your programs.

Ask the Expert

Q: What are the only lines of the PL/SQL block that are required to create a functional program?

A: The only lines of the basic PL/SQL block that are required to create a functional program are BEGIN and END.

Define PL/SQL Data Types

The use of local variables within a PL/SQL program is an important knowledge point for everyone using the language. It is a basic component of each program, and as such, it is invaluable for gaining the knowledge of what is available and how best to use it. You can now look at how you use and define variables and working storage within your PL/SQL programs.

As with all programming languages, there are characters that you use to write your programs. Each language has its own rules and restrictions when it comes to the valid characters. In the following sections, we will show you

- Valid characters when programming in PL/SQL

- Arithmetic operators

- Relational operators

Valid Characters

When programming in PL/SQL, you may use only characters as defined here:

- Characters can be typed in either upper- or lowercase. PL/SQL is case insensitive.

- All digits between 0 and 9.

- The following symbols: ( ) + - * / < > = ! ~ ; : . @ % , " ' # ^ & _ | { } ? [ ]

Some of these characters are for program commands; others serve as relational or arithmetic operators. Together they form a program.

Arithmetic Operators

Table 5-1 shows the common arithmetic operators used in PL/SQL. They are listed in the order of precedence in which they are executed (that is, by priority). When the functions appear in the same line, it means that they are executed with the same

Operator	Meaning
**	Exponent
*,/	Multiplication, Division
+,-, ||	Addition, Subtraction, Concatenation

TABLE 5-1. *Arithmetic Operators*

level of precedence, so the position of the expression determines which goes first in the operational execution.

Table 5-2 shows the common relational operators used in PL/SQL. These are the logical variables that are used to compare data. As with any comparison, they need to conform to logic hierarchies, especially when using multiple operators in your conditional clauses.

The use of variables in a PL/SQL program is usually something that is required to truly leverage the power of the language. It is here that you define how your data is to be held while you work it through your program. These variables can be the same types you have already learned about in the SQL language. However, in addition to these standard data types, there are some special ones that have been created specifically for the PL/SQL language.

NOTE
All SQL within Oracle is supported directly with PL/SQL.

One of the important features of Oracle Database 11g is the tight integration of the SQL and PL/SQL engines into one system. This means that from Oracle9i forward you can run the same commands in PL/SQL that you use in SQL. This was not true in earlier versions of PL/SQL, so take care if using these versions (it may be time to consider an upgrade). That would also qualify you as more than a beginner.

Now you can move on to the most common data types that you will use when writing PL/SQL programs:

- varchar2
- number
- date
- Boolean

Operator	Meaning
=	Equal
<> or !=	Not equal
>	Greater than
<	Less than
>=	Greater than or equal to
<=	Less than or equal to

TABLE 5-2. *Relational Operators*

You'll use these variables in PL/SQL the same way that you would use them in SQL. Assigning values to variables is very important when programming in PL/SQL or any other programming language. You can assign values to variables in any section of your program code, and you can also assign values to variables in the declare section. Defining your variable in the declare section is done to initialize values in advance of their use in the program or to define values that will be used as constants in your program. To assign a value to a variable in the declaration section, you would use the following format:

```
Variable_name      variable_type      := value;
```

NOTE
The important item that you should notice here is that you use the := to assign a value. This is the standard used in PL/SQL.

You may also define variable values in the execution and exception sections of your PL/SQL program. Within the program, you would use the following format to assign a value to a variable:

```
Variable_name      := value;
```

To assign values to variables you use, let's look at a small program that assigns values in each section of a program:

```
-- Declaration section of the program
declare
      l_counter     number := 0;        -- initiate value to 0
      l_today       date   := sysdate; -- assign system date to variable
      l_name        varchar2(50);       -- variable is defined but has no value
      l_seq_val       number := ian_seq.nextval; -- assigns the next sequence
value to the variable
--
-- Execution section of the program
begin
      l_counter := l_counter + 1; -- add one to current value of counter
      l_name := 'LUCY THE CAT';    -- set a value to character variable
-- Error (EXCEPTION) handling section of the program
exception
      -- Generic error handling to handle any type of error
      when others then
-- print out an error message
raise_application_error (-20100, 'error#' || sqlcode || ' desc: ' sqlerrm)
end;
```

NOTE
Oracle has some special variables that may be used in a PL/SQL program. In the example, we used the sqlcode and sqlerrm variables. These variables represent the Oracle error number and the Oracle error message respectively. You may use these variables to capture Oracle errors in your program.

The varchar2 Data Type

varchar2 is a variable-length alphanumeric data type. In PL/SQL, it may have a length up to 32,767 bytes. When you define the varchar2 variable in the declare section, remember to terminate the line with a semicolon (;). The following is the form of varchar2 variable declarations:

```
Variable_name        varchar2(max_length);
```

where the max_length is a positive integer, as in

```
l_name        varchar2(30);
```

You may also set an initial or default value for the variable. This is done on the same line as the variable declaration in the declare section of your program. You can do this by using the following syntax:

```
L_name        varchar2(30) := 'ABRAMSON';
```

The preceding statement will set that value of the variable L_name to the value of ABRAMSON.

The Number Data Type

The number data type is used to represent all numeric data. The format of the declaration is

```
Number_field number(length, decimal_places);
```

where the length can be from 1 to 38 numerical positions, and decimal_places represents the positions for numerical precision of the decimal place for the variable. Keep this in mind when you define your numerical variable, as in

```
L_average_amount    number(12,2);
```

This describes a variable that may hold up to ten digits (Length(12) - decimal_places(2)) and up to two decimal places. This means the variable may hold a number up to a value of 9,999,999,999.99. The number data type has a number of supported subtypes. These include DECIMAL, FLOAT, REAL, and others. These are quite familiar to people who use other languages to program for their business needs.

The Date Data Type

The date data type variable is used to store date and datetime values. The following is the format of the date declaration:

```
Date_variable      date;
```

By default, Oracle displays values using the format *DD-MON-YY*. So a value of 14-JAN-08 would be the equivalent of saying January 14, 2008. When programming in PL/SQL, you should always use this data type when performing date manipulation. It is possible when combining this data type with some built-in Oracle functions to extend the flexibility of your date manipulations. For example, let's say that you create a variable for a start date and you want to place values into this variable. Let's see how this may be done:

```
Declare
     L_start_date      date;
Begin
     L_start_date := '29-SEP-05';    -- Sets variable
                                     -- to September 29, 2009.
     L_start_date := to_date('29-SEP-2083 ', 'DD-MON-YYYY');
              -- Sets variable to September 29, 2083
     L_start_date := to_date('09-JUN-91:13:01 ', 'DD-MON-YY:HH24:MI');
              -- Sets variable to June 9, 1991, 1:01 p.m.
End;
```

So here you have set the date variable in three different forms. The first is the simplest, while the second is more complex (since it uses the to_date function), though it does allow for more flexible data declarations, since you can use a four-digit year definition. The final example shows you how to put a datetime into the variable. Again you'll use the to_date function, but you'll include the time in the value and then define it with the date mask definition.

NOTE
For more information on other Oracle built-in functions, see "Oracle Database SQL Reference," in the Oracle Database 11g documentation.

You should also familiarize yourself with the variations of the date data type. This includes the timestamp data type, which provides additional date support that may not be available with the simple date data type.

The Boolean Data Type

The final basic data type we will discuss is the Boolean data type. Simply put, this variable will hold a value of either true or false. When you use this data type, you must test its status and then do one thing if it is true and another if it is false. You can use a Boolean expression to compare arithmetic expressions or character expressions. So, if you have the following arithmetic values, you'll get

```
L_record_goals := 91;
L_season_goals := 77;
-- Therefore the following expression will be true
L_record_goals > l_season_goals
-- However the next is false
l_record_goals <= l_season_goals
```

If you wish to compare character strings, the same may be done. Here's an example:

```
l_Cognos_developer := 'Falcon';
l_Oracle_dba := 'Ruxpinnah';
-- The following expression will be true in a true Boolean value
l_Cognos_developer <> l_oracle_dba
```

It is important to understand that these comparisons provide Boolean results that may then be used during conditional program control, so you should take the time to know the difference between true and false. There are numerous other data types, but by mastering these simple ones you can already build some complex programs. In C++ and other languages, Booleans can be represented as either true/false or 1/0. In PL/SQL, the value is assigned only true or false.

Ask the Expert

Q: How do you let Oracle set the definition of a variable within PL/SQL programs based on a table's column definition?

A: The use of dynamic variable definitions based on column definitions is a very important feature that you should always utilize within PL/SQL. This ties the variable definition to a table within the database. When defining your variable, use the name of the table, the column, and the special string of %TYPE. The following is an example of using the product table's prod_id as a variable data definition:

```
v_product_id      products.prod_id%TYPE
```

By using the %TYPE variable type, we have freed our program of the need to ever redefine this field. So if the column's definition changes, so will the variable within your program.

Progress Check

1. Name four programs or facilities where you can use PL/SQL.

2. Name three sections that may be contained in a PL/SQL block.

3. What is the only required section in a PL/SQL block?

4. What data type would you use to store each of the following?

   A. 12344.50

   B. True

   C. April 11, 1963

   D. "PINK FLOYD"

   E. 42

CRITICAL SKILL 5.4

Write PL/SQL Programs in SQL*Plus

When you write PL/SQL programs, you have a couple of options for how to run a program. A program may be run directly in SQL*Plus (or some other SQL environment such as SQL Developer), or it can be stored in the database and then run from a

---

Progress Check Answers

1. Any four from among the following would be acceptable answers: Oracle Forms, Reports, Warehouse Builder, Oracle Applications, Oracle Portal, SQL*Plus, Oracle Grid Control, Oracle Pre-compilers, and Oracle Application Server.

2. The three sections that may be contained in a PL/SQL block are the Declaration, Execution, and Exception sections.

3. The Execution section is the only required section in a PL/SQL block.

4. The data types used to store each of the variables would be

   A. Number or number(8,2). The storage of a number should always be done in a number data type. You can specify the precision or simply define it as a number with no precision, when you do not know the exact nature of your data.

   B. Boolean. The boolean data type is used to store true and false information.

   C. Date. The date data type stores date and time information.

   D. Varchar2(10). Character values should be stored in the varchar2 data type. This is more effective for storing the data, yet it has a limit of 4000 bytes. If you need more than 4000 bytes, you should then use the LONG data type, which allows you to store up to 2GB of data.

   E. Number or number(2). These are the preferred data types for numbers when no decimal places are required (integers).

SQL environment or a program. When you store a program in the database, it's called a stored program or stored object. (We'll cover this later in the chapter.) For now, let's discuss how to write a program using SQL*Plus. While we illustrate this example from within the SQL*Plus environment, these programs may also be run using other SQL interfaces such as SQL Developer, TOAD, or any other product that you may prefer.

When first writing a program, you can create and modify it using the command line in SQL*Plus. To do this:

1. Log into SQL*Plus. Depending on your environment you may need to issue a sqlplus command on the command line. You should note that with Oracle Database 11*g*, the Windows version of SQL*Plus has been deprecated, so if you wish you may also perform this exercise using SQL Developer.

2. Type in your program via the command line.

3. For each line you write, press ENTER to get to the next line.

4. When you finish typing in your program, remember to terminate it with a "/" character. This tells Oracle to run the program that you just finished entering.

5. Monitor Oracle to see if your program ran successfully. If your program does run without errors (syntax errors), you will see the message "PL/SQL procedure successfully completed." If you see anything else, this is an indication that an error occurred.

6. To see the errors created by your program (if you have created a stored object as we will discuss later in this chapter), type in **Show errors**. SQL*Plus will display the errors it encountered during the current run of your program.

7. Should you receive an error, you will need to edit your program. If your SQL*Plus and Oracle environment is set up correctly, you should be able to simply enter **edit** on the command line and your program will be loaded into an editor where you can then fix it. Once you exit the editor, the program will be reloaded into the SQL buffer and may be run again.

Now let's move on to an illustration for how to construct a PL/SQL program and get some output of our results.

Ask the Expert

Q: How can I get feedback/output from my PL/SQL programs?

A: Oracle provides a built-in package named dbms_output for this purpose. Oracle supplies many of these packages that provide users with additional functionality, such as outputting data to the screen. By placing the dbms_output.put_line command into your programs, Oracle PL/SQL can then provide information to the user as shown in this chapter's examples.

To actually see this information, you must enable screen output by entering **SET SERVEROUTPUT ON** at the SQL> prompt before executing your PL/SQL routine.

Project 5-1 Create a PL/SQL Program

This will be the first PL/SQL program that you will create. The concept is straightforward; you will first declare some variables, place some values into them, and then output the data to the screen with SQL*Plus.

Step by Step

1. Log into SQL*Plus.

2. At the SQL> prompt, enter the serveroutput command: **set serveroutput on;**.

3. Enter the following PL/SQL program:

```
Declare
     L_start_date    date;
Begin
         L_start_date := '29-SEP-2005';
         dbms_output.putline (l_start_date); --show date
End;
/
```

4. You should now see the following output on your screen:

```
SQL> /
29-SEP-05
PL/SQL procedure successfully completed.
```

5. You have now completed your first PL/SQL program.

6. Take the time to add to the program and add lines that use other date formats or perform some date addition. For example, you may wish to add the following code and see the results that they provide:

```
L_start_date := to_date('14-JAN-2063', 'DD-MON-YYYY');
dbms_output.put_line (l_start_date);
L_start_date := to_date('09-JUN-91:13:01', 'DD-MON-YY:HH24:MI');
dbms_output.put_line (l_start_date);
```

Next, we need to discuss how to include database data within your PL/SQL programs.

Project Summary

This project enables you to see how to construct a PL/SQL program. You now have seen how to create, run, and then re-run it, allowing you to see the output. This is a simple example, presented to show you the basis of all PL/SQL programs.

SQL in Your PL/SQL Programs

We have looked at a lot of structure up until now. You should know that a PL/SQL program will always have a BEGIN and END statement. It may have variables, loops, or logic control, but now you need to get real database data into your programs. What gives PL/SQL its power is its tight integration with SQL. You may want the information so that you can create a report, update data, create new data, delete old data, or perform just about any other function you can think of. It is very important for you to see how you can integrate data into PL/SQL code. Without data, PL/SQL is just PL.

PL/SQL Cursors

How do you get data to your programs? Simple—select it from the database. This is the easiest way to use SQL in your program. Thus, inserting a line like the following will provide you with the ability to access data in the database:

```
select prod_name
into   v_prod_name
from products
```

Let's break down the statement and look at what it means to the program. As you look at the select statement, you can see that it looks very similar to a standard select statement. However, you should also have noticed the word into in the statement. You may be wondering what it's for? This is how you put a value into a variable using a select statement.

The following example illustrates how you include a SQL statement in your PL/SQL program:

```
1  declare
2    v_prod_name varchar2(80);
```

```
 3  begin
 4      select prod_name
 5      into   v_prod_name
 6      from products
 7      where rownum = 1;
 8    dbms_output.put_line(v_prod_name);
 9* end;
10  /
```

In addition to selecting one value from the database, you also have the ability to select more than one value and add conditions that you want to include. To do this, use the following cursor format:

```
select prod_name, prod_list_price, prod_min_price from products
where rownum < 10
```

You can use any SQL statement you want within your program. It can be a select, insert, update, or delete statement. All of these will be supported. When you use a select statement like you did in the preceding example, this is called an *implicit cursor*. An implicit cursor is a SQL statement that is contained within the executable section of the program and has an into statement (as in the case of a select statement). With an implicit cursor, Oracle will handle everything for you, but there is a cost to doing this: the program will run slower. You need to understand what you're doing because though it may not be the best way to perform a select statement, you must use an implicit cursor when you want to run a delete, update, or insert statement. So, let's move on to see a better way of doing the same thing. We will revisit your previous example so that you can compare the two.

The better way is to create an explicit cursor. An *explicit cursor* is a select statement that is declared in the declare section of a program. You do this so that Oracle will then prepare your SQL statement in advance of running your program.

Ask the Expert

Q: Why did we include rownum = 1 in our select statement?

A: The reason we include rownum = 1 when using an implicit cursor is that in this particular case the select statement will return more than 1 row. This will result in an Oracle error that terminates the processing of this PL/SQL block. To avoid this situation, we include the rownum = 1 condition.

This makes for very efficient use of memory by the program. Let's look at what the program would look like with an explicit cursor:

```
 1   declare
 2     v_prod_name varchar2(80);
 3     cursor get_data is
 4       select prod_name
 5       from products;
 6   begin
 7       open get_data;
 8       fetch get_data into v_prod_name;
 9       dbms_output.put_line(v_prod_name);
10       close get_data;
11*  end;
```

In the previous code, we converted the initial example into one that uses an explicit cursor. Notice that the select statement is now contained in the declaration section. There is also no longer an into clause. This functionality is moved into the execution section, where it is used in the fetch command.

You will also note that we introduced three new PL/SQL commands: open, fetch, and close. With these three simple commands, you can get data from your database using SQL cursors. The open command tells Oracle to reserve memory that will need to be used by the select statement. The fetch command, meanwhile, pulls the data from the first row of the result set, and the close command returns the memory back to Oracle for other uses.

NOTE
Always remember to close your cursors when you are done with them. If you don't, you may start getting memory problems, or you could get results that you don't expect.

The Cursor FOR Loop

You get a better sense of the power of the cursor by combining it with a loop. The cursor FOR loop is the result of combining the select cursor with a FOR loop (we'll go into additional detail about this loop in the next section). This allows you to retrieve multiple rows from the database if your result set should do this. It also is simpler to program, and you don't have to worry about opening or closing your cursor; Oracle handles all that within the loop. Let's look at an example of the cursor FOR loop. The important lines have been highlighted for you:

```
SQL> set serveroutput on
SQL>  declare
  2      v_prod_name varchar2(80);
  3      cursor cur_get_data is
```

```
  4      select prod_name
  5      from products;
  6  begin
  7     for i in cur_get_data
  8     LOOP
  9             dbms_output.put_line(i.prod_name);
 10     END LOOP;
 11 end;
 12 /
5MP Telephoto Digital Camera
17" LCD w/built-in HDTV Tuner
Envoy 256MB - 40GB
Y Box
Mini DV Camcorder with 3.5" Swivel LCD
Envoy Ambassador
Laptop carrying case
Home Theatre Package with DVD-Audio/Video Play ...
```

NOTE
To reference columns during a FOR loop, use the name of the loop and concatenate it with the name of the column as defined within the cursor declaration. Thus, your result will be a variable named cursor_name.fieldname (in our example, we did this using the variable i.prod_name).

The cursor FOR loop is truly PL/SQL power in action. It provides you with the ability to easily move through the result set of a select statement and perform the logic and manipulations you need to be successful.

We have just touched the surface of getting information from PL/SQL. One concept that you will need to get comfortable with is the debugging of PL/SQL programs, which can be a very complex task. Experience has taught us that finding our errors can never be taken lightly or ignored. Using a simple facility like dbms_output, you have a way of tracking the progress of your program.

NOTE
Another available facility is dbms_profiler. This package analyzes how your program is running and collects statistics on how long each line takes to execute. This helps you find code that runs slowly or inefficiently. When you need to access more advanced statistics about your programs, take the time to investigate this package and how to integrate it into your PL/SQL code. Since this is a beginner's guide, we'll only direct you to an important feature when you need its functionality.

Having seen how to write and debug programs, you can now make those programs more complex.

Handle Error Conditions in PL/SQL

As you have seen in the previous section, bad things happen to good programs. However, you also have to deal with bad or problematic data as well. To deal with problems during the processing of data, PL/SQL provides us with the robust ability to handle these types of errors. We call this type of program code *exception handling*.

To raise an error from within a PL/SQL program, use the built-in procedure named raise_application_error. The procedure requires two arguments: one is for the error number and must be between –20000 and –20999, whereas the second argument is the error that you want the user to see.

As with all exception handling, this program code is placed into the EXCEPTION section of your PL/SQL program. Thus, your program structure will now be

```
BEGIN
     -- Put Program Here
EXCEPTION
-- Put exception handlers here
END;
/
```

Table 5-3 gives you some examples of the most common errors that Oracle can help you handle.

NOTE
You must always make the Others error handle the last one in your program, since Oracle will not process any exception handles after this one. In addition, the WHEN OTHERS exception should be a last resort and should not be used as a catch-all, error-handling mechanism.

The following is the line that your program may contain to provide feedback to the user:

```
raise_application_error (-20123, 'This is an error, you have done a bad thing');
```

Exception Name	Explanation	Oracle Error
No_data_found	When a select statement returns no rows, this error may be raised. It usually occurs when you use an implicit cursor and perform a SELECT INTO.	ORA-01403
Too_many_rows	When a case that should only return a single row returns multiple rows, this exception is raised.	ORA-01422
Dup_val_on_index	This exception is raised when you try to insert a record into a table that has a primary key on it and the record that you are inserting is a duplicate of one that already exists in the table.	ORA-00001
Value_error	This error occurs when you attempt to put a value into a variable, but the value is incompatible (for example, inserting a value of 'MICHAEL BROWN' into a numerical field). It also occurs when you input a value that is too large to be held in the defined field (for instance, inputting 'JILLIAN ABRAMSON' into a character variable that is only ten characters long).	ORA-06502
Zero_divide	This error is encountered when you attempt to divide by zero.	ORA-01476
Others	This exception is used to catch any errors not handled by specific error handles.	Non-specific

TABLE 5-3.   *Built-in PL/SQL Exceptions*

So let's see how these all come together in a single program:

```
SQL> run
  1  declare
  2       l_emp_count number;
  3       i          number;  -- We will use this as our counter
```

```
 4        l_row        employee%rowtype;
 5    begin
 6            select *
 7            into l_row
 8            from    employee
 9            order by emp_name;
10   EXCEPTION
11    WHEN no_data_found then
12     raise_application_error (-20052,'Sorry no data in this table. TRY AGAIN!');
13    WHEN others then
14      raise_application_error (-20999,'Something has gone really wrong...you better
guess');
15*   end;
declare
*
ERROR at line 1:
ORA-20052: Sorry no data in this table. TRY AGAIN!
ORA-06512: at line 12
```

This program will handle instances where no data is found, as well as anything else that happens that is not a result of lack of data. So, with these simple techniques you may now handle problems that might occur in your programs.

You may also extend the functionality of the Oracle exception handling facility with your own *user-defined exceptions.*

User-defined exceptions are defined within your program code. There are three components to defining and using this exception type. They include

- Declaring the exception

- Raising the exception during program execution

- The exception handle itself

These three items must all be in place for an exception to be valid and to be used within the program. This differs from the Oracle-defined exceptions, which may be used within a program without declaring them or even raising an error condition. So let's see how this all comes together in a program:

```
Declare
      L_counter    number := 0;
      L_name employee.employee_name%type;
      Cursor get_employee_name is
      Select employee_name
      From employee;
excep_old_friend    Exception;
never_met_them              Exception;
Begin
      Open    get_employee_name;
      Fetch   get_employee_name into l_name;
      If l_name = 'CARL DUDLEY' then
            Raise excep_old_friend;
```

```
Else
     Raise excep_never_met_them;
     End if;
     Close get_employee_name;
Exception
     When excep_old_friend then
          Dbms_output.put_line('I know this person');
When    excep_old_friend then
          Dbms_output.put_line('I do not know this person');
End;
```

As you can see in this program, the definition and use of a user-defined exception is really driven by your needs. In this case, you select data from the employee table. Should the name of the person you retrieve be *Carl Dudley,* then you raise the exception that you defined called excep_old_friend. In any other case, you would raise excep_never_met_them. Based on this decision, you *raise* the exception that you want to handle for the situation.

So, let's look at the three components you need to use this exception you've created specially. First, there is the declaration of the exceptions. These go into the Declaration section. You simply name the exception and tell Oracle that they are of the type exception, just as we have done in the following lines of program code:

```
excep_old_friend   Exception;
never_met_them     Exception;
```

Next, you need to call the appropriate exception within the program code. You'll want to call the exception when something occurs—in this case, when you obtain the name of a friend or the name of a stranger.

NOTE
User-defined exceptions may be raised to handle an error or to handle a condition that may not be seen by Oracle as an error.

In your case, you are not concerned with an error; you just want to deal with a situation. Therefore, in your program code all that is needed to call a user-defined exception is to simply use the raise command followed by the name of the exception, as in the following code snippet:

```
Raise excep_old_friend;
```

You have taken the first two steps toward defining and calling your own exception (Declaration and Execution sections); all that's left is to define what the exception is going to do. This is done in the Exception section of your program. To do this, simply include the exception in the Exception section:

```
Exception
      When excep_old_friend then
            Dbms_output.put_line('I know this person');
```

In your case, you simply will output that you know this person.

This example has shown you how to set up user-defined exceptions and how to use them. The way in which you implement exceptions is limited only by your imagination.

Error Handling Using Oracle-Supplied Variables

As well as being able to define your own exceptions within your PL/SQL program, Oracle also provides some standard variables that may be used in your PL/SQL programs. These variables are available to you in many different forms depending on where you use them in your program. These variables are known as *pseudo-columns*. A pseudo-column is a column that may be used in a select statement or during the processing of data. We use the term pseudo-column so that you can consider their use similarly to the way you would use a column. They include

- Current system date (sysdate)

- Row number (rownum)

- Oracle error number (sqlcode)

- Oracle error message (sqlerrm)

In this section, we will only look at the last two, which in exception handling are the two that are often used. They provide you with access to the Oracle error number and message and will therefore allow you to write programs that may always end successfully. Even though they may still encounter an error, it's handled in a manner that is quite robust and manageable. Let's look at the same program, except this time you will add another exception handle for when any error occurs. You do this by adding the when others exception:

```
Declare
      L_counter      number := 0;
      L_name employee.employee_name%type;
      Cursor get_employee_name is
      Select employee_name
      From employee;
excep_old_friend    Exception;
never_met_them             Exception;
Begin
      Open   get_employee_name;
      Fetch  get_employee_name into l_name;
      If l_name = 'CHRISTINE LECKMAN' then
            Raise excep_old_friend;
```

```
Else
     Raise excep_never_met_them;
End if;
     Close get_employee_name;
Exception
     When excep_old_friend then
            Dbms_output.put_line('I know this person');
When excep_never_met_them then
            Dbms_output.put_line('I do not know this person');
    When others then
             Dbms_output.put_line('Oracle Error: ' || sqlcode);
             Dbms_output.put_line('Oracle error message is: '|| sqlerrm);
End;
```

As you can see, you have now added an extra error-handling condition. The one you have added to the program is the infamous when others exception. As previously discussed, this exception may be used to handle any error that occurs for which no other exception has been defined. Most importantly, it must also be the last exception in your exception section, since Oracle stops processing when it encounters an exception that meets the criteria. Therefore, if this exception is first, Oracle will stop once it hits the *when others* condition. As we mentioned before, this is a dangerous practice; you need to handle this error carefully and might even consider *not* utilizing the when others condition because it could mask the real issues with your program.

In our example, we have now used the functions sqlcode and sqlerrm. You should always consider using these variables in your program code to ensure your PL/SQL program completes in a manageable manner and provides the necessary feedback for diagnosing potential problems and errors.

Progress Check

1. What facility do you use to get output from within a PL/SQL program?

2. What is wrong with the following cursor declaration?

   ```
   Cursor get_data is;
   Select cust_id, cust_last_name
   From customers;
   ```

3. What are the two basic types of exception handles within PL/SQL?

4. To call an exception, what PL/SQL command should you use?

5. Name two pseudo-columns that help with exception feedback?

CRITICAL SKILL 5.6

Include Conditions in Your Programs

The inclusion of conditions in your programs is the heart of all advanced programming languages. In the previous section, you actually included some statements for performing these types of tasks and you may have noticed IF statements and loops. It is in this section that we now illustrate how to construct them by providing you with a step-by-step guide. Since programs are written to handle a number of different situations, the manner in which different conditions are detected and dealt with is the biggest part of program control. This section will provide you with details on the following topics:

- Program control

- Various types of IF logic structures

- CASE expressions

- Various types of looping structures

Program Control

Program control is governed by the status of the variables that it uses and the data it reads and writes from the database. As an example, picture yourself going to the Department of Motor Vehicles to renew your driver's license. Upon entering the office, you are presented with a number of directional signs. One sign is "Drivers Testing"; for this you go to the 2nd floor. Another sign tells you that "License Renewals" are on the 3rd floor. So, since you are here for a renewal, you proceed to the 3rd floor. Once you arrive in the renewal office, you are once again faced with some new choices—after all, this is a government office; it's not going to be a simple exercise. So, now you have to decide if you are going to pay by cash or credit card. Cash payments are being accepted to the right and credit cards are to the left. Noting that you have enough cash, you head to the payment wicket on the right. Let's look at Table 5-4 and see how the program control influenced your choices.

Progress Check Answers

1. The dbms_output package can be used to get output from within a PL/SQL program.

2. The extra ";" on line 1 of the cursor should not be there.

3. Built-in exceptions like when others and when no_data_found are the two basic types of exception handles within PL/SQL.

4. The raise command is used.

5. Two pseudo-columns that help with exception feedback are sqlcode and sqlerrm.

Step #	Process or Decision to Make	Next Steps	
1	Here for a driver's license transaction	Yes = 2	No = 4
2	Here for a driving test	Yes = 5	No = 3
3	Here for a license renewal	Yes = 6	No = 4
4	Ask for help	Right place = 1	Wrong place = 13
5	Go to 2nd floor	7	
6	Go to 3rd floor	9	
7	Line up for driver's test	8	
8	Pass test (we hope)	6	
9	Payment method	Cash = 10	Credit = 11
10	Cash payment wicket	12	
11	Credit-card payment wicket	12	
12	Receive new license	13	
13	Leave building, head home		

TABLE 5-4.   *Logical Flow*

IF Logic Structures

When you are writing computer programs, situations present themselves in which you must test a condition. So, when you ask a question in your program, you are usually presented with one of two answers. First, it may be true or it may be false; computer programs are quite black and white. So, in computer logic there can only be true or false answers to our questions, no maybes here. PL/SQL provides you with three distinctive IF logic structures that allow you to test for true and false conditions. In everyday life, you are presented with decisions that you need to make. The following sections show you how to do this using PL/SQL.

IF/THEN   The IF/THEN construct tests the simplest type of condition. If the condition evaluates to TRUE, then one or more lines of program code will be executed. If the condition evaluates as FALSE, then no action is taken. The following code snippet illustrates how this is performed with a PL/SQL program:

```
IF l_date > '11-APR-63' then
     l_salary :=  l_salary * 1.15; -- Increase salary by 15%
END IF;
```

In this case, you are asking that if the value of the variable l_date is greater than (>) April 11, 1963, then the salary should increase by 15 percent. This statement may also be restated using the following:

```
IF not(l_date <= '11-APR-63') then
     l_salary :=  l_salary * 1.15; -- Increase salary by 15%
END IF;
```

You may nest IF/THEN statements to increase the power of your statements. So, let's add an additional condition to limit who gets the raise:

```
IF l_date > '11-APR-63' then
IF l_last_name = 'PAKMAN' then
                    l_salary :=  l_salary * 1.15; -- Increase salary by 15%
END IF;
END IF;
```

So, not only must the date be greater than April 11th, 1963, but your last name must be equal to 'PAKMAN' in order to get the raise. This is a method we use to make sure that human resource programs ensure that programmers get a raise every year.

What you should also notice in this code is that there are now two END IF statements. This is a required construct, since you must always pair up an IF statement with an END IF. So, if you are going to have nested IF statements, you must ensure that each is paired with a matching END IF.

NOTE
Each IF statement block must have at least one line of program code. If you wish to do nothing within your program code, then simply use the NULL; command.

IF/THEN/ELSE   The IF/THEN/ELSE construct is similar to the simple IF/THEN construct. The difference here is that if the condition executes as FALSE, you perform the program statements that follow the ELSE statement. The following code illustrates this logic within PL/SQL:

```
IF l_date > '11-APR-63' then
            l_salary :=  l_salary * 1.15; -- Increase salary by 15%
ELSE
l_salary := l_salary * 1.05;  -- Increase salary by 5%
END IF;
```

In this code listing, you see the condition that if the date is greater than April 11, 1963, you will get a 15 percent salary increase. However, when the date is less than or equal to this date, you only receive a five percent increase.

As with the simple for of the IF/THEN construct, you may nest the IF/THEN/ELSE construct. Let's look at how this might appear in your PL/SQL program:

```
IF l_date > '11-APR-63' then
If l_last_name = 'PAKMAN' then
                    l_salary :=  l_salary * 1.15; -- Increase salary by 15%
ELSE
                    l_salary :=  l_salary * 1.10; -- Increase salary by 10%
END IF;
ELSE
                    l_salary := l_salary * 1.05;  -- Increase salary by 5%
END IF;
```

This leads us to another two points on using the IF statement within PL/SQL:

■ There may only be one ELSE statement within every IF statement construct.

■ There is no semicolon (;) on the line starting with ELSE.

IF/THEN/ELSIF   The final IF construct that we will show you is the IF/THEN/ELSIF one. In this case, you provide yourself with the option to test another condition where the condition is evaluated as FALSE. So, should you want to test for more than one condition without using nested IF statements, this is the type of statement you might use:

```
IF l_last_name = 'PAKMAN' then
                    l_salary :=  l_salary * 1.15; -- Increase salary by 15%
ELSIF l_last_name = 'ASTROFF' then
                    l_salary :=  l_salary * 1.10; -- Increase salary by 10%
ELSE
                    l_salary :=  l_salary * 1.05; -- Increase salary by 5%
END IF;
```

In this statement, if your last name is Pakman, you get a 15 percent raise. If it is Astroff, you get 10 percent, and the rest of us get only a 5 percent raise.

Note that there is no limit to the number of ELSIF conditions you may use within this construct. The following shows an example of using multiple ELSIF statements within the construct:

```
IF l_city = 'OTTAWA' then
     L_team_name := 'SENATORS';
ELSIF l_city = 'BOSTON' then
     L_team_name := 'BRUINS';
ELSIF l_city = 'MONTREAL' then
     L_team_name := 'CANADIENS'
ELSIF l_city = 'TORONTO' then
     L_team_name := 'MAPLE LEAFS';
END IF;
```

NOTE
There is no matching END IF statement for each ELSIF. Only a single END IF is required within this construct.

When writing your PL/SQL program, you should use indentation to simplify the reading of the program. Notice in our code segments that we use indentation to make it easier for you to read the code statements. As a rule, you should line up each IF/THEN/ELSE statement and indent the program code that lies between each of these words.

CASE Statements

The next logical step from the IF statement is the CASE statement. The CASE statement was introduced with Oracle9*i* and is an evolution in logical control. It differs from the IF/THEN/ELSE constructs in that we now can use a simple structure to logically select from a list of values. More important, it may be used to set the value of a variable. Let's explore how this is done.

First, let's look at the format you will need to follow:

```
CASE variable
     WHEN expression1 then value1
     WHEN expression2 then value2
     WHEN expression3 then value3
     WHEN expression4 then value4
     ELSE value5
END;
```

There is no limit to the number of expressions that may be defined in a CASE statement. The following is an example of the use of the CASE expression:

```
SQL> run
  1  declare
  2     val      varchar2(100);
  3     city     varchar2(20) := 'TORONTO';
  4  begin
  5     val := CASE city
  6         WHEN 'TORONTO' then 'RAPTORS'
  7         WHEN 'LOS ANGELES' then 'LAKERS'
  8         WHEN 'BOSTON' then 'CELTICS'
  9         WHEN 'CHICAGO' then 'BULLS'
 10         ELSE 'NO TEAM'
 11  END;
 12
 13     dbms_output.put_line(val); -- output to the screen
 14* end;
RAPTORS
PL/SQL procedure successfully completed.
```

Ask the Expert

Q: How do I add comments to my PL/SQL programs?

A: To add comments to your code, simply start a comment with a /* and end it with a */ or use the -- (as we have done previously). If you use the --, you need to make sure you put it on its own line, or after your program code if you place it on the same line. The following are examples of valid comments:

```
/* This is a comment */
-- This is also a comment
```

Although you may have been able to use the IF/ELSIF/THEN/ELSE construct to achieve the same purpose, the CASE statement is easier to read and is more efficient with the database.

Loops

When was the last time that you visited an amusement park? Well, if you have been to one in recent years, you will surely have seen a roller coaster. That roller coaster, if it's a really good roller coaster, probably had one or more loops. PL/SQL is that kind of ride. It is a ride that includes loops. Loops are control structures that allow you to repeat a set of commands until you decide that it is time to stop the looping.

Generally, the format that all loops take is the following:

```
LOOP
     Executable statements;
END LOOP;
```

Each time the loop is executed, the statements within the loop are executed, and the program returns to the top of the LOOP structure to do it all over again. However, if you ever want this processing to stop, you need to learn about the EXIT statement.

The EXIT statement allows you to stop executing within a loop without a condition. It then passes control back to the program and continues on after the LOOP statements.

The following is how to get out of a tight LOOP:

```
LOOP
     IF l_bank_balance >= 0 then EXIT;
     ELSE
          L_decision := 'ACCOUNT OVERDRAWN';
     END IF;
END LOOP;
```

NOTE
Without an EXIT statement in a simple LOOP, the loop will be infinite.

There are many other kinds of loops, some of which provide more control over your looping. Each has its use in PL/SQL programming and each should be learned in order to give your programming the greatest flexibility.

The WHILE Loop

The WHILE loop will continue to execute as long as the condition that you have defined continues to be true. When and if the condition becomes false, then you exit your loop. If your condition is never satisfied you will end up in a loop that will never exit. Let's look at an example:

```
WHILE l_sales_total < 100000 LOOP
     Select sales_amount into l_sale_amount from daily_sales;
     l_sales_total := l_sales_total + l_sale_amount;

END LOOP;
```

Although you may have used the EXIT command to do the same thing, it is better form to use the WHILE expression.

The FOR Loop

The FOR loop is one of the most common loops you will encounter in your PL/SQL programming and it allows you to control the number of times a loop executes. In the case of the WHILE loop, you are never quite sure how many times a loop is executed, since it will continue to loop until a condition is met. However, in the case of the FOR loop, this isn't true.

The FOR loop allows you to define the number of times to loop when you program the loop itself. You will define the value that starts your loop, as well as the value that terminates it. Let's look at its syntax:

```
FOR l_counter IN 1 .. 10
LOOP
     Statements;
END LOOP;
```

So, what is important to note in the preceding statement? First, you need to know that the variable l_counter will hold the value between 1 and 10. How do you know it will be between 1 and 10? Well, after the IN word, you place the counter's range. In this case, you want the counter to start at 1 (the low bound), and then continue to 10. You should also note that between the two integer values (1 and 10) you place two dots (..). You do this to tell Oracle that you would like it to count between these two numbers. You should also notice that we have not shown you any type of declaration section, as they are not explicitly defined, since LOOP counters are defined when they are used. You also have the ability to count backwards using the REVERSE clause. This listing shows you how the REVERSE clause may be used:

```
declare
    l_counter number;
begin
    FOR l_counter IN REVERSE 1..5
    LOOP
            dbms_output.put_line(l_counter);
    END LOOP;
end;
/
5
4
3
2
1

PL/SQL procedure successfully completed.
```

Now you can see how simple it is to use simple loops. But don't be fooled—loops have a lot of power, some of which you will see later. When you use loops like the WHILE loop or the FOR loop, you have the ability to use variables instead of hard-coded values. This allows you to have the greatest possible flexibility since you can have the database or external data provide you with the limits within your loop. Let's look at how this might work. The following example illustrates the simplest form of the FOR loop. In this case, you select the number of employees you have in your employee table and then simply show how the counter counts from 1 to the number of employees in your small company:

```
SQL> run
  1  declare
  2      l_emp_count number;
  3      i               number;  -- We will use this as our counter
  4  begin
  5    -- Select the number of employees in the l_emp_count variable
  6      select count(*) into l_emp_count from employee;
  7
  8      FOR i IN 1 .. l_emp_count  LOOP
  9            dbms_output.put_line('Employee ' || i);
 10      END LOOP;
 11* end;
```

```
Employee 1
Employee 2
Employee 3
Employee 4
Employee 5
Employee 6
PL/SQL procedure successfully completed.
```

So, as you might have guessed, you have six employees in your company. It may be small, but it's very good. However, the important thing to know is that you may use variables in your loops. The other line you may have noticed was the select statement contained in the PL/SQL block.

Project 5-2   Use Conditions and Loops in PL/SQL

In this project, you will create a PL/SQL program that will read the data in the products table and then print out the products that are priced above $50.

Step by Step

1. Log into SQL*Plus.

2. At the SQL> prompt, enter the serveroutput command: **set serveroutput on**.

3. Enter the following PL/SQL program:

```
 1  declare
 2    cursor get_data is
 3      select prod_name, prod_list_price
 4      from products;
 5  begin
 6      for i in get_data
 7      LOOP
 8       if i.prod_list_price > 50 then
 9        dbms_output.put_line(i.prod_name||' Price: '|| i.prod_list_price);
10       end if;
11      END LOOP;
12* end;
```

4. You should now see the following output on your screen:

```
SQL> /
5MP Telephoto Digital Camera Price: 899.99
17" LCD w/built-in HDTV Tuner Price: 999.99
Envoy 256MB - 40GB Price: 999.99
Y Box Price: 299.99
Mini DV Camcorder with 3.5" Swivel LCD Price: 1099.99
```

(continued)

```
Envoy Ambassador Price: 1299.99
Laptop carrying case Price: 55.99
Home Theatre Package with DVD-Audio/Video Play Price: 599.99
18" Flat Panel Graphics Monitor Price: 899.99
SIMM- 8MB PCMCIAII card Price: 112.99
SIMM- 16MB PCMCIAII card Price: 149.99
Unix/Windows 1-user pack Price: 199.99
8.3 Minitower Speaker Price: 499.99
Multimedia speakers- 5" cones Price: 67.99
Envoy External 8X CD-ROM Price: 54.99
Model NM500X High Yield Toner Cartridge Price: 192.99
Model A3827H Black Image Cartridge Price: 89.99
128MB Memory Card Price: 52.99
256MB Memory Card Price: 69.99

PL/SQL procedure successfully completed.
```

5. You may now change the criteria we have used so that we print out messages for products under $50. This is done by adding the following text in the right place in the code:

```
else
    dbms_output.put_line(i.prod_name || ' Product under 50');
```

6. More output will appear, including that of all the products.

Project Summary

This project illustrates how to use loops and conditional clauses and how you can easily select data and use it within a PL/SQL program.

CRITICAL SKILL 6.7

Create Stored Procedures—How and Why

PL/SQL is a very powerful language; one of its most important features is the ability to store programs in the database and share them with others. We generally refer to these as stored objects or stored sub/programs. There are four distinct types: procedures, functions, triggers, and packages. Up until now in this chapter, you have looked at anonymous PL/SQL blocks. Stored PL/SQL programs differ from these since they are named objects that are stored inside the database. Anonymous blocks are not stored in the database and must be loaded each time you want to run them.

You create stored programs for a number of reasons. The most important reason to create programs that are stored and named instead of anonymous ones is that it provides you with the ability to share programs and optimize performance. By storing programs, you can grant many different users the privilege of running your program. You can also simplify them and have different programs perform specific functions. These programs can then be called from a central program, which can optimize performance and programming time. This concept is very familiar to object-oriented programmers and is known as *modularity*.

If you are to truly take advantage of PL/SQL within the confines of your Oracle database, you will need to understand how to create and maintain PL/SQL stored objects. Let's look at the various types of PL/SQL stored programs.

The first stored object is called a *stored procedure*. A stored procedure is a PL/SQL program-adding construct that tells the database you want to store an object. Just as you do when you create a table, a procedure is created or updated with the create procedure command. By adding this at the beginning of a PL/SQL block, you create an object in the database known as a procedure. Another feature of stored procedures, provided to you at no extra cost, is the ability to pass values in and out of a procedure.

NOTE
You should put create or replace procedure in your create procedure commands. If you do not use the replace portion of the command, you will need to drop your procedure before trying to re-create it. By including replace, the procedure will be created if it does not exist or will be replaced if it does.

Let's look at one of the programs you have already created and convert it to a stored procedure:

```
 1   create or replace procedure print_products
 2   as
 3   declare
 4     cursor get_data is
 5       select prod_name, prod_list_price
 6       from products;
 7   begin
 8   for i in get_data
 9    LOOP
10     if i.prod_list_price > 50 then
11       dbms_output.put_line(i.prod_name || ' Price: ' || i.prod_MIN_price);
12     else
13       dbms_output.put_line(i.prod_name || ' Product under 50');
14     end if;
15   END LOOP;
16*  end;
```

Warning: Procedure created with compilation errors.

Now it looks like we have a couple of errors. Even authors get errors when we write PL/SQL. To see what errors you have received from your program, simply enter **show errors**. Oracle will then show you the errors that have occurred during the compiling of your program. Let's see what we did wrong:

SQL> **show errors**

```
Errors for PROCEDURE PRINT_PRODUCTS:

LINE/COL ERROR
-------- ----------------------------------------------------------------
3/1      PLS-00103: Encountered the symbol "DECLARE" when expecting one of
         the following:
         begin function package pragma procedure subtype type use
         <an identifier> <a double-quoted delimited-identifier> form
         current cursor external language
         The symbol "begin" was substituted for "DECLARE" to continue.

16/4     PLS-00103: Encountered the symbol "end-of-file" when expecting
         one of the following:
         begin case declare end exception exit for goto if loop mod
         null pragma raise return select update while with
         <an identifier> <a double-quoted delimited-identifier>
         <a bind variable> << close current delete fetch lock insert
         open rollback savepoint set sql execute commit forall merge
         <a single-quoted SQL string> pipe
         <an alternatively-quoted SQL string>
```

It looks like we have errors on lines 3 and 16. When creating a stored object, you do not always need to include the declare statement since PL/SQL understands that, based on the way the program is structured, after a create statement it expects to see the reserved word as, which will be followed by the Declaration section. So you can think of it this way: as replaces declare when creating a stored object. Let's now look at the repaired PL/SQL code. The lines we changed are highlighted in bold:

```
 1   create or replace procedure print_products
 2   as
 3     cursor get_data is
 4       select prod_name, prod_list_price
 5       from products;
 6   begin
 7       for i in get_data
 8       LOOP
 9       if i.prod_list_price > 50 then
10         dbms_output.put_line(i.prod_name ||' Price: '|| i.prod_LIST_price);
11       else
12         dbms_output.put_line(i.prod_name || ' Product under 50');
13       end if;
14       END LOOP;
15*  end;
SQL> /

Procedure created.
```

That's good news. The program has compiled and will now run when we call it. Let's look at how to call a procedure from SQL*Plus. Using the execute command, you may run a stored program:

```
SQL>> execute print_products
PL/SQL procedure successfully completed.
```

Ask the Expert

Q: I get an error "ORA-20000: ORU-10027: buffer overflow, limit of 2000 bytes" when running my PL/SQL programs that use dbms_output. How can I fix this problem?

A: The default buffer size for the DBMS_OUTPUT package is 2000 bytes. This is usually sufficient for most testing purposes. However, if you need to increase this, you can do it through the serveroutput command. One parameter it has is size, whose value may be set to between 2000 and 1,000,000 bytes. You perform this by issuing the following command:

```
SQL> set serveroutput on size 100000
```

You have added a parameter to your program to show you how to get information into it. You use parameters within the program when you supply data to the procedure, and you can then return a value to the program that calls it through another output parameter. It is also possible to define parameters as both input and output. However, to simplify our parameters, you usually define them for only one of the two purposes. In this case, you will use SQL*Plus to call your procedure since it works. Your example will input a character that will be used to find only products that begin with the input string:

```
1   create or replace procedure print_products
2   (FIRST_CHARACTER IN VARCHAR)
3   as
4     cursor get_data is
5       select prod_name, prod_list_price
6       from products
7       where prod_name like FIRST_CHARACTER || '%';
8   begin
9   for i in get_data
10    LOOP
11     if i.prod_list_price > 50 then
12      dbms_output.put_line(i.prod_name ||' Price: '|| i.prod_LiST_price);
13     else
14      dbms_output.put_line(i.prod_name || ' Product under 50');
15     end if;
16    END LOOP;
17* end print_products;
```

Now, let's see how to describe your procedure, as indicated by the bold text in the next listing. Here, you learn the name of the program and get a list of any parameters you may need to pass:

```
SQL> describe print_products
PROCEDURE print_products
 Argument Name                   Type                    In/Out Default?
 ------------------------------- ----------------------- ------ --------
 FIRST_CHARACTER                 VARCHAR2                IN
```

Next, you need to run the procedure. In this case, you are running it in SQL*Plus. When in this facility, if you want to receive data from a program, you need to declare a variable. This is done in the first line of the following listing. You will then run the program with the execute command:

```
SQL> exec print_products ('A');
Adventures with Numbers Product under 50

PL/SQL procedure successfully completed.
```

As you can tell, the program was called print_products. You want to print the products that begin with an "A." The results show you that you only have one product that begins with the character "A." As you may have gleaned from the results, the program has functioned as expected.

Now that you have learned to create stored objects in Oracle Database 11*g*, let's look at a specialized program, called a function, which can extend the functionality of the database.

Progress Check

1. What type of IF structure should be used if you had a single test and only one alternate choice?

2. What is wrong with the following IF structure? What other way can this type of logic be implemented with Oracle Database 11*g*?

```
IF surname = 'ABRAMSON' then
     Salary = salary * 1.12;
IF surname = 'ABBEY' then
     Salary = salary * 1.22;
IF surname = 'COREY' then
     Salary = salary * 2.5;
END IF;
```

3. True or False: When naming your stored programs, you must follow the same rules as naming a table.

4. What are the three types of procedure parameters you can have?

5. What SQL*Plus command do you use to run your stored programs?

CRITICAL SKILL 5.8

Create and Use Functions

You may also create stored objects that can be used within a select command. Oracle provides us with functions. There are functions to trim spaces from a field, or replace one character with another. All of these provide us with an ability to extend the capabilities of Oracle itself.

Functions are very much like stored procedures. The main difference is that functions may be used within a select statement in the column list or may also be used in the where clause.

When creating a function, you perform a create or replace function command. You can have variables input to the function and return a value to the calling statement. A function must return a value. The data type of the returned value must be defined when creating the function. This is how a function differs from a procedure. The function will then perform its task during regular processing, allowing you to utilize the results along with your regular data, thus extending the value of your data and your database.

Project 5-3   Create and Use a Function

The following project will walk you through the process of defining a function. Then, use the function in two select statements. The first will use the function in the returned columns and the next will use it as a data constraint. The function that you

(continued)

Progress Check Answers

1. You would use the IF/THEN/ELSE structure.

2. We should not use chained IF statements, but instead use ELSIF in the secondary IF statements. The best way to implement this type of logic is to employ a CASE statement.

3. True. When naming your stored programs you must follow the same rules as naming a table.

4. You can have any or all of the following: INPUT, OUTPUT, or INPUT&OUTPUT.

5. Use the execute command to run your stored programs.

create will perform the simple task of adding a 15 percent tax to the list price, giving the price with taxes included.

Step by Step

1. Log into SQL*Plus.

2. At the SQL> prompt, type in the following command:

```
create or replace function GetProductTaxIn
(in_product_id number)
return number
is
    v_price number;
    cursor get_price_tax  is
    select nvl(round(prod_list_price * 1.15,2),0)
    from    products
    where   prod_id = in_product_id;
begin
        open get_price_tax;
        fetch get_price_tax into v_price;
        return v_price;
    exception
        when others then v_price := 0;
        return v_price;
    end;
```

```
Function created.
```

3. If you receive any errors, you will need to fix them before you move on.

4. Create a select statement that uses the function in the columns specification. The following is an example:

```
select prod_id, prod_list_price, GetProductTaxIn(Prod_id)
from products
```

5. Your results may look similar to this:

```
PROD_ID PROD_LIST_PRICE GETPRODUCTTAXIN(PROD_ID)
---------- --------------- ------------------------
        13          899.99                  1034.99
        14          999.99                  1149.99
        15          999.99                  1149.99
        16          299.99                   344.99
        17         1099.99                  1264.99
        18         1299.99                  1494.99
        19           55.99                    64.39
```

20	599.99	689.99
21	899.99	1034.99
22	24.99	28.74
23	21.99	25.29

. . .

6. Now use the function in the where clause of a SQL statement. The following is an example of using the function within a where clause:

```
select prod_id, prod_list_price, GetProductTaxIn(Prod_id)
  from products
where GetProductTaxIn(Prod_id)>= 500
```

Project Summary

This project illustrates how you can extend the functionality of your database as well as add value to your organization by building standard rules that can be utilized by everyone using your database.

Functions provide us all with the ability to define standard rules and derivations for our user community and ensure that programs perform predictably and optimally.

CRITICAL SKILL 5.9

Call PL/SQL Programs

Up to this point in the chapter, you have done the following:

- Defined a PL/SQL block

- Defined a PL/SQL program

- Created a stored program

- Debugged your code

This is fine if you want to write every program and have it run as a simple standalone program. However, as with many programming languages it is important to write a number of separate programs that perform specific tasks, rather than a single program that performs all of your tasks. So, when writing PL/SQL programs, you should think the same way. Have programs that perform table maintenance, that perform complex logic, or simply read data from tables or files. This leads you to how to call programs from other programs, a process similar to calling subroutines within C programs. Procedures may be called from programs ranging from Oracle Forms to perl scripts, but for this section we will simply show you how to call procedures from each other.

To call a procedure from another, you can use your previous procedure, named print_products. Let's create another procedure that calls this procedure:

```
create or replace procedure call_print_prods
as
begin
  for l_alpha IN 65 .. 90
  LOOP
   print_products(chr(l_alpha));
  END LOOP;
end;
/
```

You have created a new procedure. It loops through the values of 65 to 90, the ASCII values for A to Z. Using the CHR function, you can convert the value to an ASCII character. You need to do this because you cannot loop through character values. So, the procedure will loop through the values calling the print_products procedure each time. This calling of programs can be looped extensively and can be organized into efficient and simple program units. This is similar to modularization seen in object-oriented programming language.

As you can tell, Oracle's PL/SQL is a powerful and deep language. In this chapter, we've helped provide you with the ability to start writing programs and to incorporate some complex logic using the basic features of the language. As with any language, you can achieve a significant amount of productivity with only a limited number of commands. We encourage you to use this as a starting point and build upon it to ultimately create the programs you and your organization will need.

☑ Chapter 5 Mastery Check

1. Where is PL/SQL executed?

2. Which type of PL/SQL statement would you use to increase the price values by 15 percent for items with more than 1500 in stock and by 20 percent for items with fewer than 500 in stock?

    A. A cursor FOR loop

    B. An IF/THEN/ELSE command

    C. An insert statement

    D. An update statement

3. What is the fetch command used for?

4. What will the following command do?

```
V_PRICE_TOLERANCE := 500;
```

5. What is wrong with this function definition?

```
CREATE OR REPLACE FUNCTION raise_price
   (original_price IN NUMBER)
RETURN number
IS
BEGIN
   RETURN (original_price * 1.25);
END lower_price;
```

6. What is the advantage of using the %TYPE attribute when defining PL/SQL variables?

7. What Oracle Database 11*g* facility, besides PL/SQL, supports exception handling based on error numbers?

8. A commit that is issued in a PL/SQL program will commit what?

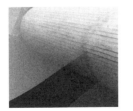

CHAPTER
6

The Database Administrator

CRITICAL SKILLS

6.1 Learn What a DBA Does

6.2 Perform Day-to-Day Operations

6.3 Understand the Oracle Database 11*g* Infrastructure

6.4 Operate Modes for an Oracle Database 11*g*

6.5 Get Started with Oracle Enterprise Manager

6.6 Manage Database Objects

6.7 Manage Space

6.8 Manage Users

6.9 Manage Privileges for Database Users

o, you've decided to be a Database Administrator (DBA). Great choice! On top of that, you've chosen Oracle as the Database Management System (DBMS) that you want to work with. Even better! All you need to figure out now is what to learn in order to do the job. Reading this book is a great start. However, a DBA's job cannot be learned entirely in a few short months. It is a work in progress and it can take several years to become really good at it. Don't get us wrong—you can learn the basics that will make you a productive DBA in a few short months. However, there is a great deal to learn, and you won't become really good at this job until you've actually run the utility, executed the SQL, or performed the task. In other words, don't just read this book—try out the examples and don't be afraid to make mistakes.

CRITICAL SKILL 6.1

Learn What a DBA Does

The role of a DBA is more of a career than just a job. Those of us who have been doing this for many years are always learning new things and are just trying to keep up! That's the exciting thing about being a DBA: the job keeps changing. Databases are growing at a phenomenal pace, the number of users is increasing, availability requirements are striving for that magical 24/7 mark, and security has become a much greater concern. As you will see in this book, databases now include more than just data. Knowledge of databases also encompasses the Internet, grid computing, XML, storage management, clustering, and Java. So, how long will it take you to learn how to be a DBA? The answer is for as long as you're planning to practice this career.

There are some concrete steps that you can take to jumpstart your learning process. Undertaking an Oracle Certification will provide you with a structured program offering you clear steps for learning the details of the job. Instructor-led courses as well as CD- and Internet-based classes can help you through the process. Getting involved in user groups in order to learn from other DBA experiences is highly recommended. Also, read as much as you can and then get your hands on a test database and practice what you've learned.

Applications come and go, but data stays around. All of the information that makes your company valuable is (or should be) stored in a database. Customer, vendor, employee, and financial data, as well as every other kind of corporate data, is stored in a database; your company would have great difficulty surviving if any of that data was lost. Learn your job well. People are depending on you.

There is good news for DBAs: Oracle has tools to help you do your job and manage your databases. These tools have existed for many versions of Oracle and have improved with each release to the point where the Oracle Database 11*g* offerings are extensive. You will have the option of doing your job using either a graphical user interface (GUI) or a command-line interface. We recommend learning both. In many cases, you will need to use the command-line interface to schedule work through scripts. The GUI, on the other hand, can be used for performing day-to-day operations and can also be used as a great learning tool the first time you perform an operation. Often you will be able to generate the low-level commands from the GUI and can then copy them to a file to be used later on.

Either with the command line or with GUI tools, DBAs will need to perform many tasks, from managing users to backing up the database. Performing some tasks might have gotten easier with the improved management tools; however, areas such as high availability, securing the database from data to backups, and managing new features of the database have gotten more complex. A DBA's skill set now must include understanding these areas and how to design the architecture of the database environment to meet requirements coming from the business.

As we've mentioned previously, there is a great deal that you will need to know in order to be able to provide well-rounded coverage of your Oracle environment. Because of this, we have categorized the specialized areas of database management so that you will be aware of the whole picture and can break your work into well-defined groupings.

CRITICAL SKILL 6.2
Perform Day-to-Day Operations

In order to properly perform the role of Database Administrator, you will need to develop and implement solutions that cover all areas of this discipline. The amazing part of this job is that you may be asked to do many, or perhaps all, of the different aspects of your job on any given day. Your daily tasks will vary from doing high-level architecture and design to performing low-level tasks. Let's take a look at the things that you will be getting involved in.

Architecture and Design

DBAs should be involved with the architecture and design of new applications, databases, and even technical infrastructure changes. Decisions made here will have a large impact on database performance and scalability, while database knowledge will help you choose a better technical implementation. Data design tools such as Oracle Designer can assist the DBA.

Capacity Planning

Short- and long-range planning needs to be performed on your databases and applications. You should focus on performance and sizing characteristics of your systems that will help to determine upcoming storage, CPU, memory, and network needs. This is an area that is often neglected and can lead to big problems if it is not done properly.

Backup and Recovery

A backup and recovery plan is, of course, critical for protecting your corporate data. You need to ensure that the data can be recovered quickly to the nearest point in time as possible. There is also a performance aspect to this, since backups must be performed using minimal resources while the database is up and running and recoveries need to be performed within a time limit predefined by Service Level Agreements (SLAs) developed to meet customers' requirements. A complete backup and recovery implementation should include local recovery and remote recovery that is also referred to as disaster recovery planning (DRP). You will see more on backup and recovery in Chapter 7.

Security

This is an area that has become very sensitive due to the number of users that can access your databases and the amount of external, web-based access. Database users need to be authenticated so that you know with certainty who is accessing your database. The users must then be given authorization to use the resources that they need to do their job by being granting access to the objects in Oracle. However, despite this need for permissions and access in order to do their jobs, a best practice is to only grant the minimum amount of permissions and access for the role or user. This can be managed with Oracle Enterprise Manager, as you'll see in some examples of this later in this chapter. External users require extra web-based security that is beyond the scope of this book.

Performance and Tuning

Performance and tuning is arguably the most exciting area of database management. Changes here are noticed almost immediately and every experienced DBA has stories about small changes they've made that resulted in large performance gains. On the other hand, every performance glitch in the environment will be blamed on the database and you will need to learn how to deal with this. Automatic Workload Repository (AWR) Reports, Statspack, OEM Performance Management, and third-party tools will assist you in this area. There is a lot to learn here, but the proper tools will simplify this considerably.

Managing Database Objects

You need to manage all schema objects, such as tables, indexes, views, synonyms, sequences, and clusters, as well as source types, such as packages, procedures, functions, and triggers, to ensure they are valid and organized in a fashion that will deliver adequate performance and have adequate space. The space requirements of schema objects are directly related to the tablespaces and data files that are growing at incredible rates. Using OEM, this can be simplified, something you'll see examples of later in this chapter.

Storage Management

Databases are growing at incredible rates. You need to carefully manage space and pay particular attention to the space used by data files and archive logs. Online utilities are supported to help with reorganization of indexes and tables while they remain online. Reorgs use considerable resources, however, so do not perform these operations unless it is necessary. See the section "Manage Space," later in the chapter, for more on this.

TIP
Do not reorg your database unless you absolutely need to.

Change Management

Being able to upgrade or change the database is a skill that requires knowledge of many areas. Upgrades to the database schema, the procedural logic in the database, and the database software must all be performed in a controlled manner. Change control procedures and tools such as Oracle's Change Manager and third-party offerings will assist you.

Schedule Jobs

Oracle Database 11*g* comes with a new scheduler that allows you to schedule a job for a specific date and time, and to categorize jobs into job classes that can then be prioritized. This means that resources can be controlled by job class. Of course, other native scheduling systems such as Task Scheduler in Windows and crontab in UNIX can be used, as well as other third-party offerings.

Jobs can include any of the database maintenance tasks such as backups and monitoring scripts. Grouping the monitoring and maintenance jobs into a job class can give them a lower priority as opposed to an application batch job that needs to finish in a short batch window.

Network Management

Oracle Networking is a fundamental component of the database that you will need to become comfortable with. Database connectivity options like tnsnames, the Oracle Internet Directory (OID), and the Oracle Listener require planning to ensure that performance and security requirements are met in a way that is simple to manage. Details of this are discussed in Chapter 3.

Troubleshooting

Though troubleshooting may not be what you'd consider a classic area of Database Management, it is one area that you will encounter daily. You will need tools to help you with this. Oracle MetaLink technical support, available to customers who purchase the service, is invaluable. Oracle alert logs and dump files will also help you greatly. Experience will be your biggest ally here and the sooner you dive into database support, the faster you will progress.

You've seen the areas of database management that need to be handled; now it's time to look at the Oracle schema and storage infrastructure.

CRITICAL SKILL 6.3

Understand the Oracle Database 11*g* Infrastructure

Oracle's memory and process infrastructure have already been discussed in Chapter 1. In this section, you will take a look at the Oracle schema and storage infrastructure, since these are a large part of what you will be required to manage.

Schemas

An Oracle database can have many schemas contained in it. The schema is a logical structure that contains objects like segments, views, procedures, functions, packages, triggers, user-defined objects, collection types, sequences, synonyms, and database links. A *segment* is a data structure that can be a table, index, or temporary or undo segment. The *schema name* is the user that controls the schema. Examples of schemas are the SYSTEM, SYS, SCOTT, and SH schemas. Figure 6-1 shows the relationship between these schema objects.

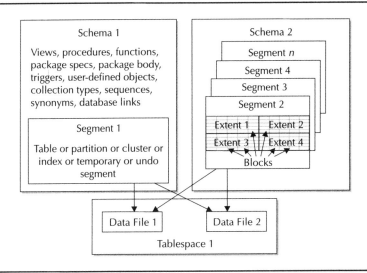

FIGURE 6-1. *The database and user schemas*

Segments, Extents, and Blocks

As you can see in Figure 6-1, a schema can have many segments and many segment types. Each segment is a single instance of a table, partition, cluster, index, or temporary or undo segment. So, for example, a table with two indexes is implemented as three segments in the schema. A segment is broken down further into *extents*, which are a collection of contiguous data blocks. As data is added to Oracle, it will first fill the blocks in the allocated extents and once those extents are full, new extents can be added to the segment as long as space allows. Oracle segment types are listed here:

- **Tables.** This is where the data is kept in rows and columns. This is the heart of your database with tables implemented in one schema and one tablespace. The exception to this is a special type of table called a partitioned table, where the table can be split into different ranges or sets of values called a *partition,* with each partition implemented in a different tablespace. Remember, however, that each partition is itself a segment and each segment can only reside in one tablespace. Clustered tables are another special case where two tables with a close link between them can have their data stored together in a single block to improve join operations.

- **Indexes.** These are optionally built on tables for performance reasons and to help implement integrity constraints such as primary keys and uniqueness.

- **Temporary segments.** Oracle uses these as a temporary storage area to run a SQL statement. For example, they may be used for sorting data and then discarded once a query or transaction is complete.

- **Undo segments.** These are used to manage the before image of changes, which allows data to roll back if needed and helps provide data consistency for users querying data that is being changed. You'll learn more about this in Chapter 7.

Segments can be thought of as physical structures since they actually are used to store data that is kept in a tablespace (although some of this is temporary in nature). There are other structures stored in the schema that are more logical in nature.

Logical Schema Structures

Not everything stored in a database and schema is data. Oracle also manages source modules and supporting structures (such as sequences) that are used to populate new unique and primary key values when inserting data into the database. These objects belong to a schema and are stored in the Oracle Catalog. These, as well as view properties of the objects, can all be easily managed through OEM, as

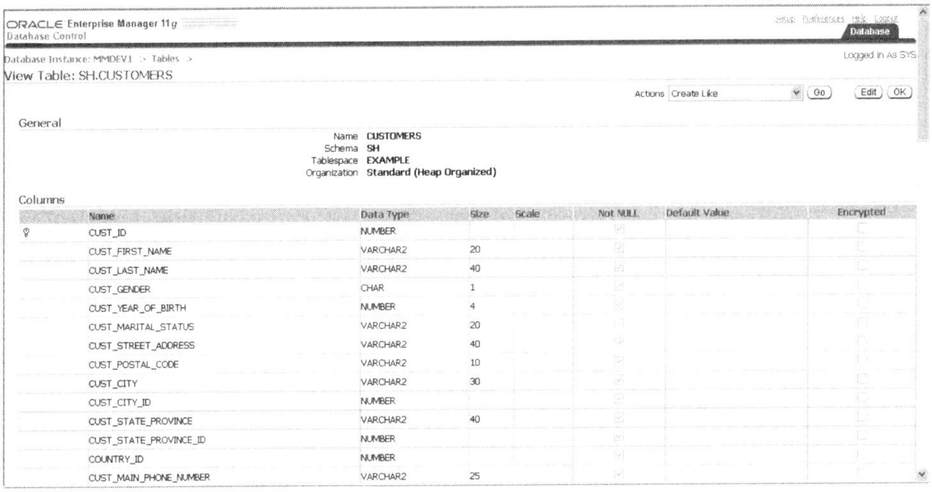

FIGURE 6-2. *Enterprise Manager table definition view*

shown in Figure 6-2. Take a look at the following for a brief description of these logical structures:

- **Views.** These give you the capability of subsetting a table and combining multiple tables through a single named object. They can be thought of as a *stored query*. With the exception of a special type of view called a materialized view, which is used for data warehousing, data is not stored in views. They are simply a new way of defining access to the underlying tables. These can be used for security, performance, and ease-of-use.

- **Synonyms.** These are used to create a new name or alias for another database object such as a table, view, another synonym, and sources such as a procedure, package, function, java class, and so on. They can be used to simplify access. As with views, data is not stored in a synonym.

- **Sequences.** These are used to generate new unique numbers that can be used by applications when inserting data into tables.

- **Source programs.** These can be stored in the catalog and written either in Oracle's proprietary PL/SQL or in Java. PL/SQL source types include business logic that can be written as Packages, Procedures, and Functions. Triggers can also be used to implement business logic, but are often used to implement data integrity since they are not executed directly by a user or source program, but rather are automatically executed when an action is performed on the database. Java Sources and Java Classes are also implemented directly in Oracle. This server-side support of application logic improves performance since the logic resides with the data and it also improves performance.

■ **User types.** These can be created by you to support object-oriented development. Array types, Object types, and Table types can all be created by you. Also, the Oracle XML Schema Processor supports XML processing by adding data types to XML documents that can be used to ensure the integrity of data in XML documents.

So now that you have seen all of the schema objects, it's time to tie these together to your storage architecture.

Storage Structures

As shown earlier in Figure 6-1, the physical schema objects are stored as segments in the database. Each segment can only be stored in a single tablespace, with a tablespace being made up of one or more data files. If a tablespace is running out of space, you can expand the data files it is made up of, or you can also add a new data file to the tablespace. A data file can only store data for a single tablespace.

A single tablespace can store data for multiple segments and in fact for several segment types. Segments from multiple schemas can also exist in the same tablespace. So, for example, table_a from schema1 and index_b from schema2 can both be implemented in the same tablespace. Oh, and by the way, a tablespace can only store data for a single database.

The logical structures such as views and source code are stored in the Oracle catalog, but are part of a schema. So, this means that the Oracle-supplied SH schema can contain all of the objects that it needs to run the entire application under its own schema name. This provides strong security and management benefits.

Progress Check

1. Name five areas that you will need to address as a DBA.

2. What is a schema and what does it contain?

3. Can a tablespace store more than one segment type?

4. List an example of nondata structures or logical structures in a database.

Progress Check Answers

1. As a DBA, you will need to address architecture, capacity planning, backup and recovery, security, and performance, among other things.

2. A *schema* is a logical structure that contains objects like segments, views, procedures, functions, packages, triggers, user-defined objects, collection types, sequences, synonyms, and database links.

3. A single tablespace can store data for multiple segments and different segment types. Segments from multiple schemas can also exist in the same tablespace. So, for example, table_a from schema1 and index_b from schema2 can be implemented as two segments in the same tablespace.

4. Source programs such as triggers, stored procedures, functions, and packages are logical structures. Other examples include views, synonyms, sequences, and types.

Operate Modes of an Oracle Database 11*g*

Oracle is a software package like many others that you may have used. However, when you run most programs, they run one and only one way. So, when I open my accounting software, I run it the same way all the time. However, you have options with Oracle. This section discusses the many ways that you can run Oracle. Some of these methods will be important to administrators, while others will allow for full use. This feature is important when you need to perform both critical and noncritical activities, and not interfere with your users or your data.

Modes of Operation

Oracle has several modes of operation. In most cases, when you start Oracle, you will simply issue the command:

```
> Startup;
```

This command actually takes Oracle through three distinct startup phases automatically, though you can also choose to explicitly step through these phases:

1. **nomount phase**   In this phase, the database reads the spfile or the init.ora parameter file and starts up the Oracle memory structures as well as the background processes. The instance is started, but the database is not yet associated with the newly started instance. This is usually used in cases where you need to re-create the control file. The command to perform this is

   ```
   > startup nomount;
   ```

2. **mount phase**   You use this phase in order to associate a database with the instance; the instance "mounts" the database. The previously read parameter file is used to find those control files, which contain the name of the data files and redo logs. The database is then mounted to allow some maintenance activities to be performed. Data files and redo logs are not opened when the database is in mount mode, so the database is not yet accessible by end users for normal tasks. Commands to mount a database are

   ```
   > startup mount;
   > alter database mount;
   ```

3. **open phase**   This is when Oracle opens the data files and redo logs, making the database available for normal operations. Your redo logs must exist in order for the database to open. If they do not, the resetlogs command must be used to create new redo logs in the location specified in the control files:

   ```
   > Startup {open} {resetlogs};
   > alter database open;
   ```

Other Ways to Open the Database

There are other options for opening a database. For example, you may want to open it in read-only mode so that no database changes (inserts, updates, or deletes) can be performed. There are also the upgrade/downgrade options that allow a database to be opened to perform a downgrade or upgrade to another version of Oracle:

```
> alter database open read only;
```

A common option you will use to perform maintenance will be to open the database in *restricted mode*. When you issue the command startup restrict, only users with both the create session and restricted session privileges will be able to use the database. So, as a DBA this is a helpful way to open the database that only you can use:

```
> startup restrict;
```

The database can be placed in a state where only the sys and system users can query the database without stopping the database and performing a subsequent startup restrict. The activities of other users continue until they become inactive. This can be performed using the quiesce option of alter system when the Database Resource Manager option has been set up:

```
> alter system quiesce restrict;
> alter system unquiesce;
```

Forcing a Startup

Over time, you will run into situations where Oracle has not shut down properly and you are unable to restart it. In these rare instances, you will need to use the force option of the startup command. This will first perform a "shutdown abort," which forces the database to shut down (see the next section for more information on this) followed by a database startup:

```
> startup force
```

Database and Instance Shutdown

When shutting down an instance, perform these steps, which are the reverse from those you just saw when opening a database:

1. Close the database (including the data files and redo logs), so that it is no longer usable for normal tasks.

2. Unmount the database from the instance so that only the instance memory structures and background tasks are left running without a database associated with them.

3. Shut down the instance to close the control files.

In order to shut down a database, four different approaches can be used: shutdown normal, immediate, transactional, and abort.

- **Normal** is, in a sense, the perfect way to shut down, since this approach will wait for all users to disconnect from the database and all transactions to complete before the shutdown occurs. Once this command has been issued, new users are not allowed into the system. This can be impractical in cases where users remain on the system for long periods of time:

  ```
  > shutdown normal;
  ```

- **Immediate** is a practical shutdown approach that also leaves the database in a consistent state. When the database is put through a "shutdown immediate," all current transactions are rolled back and users are disconnected. No new transactions are allowed into the system. This will be relatively quick if the rollback operations are small and it's an excellent way to shut down the database before performing a database backup:

  ```
  > shutdown immediate;
  ```

- A **transactional shutdown** is similar to the immediate variety except that running transactions are allowed to complete. So, once transactions have been committed, the user running it is disconnected. This is useful in cases where you do not want to shut down until currently running transactions have finished or in cases where it will be quicker to complete existing transactions than it will be to roll them back:

  ```
  > shutdown transactional;
  ```

- **Abort** is the least graceful shutdown option of the four. When this is used, all transactions are ended immediately without waiting for a rollback or commit and all users are instantly disconnected while the database is brought down. Use this only if you are experiencing problems shutting down the database using one of the three options described previously or in cases where you need to shut down the database immediately. The database needs to go through recovery procedures the next time it is restarted. After a shutdown abort has been performed, you should try to immediately start up the database so that you can then perform a shutdown (normal, immediate, or transactional) to bring the database down in the proper manner:

  ```
  > shutdown abort;
  ```

OEM can help with instance and database startup and shutdown, as shown in Figure 6-3. First, open OEM in a web browser. Then, on the Home tab under the General section, choose Shutdown (or Startup, depending on if the database is currently running). The advanced options allow for the different types of shutdown.

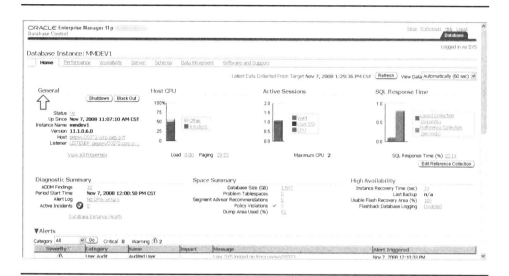

FIGURE 6-3. *Enterprise Manager Home page view*

Get Started with Oracle Enterprise Manager

Oracle Enterprise Manager (OEM) is a great tool for assisting the beginner DBA to become an experienced one. You should, however, also learn the low-level commands that will allow you to do your job through an interface like SQL*Plus. OEM can help you with this by showing you the SQL that it has generated when you select the Show Sql button that exists on many windows. Given how many options OEM has to help you do your job as a DBA, you should take a quick look at them here.

Oracle Enterprise Manager can be used to manage all of the aspects of the databases. As shown in Figure 6-3, you can see the Home page of Enterprise Manager and details about the current state of the database. The tabs show the different areas of database that can be managed for performance, availability, server, schema, and data movement.

Instance Configuration

Figure 6-3 shows you the state of an instance and server. By selecting the Server tab from the Home page (shown later in Figure 6-6), you can see different areas to manage the parameters, memory settings, recovery options, resource monitors in effect, and undo information.

User Sessions

Now that you have a good handle on managing instances and databases, you can drill down to your user sessions to see exactly what is going on inside the database. By choosing a session, you can see some general information such as the user session ID, when the user logged in, and what the OS username and terminal name are for this user. As you can see from Figure 6-4, you can also see the SQL that is currently running, along with the explain plan being used. You can follow the order that each explain step is being performed in by the Step # column and can step through the plan or see it in a graphical layout using the far right column. You can also manage sessions and disconnect users by right-clicking the username and issuing the kill session command. The command name may sound a bit harsh, but it does get the idea across.

Resource Consumer Groups

Next, you can select the Resource Consumer Groups item to see all of the groups that exist. A resource consumer group provides a way to group together users so that they can share similar processing requirements. The DATABASE_RESOURCE_MANAGER package is used to allocate the maximum amount of CPU that a session can use or to set a limit for parallel execution for a session or to set the number of sessions that can be active for a consumer group as a few examples of this capability. OEM can assist in managing these groups by giving you an easy way to add new

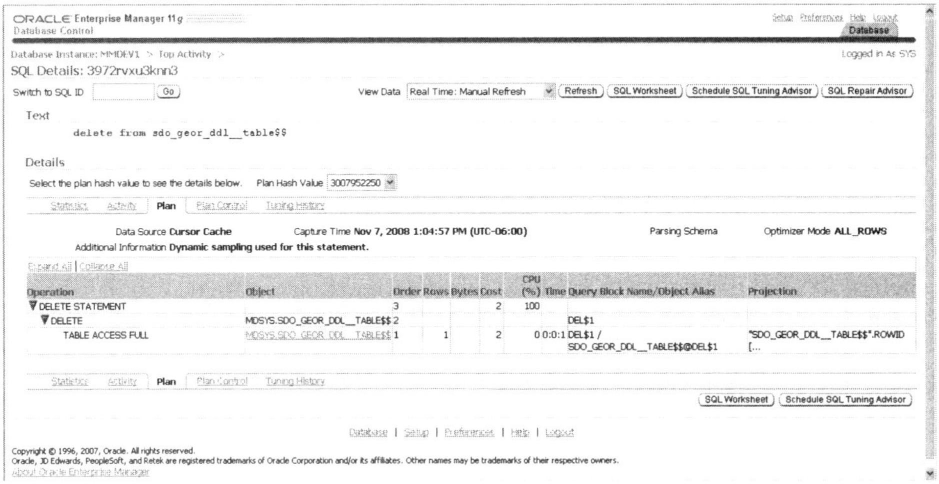

FIGURE 6-4. *SQL explain plan*

groups and edit those that exist. This panel allows you to enter a description of the group and attach users and database roles to a group. If you look at Figure 6-5, you will see all of the resource consumer groups listed. If you select one of these consumer groups, you will be presented with the capabilities to manage users, roles, and general information about the group.

A resource plan builds on the resource consumer groups by providing a way to define the way that system resources will be allocated to the resource consumer groups that we just discussed. Figure 6-5 shows a list of the groups and subplans that can be set up here. Also in the figure you can see the tabs to define other options, such as maximum parallelism, concurrently active sessions in the session pool, undo pool space, and execution time limits for the group. Group switching allows for a session to change groups after a predefined amount of execution time has been reached. Presumably, you would move the user to a lower priority group to free resources to other sessions. The resource plan schedule can be used to set daily schedules to enable and disable resource plans.

Schema, Security, and Storage Management

The next items on the OEM console are schema, security, and storage management. We will visit these in Critical Skill sections 6.6, 6.7, and 6.8–6.9, respectively. It is worth mentioning now, however, that all three of these can be completely managed through OEM.

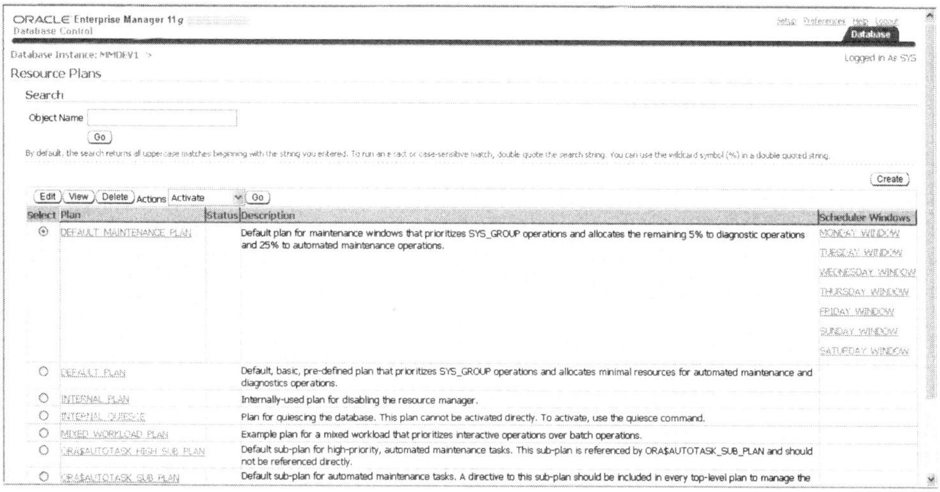

FIGURE 6-5. *Enterprise Manager resource group view*

Distributed Management

Some Oracle distributed capabilities are handled through the Distributed option. These include the ability to

- Manage in-doubt transactions that can result from two-phase commit.

- Create, edit, and drop database links.

- Use streams to implement messaging.

- Use advanced queues and replication to pass messages and data to applications.

This can be a difficult area to manage and having a tool such as the OEM Console to help you out with this is a very welcome feature.

Warehouse Features

Warehouse options such as summary management, materialized views, and dimensions can all be dealt with through OEM, as was shown in Figure 6-5.

Other Tools

The Server tab from the Home page, shown in Figure 6-6, will take you to a list of different tools. This includes more advanced tools for managing the environment. Let's very quickly review the tools that are included here:

- Database tools enable you to analyze data and performance, and manage tablespaces and parameters. The backup and recovery tools are available under the Availability tab. Statistics management is also an important area for running statistics and getting information about the workload repository.

- Oracle Scheduler provides tools to set up jobs and manage schedules. Job classes can be set up here, as well as standard maintenance jobs to be automated.

- Tuning facilities such as performance manager, outline management, and tablespace maps are provided through Query Optimizer.

As you can see from this overview of OEM console capabilities, many of the tools that you need to perform your day-to-day tasks can be found in this one console. Now that you have confidence that there's a toolset to support you, let's take a quick look at what you need to think about when managing database objects.

FIGURE 6-6.   *Enterprise Manager Server tab view with configuration options*

CRITICAL SKILL 6.6

Manage Database Objects

A large part of your job as a DBA will be to manage the objects that exist in a database. Let's look at the objects that you need to concern yourself with and discuss the main management issues that you will have in each of these areas.

Control Files

It is critical to the database that you have at least one valid control file for your database. These are small files and can be multiplexed by the Oracle instance. Ensuring that you have at least three copies of the control files (remember, they are small), as well as text and binary backups whenever a data file, log file, or tablespace is changed and on a regularly scheduled basis (at least daily), will go a long way towards ensuring that your control files are in good shape. Control files will be discussed in more detail in Chapter 7.

Redo Logs

Redo logs are necessary to ensure database integrity and should be duplexed in Oracle. Oracle mirroring helps even if your redo logs are mirrored by your storage subsystem since Oracle will use the alternate redo log if one should become corrupt. You will need to ensure that you have enough redo logs and that they are sized properly to support database performance. How large should your redo logs be? They should be large enough that a log switch does not usually occur more than once every 15 minutes due to the checkpointing that occurs during a log switch and the overhead that is incurred during this operation. How many redo logs should you have? You should have enough redo logs that the system will not wrap around to a log that has not yet completed a checkpoint or completed archiving (for systems in archivelog mode). Redo logs can be added, deleted, and switched through OEM.

Undo Management

The Undo segment is where the before images of changed rows are stored. Oracle will manage your undo segments for you, but you need to determine how large to make the tablespace that the Undo segment is stored in. The size that you make this depends on the length of time that you want the undo information to be available to you. If you look at Figure 6-7, you will see how OEM helps you determine the length of time that Undo can be retained, based on the system activity and Undo tablespace. This is in the Configuration section for an instance. If the tablespace is not the correct size, it can be changed using the Storage feature of OEM, which you will see later in this chapter.

If you choose to implement user-managed rollback segments, then these can be managed in the Storage section of OEM by choosing Rollback Segments and then selecting the segment name that you want to manage.

NOTE
When using user-managed rollback segments, the system rollback segment will always exist, but should never be used as a rollback segment for user processes.

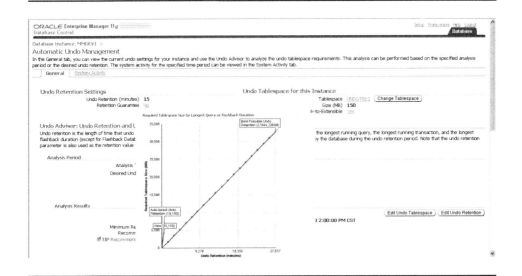

FIGURE 6-7. *Enterprise Manager Automatic Undo Management view*

Schema Objects

Schema objects were discussed earlier in this chapter where you saw that you can manage schema objects through OEM. There are also some things that you may want to do with your own SQL scripts that run as scheduled jobs. When managing schemas, you need to ensure that those physical objects that take up a great deal of space do in fact have enough space to grow. These include tables, indexes, clusters, and partitioned tables. Manage these objects through the tablespaces where they are implemented and ensure that there is enough room to grow. Just because an object may have hundreds of extents doesn't mean that a reorganization of the object is necessary. You only need to reorg if there are a large number of chained or migrated rows. It is also possible for the reorgs to gain back unused space. Indexes, on the other hand, will need to be rebuilt more frequently and do provide some performance benefits. These rebuilds and reorganizations of indexes can normally be done online and are easy to take care of during a time when there is not much going on in the database. You will find out more about managing space in the next section.

Figure 6-2, seen earlier, is an example of how the SH.Customers table can be managed through OEM. Note the Storage tab that allows you to change the table's storage parameters. You should also try to maintain statistics on your tables and indexes so they are up-to-date. This will assist the optimizer make better decisions when choosing access paths for your queries and can be used to validate the structures. In Oracle Database 11*g*, a scheduler job called gather_stats_job will run during a maintenance window between 10:00 P.M. and 6:00 A.M., by default, and will run statistics for those objects in cases where they have not been collected yet or are stale, which are statistics that are old due to recent changes in data. Setting the Oracle Database 11*g* initialization parameter statistics_level to typical (the default) will allow Oracle to automatically update statistics as a background task on a regular basis and is the recommended approach for gathering statistics. In pre–Oracle Database 11*g* releases, the DBMS_STATS package should be run manually or it can be turned on at a table level by using the Monitoring keyword in a CREATE or ALTER table. Monitoring is a deprecated feature in Oracle Database 11*g* and the keyword (along with "nomonitoring") will be ignored.

Triggers, views, synonyms, procedures, functions, and packages are logical schema objects that do not take up a lot of space in the tablespace; however, these objects need to be watched to ensure they are not invalid. They can become invalid with an ALTER table statement or changes in structure to any dependent objects. These objects should be valid, and you can check this with the SQL statement that follows:

```
select owner, object_name, object_type
from dba_objects where status ^= 'VALID';
```

You've looked at many of the database objects that will require your attention. Let's now explore one area that requires special attention due to the size of today's databases.

Ask the Expert

Q: Why is it important for DBAs to get involved with the architecture and design of a new system?

A: Decisions made on the technical infrastructure as well as data and application designs will have a large impact on database performance and scalability. Database knowledge will help choose a better technical implementation. Once chosen, these can be difficult to change.

Q: Which method do you normally use to shut down a database?

A: Although the shutdown normal operation is a recommended approach, it is often impractical since you need users to disconnect themselves. The approach that we prefer is to perform a checkpoint using the command alter system checkpoint, which will write data out to data files and speed up the restart. Then perform a shutdown abort, immediately followed by a startup restrict and shutdown immediate. This is a fast, guaranteed shutdown that leaves the database in a consistent state once all of the steps have been completed.

Q: What is the best way to become a good Oracle DBA quickly and then to keep improving?

A: There are many things that you will need to do and many skills that you'll need to develop to do this job. First, learning the basic DBA skills, which you can get from books such as this, as well as from courses, will give you a head start. Practicing what you see is probably the quickest and most practical way to learn. Getting involved in supporting some databases in development and production will force you to learn very quickly. Then, working on development systems for different types of applications will help to round out your skills. Keep reading and learning and never assume that you know it all and you will do very well.

CRITICAL SKILL 6.7

Manage Space

The challenge of managing data in your Oracle Database 11*g* is one that provides you with options. In this section, you will look at the methods that have been used in the many versions of the database to manage your information. Today's version of the database provides you with options. The first that you will discuss is managing your data and the files in which they reside in a manual way. Another option, Automatic Storage Management, is discussed in Chapter 8.

Archive Logs

When you put the database in archive logging mode, the redo logs are written out to a directory that is named in the SPFILE. If that directory becomes full and the database attempts to write another archive log, the database activity will be suspended until sufficient space is made available for the new file. Create a large directory and schedule jobs to move the archive log files from online storage to tape before you encounter a space issue. Recovery Manager (RMAN), a utility used for backup and recovery, does a nice job of helping you manage this. Please see Chapter 7 for more information on backing up the archive log files to tape and managing these files.

Tablespaces and Data Files

Space should be managed at the data file and tablespace level rather than at a lower level such as a table or index. Using locally managed tablespaces with uniform extent sizes will simplify your management. Do not worry that you have multiple extents in a tablespace or for an object. This does not create a performance issue since the extents contain a number of blocks that must be contiguous, and the extents will be reused and created as needed. You can see the amount of space available in your data files or tablespaces in OEM, as in Figure 6-8. This shows the amount of free space available in the currently allocated space. If you have used the autoextend feature to allow a data file to extend in size when more space is needed, the extra space is not shown in this graph.

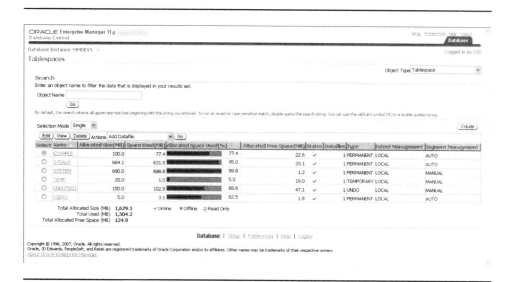

FIGURE 6-8. *Tablespace view in Enterprise Manager*

TIP
Do not autoextend temporary and undo tablespaces, since they will quickly grow to use all of the space to which they can autoextend.

What do you do if you run out of space in a data file? Just enter OEM, click the data file, and choose the Storage tab. Once there, you can change the autoextend feature and enter the size of the extensions that you would like. Do not forget to limit the size of the data file so that it doesn't grow until it uses all of your space. After you've completed this, click Apply and you're done. If you select the Show SQL button, you can see the alter database syntax, which is also shown next:

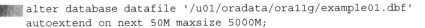

```
alter database datafile '/u01/oradata/ora11g/example01.dbf'
autoextend on next 50M maxsize 5000M;
```

You can write your own scripts to compare the amount of allocated space for a data file in view dba_data_files to the amount of free space, as shown in view dba_free_space.

OEM also provides you with a more detailed map of how space is used. In OEM, select a tablespace and then navigate from Tools to Tuning Features, finally choosing Tablespace Map. This opens a graphical layout showing each segment in the tablespace. From the tablespace map, you can choose the Tablespace Analysis Report tab for a written report on the space being used.

Managing the database objects discussed earlier will be a large part of your role as a DBA. In the next section, you'll take a look at setting up and managing users. After all, without database users, there is no point in doing any of this!

Progress Check

1. What's better: shutdown transactional or shutdown immediate?

2. Do you only need to worry about logical schema objects that take up a large amount of space?

3. What happens if your archive log directory becomes full?

4. Why would you want to use a command-line interface rather than a GUI to perform your tasks as a DBA?

5. Under what circumstances would you bother to start up the database in nomount mode?

CRITICAL SKILL 6.8

Manage Users

Before you can do anything in Oracle, you need to have a user ID created to enable you to log into Oracle. As a DBA, you will begin with the SYS or SYSTEM accounts since these accounts both have the DBA role and exist in all Oracle databases. They are often used to perform database administration tasks. The SYS account is also granted the sysdba privilege and is the schema that the Oracle catalog is stored in. You should only use the SYS account when you need to perform a task as SYS or need the sysdba privilege. If your database was created using the Database Configuration Assistant (dbca), then you will also automatically get the SYSMAN and DBSNMP accounts. SYSMAN is used to administer Oracle Enterprise Manager (OEM) and DBSNMP is used by the agent that OEM employs to monitor Oracle databases. Several other accounts will also be set up for the "example" schemas, such as the Sales History ('SH') user that you will see utilized throughout this book. The OUTLN schema will be created to allow you to use query plan stability through the stored outline feature.

Depending on the options you choose when creating your database, other accounts may be set up for you. For example, if you install the OLAP option, the OLAPSYS account will be created.

Create a User

When you create a user, you can use either the create user syntax or the OEM, which is an easier approach. In order to create a user, you will need to decide the following:

- The default tablespace where segments created by this user will be placed unless a tablespace name is used in the DDL to override this.

Progress Check Answers

1. Both leave your database in a consistent state. It depends on how long your transactions will take to complete or roll back. If all things are equal, and you think that it will take as long to commit the transactions that are already running, then you should use "shutdown transactional" since commits will be allowed to complete and no data will be lost.

2. No; logical schema objects also need to be watched to ensure they are in a valid state.

3. If database attempts to write an archive log after the directory has become full, the database activity will be suspended until sufficient space is made available for the new file.

4. You may want to place the command in a script that is scheduled or run as a repetitive task.

5. When started in nomount mode, the parameter file is read, and memory structures and processes are started for the instance. The database is not yet associated with the instance. You would use this in circumstances when you need to re-create the control file.

■ Whether to expire the password so that the user needs to change it the first time they log into Oracle.

■ A temporary tablespace to store internal data used by Oracle while queries are running. Sort operations make use of the temporary tablespace if there is not enough room in the SGA to perform the sort operation.

■ Whether to employ user quotas on tablespaces, which put a limit on the amount of space that a user's objects can take up in that tablespace.

■ The authentication type, which allows you to specify whether you want Oracle to force the user to specify a password when they log in, or you can trust the operating system to do this for you.

■ The initial password that the user will log in with. The user must change this during the first logon if you chose to expire the password in advance of the user's first logon.

■ Privileges to grant to the user. These can be direct privileges or roles. You'll see these discussed in the next section.

■ A profile for the user, which can be employed to manage the user's session by limiting resources that sessions can use, and that help implement corporate password policies. You will also see this in the next section.

■ The account status of the user (*lock* or *unlock*) as it is created.

The OEM console in Figure 6-9 shows the options available to you to create and edit a user. For each user, there are eight separate tabs that allow you to easily enter a user's information. You can see the SQL that will be generated by selecting the Show SQL button at the bottom of the panel. Another great option allows you to model a user and create another user like one that already exists. To do this, click the user that you want to model, select Object from the top of the panel, and then select the Create Like option.

Here is a sample CREATE USER statement:

```
CREATE USER "NEWUSER" PROFILE "DEFAULT" IDENTIFIED BY "newpassword"
PASSWORD EXPIRE DEFAULT TABLESPACE "USERS" TEMPORARY TABLESPACE "TEMP"
QUOTA UNLIMITED ON TEMP QUOTA UNLIMITED ON USERS
ACCOUNT UNLOCK;
GRANT "CONNECT" TO "NEWUSER";
```

Edit Users

Once a user has been created, you will be asked at different times to alter it in order to change quotas or reset passwords or unlock an account. This can be easily performed through OEM by selecting the User, choosing the option you want to change through the GUI, and then applying the change.

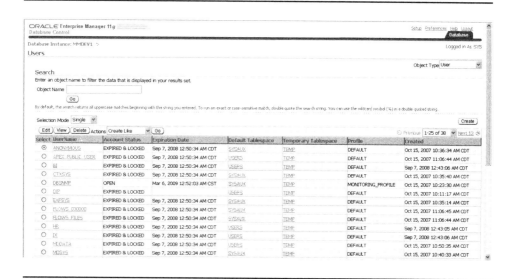

FIGURE 6-9. *User Management view*

Editing users can also be performed using the ALTER USER statement, as shown next, where a user account is unlocked, the password is changed, and a tablespace quota is increased:

```
ALTER USER "username"  IDENTIFIED BY "newpwd" QUOTA UNLIMITED
ON TOOLS ACCOUNT UNLOCK;
```

You've now created a user and it's time to grant them some privileges. Let's see how you do this in the next section.

CRITICAL SKILL 6.9
Manage Privileges for Database Users

Creating a user in Oracle has accomplished the first part of user setup, which is authentication. You have a user ID and password and have authorized this user to use an Oracle database. Once the user logs in, however, they will not be able to do very much because they will not have privileges that allow them to access any objects. This leads you to the second step of setting up a user: authorization. In order to authorize a user to perform their tasks, you need to grant access.

Grant Authority

You now need to give permission to the user to do things in Oracle. Actions like accessing a table or executing a procedure or running a utility require you to "grant" the authority to that user. When you perform a grant, you can specify four things:

- The user that is being granted the authority.

- The object that is being granted. Examples of these are a table, procedure, or role.

- The type of access being granted, such as select, insert, update, or delete on a table, or execute on a procedure, function, or package.

- Whether this user has authority to then grant the same authority to other users. By default, they do not, but this can be added by using the With Grant option.

Here are two examples that grant a user "NEWUSER" access to a table and then to a package:

```
GRANT SELECT ON "TABLE_NAME" TO "NEWUSER" WITH GRANT OPTION;
GRANT INSERT ON "TABLE_NAME" TO "NEWUSER" WITH GRANT OPTION;
GRANT EXECUTE ON "PROCEDURE_NAME" TO "NEWUSER"
```

Types of Grants

There are two types of grants that can be given to a user: system privileges and object privileges.

- System privileges are predefined Oracle privileges granting authority to overall system objects; for example, using ANY or ability to execute types of statements rather than relating to an individual object or schema. The ability to perform a create tablespace, create session, or alter system or to back up any table are just a few examples of some system-level privileges that can be granted to a user. There are over 150 different system privileges, which can be viewed by looking at the DBA_SYS_PRIVS view.

- Object privileges are a lower-level authority where a named object is granted to a user. So, the ability to perform an operation on a particular table, or execute an individual function, package, or procedure is an object privilege, as opposed to the ability to execute any procedure or select any table, which is a system-level privilege.

Take Away Authority

What is given can be taken away. In order to take privileges away from a user, you use the REVOKE command; the syntax is very similar to the syntax you use when issuing a grant. Here are two examples of a REVOKE operation:

```
REVOKE INSERT ON "TABLE_NAME" FROM "NEWUSER";
REVOKE EXECUTE ON "TABLE_NAME" FROM "NEWUSER";
```

Roles

When you think of the number of privileges that need to be managed in situations where you have thousands of database objects as well as thousands of users, you quickly realize that it would be nice to organize the privileges into groups that can be easily managed. This is where roles come into play.

A "role" is used to group privileges together into a predefined group that can be granted to users. So, rather than granting object and system privileges individually to every user in your system, you can grant them to a role, which in turn is granted to the user. With the amount of system privileges that can be granted as well as several thousand objects that could be in a schema, using roles makes it at least a little easier to manage grants and permissions.

Oracle-defined Roles

Some special roles are created by Oracle through the install process or by running Oracle-supplied scripts. The DBA, Connect, Resource, Imp_Full_Database, and Select_Catalog_Role are some examples of roles that are supplied by Oracle and should not be changed.

Create and Grant a Role

Roles are created using the create statement in the same manner as creating users. You can also revoke privileges from roles and drop roles when they are no longer needed. Roles can also be granted to other roles. You can see an example of this next where the Oracle role CONNECT is granted to the newly created role TESTROLE, along with a system and object privilege:

```
CREATE ROLE "TESTROLE";
GRANT CONNECT TO "TESTROLE"
GRANT EXECUTE ANY PROCEDURE TO "TESTROLE"
GRANT SELECT ON "table_name" TO "TESTROLE"
```

The new role can then be granted to a user as shown next, where TESTROLE is granted to user TESTUSER:

```
Grant "TESTROLE" to "TESTUSER";
```

The TESTROLE is then dropped since it is no longer required:

```
DROP ROLE "TESTROLE";
```

Now that you've created users and roles, you can fine-tune our management of these by implementing some user policies through *profiles,* which you will explore next.

Profiles

A profile can be used to implement the management for strong passwords as well as establish limits in resources for a user. When you created the user NEWUSER earlier, a password was supplied along with the DEFAULT profile. Using this DEFAULT profile, the user never needs to change their password and there are no limits placed on any system resources. You can create new profiles to implement your corporate password policies in Oracle. For example, you can specify the number of days after which a user must change their password. You can also establish a rule where a password cannot be reused within a certain period of time and must contain a certain number of changes. A function can be used to ensure that a complex password is created by the user. For example, you may require that a password be more than eight characters long, use alpha, numeric, and special characters, and that it does not repeat a character more than twice. This can all be implemented in a function. An account can be locked after a specified number of login attempts and can remain locked for the number of days defined in the profile.

System limits for a user can also be implemented by a profile. These include limiting system resources such as those for CPU, connect, and idle time as well as the number of sessions employed by the user, limits on reads, and the SGA used. You should note, however, that the Database Resource Manager is the preferred way to limit resources and that you should use profiles to manage passwords.

The following is an example of the creation of a new profile that will lock an account after three failed login attempts and will keep the account locked indefinitely. The password needs to be changed every 60 days and the new password will be verified by your custom function COMPLEX_PASSWORD. The old password cannot be reused for 120 days:

```
CREATE PROFILE "NEWPOLICY"
FAILED_LOGIN_ATTEMPTS 3
PASSWORD_LOCK_TIME UNLIMITED
PASSWORD_LIFE_TIME 60
PASSWORD_REUSE_TIME 120
PASSWORD_VERIFY_FUNCTION COMPLEX_PASSWORD
```

Now, let's add this profile to user NEWUSER:

```
ALTER USER NEWUSER PROFILE NEWPOLICY;
```

Tie It All Together

As you have seen in this chapter, there is a great deal that a DBA needs to be aware of to properly manage a database. The good news is that you will have tools such as OEM to help you. Do your best to keep your environment as simple as you possibly can! You will be glad that you did as your overall database environment continues to grow.

Project 6-1   Create Essential Objects

This project will walk you through the creation of the essential storage and schema objects after a database has been created, which in this project will be called ora11*g*. You will create a new tablespace called NEW_TS and will then add a user NEW_USER who will be given a quota for this tablespace in order to be able to create objects in the tablespace. You will then create a role called NEW_ROLE and grant privileges to it. Afterward, you'll grant this role to the new user. A table and index will be created on this tablespace by the new user. Lastly, you will resize the undo tablespace to make it larger. You will see how to do this in OEM and the generated SQL will also be shown to you so you can do this in SQL*Plus.

Step by Step

1. You have been asked to create a new user named NEW_USER who will need to create objects in a new tablespace called NEW_TS that should be sized at 5MB. Your first step will be to create the tablespace. In OEM, log in as user SYSTEM, go to database ora11g, choose storage, then choose tablespace and select an existing tablespace to model. Under Objects in the toolbar, select the Create Like option to model your new tablespace after the existing one. Enter the new tablespace name, data file name, and all properties including the size. Make this a locally managed tablespace 5MB in size with uniform extents 96KB in size. If you choose the Show SQL button, you will see the generated SQL. It should look something like the following SQL. You can either apply the change in OEM or you can copy and paste the generated SQL and run it in SQL*Plus:

```
CREATE TABLESPACE "NEW_TS" LOGGING
DATAFILE 'C:\ORACLE\ORA11\ORA11g\NEW_TS1.ora' SIZE 2M
REUSE AUTOEXTEND ON
NEXT  1280K MAXSIZE  32767M EXTENT MANAGEMENT LOCAL
UNIFORM SIZE 96K SEGMENT SPACE MANAGEMENT  AUTO;
```

2. Now you will create NEW_USER. As with the preceding tablespace creation, you can model an existing user. In OEM, go to Security and then to User, choose an existing user to model, and select Object from the toolbar. Once again, use the Create Like feature. The user should now have a password of new_password, which will be unlocked. Set the default tablespace to NEW_TS:

```
CREATE USER "NEW_USER"  PROFILE "DEFAULT" IDENTIFIED
BY "new_password" PASSWORD EXPIRE DEFAULT TABLESPACE "NEW_TS"
TEMPORARY TABLESPACE "TEMP" QUOTA UNLIMITED    ON "TEMP";
```

3. Create a role called NEW_ROLE. In OEM, go to security, and then choose Role. Under Object in the toolbar, select Create and enter the role name:

```
CREATE ROLE "NEW_ROLE"  NOT IDENTIFIED;
```

(continued)

4. Grant the CREATE TABLE system privilege, the OLAP_USER role, and the object privilege SELECT on table SQLPLUS_PRODUCT_PROFILE to NEW_ROLE. In OEM, go to Role and choose NEW_ROLE. Use the tabs System, Object, and Role to choose the objects listed here. Click the Apply button to make the changes. The generated SQL will look like the three grants listed next:

```
GRANT CREATE TABLE TO "NEW_ROLE";
GRANT SELECT ON  "SYSTEM"."SQLPLUS_PRODUCT_PROFILE"
TO "NEW_ROLE";
GRANT "OLAP_USER" TO "NEW_ROLE";
```

5. Grant NEW_ROLE and connect to NEW_USER. Also, give NEW_USER an unlimited quota on NEW_TS to allow for objects to be created in the tablespace. In OEM, navigate to Users and choose NEW_USER. Once there, choose the Role tab and select NEW_ROLE, and then select the down arrow. Click the Apply button to make the change:

```
GRANT "NEW_ROLE" TO "NEW_USER";
ALTER USER "NEW_USER" DEFAULT ROLE  ALL;
ALTER USER "NEW_USER"  QUOTA UNLIMITED ON "NEW_TS";
```

6. You will now log into the database as NEW_USER and can use OEM with the NEW_USER account. Once in OEM, you will create a table called NEW_TABLE with columns col01 as number(15) and col02 as varchar2(30). In OEM, in the toolbar, select Object and under that choose Create, and then choose Table. Make sure the table is created in NEW_TS. Follow the screens to add col01 and col02. You will then create a primary key called NEW_TABLE_PK using col01. Follow the screens and choose the options you would like. We recommend that you name any keys and constraints rather than relying on system defaults. Choose Finish and you have created a new table with a primary key!

```
CREATE TABLE "NEW_USER"."NEW_TABLE"
("COL01" NUMBER(15) NOT NULL,
 "COL02" VARCHAR2(30) NOT NULL,
CONSTRAINT "NEW_TABLE_PK" PRIMARY KEY("COL01"),
CONSTRAINT "NEW_TABLE_U1" UNIQUE("COL01"))
TABLESPACE "NEW_TS";
```

7. You now have one last task: resizing the undo tablespace to add 100MB to it. Log into OEM as user System and choose the data file under the undo tablespace. Enter the new size and click Apply. It's as easy as that. The SQL to increase this from 50MB to 150MB is shown here:

```
ALTER DATABASE DATAFILE '/u01/oradata/ORA11g/UNDOTBS01.DBF'
RESIZE  150M;
```

Project Summary

This project has taken you through the basic steps of creating an environment for a new user, including using roles and granting privileges. You've seen how to manage users as well as space and have even created objects. Armed with these capabilities, you are now on your way to being a productive DBA. Congratulations!

☑ Chapter 6 Mastery Check

1. What is the benefit of a role?

2. Should a table that is in tens or hundreds of extents be reorganized?

3. What is the preferred method for collecting object statistics?

4. What is a segment?

5. What is an extent?

6. Name two reasons for implementing an index.

7. How can you place a database in maintenance mode without first shutting it down?

8. How can you limit the resources that a particular user can consume, and how does this work?

9. When managing undo segments, what are the things that you need to think about?

10. What is likely to happen if you turn on the autoextend property for undo and temporary tablespaces with a maxsize set to unlimited?

11. What is special about the SYS user account, and how does it differ from SYSTEM?

12. What are temporary tablespaces used for?

13. What are the two aspects of security that are covered in Oracle's implementation?

14. Name and describe the types of privileges that can be granted to a user.

15. How would you implement your corporate password policy in Oracle?

CHAPTER
7

Backup and Recovery

CRITICAL SKILLS

his chapter discusses many concepts that are very important to Oracle DBAs and to Oracle users. Backing up your data is crucial, and in this chapter you'll learn how to do this, as well as how to recover when things go wrong. As we have said before, the best way to learn is to do, and backup and recovery are tasks that every DBA must learn and, more importantly, practice. Just remember, if you do plan to perform the exercises and examples in this chapter, do it on a database that is not being used or create one just for this purpose...just in case.

CRITICAL SKILL 7.1

Understand Oracle Backup and Recovery Fundamentals

As you should already know, data is a valuable asset. To ensure that you can protect your investment, it is important to insure your valuable property and Oracle Database 11*g* provides numerous features to enable you to protect your investment. The ability to back up your data in case of a failure is invaluable; now you have the chance to back up your data without interruption to your business processes. Just as important as backing up your data is the ability to recover quickly from a failure. Whether you lose data due to hardware, software, or human failures, the time needed for recovery costs businesses opportunity and money. This chapter introduces you to the ways Oracle supports the backing up and recovering of data.

Where Do I Start?

Oracle's implementation of backup and recovery is an extensive one that provides you with the advantage of having many options that you can use. This is a good thing, but can leave you wondering, "Where should I start and which options are best for me?" This chapter will take you on a quick tour of backup and recovery and should leave you with a good understanding of how this is implemented in Oracle. As you review the backup and recovery utilities presented in this chapter, keep in mind that we strongly recommend using Recovery Manager (RMAN) for performing backup and recovery (we'll explain why later).

One of the most important elements of an advanced database management system (DBMS) is the capability to perform backup and recovery in a manner that guarantees data will not be lost. Oracle provides you with many options, from basic backup and recovery through advanced facilities to keep the database up in a high-availability environment. As a DBA, when you need to deal with a situation where the database is corrupted and needs to be recovered, there is nothing more comforting than knowing that you have valid backups for recovery and that you know how to use them!

In this chapter, you will see basic approaches and sound practices for performing backup and recovery. We will cover some examples and provide you with scripts you can use to start implementing your own backup and recovery procedures.

Three fundamental types of backups and recoveries can be performed in Oracle:

- **Physical backup and recovery** This is performed on the entire database, tablespaces, or even at the data file level without regard for the underlying logical data structures such as tables or schemas. All of the database files are backed up together so they may be recovered simultaneously. These are often referred to as hot or cold backups and they will be covered in more detail later on in the chapter.

- **Logical backup and recovery** This is performed by choosing specific logical database structures such as named tables, indexes, and perhaps even schemas. They allow you to restore the database in a more granular fashion than is possible with a physical backup. Logical backups are implemented by tools such as Oracle's Data Pump Export and Data Pump Import facilities. You should note that you cannot use a logical backup for a recovery; you can only use it for a restore.

- **Recovery Manager (RMAN)** This Oracle tool allows you to perform physical database backups in a more controlled manner. With RMAN, the backups and recoveries are managed for you through the RMAN toolset, as well as with a GUI interface using Enterprise Management. Syntax is simplified and the scripting is powerful and consistent across platforms. This is the toolset that Oracle has been investing in and moving toward since Oracle 8 and it is the recovery toolset that we recommend you use.

TIP
Which types of backups should you use: physical or logical? That's easy! Use both, whenever possible. Always try to have more than one way to restore or recover data when faced with this task. Having a logical and physical backup on hand provides you, the DBA, with more options when presented with a recovery scenario.

Backup Architecture

There are many types of failures and corruptions that can occur and impact the database, including server, network, and media failures that may render the database inoperable. They can come in the form of data corruptions caused by software failures in the OS, in Oracle, or in the application. Human error can also create problems with the database (but these errors are never the result of the DBA, of course).

In order to understand the type of backup and recovery needed for a given situation, it's important to understand Oracle's database architecture fundamentals. The database architecture, as it relates to backup and recovery principles, includes many components. Let's examine those structures critical to performing Oracle backup and recovery.

Oracle Binaries

Oracle binaries are the programs that make up Oracle software and perform the logic of the Oracle database. This should be backed up after the install of every release and product patch. A patch is software containing fixes for known problems and, in some cases, enhancements to major versions or releases of the database. Patches are installed over the top of a release and, in some cases, after other patches have already been applied.

Though you can always reinstall the software, you should back up your Oracle binaries for the following reasons:

- Installs of software are slower than file restores.

- CDs and web sites that contain the software for download may not be available.

- You may not remember the exact patch level applied to a particular server.

This means that the Oracle binaries should be backed up after every software change and on a regularly scheduled basis. At a minimum, there should be a weekly backup.

Parameter Files

The text-based init.ora parameter file and executable Server Parameter file (spfile) contain a list of directives for how the instance will operate once it has been started. All parameters that define the database are either stored in these files, derived from parameters that are stored here, or set to system defaults. These files are not volatile, but should be backed up so that the current state of the database can be re-created from a consistent set of backups. Not having a backed-up parameter file forces you to guess which parameters the database is using.

TIP
Back up the init.ora file and spfile on a nightly basis.

Control Files

Introduced in Chapter 1, the *control file* contains information that assists the recovery process. The history of archive logs, the name of the current online redo log file, and data file header checkpoint data are some of the types of information maintained by the control file. This is a small but critical piece of the database without which Oracle cannot run! Because of this, control files should be multiplexed so that at least three copies are used. A text version of this file and a binary version should both be backed up.

TIP

Back up a text and binary version of the control files with your regular database backups, as well as every time you alter a data file, tablespace, or redo log.

```
alter database backup controlfile to trace;          --text backup
alter database backup controlfile to '/directory/file'; --binary backup
```

Redo Logs

When data is changed in Oracle, data buffers are changed to reflect the change in tables and indexes. For performance purposes, these are usually not written out to the physical disk immediately. In order to protect the data, change records are written out to allow changes to be undone (undo records) when a transaction is rolled back, or redone (redo records) for the purpose of forward recovery. At transaction commit time, all redo records that make up the transaction have been written to the redo log files along with a unique system change number (scn) and the time of the change. Once redo logs have been written, data protection is guaranteed. The changes to the data files are in the buffer and can be written out at a later time. Multiple log files in a database are used in a round-robin format. So, once one redo log file fills up, the next redo log will then be used until it is full, followed by the next one and so on until finally the first redo log will be used again; this is a continuous cycle. Redo logs should be multiplexed so that each redo log can be a group of two or more identical members. In this manner, if there is a problem with one file being corrupted, the database can still operate as long as the other file(s) remain intact. The redo logs are absolutely required by Oracle to ensure that changes to the data aren't lost.

Figure 7-1 shows how the redo logs are being used and cycling through each log. Starting at the left side of Figure 7-1, you can see that after the redo log file is full, it moves to the next log group. It will continue to cycle through all of the log groups. Each group has two files in the group, and the LGWR process will write to both, creating a copy. The archive process copies the log files to the archive log files so that the redo file is available to be overwritten as it cycles through.

Undo Segments

When data is changed, as mentioned earlier, "before images" of the data are created to allow a transaction to roll back. This is accomplished through undo records being written to undo segments (also called *rollback segments*) and undo tablespaces.

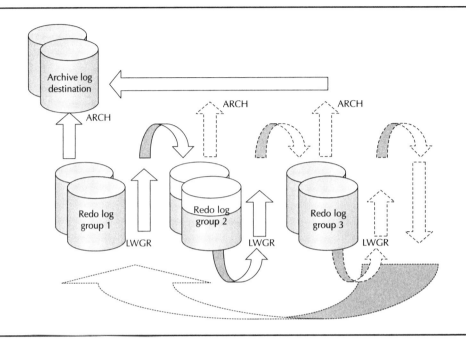

FIGURE 7-1. *Redo logs*

Undo tablespaces are managed in the same way as any other tablespace and the data is subsequently logged as redo logs. Rollback segments allow changes to be undone, either for system reasons, perhaps due to a transaction that has failed, or because the application has explicitly requested that a rollback be performed. Undo or rollback tablespaces need to be included as part of your backup strategy.

Checkpoints

As you've seen, the redo logs and database data are not written out at the same time. The redo logs are guaranteed to be written out at commit time, but the data is not written to disk simultaneously. If that's the case, just when is the data written from the buffers to the data files? This is determined by an Oracle process called the database writer (dbw0) process, which manages the writing of information to the database. dbw0 writes changes to the data files to free up *dirty buffers* (buffers that have changed data in them) to allow more changes to occur. A checkpoint is a background event that ensures all of the changed data has been written to the data files.

Archive Logs

Archive logs are the mechanism used to provide continuous availability to an Oracle database by allowing you to back up the database while it is running. This is known as a *hot backup.* They also allow you to recover databases by performing a "roll-forward" of changes using redo logs up to either the current point in time or a time that you specify the database should be rolled forward to. This cannot be done with online redo logs, because they are written to sequentially and eventually wrapped-around. When that occurs, the previous records that existed in the wrapped redo file are overwritten. By placing the database in archive log mode, online redo logs can be written out to files to be kept indefinitely. The files can then be named with sequential incrementing names so that you know the order they should be applied in. As with redo logs, archive logs can be multiplexed. In other words, more than one copy of each archive log can be written to different locations. Refer back to Figure 7-1, as it also demonstrates the redo logs being written to the archive log location.

Data Files, Tablespaces, Segments, Extents, and Blocks

Data files are the low-level structures that make up what you probably think of as a database. To put it simply, the tables and indexes that make up your applications are stored in tablespaces and each tablespace is created on one or more data files. A particular data file will store data for one tablespace and a tablespace can contain many tables and indexes. Tables and indexes are a subset of a type of database object called a *segment.* Examples of segments are indexes, tables, rollback/undos, clusters,

Ask the Expert

Q: What would happen if I restored the redo logs before I performed a point-in-time recovery? It seems like this is the best approach to use.

A: There is an end-of-redo marker on the online redo logs that will stop the recovery immediately. Oracle will think the forward recovery is complete and archive logs will not be applied. The current redo logs should also not be overwritten by the backups because the current redo logs contain the last pieces of the recovery information. This means that the recovery will not be restored completely and an incomplete recovery will need to be done.

Q: How can I find out the state of a file when a backup control file was taken? I need to know which files are read-write, read-only, or offline, but how can I do that?

A: Whenever you back up a control file, run a sql script that queries dba_data_files and writes the status of all of your data files to a separate file that is kept with the backup control file. We will show you an example of this in the following section.

lobindexes, and lobsegments. A segment is made up of extents that are a collection of contiguous blocks. Take a look at Figure 7-2 for a picture of these breakdowns of the storage structure. So, to put this into a single sentence, a tablespace is created on one or more data files and consists of one or more segments made up of one or more extents that are a contiguous collection of blocks. Got it? Good. It's an important set of relationships to understand.

From a backup and recovery point-of-view, it's important to be aware of the relationship between tables, tablespaces, and data files. You should employ a naming standard that makes it easy to determine the tablespace that a data file supports. Whenever you perform a backup where you are not backing up the entire database at the same time, it is important to consider any referential integrity constraints enforced by the backup or application that must be honored. If you're just backing up a set of tables, or one tablespace but not another, are you getting all that is needed for valid restore of the application?

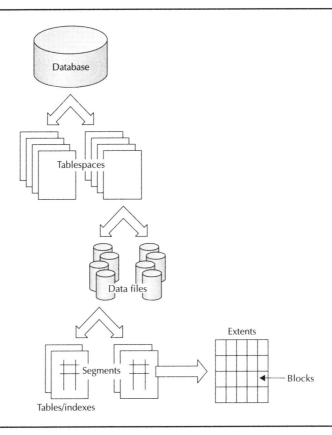

FIGURE 7-2. *A database's storage structure is not just made up of tables, but tablespaces that are comprised of data files that are made up of segments built of blocks.*

Dump Files

There are three types of dump files that contain information about errors that occur in the database. *Background dumps* are written out by Oracle background processes when an error occurs. *User dumps* are files written for user processes for the purpose of debugging. *Core dumps* are a place where Oracle dumps core files in a UNIX environment. These may be worth backing up as a history of problems that have occurred to help you troubleshoot future issues. One particular file that should be backed up regularly is a special trace file called an *alert log*. This file reports on a great deal of activity, such as when the database is stopped and started, when checkpoints occurred, and the system change number (or scn, a unique number given to every change in the database), where the current incarnation or version of the database began. This is all valuable information that can be of great assistance when it comes time to recover your database.

TIP
Back up your alert log with your regular database backups. The location of the alert log can be found by looking at the value of the parameter background_dump_dest. Since this is a regular file, a file system backup of this directory is a valid option and would back up the alert log.

You have now seen the structures that are critical to your backup and recovery operations. Armed with this knowledge, you are ready to learn about user-manager backup and recovery.

Progress Check

1. Name some files that should be backed up as part of your strategy.

2. What does multiplexing mean and which objects should be multiplexed?

3. Why would you want to use archive logging?

Progress Check Answers

1. Some files that should be backed up include parameter, control, undo, archive log, data, online redo, dump, and trace files.

2. Multiplexing is a term to describe data that's written to more than one location or file at the same time. Redo logs, archive logs, and control files should be multiplexed and each copy should go to a different disk to protect against the loss of one disk.

3. Archive logging allows you to perform full recovery of the database. Without archive logs, no recovery is possible (only restores can be performed). Also, the database can be backed up while it is up and running. It is needed to deliver high availability.

Learn about Oracle User-Managed Backup and Recovery

Oracle supports backing up data in a number of ways. This section discusses how and why to use user-managed backups. These backups are by nature handled more mechanically than other methods and are just as effective. The information presented here is also needed to recover your first database. Please remember that you should try this on test databases before trying your first backup and ultimate recovery on a business database.

Types of User-Managed Backups

User-managed database backups can be performed as either cold or hot physical backups. A *cold backup* means that all users are disconnected from the database and it is shut down in order to perform the backup. A *hot backup* is performed while the database is up and end users can remain connected to the database. In fact, they can be changing the very data that is being backed up! Let's examine these two situations in more detail.

Cold Backups

Cold backups are the simplest type of backup operation you can perform. Cold backups are performed with the database completely shut down so that the data files are in a consistent state and nothing is being accessed or changed. Once that is done, all database files should be backed up to disk or tape. Once the file copies are complete, the database can be started and users can resume their activity. The database does not need to be in archive log mode in order to perform a cold backup, but without archive logging, the database can only be restored to the point in time that the cold backup was done. Cold backups are a simple option and are limited in the way they must be run, but once you have a cold backup, it can be easier to work with and can provide a fair degree of functionality.

In order to perform a cold backup, the database must be shut down in a consistent manner. In other words, the database should be shut down by issuing one of the following commands:

- shutdown normal
- shutdown immediate
- shutdown transactional

Do not perform a cold backup of the database immediately after a shutdown abort. If you must shut down the database in this manner, follow it up with a startup restrict (to not allow user access), so that the recovery process of the transactions that were in progress before the abort can complete. Then execute a shutdown [immediate, transactional, normal]. In this way, you can be confident that you have a database wherein all of the transactions have completed or rolled back and the data is in a consistent state. When the database has been shut down, copy the files to another location on disk or to tape. The files that you should back up include

- All database data files and tablespaces including system, temp, and rollback/undo

- Control files, backup binary control files, and text control files

- Archive logs if they are being used

- Alert logs

- Oracle password files if they exist

- Parameter files init<SID>.ora and spfile

- Redo logs—but you should be careful whenever restoring redo logs since the restore of a redo log could overwrite existing current redo logs containing the final entries in the redo stream needed to complete the recovery. Because of this, Oracle recommends that you do not back up redo logs.

Once the backups have been completed, the database can be restarted. If the backups were made to disk, these files can later be backed up to tape after the database is restarted.

Hot Backups

A hot backup is a backup done while the database is up and running. The entire database can be backed up or a subset of the tablespaces or data files can be backed up at one time. While this is happening, end users can continue to perform all of their normal operations against it. In order to do this, the database must be running in archivelog mode. This is done by setting the parameter log_archive_start = true and then running the sql statement alter database archivelog while the database is mounted. The tablespaces to be backed up are put in backup mode with the alter tablespace tablespace_name begin backup command. The whole database can also be put into backup mode at the same time with alter database begin backup and end backup. But when at a tablespace level it is recommended to put the tablespaces into backup mode one at a time. The data files are then copied using OS copies, and the backup is completed with the alter tablespace tablespace_name end backup command. This looks like the following:

```
alter tablespace <tablespace_name> begin backup;
[os file copy command such as cp in unix or ocopy in Windows]
alter tablespace <tablespace_name> end backup;
```

Once the backup is complete, you will need to ensure that all of the log records created during the backup operation have been subsequently archived. Do this with the sql statement archive log current. This command ensures that all redo logs have been archived and it will wait for the archive to complete. You should note that the ocopy utility is required in Windows environments to allow a file to be shared between the copy utility and Oracle. Ocopy is a command-line utility used to back up files to disk when the database is down or tablespace is offline. It is not needed in UNIX environments.

After a hot backup has been successfully completed, the database can be recovered to a particular point in time by restoring the data files from the hot backup and rolling forward archive logs to the time required. Online redo logs should never be backed up during a hot backup. Rather, you should archive the current redo logs and back those up. As a result, you will create the redo logs at the end of recovery when an alter database open resetlogs is performed (resetlogs is discussed later in this chapter, in the section "Recovery Using Backup Control Files").

In order to recover from a hot or cold backup, it is important to remember that all of the files that make up the database must be recovered to the same point in time in order to keep the entire database consistent. The exception to this rule is that read-only tablespaces can be restored to the point that they were made read-only. This makes sense since the tablespace cannot be changed once it has been made read-only. In order to recover a tablespace that is open for read-write operations to a point in time that is different from the rest of the database, a special operation called Tablespace Point In Time Recovery (TSPITR) must be performed. However, this operation requires a clone database and is beyond the scope of this chapter.

Whenever a tablespace status changes to read-only or read-write, it should be backed up. You will need to keep track of these backups so that you know where they are when it comes time to use them in a recovery situation. Consider backing up "read only" tablespaces periodically to deal with potential expiry dates on tape, as well as other tape management problems that could result from older tapes.

TIP
Run hot backups when the system is not busy. Also, only put one tablespace between the begin and end backup operations to reduce the amount of system overhead associated with this activity, since system logging is increased on tablespaces that are in backup mode. You can group multiple tablespaces together in cases where change activity will not be high on them during the backup.

Hot backups and archivelogs will be a requirement of every system that has true high-availability requirements.

Recovery from a Cold Backup

Database recovery can be broken into two distinct steps: the first step involves file restores where files are copied from tape or a disk backup to a location on disk where the actual database resides. This is the location of files pointed to by the control files. The second step is forward recovery, where the archive logs can be processed and applied to the database, making the data as current as possible. In the case of the database in noarchivelog mode (which is often the case where cold backups are concerned), there are no logs to recover with, so all data files, control files, and redo logs are simply restored to their proper location. Other files, such as the init.ora and spfile parameter files, as well as password files, must also be in the proper place.

Restoring a database from a cold backup is one of the simpler things you can do as a DBA; this simplicity is perhaps the biggest benefit of performing a cold backup. A cold backup of a database that is in archivelog mode can be recovered, but there is no recovery from a hot backup that isn't in archivelog mode (note that a hot backup is only performed on databases in archivelog mode): there are only file restores. Once these files have been restored, the database can be started. That's it!

Ask the Expert

Q: Why would I ever want to use cold backups if hot backups are so powerful?

A: There are situations when you only need to restore a database from a cold backup and high availability is not a concern. In these cases, you can consider using a cold backup.

Q: What is the downside to performing hot backups and running in archivelog mode, if any?

A: You will need to manage the archive log files, but RMAN can help you with this (more information can be found later in this chapter in the "Archive Log Management" section). There is also extra logging that occurs when a tablespace is placed in the backup mode. This can be overcome by scheduling backups when the database is not busy or by using RMAN, which does not place tablespaces in backup mode. Restorations from hot backup require more care and practice, but the benefits to hot backups outweigh the disadvantages by a great deal.

Recovery from a Hot Backup

This is one of the places where you will earn your stripes as a DBA, since you will always need to perform recovery from a hot backup. To clarify this point, recovery can be performed on any database that is in archivelog mode, whether the backup was a hot or cold one, but hot backups always require that recovery be performed. There are two fundamental types of recovery: *complete recovery* and *incomplete recovery.*

Complete recovery describes a recovery where the database is restored and then recovered forward using all available archive logs. You are performing as complete a recovery as you can, with no data loss. Complete recovery can be performed at the database, tablespace, data file, or block level.

Incomplete or point-in-time recovery is where the database is restored and then optionally rolled forward to a predetermined point in time or system change number (scn) by applying some, but not all, of the logs. This produces a version of the database that is not current and is often done to bring the database back to a time before a problem occurred. There are three fundamental types of incomplete recovery:

- **Cancel-based recovery** runs until you issue a cancel command.

- **Timestamp recovery** applies to all of the logs until a timestamp you enter is reached.

- **Change-based recovery** applies to all of the logs until a scn you enter is reached.

Examples of these are shown next:

```
SQL> recover database until cancel;
SQL> recover database until change 1234567;
SQL> recover database until time '2004-04-15:14:33:00';
```

TIP
When performing a recovery, always try to recover as much data as possible by running a complete recovery or by applying archive logs to the latest timestamp or scn that you possibly can.

Seven Steps to Recovery

The fundamental steps for performing a recovery are summed up here:

1. Restore data files from tape or a backup location on disk to the location where the database file should reside.

2. Startup nomount. This step reads the parameter file, allocates the memory structure of the SGA, and starts the background Oracle processes. Also, the alert log and trace files are opened. Note that the data files are not open during a Startup nomount. (This step has to be performed if the control file needs to be rebuilt.)

3. Create the control file. This step is optional and only needed if the control file is unavailable. A text version of the control file should be used to create a new binary version of the control file.

4. Ensure that all the data files to recover are online. Read-only data files once restored do not need to be recovered since no data will have changed in these files.

5. Mount the database. This step associates a database with the instance that was started in step 2. The database, however, is not opened at this time. The control file listed in the parameter file is opened and all database files are located.

6. Recover the database by locating and applying the archive logs.

7. Open the database. The database, including the redo logs and data files, is opened with the Startup Open command.

In some cases, you only need to recover a single tablespace or data file without touching the rest of the database. These must be complete recoveries and the tablespace or data file must be taken offline to perform this. A block level recovery can also be performed, but only by RMAN and only with the data file online. This feature allows you to recover a small number of corrupt blocks of a data file and is one of the great reasons to use RMAN!

TIP
If a database crashes in the middle of a hot backup, and the data file is still in backup mode, it will appear that the data file will need recovery. However, it will just need to be changed out of backup mode to allow the database to come up properly and continue. Check the status of the data file in v$backup before performing a recovery.

Recovery Using Backup Control Files

You can create both a text version of the control file and a binary version of the control file as backups. When recovering the database, you should try to use the current control file. If that is not possible, then your next option should be to try to use a backup control file since it contains useful information that assists recovery that is not included in the text-based control file. With a backup control file, you will need to perform media recovery and use the using backup control file syntax when performing the recover database command. A resetlogs command will then need to be performed when the database is opened, which will create new redo logs as well as a new version, or incarnation, of the database. You also need to know the status of data files when the backup control file was created. If a data file had a status of read-write when the backup control file was created (but should be opened as a read-only file), then it should be taken offline before recovery begins. Backup control files are a useful and sometimes required feature, but can complicate your database recovery.

TIP
Always back up the database after performing an incomplete recovery and opening the database with the Resetlogs option. The backups before this recovery are not easily useable, so taking another backup after the resetlogs option will make a simple restore possible if there is a need to recover after this point.

CRITICAL SKILL 7.3

Write a Database Backup

When you decide to use a user-managed backup strategy rather than RMAN, you will need to develop scripts to perform hot or cold backups. One of the most important things you should do to simplify your maintenance requirements is to develop scripts that are generated from the Oracle catalog. If done properly, you won't need to change your backup scripts every time you add a new file or change the location of a file.

TIP
Automate your backups with scripts that are generated from the Oracle Catalog.

Whenever you perform a backup, it is extremely useful to know the status of your database including the data files and parameters in effect. Information such as which data files are open in read-only mode at backup time is invaluable, as is a listing of the file locations and sizes. Next we'll show you a simple example of some SQL queries that provide information about the state of a database when you need to restore:

```
select * from dba_tablespaces;   -- Tablespace Information
select * from dba_data_files;    -- Data file Information
select * from v$datafile;        -- More data file information
select * from v$logfile;         -- log file information
select * from v$log;             -- more log file information
select * from v$controlfile;     -- control file information
select * from v$parameter;       -- database parameters in effect
select * from v$nls_parameters;  -- language characters in effect
-- Get the log history information for the past 3 days
select * from v$log_history where first_time > sysdate - 3;
```

The preceding should be spooled to the backup directory and kept with your backups. You can list the specific columns you want to see in the previous queries, but when it comes to needing information during a high-pressure recovery, we would rather you err on the side of having a little too much information than risk missing a piece of information that would be useful. Once you have this information, your backup can be performed. The following is an example of a hot backup SQL script. This script must be executed on a database running in archivelog mode:

```
set echo on;
spool /u02/backup/ora11g/hotBackup1.lst;
alter system archive log current;
alter tablespace INDX begin backup;
! cp /u01/oradata/ora11g/indx01.dbf /u02/backup/ora11g
alter tablespace INDX end backup;
alter tablespace TABLESPACE_n begin backup;
! cp /u01/oradata/ora11g/tablespace_n01.dbf /u02/backup/ora11g
! cp /u01/oradata/ora11g/tablespace_n02.dbf /u02/backup/ora11g
alter tablespace TABLESPACE_n end backup;
... more tablespaces ...
alter tablespace SYSTEM begin backup;
! cp /u01/oradata/ora11g/system01.dbf /u02/backup/ora11g
alter tablespace SYSTEM end backup;
-- Backup the log file
alter system archive log current;
--  Create 3 copies of a binary controlfile backup.
alter database backup controlfile to
   /u02/backup/ora11g/CONTROL01.CTL' reuse;
alter database backup controlfile to
   /u02/backup/ora11g/CONTROL02.CTL' reuse;
alter database backup controlfile to
   /u02/backup/ora11g/CONTROL03.CTL' reuse;

-- Create a text version of a controlfile backup
alter database backup controlfile to trace;
spool off;
exit;
```

This is a SQL script that can be run from a UNIX shell script or a Windows command file. To run this in Windows environments, the file copies are performed using the host start /wait c:\oracle\ora11g\bin\ocopy.exe command rather than with the UNIX ! cp command, which hosts out and runs the UNIX version of copy. The ocopy command is an Oracle copy utility that must be run under Windows to allow file sharing to occur during hot backups. The standard DOS copy command does not allow this.

Cold backups are similar to the preceding except that the begin backup and end backup commands are not needed. The copy commands are surrounded by a consistent database shutdown before the copies have started, with a startup after the copies have completed. Note that in Windows environments, you should use the standard "copy" utility for cold backups.

You should also add your parameter files, dump files, alert logs, and your own DBA scripts that perform backup, recovery, and monitoring to your backups. Once you've added those, you'll have everything backed up except for your archive logs. Let's see how to manage those next.

CRITICAL SKILL 7.4

Back Up Archived Redo Logs

Managing archive logs is one of the more difficult tasks on a busy Oracle database. You will want to have archive logs available to you in case they are needed for a database recovery. At the same time, the archive logs must be written to disk and if disk space fills up, the instance will stop processing requests until more space becomes available. Trying to balance both of these competing requirements can be tricky, especially if your system writes a large number of log records.

To meet the first requirement of having the archive logs available to your online system in the event of a recovery, try to keep archive logs since the last backup (or, even better, the last two backups) on disk. If you are unable to keep archive logs online due to space issues, then you will need to write a script that regularly backs up the archive logs to tape and deletes them from disk. An example of a space management script that backs up archive logs once the archive directory is over 50 percent full is shown next:

```
#Pseudo-shell-code for free archive log space
# Check used and free space: this is a very simple script
# df -k  (on linux: location of fields varies by platform)
# Filesystem    1k-blocks Used      Available Use%    Mounted on
# /dev/hda3     3763404   102676    3469556   3%        /
Log_arch_dest='/u01/oradata/db01/arch'
arch_dir_mountPoint=`df -k ${log_arch_dest}|grep -v blocks|
    awk '{print $6}'`
arch_dir_freeSpace=`df -k ${log_arch_dest}|grep -v blocks|
    awk '{print $4}'`
arch_dir_used=`df -k ${LOG_ARCH_DEST}|grep -v blocks|
```

```
      awk '{print $3}'`
if [${arch_dir_freeSpace} -le  ${arch_dir_Used}]; then
 echo "Place archiving logic here"
fi
```

All of this is unnecessary when you use RMAN, since it will back up archive logs to tape, delete the files on disk, and manage the tape files in the RMAN repository. You will see more of this later in the "Get Started with Recovery Manager" section.

CRITICAL SKILL 7.5

Get Started with Oracle Data Pump

Oracle Data Pump is a utility available since Oracle Database 10*g* that can be used to move data and *metadata* from one database to another. (Metadata is the "data about the data," or in Oracle terms, the catalog information.) In earlier versions of Oracle, Export and Import were the utilities for this; their interface is similar to the new utilities, Data Pump Export and Data Pump Import, though they are completely separate utilities. The performance of Oracle's new utilities Data Pump Export and Data Pump Import will increase greatly over the old Export and Import utilities and can also take advantage of parallelism to accomplish this. The Data Pump Export and Import utilities use the expdp and impdp commands, respectively. You are encouraged to use these rather than the pre–Oracle Database 10*g* exp and imp utilities, since those do not support all Oracle Database 11*g* features, while the Data Pump utilities do.

The Data Pump output files are written in a proprietary format that can only be read by the Data Pump Import utility. Now with Oracle 11*g*, the export files can be encrypted and compressed as they are exported. The compression of the export file can shrink the file from 10–15 percent. Encryption of the export can be done at a file level—or even at the level of table columns—to protect the sensitive data in these tables.

Data Pump will allow a subset of data and metadata to be moved through filters implemented in the Export and Import parameters. The Data Pump Export utility unloads data, metadata, and control information from the database into one or more operating system files that are called dump files. These can be imported into a target database that resides on another server and a totally different operating system.

The Data Pump Import utility can read these dump files and load a target database with metadata, data, and all objects that have been previously exported. For example, table DDL, security in the form of grants, objects such as triggers, stored procedures, and views can also be imported, among other things. In fact, an entire target database can be created from a Data Pump Full Export using the Import utility. Some useful options provided through Data Pump are

- The ability to view object DDL without running it using the SQLFILE parameter

- The network import, which allows a Data Pump Import to occur using a source database rather than a dump file set

- The ability to restart Data Pump jobs using the start_job parameter to restart import jobs

- Using the Parallel parameter to define the maximum number of threads and degrees of parallelism for export and import jobs

- The ability to monitor jobs by detaching and reattaching to running jobs

- The ability to estimate the amount of space an export file will occupy by using the estimate_only clause

The Data Pump Export and Import for data and metadata are performed using the Data Pump application programming interface (API) and use procedures in the DBMS_DATAPUMP PL/SQL package. The metadata API is implemented through the DBMS_METADATA package. This package retrieves metadata in an XML format that can be used in many ways. For example, XML can be transformed into DDL or Extensible Stylesheet Language Transformation (XSLT) and the XML itself can be used to create an object. There is a new Remap attribute that allows the attributes of an object to be changed; for example, schema names can be changed using this feature. The Data Pump API supports all objects needed to perform a full export.

There are three ways to perform Data Pump Export and Import utilities. There is the command-line interface, where export and import parameters are listed on a command line or in a script. A variation of the command-line interface is to add a parameter file using the parfile parameter, which points to a different file where all of the import or export parameters are listed. An interactive-command interface can also be used by entering CTRL-C during an import or export run which will then allow you to enter commands when prompted.

Let's now explore some details about actually running Data Pump exports and imports.

CRITICAL SKILL 7.6

Use Oracle Data Pump Export

There are five mutually exclusive modes for performing the Oracle Data Pump Export:

- **Full Export** is where the entire database is exported using the full parameter. This can be used to completely rebuild the database if needed.

- **Schema Export** is the default mode; it allows you to export one or more schemas in the database. The schemas parameter is used to run this. Please note that objects in other schemas related or dependent on objects in this schema are not exported unless the other schema is also mentioned in the schema list.

- **Table Export** allows for the export of tables or partitions and their dependent objects using the tables parameter.

- **Tablespace Export** can be used to unload all of the tables that have been created in the given tablespace set using the tablespaces parameter.

- **Transportable Tablespace** mode differs from the preceding bullet in that only the metadata is exported from the database for a given tablespace set. This uses the transport_tablespaces parameter.

The exp_full_database role must be granted to a user performing a full or tablespace export or, alternatively, an export of a schema or table that is outside of the user's schema.

A feature of the Data Pump Export is that filters can be used on both data and metadata. The data filters are applied with the query parameter, and the filter is executed once per table per job. For metadata, either the exclude or include parameters can be used and are mutually exclusive commands. When filters are applied to metadata, the objects that are included will also have their dependent objects. For example, tables will also have indexes, triggers, grants, and constraints included with them. You can use the datapump_paths view to see which objects can be filtered on. When multiple filters are applied to an object, they are processed with an and condition between them. When using filters, we recommend using the parfile parameter and placing all parameters in the parfile including the filter operators.

The parameters for the Data Pump Export command can be seen using the command expdp help=y. A subset of the output from this, which contains the parameters along with a brief description, is shown next.

```
C:\Users\iabramson>expdp help=y

The Data Pump export utility provides a mechanism for transferring
data objects between Oracle databases. The utility is invoked with
the following command:

   Example: expdp scott/tiger DIRECTORY=dmpdir DUMPFILE=scott.dmp

You can control how Export runs by entering the 'expdp' command
followed by various parameters. To specify parameters, you use
keywords:

   Format:  expdp KEYWORD=value
            or KEYWORD=(value1,value2,...,valueN)
   Example: expdp scott/tiger DUMPFILE=scott.dmp
            DIRECTORY=dmpdir SCHEMAS=scott
          or TABLES=(T1:P1,T1:P2), if T1 is partitioned table

USERID must be the first parameter on the command line.

Keyword                 Description (Default)
----------------------------------------------------------------
ATTACH                  Attach to existing job, e.g. ATTACH [=job name].
```

COMPRESSION	Reduce size of dumpfile contents where valid keyword values are: ALL, (METADATA_ONLY), DATA_ONLY and NONE.
CONTENT	Specifies data to unload where the valid keyword values are: (ALL), DATA_ONLY, and METADATA_ONLY.
DATA_OPTIONS	Data layer flags where the only valid value is: XML_CLOBS-write XML datatype in CLOB format
DIRECTORY	Directory object to be used for dumpfiles and logfiles.
DUMPFILE	List of destination dump files (expdat.dmp), e.g. DUMPFILE=scott1.dmp, scott2.dmp, dmpdir:scott3.dmp.
ENCRYPTION	Encrypt part or all of the dump file where valid keyword values are: ALL, DATA_ONLY, METADATA_ONLY,ENCRYPTED_COLUMNS_ONLY, or NONE.
ENCRYPTION_ALGORITHM	Specify how encryption should be done where valid keyword values are: (AES128), AES192, and AES256.
ENCRYPTION_MODE	Method of generating encryption key where valid keyword values are: DUAL, PASSWORD, and (TRANSPARENT).
ENCRYPTION_PASSWORD	Password key for creating encrypted column data.
ESTIMATE	Calculate job estimates where the valid keyword values are: (BLOCKS) and STATISTICS.
ESTIMATE_ONLY	Calculate job estimates without performing the export.
EXCLUDE	Exclude specific object types, e.g. EXCLUDE=TABLE:EMP.
FILESIZE	Specify the size of each dumpfile in units of bytes.
FLASHBACK_SCN	SCN used to set session snapshot back to.
FLASHBACK_TIME	Time used to get the SCN closest to the specified time.
FULL	Export entire database (N).
HELP	Display Help messages (N).
INCLUDE	Include specific object types, e.g. INCLUDE=TABLE_DATA.
JOB_NAME	Name of export job to create.
LOGFILE	Log file name (export.log).
NETWORK_LINK	Name of remote database link to the source system.
NOLOGFILE	Do not write logfile (N).
PARALLEL	Change the number of active workers for current job.
PARFILE	Specify parameter file.
QUERY	Predicate clause used to export a subset of a table.
REMAP_DATA	Specify a data conversion function, e.g. REMAP_DATA=EMP.EMPNO:REMAPPKG.EMPNO.
REUSE_DUMPFILES	Overwrite destination dump file if it exists (N).
SAMPLE	Percentage of data to be exported;

SCHEMAS	List of schemas to export (login schema).
STATUS	Frequency (secs) job status is to be monitored where the default (0) will show new status when available.
TABLES	Identifies a list of tables to export - one schema only.
TABLESPACES	Identifies a list of tablespaces to export.
TRANSPORTABLE	Specify whether transportable method can be used where valid keyword values are: ALWAYS, (NEVER).
TRANSPORT_FULL_CHECK	Verify storage segments of all tables (N).
TRANSPORT_TABLESPACES	List of tablespaces from which metadata will be unloaded.
VERSION	Version of objects to export where valid keywords are: (COMPATIBLE), LATEST, or any valid database version.

The following commands are valid while in interactive mode.
Note: abbreviations are allowed

Command	Description
ADD_FILE	Add dumpfile to dumpfile set.
CONTINUE_CLIENT	Return to logging mode. Job will be re-started if idle.
EXIT_CLIENT	Quit client session and leave job running.
FILESIZE	Default filesize (bytes) for subsequent ADD_FILE commands.
HELP	Summarize interactive commands.
KILL_JOB	Detach and delete job.
PARALLEL	Change the number of active workers for current job. PARALLEL=<number of workers>.
REUSE_DUMPFILES	Overwrite destination dump file if it exists (N).
START_JOB	Start/resume current job
STATUS	Frequency (secs) job status is to be monitored where the default (0) will show new status when available. STATUS[=interval]
STOP_JOB	Orderly shutdown of job execution and exits the client. STOP_JOB=IMMEDIATE performs an immediate shutdown of the Data Pump job.

The values in brackets in the preceding list are the default values in use for the parameter. Some parameters worth noting are explored further in the following bullet points:

- DIRECTORY is the directory that is created using the sql create directory syntax in Oracle and it's the location that the dump file is written to. The default name is DPUMP_DIR. Without a directory the export will fail; the directory is where the dump file and log file will be stored. For example, set this as follows:

```
create or replace directory DPUMP_DIR as '\u01\';
grant read, write on dpump_dir to export_user;
```

■ ESTIMATE allows you to see how much disk space each table in the export job will consume. The options for ESTIMATE include BLOCK and STATISTICS, which specify if Data Pump will use either a sample of blocks or table statistics to determine the size of the export.

■ EXCLUDE can be used to exclude metadata, dependent objects, and data to be exported or imported. The exclude parameter can exclude tables, constraints, stored procedures, grants, and schemas. This doesn't exclude data from a table; to exclude data, you must use data filtering through a query and where clause.

■ FLASHBACK_SCN and _TIME directs the export to unload data that is consistent with the time or scn listed.

■ INCLUDE is used to list metadata objects and dependent data that will be exported. This can include object types and object names. Only objects explicitly listed in the INCLUDE statement will be exported.

■ NETWORK_LINK allows an import into a target database directly from a source database rather than from a dump file.

■ PARALLEL is a performance option that can be used to specify the maximum number of threads that can be used to speed up an export by running it in parallel.

■ PARFILE can be included to point to another file that includes export parameters. Use this when filtering data and metadata using the exclude, include, or query parameters.

■ QUERY can be used to apply syntax similar to qualifiers that you would use in a select...where clause to filter the rows to be exported.

■ TRANSPORT_TABLESPACES (TTS) is the parameter used to specify the tablespaces that will have their metadata exported during a transportable tablespace operation. When this is done, the tablespaces in the source database should be placed in read-only mode and their underlying data files copied to a new location. The data file copies are performed at the OS level. The only exportx is that of the metadata. The data file copies and exported metadata can be used to plug in the tablespaces to a target database. The tablespaces must be a self-contained set and the transport_full_check parameter can be used to ensure this is the case.

- ADD_FILE is valuable if an export operation fills the current dump file. If working in interactive mode when this occurs, you will be prompted to add a new dump file and will be able to do so. Otherwise, additional files can be added when the job is defined.

- START_ JOB allows you to start a job to which you are attached. This allows you to restart an export after a previous failure and is valuable for long-running jobs.

Next we'll cover some examples. To perform a full database export and compress the full export file using Data Pump, run the following:

```
expdp system/manager DUMPFILE=expdat.dmp FULL=y LOGFILE=export.log
COMPRESSION=ALL
```

A Schema Level Export of the Sales History (SH) schema can be performed as follows:

```
expdp system/manager DUMPFILE=expdat.dmp SCHEMAS=sh LOGFILE=export.log
```

A single table can be exported, as shown next with the sh.customers table:

```
expdp system/manager DUMPFILE=expdat.dmp TABLES=sh.customers
LOGFILE=export.log
```

Here is an example of data filtering where the tables in the SH schema are exported, except for the PROMOTIONS table and CUSTOMERS table which has one row exported:

```
expdp sh/sh parfile=exp.par
```

The contents of the exp.par file are shown here:

```
DIRECTORY=DPUMP_DIR
DUMPFILE=testsh.dmp
CONTENT=DATA_ONLY
EXCLUDE=TABLE:"in ('PROMOTIONS')"
QUERY=customers:"where cust_id=1"
```

The Data Pump Export utility is valuable for performing backups of a database or objects in a database, as well as for moving data from one database to another. Experiment with the different parameters and test your exports by performing imports to another database to ensure that the entire export and import stream is working properly.

Work with Oracle Data Pump Import

You've successfully performed exports and they seem to have worked, but that's only half of the job. You now need to perform the ultimate test of whether those exports worked by performing Data Pump Imports.

Imports are performed using the impdp command, which is new since Oracle Database 10*g*. As with Data Pump Export, this utility has similar functionality with the import utility found in pre–Oracle Database 10*g* versions. There are five modes for performing the Oracle Data Pump Import, described next. The modes correspond to the export modes, but an import can be run using an export of the exact same mode or an export mode that is a higher level in the hierarchy. For example, a table-mode import can be performed using a source that is a Full, Schema, Tablespace, or Table mode export dump file as well as a Network_Link. These modes are mutually exclusive and explained in detail next:

- **Full Import**   The entire database is imported using the FULL parameter. This can be used to completely rebuild the database if needed. This can be run using a source dump file or a source database using a Network_Link.

- **Schema Import**   The default mode allows you to import one or more schemas in the database using the SCHEMAS parameter. Objects in other schemas that are dependent on objects in this schema are not imported unless the other schema is also mentioned in the schema list. The source for this can be a full export dump file or a schema level export dump file or another database using a Network_Link.

- **Table Import**   This allows for the import of tables or partitions and their dependent objects using the TABLES parameter. To import tables that are not in your schema, the imp_full_database role must be granted to you. The source for this can be a Full, Schema, Table, or Tablespace level dump file, or another database using a Network_Link.

- **Tablespace Import**   This can be used to load all of the tables that have been created in the given tablespace set using the TABLESPACES parameter. The source for this can be a Full, Schema, Table, or Tablespace level dump file, or another database using a Network_Link.

- **Transportable Tablespace (TTS)**   This differs from its siblings in that only the metadata is imported to the database for a given tablespace set, and it uses the TRANSPORT_TABLESPACES parameter. The metadata that was exported using a TTS export are imported into the target database and the data files need to be copied into the correct location as specified by the metadata (note that the paths can be changed). The source for this can be a transportable tablespace export dump file or a source database.

The parameters available with Data Pump Import can be seen using the command impdp help=y. A subset of the output from this, which contains the parameters along with a brief description, is shown next.

```
>impdp help=y
Keyword                   Description (Default)
----------------------------------------------------------------
ATTACH                    Attach to existing job, e.g., ATTACH [=job name].
CONTENT                   Specifies data to load where the valid keywords
                          are (ALL), DATA_ONLY, and METADATA_ONLY.
DIRECTORY                 Directory object to be used for dump, log, and
                          sql files.
DUMPFILE                  List of dumpfiles to import from (expdat.dmp),
                          e.g., DUMPFILE=scott1.dmp, scott2.dmp,
                          dmpdir:scott3.dmp.
ESTIMATE                  Calculate job estimates where the valid keywords
                          are (BLOCKS), SAMPLING, and STATISTICS.
EXCLUDE                   Exclude specific object types, e.g.,
                          EXCLUDE=TABLE:EMP.
FLASHBACK_SCN             SCN used to reset the session snapshot.
FLASHBACK_TIME            Time used to get the SCN closest to the
                          specified time.
FULL                      Import everything from source (Y).
HELP                      Display help messages (N).
INCLUDE                   Include specific object types, e.g.,
                          INCLUDE=TABLE_DATA.
JOB_NAME                  Name of import job to create.
LOGFILE                   Log file name (import.log).
NETWORK_LINK              Name of remote database link to the source
                          system.
NOLOGFILE                 Do not write logfile.
PARALLEL                  Change the number of active workers for current
                          job.
PARFILE                   Specify parameter file.
QUERY                     Predicate clause used to import a subset
                          of a table.
REMAP_DATAFILE            Redefine datafile references in all DDL
                          statements.
REMAP_SCHEMA              Objects from one schema are loaded into
                          another schema.
REMAP_TABLESPACE          Tablespace object is remapped to another
                          tablespace.
REUSE_DATAFILES           Tablespace will be initialized if it already
                          exists (N).
SCHEMAS                   List of schemas to import.
SKIP_UNUSABLE_INDEXES     Skip indexes that were set to the Index Unusable
                          state.
SQLFILE                   Write all the SQL DDL to a specified file.
```

STATUS	Frequency (secs) job status is to be monitored where the default (0) will show new status when available.
TABLE_EXISTS_ACTION	Action to take if imported object already exists. Valid keywords: (SKIP), APPEND, REPLACE, and TRUNCATE.
TABLES	Identifies a list of tables to import.
TABLESPACES	Identifies a list of tablespaces to import.
TRANSFORM	Metadata transform to apply (Y/N) to specific objects. Valid transform keywords: SEGMENT_ATTRIBUTES and STORAGE. e.g., TRANSFORM=SEGMENT_ATTRIBUTES:N:TABLE.
TRANSPORT_DATAFILES	List of datafiles to be imported by transportable mode.
TRANSPORT_FULL_CHECK	Verify storage segments of all tables (N).
TRANSPORT_TABLESPACES	List of tablespaces from which metadata will be loaded. Only valid in NETWORK_LINK mode import operations.
VERSION	Version of objects to export where valid keywords are (COMPATIBLE), LATEST, or any valid database version. Only valid for NETWORK_LINK and SQLFILE.

```
The following commands are valid while in interactive mode.
Command             Description (Default)
------------------------------------------  ----------------------
```

Command	Description (Default)
CONTINUE_CLIENT	Return to logging mode. Job will be re-started if idle.
EXIT_CLIENT	Quit client session and leave job running.
HELP	Summarize interactive commands.
KILL_JOB	Detach and delete job.
PARALLEL	Change the number of active workers for current job. PARALLEL=<number of workers>.
START_JOB	Start/resume current job.
STATUS	Frequency (secs) job status is to be monitored where the default (0) will show new status when available STATUS=[interval]
STOP_JOB	Stops job execution and exits the client.

The values in brackets in the preceding list are the default values in use for the parameter. Some parameters worth noting are as follows:

- EXCLUDE can be used to exclude metadata and dependent objects and data to be imported. To exclude data only, you must use data filtering through a query. Once an object has been excluded, all of its dependent objects will also be excluded.

- FLASHBACK_SCN and _TIME specify the system change number (scn) or time that the import will use as a point of consistency. In other words, the import will be performed in a manner in which the data is consistent with the time or scn listed. This is only used with a Network_Link, and specifies the scn or time from the source database.

■ INCLUDE is used to include metadata objects and dependent data during an import. This can include object types as well as object names. Only objects explicitly listed in the include statement will be imported. Employ a parfile when using this option.

■ NETWORK_LINK allows for an import into a target database directly from a source database rather than from a dump file that was previously exported.

■ PARALLEL is a performance option that specifies the maximum number of threads that can be used to speed up an import by running it in parallel.

■ PARFILE can be included to point to another file that includes import parameters. Use this when filtering data and metadata using the exclude, include, or query parameters.

■ QUERY is used to apply syntax similar to qualifiers that you would use in a select...where clause to filter rows to be imported. Use a parfile with this parameter.

■ Remap parameters include REMAP_DATAFILE, REMAP_SCHEMA, REMAP_TABLESPACE, and REMAP_DATAFILES. These allow you to change the names of data files, schemas, and tablespaces when moving objects from one database to another.

■ REUSE_DATAFILES should be used with extreme caution. When set to Y, existing data files will be used and data will be overwritten when a Create Tablespace operation is performed. The default is N, and a create tablespace command will fail when a dependent data file exists.

■ SQLFILE names a file where all of the DDL that would be executed will be written. So, rather than executing the DDL, it writes the statements to the SQLFILE named here.

■ TRANSPORT_TABLESPACES (TTS) specifies tablespaces that will have their metadata imported during a TTS operation. The data file copies and previously exported metadata can be used to plug in the tablespaces to a target database.

When exporting and importing, filters can be used on both data and metadata to restrict the rows to be imported. For data, restrictions on the rows to be imported are implemented with the query parameter, and the filter is executed once per table per job. For metadata, either the exclude or include parameters can be used and these are mutually exclusive commands. When filters are applied to metadata, the objects that are included will also have their dependent objects included.

Let's look at an example of data filtering where all data from all tables in the SH schema are exported except for the SALES table. We will then use the dump file created by this export in a separate import job that renames the schema and only imports one table. Here are the export script and parameter files:

```
expdp system/manager parfile=exp.par
```

Contents of the exp.par parameter file are shown here:

```
DIRECTORY=DPUMP_DIR
DUMPFILE=testsh.dmp
SCHEMAS=SH
EXCLUDE=TABLE:"in ('SALES')"
```

An import that uses the preceding dump file is shown next. Notice that we are importing a single table into a different schema SHNEW as specified by the REMAP_SCHEMA command. If the table already exists, then this will be skipped and the import will continue through the TABLE_EXISTS_ACTION parameter. Note that the SHNEW schema must already exist in the database with the proper authority to create all of the objects in it since this was a schema level export. In order to create the SHNEW schema with Data Pump Import, a full export would need to be run:

```
impdp system/manager parfile=imp.par
```

Contents of the imp.par file are shown here:

```
DIRECTORY=DPUMP_DIR
DUMPFILE=testsh.dmp
REMAP_SCHEMA=SH:SHNEW
TABLES=SH.PRODUCTS
TABLE_EXISTS_ACTION=SKIP
```

Progress Check ⏚

1. Describe the data and metadata that is exported with the following command:

   ```
   expdb system/manager dumpfile=testsh.dmp schemas=sh
   logfile = testsh.txt compression=DATA_ONLY
   ```

2. What is the result of the following export?

   ```
   expdb system/manager dumpfile=testsh.dmp full=Y
   EXCLUDE=TABLE:"LIKE'%'"
   ```

3. Why would you run a Data Pump export rather than an original Oracle export?

4. How does a transportable tablespace export and import differ from the others?

5. What makes the metadata export and import so useful and flexible?

CRITICAL SKILL 7.8

Use Traditional Export and Import

The original (non–Data Pump) Export and Import utilities that were used in previous versions can be found in Oracle Database 11*g*. However, we strongly recommend that you use the new Data Pump utilities, since they support all Oracle Database 11*g* features and will increase performance. Here, we'll briefly review the original Export and Import utilities since you'll be using them with earlier versions of Oracle.

Before running the original export and import, the catexp.sql catalog script needs to be run to prepare Oracle for these utilities and is invoked from the catalog.sql script. These scripts can be found in the ORACLE_HOME/rdbms/admin directory.

Once the catalog has been set up for export and import, you are ready to run the utilities. As with Data Pump, these utilities can be run as a command-line interface, by using parameter files or interactive commands.

To run an original export, issue the exp executable in a manner similar to using Data Pump. Use the following syntax to run a command-line export or an export using a parameter file or an interactive export, respectively:

```
exp user/password@SID parameter_list
exp PARFILE
exp system/manager full=y grants=y rows=y triggers=y buffer=10000000
direct=n consistent=Y constraints=Y compress=Y file=shexp.dmp
log=shexp.log
```

This can be transformed to a *user* export by replacing full=y with the owner parameter:

```
exp    (and respond interactively to the export requests)
```

To find all of the export and import syntax, issue the following command:

```
exp help=y
```

Progress Check Answers

1. The entire schema, including metadata and all table data, is exported to file testsh.dmp.

2. Although the FULL=Y option is used, all tables were excluded through the wildcard LIKE '%'. No tables were exported, nor were any table dependencies and metadata.

3. The Data Pump export provides considerable performance enhancements such as parallelism, and it supports all Oracle Database 11*g* features.

4. Data is not exported and imported using Transportable Tablespaces (TTS). Rather, all of the metadata associated with the objects are exported from the source database and imported into the target. The data files in the source database are placed in read-only mode and the files are copied to the target location before the TTS Import step begins.

5. The metadata is retrieved in XML format that can be used in many different ways. The REMAP_SCHEMA parameter facilitates object renames.

To run an original import, issue the imp executable in a manner similar to using Data Pump. Use the same syntax as for export in the previous example, except that the utility to be run is imp. The three types of import can be run as shown next:

```
imp user/password@SID parameter_list
imp PARFILE
imp system/manager FROMUSER=SH TOUSER=SHNEW ignore=y compile=y
destroy=n grants=y rows=y buffer=10000000 constraints=y
file=shexp.dmp log=shimp.log
imp    (and respond interactively to the export requests)
```

To find all of the export syntax, issue the following command:

```
imp help=y
```

The parameters for export and import are a little different than the Data Pump ones, but as with Data Pump, these can be run in different, mutually exclusive modes. They are

- Full export and import
- User export and import
- Table export and import
- transportable_tablespace export and import

These utilities can also be run in Direct Path or Conventional Path mode. Conventional Path performs the utilities as SQL statements that are more versatile than Direct Path exports. These can be used to move data across different server platform types or different Oracle versions. Direct path exports and imports are much faster than conventional ones, but they are also less versatile. A direct path export and import needs to be run on the same Oracle version and the same server platform. Conventional is the default and Direct is run with the DIRECT=Y parameter.

CRITICAL SKILL 7.9

Get Started with Recovery Manager

You have seen different ways to provide backup and recovery in this section as a matter of background and completeness. We will now look into the method that Oracle recommends you should be using or at least migrating to. This is *Recovery Manager (RMAN)*. The RMAN utility has been available since Oracle8*i* and has been improving steadily with each new release. With Oracle 11*g*, there are significant improvements with performance of RMAN, as well as enhancements to features that make validation of backup sets and copying of databases simpler.

RMAN is an Oracle tool that manages all backup and recovery activities, including backup, copy, restore and recovery of data files, control files, and archived redo logs. It is included with the Oracle server at no extra charge; Enterprise Manager's backup and recovery is based on RMAN. RMAN provides many benefits over other types of Oracle backup and recovery. It can

- Perform full and incremental backups
- Create backup scripting and automation
- Use its powerful reporting capabilities
- Be used in either a GUI or command-line mode
- Compress backups so that only blocks that have been written to are included
- Keep tablespaces from being put into backup mode, so no extra redo is generated.
- Verify backups and detect corrupt blocks
- Parallel and verify backups
- Back up data files, control files, archive redo logs, backup pieces, and spfiles
- Allow online restores of corrupt blocks
- Clone a database using the DUPLICATE command

RMAN Architecture

The RMAN architecture, shown in Figure 7-3, includes a target database, repository, and Media Management Layer, as well as Server Processes, Channels, Backup Sets, and Backup Pieces. The target database is the database that is either being backed up or restored. RMAN connects to the target database using server sessions.

The repository is a separate database or schema that contains the metadata about your target database, as well as all of the backup and recovery information connected with that database for maintenance purposes. It can keep track of all of the information about every backup that you perform, including all of the file information, the time of the backup, and the database *incarnation* (the database version) at the time of the backup. This information can all be used to restore files and recover the database by issuing very simple restore and recovery commands. All of the information needed to complete these operations is stored in the repository. This repository can be implemented in one of two ways:

- By using control files
- As a recovery catalog database

RMAN client

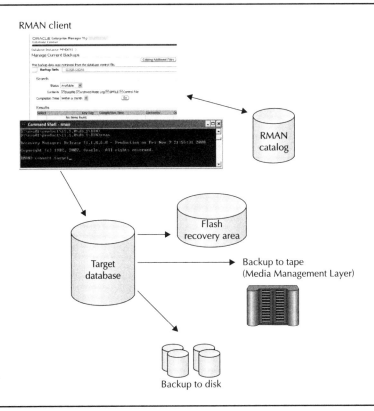

FIGURE 7-3. *RMAN architecture*

Control files are the default option for implementing a repository since backup information is written to control files making the recovery catalog optional. Using a control file, however, limits the functionality of RMAN, while a recovery catalog provides you with the use of all RMAN features (this option is strongly recommended). Some of the advantages that a recovery catalog gives include the following:

- The catalog will store the physical structure of the target database, as well as backups of data files, control files, and archive logs.

- You can store scripts of common tasks.

- Multiple databases can be managed from one location.

- Complete reporting capabilities

- Access to a longer history of backups and metadata

- Ability to perform recovery when control files are lost

■ A complete set of options when you try to restore from previous backup sets

■ More recovery flexibility and options

One disadvantage of using an RMAN recovery is that it needs to be managed itself. However, this is a small database or schema, so maintenance is minimal. Also, one RMAN catalog can manage multiple databases. Backups can be performed easily through a hot backup or database export. You also need to keep the recovery catalog in sync with the control files, which is performed with the RMAN-provided resync command.

TIP
When using RMAN, use the recovery catalog if it provides you with specific needed features that are above and beyond those provided by the control file.

The Media Management Layer (MML) is the third-party software that manages the reading, writing, loading, and labeling of backups to tape. This can be integrated with RMAN to streamline the process of backup, restore, and recovery from the database through to the tape library and keeps track of where files are cataloged on tape.

Oracle publishes a media management API that third-party vendors use to build software that works with RMAN. Tapes will, over time, become unavailable to the system after backups have been performed; the RMAN MML option will perform crosschecks to determine if backup pieces are still available to the system. Missing backups will be marked as "Expired." This can be run as follows:

`RMAN> crosscheck backup;`

The preceding code checks that the RMAN catalog is in sync with the backup files on disk or the media management catalog.

Channels are server processes that are used to read and write backup files, connect to your target database and to the catalog, and to allocate and open an I/O channel for backup or recovery using tape (called *sbt* in RMAN) or disk. Many configuration options can be set up through channels, such as implementing a degree of parallelism for a backup operation or configuring default settings to be used for a specific channel. Allocating a channel starts a server process at the target server and establishes a connection between the RMAN and the target. A channel can do things such as determine the maximum size of files, the maximum rate files are read, the maximum number of files open at one time, the number of processes accessing a device simultaneously, or the type of I/O device disk or sbt_tape. A channel will be allocated for you automatically using default options unless you explicitly allocate a channel and specify overriding options for the channel in effect.

Backup sets are a complete set of backup pieces that constitute a full or incremental backup of the objects specified in the Backup command. Each backup creates a backup set that is composed of one or more backup pieces which are just the backups of a number of data files. The backup sets are in an RMAN proprietary format.

Set Up a Recovery Catalog and Target Database

Setting up a recovery catalog is a very simple process. This can be done through the Enterprise Manager GUI or through some simple commands in SQL*Plus and the RMAN command-line interface. In SQL*Plus, all you need to do is to create a tablespace to store the catalog data in, create an RMAN user, and then grant the recovery_catalog_owner role to the RMAN user. In RMAN, run the create catalog statement:

```
SQL>create tablespace rcatts datafile '/u01/oradata/rcatts.dbf'
size 1024M;
SQL>create user rcat identified by rcat temporary tablespace temp
default tablespace rcatts quota unlimited on rcatts;
SQL>grant connect, resource, recovery_catalog_owner to rcat;
```

In the RMAN command-line interface, log in and create the catalog:

```
$ rman catalog=rmancat/rmancat
RMAN> create catalog
```

Now you need to register the target database in the catalog. To do this, connect to the target and the catalog database and then register the target database in the catalog. This can be done from either location. The target connection must have a user ID with sysdba privileges, so an Oracle password file must be created using the orapwd utility. As described in Chapter 3, you also need to create the Oracle networking configuration using tnsnames or an equivalent for both the target and recovery catalog instances:

```
$ rman
RMAN> connect catalog rmancat/rmancat@sid
RMAN> connect target sys/pwd@sid
RMAN> register database;
```

Key RMAN Features

You are now ready to start using RMAN, but before going too far, let's take a quick tour of some RMAN features.

Stored Scripts

A *stored script* is a set of RMAN commands that are stored in the recovery catalog. These can be used to perform tasks such as backup restore, recovery, or reporting. This option allows you to develop, test, and save commands, as well as minimize the potential for operator errors. Each script relates to one target database only. The following is a sample stored script that allocates a channel and performs an incremental level 0 full database backup. The current log is archived and all archive logs are then backed up and deleted:

```
RMAN> create script b_whole_l1 {
allocate channel c1 type disk;
backup
       incremental level 0
       format "/u01/backup/b_t%t_s%s_p%p"
       database plus archivelog;
 }
```

Archive Log Management

As shown in the preceding script, RMAN can back up archive logs to tape and then delete the online versions once they have been successfully backed up. This is a great space saver!

Backup and Restore Optimization

RMAN can optimize backups so files that have not changed are not backed up. This will save you from performing repeated backups of read-only files. Also, new with Oracle 11g, the data in the UNDO tablespace that is already committed and is not needed for recovery is not backed up. In the same manner, restores are optimized so that online files that have not been changed since the last backup will not be restored. This also allows restores to be restartable because the changes are tracked and the restore process can continue where it left off.

```
configure backup optimization {ON | OFF | CLEAR}
```

Corruption and Verification Checks

When RMAN moves a backup piece to another location, it verifies that the backup piece is not corrupt; a multiplexed copy will be used if a corruption is found. Archive logs are also checked in the same manner, with another archive log location used if a corruption is found. As part of backup, RMAN checks every data file block, performs verification checks, and logs the corrupted blocks. These can be viewed in the views v$backup_corruption for backup command; if the copy command is used, any corrupt block information will be in v$copy_corruption view. Each corrupt block encountered is also recorded in the control file and alert log. RMAN will not allow an unusable backup or corrupt restore to be performed.

Using VALIDATE, block corruption can be detected on backup sets and data files. On a restore the backup set can even be verified that there is no corruption before running the restore. VALIDATE can be run against the database, backup sets, or data files:

```
RMAN > validate database;
RMAN > validate backupset 7;
RMAN > validate datafile 10;
```

The validate command can also be used with the backup command to check for physical corruptions in the database as RMAN is backing up the data. The same thing is done with the restore command to make sure that the backup set can be used to restore the database. If there are no errors that appear after using validate restore, you should be able to use that backup set successfully. Otherwise, errors will appear either because of corruption to the backup set or because of missing data files that are needed for the recovery:

```
RMAN > backup validate database archive log all;
RMAN > restore database validate;
RMAN > restore archive log all validate;
```

Configuration and Default Settings

RMAN allows you to set defaults once for all of your backup and recovery jobs using the configure command. (These can be overridden when needed.) The configure settings are stored in the control file and recovery catalog once synched, and can all be displayed with the show all command in RMAN. An example of an extremely valuable setting is the one that follows which directs RMAN to automatically back up the control file after every backup, or every copy in RMAN, or in a Run block:

```
configure controlfile autobackup;
```

Channels can be allocated automatically by RMAN, and when configuration defaults are applied to a channel these can also be applied automatically. To configure a channel to have a default file format, a configure command such as the one listed next can be issued:

```
Configure channel 1 device type disk format
'/orarecover/backup/db01/tp_%U';
```

Redundancy vs. Recovery Windows

An important backup management consideration is to determine how long backups should be kept and then to automate the implementation of your policy. RMAN helps you with this through the mutually exclusive commands *redundancy* and *recovery window*. Redundancy specifies the number of backups to be kept before RMAN will start to delete backup files. This is very good for controlling disk space. For example, to start deleting backups after four backups have been taken, issue the following command:

```
configure retention policy to redundancy 4;
```

A recovery window specifies the amount of time that point-in-time recovery should be able to go back to, which is specified in days. To make point-in-time recovery possible up to the last 15 days and to make backups taken more than 14 days ago obsolete, issue the following command:

```
configure retention policy to recovery window of 15 days;
```

Block Media Recovery

Individual blocks can now be recovered from backups and this option is only available with RMAN. The database stays up while the blocks are being recovered but the blocks being recovered remain unavailable until the recovery is complete. This speeds up recovery if only a small number of blocks need to be recovered. The DBA specifies which block to recover by entering a corrupt block address that can be found in the v$backup_corruption view, the v$copy_corruption view, or in the alert log.

Trial Recovery

A trial recovery can be performed, which lets you find all of the corrupt blocks in a database. You perform a trial recovery by adding the parameter test to the end of a recover command.

Reporting

A major advantage of RMAN is that it gives you the ability to run lists and reports on the repository. Lists allow you to display the contents of the RMAN repository, such as image copies (exact copy of a data file), archive log files, or control files that can be used for a recovery or creating different incarnations of the database, among other things. Reports provide a more detailed analysis and can help you determine what should be done. Reports help identify objects that have not been backed up lately, backups that are obsolete and can be deleted, or data files that are not recoverable, to mention a few. Such reports and lists are valuable in managing your backup and recovery environment.

To list backup sets and their detailed files and pieces, run the following:

```
List backup by file
```

To report on backups that are no longer needed because they exceed the retention policy:

```
Report obsolete
```

Along with the LIST command for seeing the information about the backup sets, you can also preview the restore and see the summary for the restore:

```
Restore database preview summary
```

Backups

Oracle RMAN backups can be performed either as image copies or as backups. Image copies are a complete copy of the binary data files used in the database and can be used by both RMAN or user-managed backup and recovery. Backup sets, on the other hand, are in a proprietary RMAN format, with each set consisting of one or more files called *backup pieces*. These backups can only be used by RMAN, but have the advantage of performing unused block compression and incremental backups. Image copies can only be made to disk, while backup sets can be made to disk or tape.

When performing database backups, RMAN supports both full and incremental backups. A *full* backup will copy all used blocks in the data files specified. An *incremental* backup, on the other hand, only backs up those blocks that have changed since the previous incremental backup. Incremental backups require a *level 0* backup, which is similar to a full backup except that it serves as a baseline to allow future incremental backups. Incremental backups can save recovery time when compared to the time that may be needed to apply archive logs, and they take up less disk space and network resources than full backups. Believe it or not, before Oracle Database 11*g*, incremental backups ran as slow as or slower than full backups because table scans needed to be performed to find the blocks that had changed. This has changed with Oracle Database 11*g* and has continued to improve because a block-change tracking file consisting of bitmaps is used, rather than performing full table scans to discover changed blocks.

In order to back up a database, the target database must be either open or mounted so that RMAN can access the control file before performing a backup. If the database is mounted, it needs to have a consistent backup (that is, it must NOT have been abnormally terminated), and the control file must be current. Backups can be performed as either offline or online, and the target database must be placed in archivelog mode to allow you to perform online backups.

- **Offline Backup**   This performs an immediate or normal shutdown, followed by a startup mount. This does not require archivelog mode.

- **Online Backup**   For this to be done, the database must be open and in archivelog mode.

To help manage your backup and recovery space, a *Flash Recovery Area* should be created as the storage area for most of your backup and recovery files. Archive logs can be placed here; if possible, the Flash Recovery Area should be large enough to handle two complete backup cycles for your database, including the archive logs. The backup retention policy for either recovery window or redundancy is used to manage space in the Flash Recovery Area. The Flash Recovery Area is an Oracle-managed area that can be used to store all of the files required for backup and recovery, including RMAN backups.

RMAN Using Enterprise Manager

We just walked you through some basic setup and features of RMAN; using RMAN in Enterprise Manager is just as simple. Under backup settings (see the following illustration), you can choose whether backups go to disk or tape, the level of parallelism, and whether they are compressed or an image copy. The backups can be tested here as well.

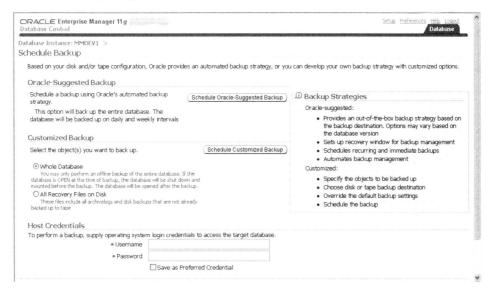

Scheduling the backups can be planned on the Schedule Backup screen (shown next) after configuring what is to be backed up and where.

Just as with using the list or preview of the RMAN backup sets, you can manage Oracle backups under Enterprise Manager in the following screen. You can review the backup sets that are available and what is current. Settings are available for backup sets as well as for image copies. It is also a good way to manage obsolete and expired sets and files. Crosschecking is an option here too, which will resynchronize the RMAN catalog with the available files.

Performing a recovery using Oracle Enterprise Manager, as shown in the following illustration, allows for either complete recovery or point in time. There is also an advisor to help manage the recovery process and help you detect to what point the database might need recovery.

Now that you're familiar with the options available through RMAN as well as some of the features available through Oracle Enterprise Manager, you're ready to back up a database.

Performing Backups

There are a number of ways that RMAN backups can be performed. In this section, you will see several examples of the basic set of backups. Namely, you will see an example of a database, data file, tablespace, and incremental backup, as well as an image copy.

Database Backup

An RMAN database backup can be as simple or as complex as you want to make it. In its simplest form, you can preconfigure channel defaults as discussed previously, connect to the catalog and the target, and then run the backup command:

```
RMAN > connect catalog rmancat/rmancat@test2
RMAN > connect target sys/lexus4me@TEST1
RMAN > backup database;
```

Data File Backup

It doesn't get any easier than that! Let's now look at a backup that allocates one channel and backs up three data files using parallelism. The archive logs are then backed up:

```
RMAN > run {
RMAN > configure device type disk parallelism 3;
RMAN > allocate channel c1 type disk;
RMAN > allocate channel c2 type disk;
RMAN > allocate channel c3 type disk;
RMAN > backup database plus archivelog;}
```

Tablespace Backup

A tablespace backup is performed along with a backup of the control file and archivelog. Of course, the tablespace backup is implemented by RMAN as a series of data file backups:

```
RMAN > backup tablespace EXAMPLE include controlfile plus archivelog;
```

Incremental Backup

You can configure default settings for a channel and then perform an incremental level 1 backup. You need to perform an incremental level 0 backup first to provide a baseline for this incremental to be compared to. If an incremental level 0 does not exist, then this level 1 backup will be changed to level 0. Check the output of your backup run to make sure that the backup ran exactly as you expected it to. Backup optimization will be used to ignore any data files that have not changed since the last backup was performed. A backup script will be used in this example:

```
replace script BackupTEST1 {
configure backup optimization on;
configure channel device type disk;
sql 'alter system archive log current';
backup database incremental 2 cumulative database;
release channel d1;
}
run {execute script BackupTEST1;}
```

Image Copy

An image copy can be performed using the RMAN copy command. Next you'll see a copy of a system data file to a named location. As you can see, there are no begin backup and end backup statements. The syntax is simple and RMAN performs the copy without incurring extra logging overhead:

```
RMAN > run { allocate channel c1 type disk;
RMAN > copy datafile 1 to '/u01/back/system.dbf';}
```

You've only done the first part of the job, but as you can see, the commands are relatively simple. We now need to think about how to use these backups in a recovery situation. Fortunately, the RMAN toolset also simplifies our restores and recoveries a great deal! Let's take a look at an example of how we can recover a database with RMAN.

Restore and Recovery

RMAN can automate file restores and can be used to restore data files, control files, and archived redo logs. In this example, you will see a full restore and recovery where the control file is restored from backup and the archive logs that we need are also restored. We have changed the archive log directory destination to write the archive log restores to. Notice that there is no mention of file names in this script. The recovery catalog has kept track of all of the files for us and if files were stored on tape, the Media Management Layer software may have also assisted with this:

```
RMAN> connect catalog rmancat/rmancat@ora11g
RMAN> connect target sys/change_on_install@ora11g

MAN> replace script fullRestoreTEST1 {
allocate channel ch1 type disk;
# Set a new location for logs
set archivelog destination to '/TD70/sandbox/TEST1/arch';
startup nomount;
 restore controlfile;
alter database mount;
restore database;
```

```
recover database;
alter database open resetlogs;
release channel ch1;
}
host 'echo "start `date`"';
run {execute script fullRestoreTEST1;}
host 'echo "stop `date`"';
exit
```

That's it! This script is simple and very powerful. We've now covered some basic RMAN backup options to give you an overview of how you can use RMAN on your databases. You should now test out various backup and recovery options to see how they function and how well the different options work in your environment. The settings that you use on one set of servers may not be the ones you will use on another, so testing your RMAN backup and recovery setup is essential!

Project 7-1 RMAN End to End

This project will have you using RMAN from start to finish. We will first assume that you have two Oracle databases to work with: the target database will be called ora11g in this project and the catalog database will be called oracat. You will first set up the RMAN catalog and then connect to the target database and register that database in the catalog. A full database backup will be performed, and once that has been successfully completed, you will use that backup to perform a full database restore using RMAN. Look carefully at the output that RMAN produces to help better understand what is going on behind the scenes. Once you've completed this project, you will have used RMAN from end to end and will be comfortable with basic RMAN functionality.

Step by Step

1. In SQL*Plus, create the RMAN tablespace, catalog, and user named rcat. Grant the authority that user rcat needs to perform all RMAN operations:

```
> export ORACLE_SID=oracat
SQL> sqlplus /nolog
SQL> connect sys/change_on_install as sysdba
SQL> create tablespace rcatts datafile
'/u01/oradata/oracat/rcatts.dbf' size 50M;
SQL> create user rcat identified by rcat temporary tablespace
temp default
SQL> tablespace rcatts quota unlimited on rcat;
SQL> grant connect, resource, recovery_catalog_owner to rcat;
SQL> exit
```

(continued)

2. Your RMAN environment and user have now been created, so you need to go into RMAN to create the recovery catalog. Note that you are using a recovery catalog here rather than the control file; we strongly encourage using this approach. You first log into the catalog, connect with the rcat user, and then run the create catalog command:

```
> rman catalog=rcat/rcat@oracat
RMAN> catalog rcat/rcat@oracat
RMAN> create catalog;
RMAN> exit;
```

3. Register the target database ora11g with the RMAN catalog. Once you've completed this, you will be connected to both the target database and a fully functional catalog and will be ready to begin issuing RMAN commands:

```
RMAN> connect catalog rcat/rcat@oracat
RMAN> connect target sys/manager@ora11g
RMAN> register database;
```

4. It's now time to back up your entire database. You'll start by applying a couple of configuration settings to set the default backup device to disk and to state that you always want to back up the control file and spfile with every backup. The spfile is automatically included with control file backups. Once these are configured, you can back up the database, archivelogs, control file, and spfile. This sounds like a lot of work, but just look at how easy this is to do with RMAN:

```
RMAN> configure default device type to disk;
RMAN> configure controlfile autobackup on;
RMAN> backup database plus archivelog;
RMAN> exit;
```

5. Once the backup has completed successfully, you'll want to set up the environment for a restore. To do this, shut down the database and delete all of the data files, archive logs, control files, and the spfile SPFILEORA11G.ora for the target database.

6. Now for the big test! The database restore and recovery is the one thing that absolutely tests how well we've done everything so far. Once again in RMAN, connect to the catalog and target and then put the database in nomount mode. Once that's done, restore the archive logs and control files, and then mount the database. You should now see these files in their proper location. Restore the database and watch the files being created in another window. Once that's complete, recover the database and open it up:

```
RMAN> connect catalog rcat/rcat@oracat
RMAN> connect target sys/manager@ora11g
RMAN> startup nomount;
RMAN> restore archivelog all;
RMAN> restore controlfile;
```

```
RMAN> alter database mount;
RMAN> restore database;
RMAN> recover database;
RMAN> alter database open resetlogs;
```

The resetlogs step at the end of the listing is needed to create new log files. This creates a new incarnation (that is, version) of the database and it should be backed up immediately.

Project Summary

This project has taken you from the very first step of setting up RMAN through a full backup, restore, and recovery. Congratulations! You have successfully completed the RMAN fundamentals and are now ready to explore it further and exploit this powerful tool in your own environment.

☑ Chapter 7 Mastery Check

1. What are some advantages of cold backups, and when would you use them?

2. What are disadvantages of cold backups?

3. Describe the difference between a logical and a physical backup.

4. Name three different types of backups.

5. What is the difference between an RMAN backup and an RMAN image copy?

6. Under what situations should redo logs be restored in a recovery situation?

7. Name three interfaces that can be used to perform a Data Pump Export and Import.

8. List some advantages of using RMAN.

9. Why would RMAN's recovery catalog be used to implement the repository rather than a control file?

10. Are there any disadvantages to an RMAN recovery catalog?

11. How can default settings be set up by you for future runs of RMAN?

12. What is an RMAN backup set and how does it relate to a backup piece?

13. Describe the ways in which corrupt blocks can be detected and recovered.

14. What are some advantages to incremental image copies?

15. When performing a recovery from a hot backup, do all files and tablespaces need to be brought forward to the same point in time?

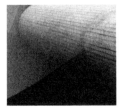

CHAPTER
8

High Availability: RAC, ASM, and Data Guard

CRITICAL SKILLS

igh availability and reducing planned (or even unplanned) downtime is a goal of database systems, especially in environments that require accessibility 24x7. It is unacceptable to have databases go down for maintenance or even for hardware failures, since these outages can cause significant losses to the business. Luckily, Oracle 11*g* is here to save the day with high availability features such as Real Application Clusters (RAC), Automatic Storage Management (ASM), and Data Guard. In architecting database environments, the combinations of RAC and Data Guard will provide instance failover and even disaster recovery to an offsite standby server. In planning the configurations and combinations, you must look at cost-effective ways to provide the business with the availability that they require. Examining the features and how to implement them will assist you in providing a plan for a reliable, scalable, and stable environment that can handle the loss of a piece of hardware or be recoverable in the event of an unplanned circumstance. Let's also not forget the need for maintenance of the databases in Oracle 11*g*. With the rolling patches working by patching one node of a cluster and then continuing to the next node so at least one node is available while patching, even the planned maintenance window now becomes smaller.

CRITICAL SKILL 8.1

Define High Availability

What does high availability mean to the business? What is the level of risk tolerance? How much data loss is acceptable? Are there current issues with backups or reporting? These are all questions that need to be asked to start mapping out the components that are needed. You may decide that absolutely no data loss can be tolerated or, alternatively, that it is fine if the application is down for a day or two.

Also, it helps to look at what kind of outages can happen and then build in fault tolerance for these situations. Examples of unplanned outages are hardware failures, such as disk or server failures; human error, such as dropping a data file or making a bad change; and network and site failures. Then, add on to these examples the planned outages needed for applying patches, database changes and migrations, and application changes that might include table and database object changes and upgrades. Look for the areas in the system with single points of failure and then match up solutions to start to eliminate those areas.

This chapter just touches on a couple of areas necessary for building a highly available environment: Real Application Clusters, Automatic Storage Management, and Data Guard. Understanding these components, plus researching other Oracle options such as Flashback Query, Transaction and Database, Flash Recovery Area, Data Recovery Advisor, and Secure Backups, will assist in synching up the environment with the business needs in the area of availability.

So, in looking at the application and the business needs, if there are planned outages for maintenance to allow for downtime to patch the environment, rolling patches might not be as much of a concern. Instead, a solution for testing application changes as well as the patches might be possible via Flashback technologies or the ability to test application changes on a production-like server. If the business doesn't allow for downtime or a regular maintenance window, and you know each minute down will cost the company a serious amount of money, you can use a combination of components for the solution: rolling patches, prevention of outages from hardware failures, having failover servers through clusters, and Data Guard.

Working with the business teams and having some understanding of different options available for architecting a solution that meets budget restrictions and business needs will take some discussions and planning. The rest of this chapter will give you an understanding of some of these areas and what it takes to implement them.

CRITICAL SKILL 8.2

Understand Real Application Clusters

Oracle Real Application Clusters (RAC) provides a database environment that is highly available as well as scalable. If a server in the cluster fails, the database instance will continue to run on the remaining servers or nodes in the cluster. With Oracle 11*g* Clusterware, implementing a new cluster node is made simple. RAC provides possibilities for scaling applications further than the resources of a single server, which means that the environment can start with what is currently needed and then servers can be added as necessary. Oracle 9*i* introduced the Oracle Real Application Clusters; with each subsequent release, management as well as implementation of RAC have become more straightforward, with new features providing a stable and good performance environment.

In Oracle 11*g*, Oracle introduced rolling patches for the RAC environment. Previously, it was possible to provide ways to minimize downtime by failing over to another node for patching, but it would still require an outage to finish patching all of the nodes in a cluster. Now with Oracle 11*g*, the patches can be applied allowing other servers to continue working even with the non-patched version. Reducing any outages, planned or unplanned, in companies with 24x7 operations is key. Along the same lines of the rolling patches, the deployment of new RAC instances and nodes has been significantly enhanced in 11*g*. The Oracle Clusterware is the piece that helps in setting up new servers and can clone an existing ORACLE_HOME and database instances. Also, it can convert a single node Oracle database into a RAC environment with multiple nodes.

The RAC environment consists of one or more server nodes; of course a single server cluster doesn't provide high availability, because there is nowhere to failover to. The servers or nodes are connected through a private network, also referred to as an *interconnect*. The nodes share the same set of disks, and if one node fails, the other nodes in a cluster take over.

A typical RAC environment has a set of disks that are shared by all servers; each server has at least two network ports: one for outside connections and one for the interconnect (the private network between nodes and a cluster manager). The shared disk cannot just be a simple file system because it needs to be cluster aware, which is the reason for Oracle Clusterware. Oracle 11*g* made several improvements with the Oracle Clusterware, which now provides several interfaces for managing the cluster. RAC still supports third-party cluster managers, but the Oracle Clusterware provides the hooks for the new features for provisioning or deployment of new nodes and the rolling patches. The Oracle Clusterware is also necessary for Automatic Storage Management (ASM), which will be discussed in the later part of this chapter.

The shared disk for the clusterware is comprised of two components: a voting disk for recording disk membership and an Oracle Cluster Registry (OCR) that contains the cluster configurations. The voting disk needs to be shared and can be raw devices, Oracle Cluster File System files, ASM, or NTFS partitions. The Oracle Clusterware is the key piece that allows all of the servers to operate together.

Without the interconnect, the servers do not have a way to talk to each other; without the clustered disk they have no way to have another node to access the same information. As seen in Figure 8-1, this is a basic setup with these key components. Next we will look at how to set up and install these pieces of the RAC environment.

CRITICAL SKILL 8.3
Install RAC

Before runInstaller or setup.exe is even executed, a checklist of pre-installation steps needs to be completed. These vary from network setup to making sure the proper disk is in place. Also before the database is even installed on one of the nodes for

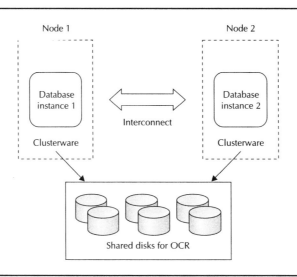

FIGURE 8-1. *RAC components*

RAC, the clusterware needs to be present. Several of these steps only need to be done once to set up the backbone of the RAC environment no matter how many nodes are being installed. Then tools for cloning the configuration can be used for deployment of new nodes in the cluster.

Each server needs to be set up with the needed kernel parameters and system parameters that are required for the operating system. (Please refer back to Chapter 2 for more details on installing Oracle.) Just as there were steps that needed to be completed for that install, network addresses and the shared disks need to be configured before Clusterware is installed.

Configurations for network addresses and connections are different from a standalone database. There are three different IP addresses that are needed: the virtual network, the private network (interconnect), and the normal or public network. The hosts need a non-domain name listed for each node in the /etc/hosts files on the nodes as well as the IP addresses. That is, each host will have at least three listings in the /etc/hosts files, and each one will have its own unique IP address and alias or name for the host.

```
cat /etc/hosts
#eth0 - Public Network
mmrac1.domain1.com            mmrac1
mmrac2.domain1.com            mmrac2
#eth1 - Private/Interconnect Network
10.0.0.1       mmrac1priv.domain1.com       mmrac1priv
10.0.0.2       mmrac2priv.domain1.com       mmrac2priv
#VIPs - Virtual Nework
192.168.10.104    mmrac1vip.domain1.com        mmrac1vip
192.168.10.05     mmrac2vip.domain1.com        mmrac2vip
```

The public and private networks need to be configured on the same adapter for all of the nodes. So from the example host file, all of the nodes in the cluster must have eth0 set to the public network and eth1 to the private. These nodes should be tested and reachable by pinging them. The interconnect network should be reserved for traffic between the nodes only, and it is even recommended that it have its own physically separate network. (This means with hardware setup there should have been at least two network adaptors installed.) This will certainly help with the performance of the cache fusion, which is the memory sharing of the buffer caches between the nodes.

The shared disk needs to be available to be able record the configuration about the cluster being installed. This disk will house the Oracle Cluster Registry and the cluster membership.

There should be multiple voting disks available to the Oracle Cluster; if not added at installation, disks can be added, backed up, and restored if necessary. To add disks, the following must be run as root; the path is the fully qualified name for the disk that is being added:

```
crsctl add votedisk css path -force
```

Verify by pulling a current list of voting disks:

```
crsctl query css votedisk
```

To back up voting disks in Linux/Unix, run the following:

```
dd if=voting_disk_name of=backup_file_name
```

In Windows, use the following:

```
ocopy voting_disk_name backup_file_name
```

To restore voting disks in Linux/Unix, run the following:

```
dd if=backup_file_name of=voting_disk_name
```

In Windows, use the following:

```
ocopy backup_file_name voting_disk_name
```

With all of these different pieces needed before RAC can even be installed, the importance of verifying and checking the configurations is extremely high. When installing the clusterware, it is critical that the initial configuration of the virtual and private networks is set up properly. Verifying the network, disk, operating system, and hardware prerequisites is the first step for installation. The clusterware will not install properly if any of these requirements is missing. The option to install the Real Application Cluster when installing the Oracle software will not be available if the clusterware is not installed or installed correctly.

The Cluster Verification Utility (CVU) assists in this area and should be run before attempting to install the clusterware. It will verify the hardware and operating system prerequisites as well as the network configurations. From the software install directory run the following:

```
./runcluvfy.sh stage -pre crsinst -n mmrac1, mmrac2
```

Unknown outputs could mean that the user doesn't have privileges it needs to run the check, or a node is unavailable or having resource errors. Running cluvfy checks after clusterware is installed to verify the install and other prerequisites before the Oracle database install. Failures should be addressed here before attempting the database install, otherwise you may find yourself uninstalling and reinstalling many more times than necessary.

NOTE
Setting up users for the installs of Oracle Software, it might be wise to plan to have different logins for Clusterware and ASM. Using ASM and Clusterware, they should be set up in different Oracle homes from the instance and can have separate Oracle Software owners, which would be a best practice for security. You can create users such as crs, asm, and oracle, but they must share the same Oracle Software Inventory and have the oinstall group as primary.

Now that the requirements are in place, the installation of the clusterware is ready to go; by using the Oracle installer, the option should be available to install clusterware. If the installation of clusterware does not come up, then go back through and run the Cluster Verification Utility and fix any issues first. Figure 8-2 shows the network information that was configured for the three network addresses as well as the name of the cluster being defined.

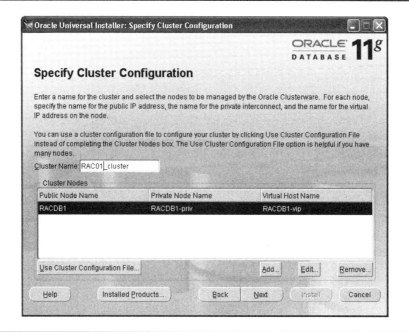

FIGURE 8-2. *Clusterware install*

After your clusterware is successfully installed, it's time to install Oracle Database because the framework has already been completed on the nodes. From the first node in the cluster, run the Oracle installer (runInstaller on linux/unix, setup.exe on Windows). Install the Enterprise Edition, which follows along the same path as a single instance, except for the Cluster installation choices (see Figure 8-3) after the location of the install information. The recommended path would be to just do a software install without creating the database, so that the software install can first be verified. Then, you can use the database configuration assistance to create the database on the nodes of the cluster.

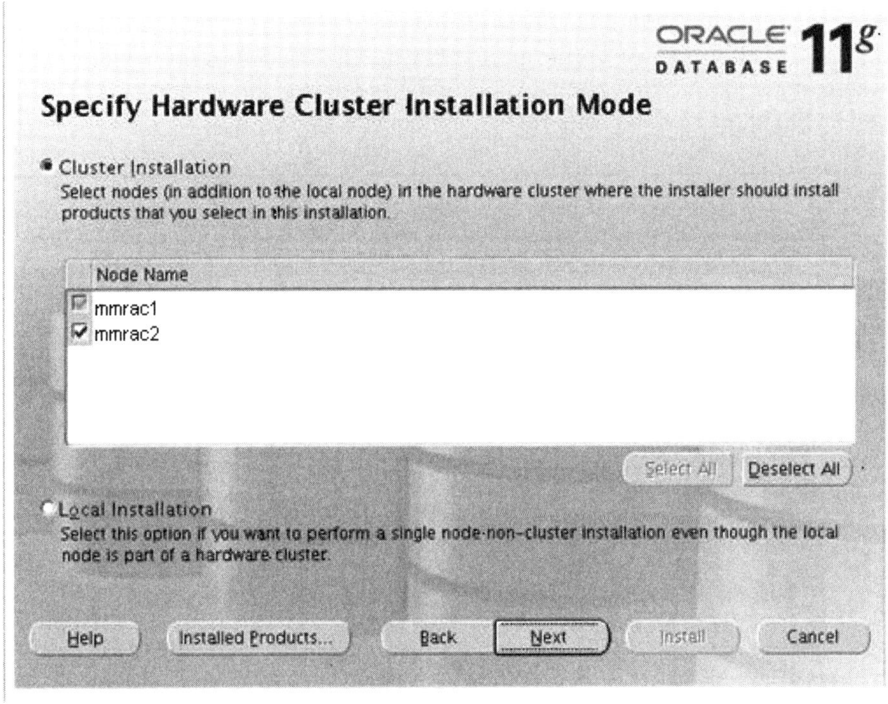

FIGURE 8-3. *RAC install*

Progress Check ⏱

1. How does RAC provide high availability?

2. What does the clusterware use the shared disks for?

3. What is the Cluster Verification Utility?

4. True or False: RAC components are shared disk, with at least two network connections and clusterware.

5. What is the private network used for in the RAC environment?

CRITICAL SKILL 8.4

Test RAC

RAC environments should first be created for testing and proving concepts for how the failover works for different applications. The RAC test environments should continue to be available for testing for production systems, because different workloads and failover can't be tested as against a single node. After the installs of the clusterware and database nodes, it's useful to test several different scenarios of failover in order to verify the install as well as to determine how the application fails over.

Create a test list and establish the pieces of the application that need to be part of that testing. Testing should include hardware, interconnect, disk, and operating system failures. Simulations of most of these failures are possible in the environment. Here is an example test list:

■ **Interconnect** Disconnect network cable from network adapter.

Progress Check Answers

1. Failover to another node when there are hardware issues with one of the nodes.

2. Oracle Cluster Registry and voting disk.

3. The utility you run to verify the environment before running the clusterware install.

4. TRUE

5. The private network is used for the interconnect, which allows the nodes to talk to each other directly and does a health check of the nodes.

- **Transaction failover when node fails**   Connect to one node, run the transaction, and then shut down the node; try with selects, inserts, updates and deletes.

- **Backups and restores**

- **Loss of a data file or disk**

- **Test load balancing of transactions**   Verify that the services are valid and are allowing for work load balancing.

Workload Manager

Using RAC databases on the backend of applications doesn't necessarily mean that the application is RAC aware. The application as a whole may not fail over, even though the database is failing over current transactions and connections. There might be a small outage when one of the nodes needs to fail over. However, with server calls about the failover, these events can be used to trigger automated processes for reconnecting or restarting application pieces. These are the Fast Application Notification events and can be used for failover and for workload balancing.

In Oracle 10*g*, having different pieces of the application connect to different nodes helped with load balancing in some ways, but now, thanks to the improvements in Oracle 11*g*, the Oracle Clusterware and the Load Balancing Advisor workload can be distributed across the RAC environment more effectively. Application workloads connect via a service, and it is by these services that load balancing as well as the failover is handled. The services are designed to be integrated with several areas of the database, and not just CPU resources. The advisor bases information on SERVICE_TIME and THROUGHPUT.

Ask the Expert

Q: Is tuning a RAC environment different than tuning single instances?

A: For a first look at tuning the RAC performance, the beginning steps are the same as with a single instance. The next step would be to look at interconnect performance and issues. The tools available to tune single instances are RAC aware, such as Automatic Workload Repository (AWR) reports, which detail the information collected about performance statistics, waits, long running SQL statements, and other details about how the database resources are being used. Oracle Enterprise Manager also provides good insight into issues, enabling you to see things at a cluster level.

ASM

As mentioned with the RAC environment, Automatic Storage Management (ASM) is both the file and disk manager for the Oracle database files. Now you might be thinking that this seems like a more advanced topic, and possibly too detailed for a beginner's guide. However, ASM is an important component in a highly available database environment and for addressing performance issues and management of Oracle files. Even after years of working with applications and databases, there is always I/O contention, and reading and writing to disk is a main part of what a database does. So, a database administrator ends up understanding more about disk, mirroring, and striping than they might really want to know. Debating different RAID strategies and optimizing I/O may seem like intermediate topics, but even some of these areas are handled by ASM and have simplified the management of the Oracle disk and file needs.

There are several more in-depth discussions and topics revolving around ASM, but this chapter will provide only a general introduction as well as the basic configuration and how to get started with ASM.

In large databases, the number of data files for an instance can grow out of control; even a tablespace for a large environment can become unmanageable. Then, any disk migrations or moving of tablespaces becomes a very difficult task and leaves areas of vulnerabilities open due to the sheer number of data files. ASM manages the files using disk groups, and disks are added to the disk groups even while the database is open and running and the ASM instance is being accessed.

CRITICAL SKILL 8.5

Set Up the ASM Instance

In Oracle 11*g*, the ASM instance can now be set up as a cluster for providing rolling patches, and one ASM instance manages the files for one RAC node or one single Oracle server. An ASM instance can manage the following files for all of the instances on each cluster node: control files, data files, tempfiles, spfiles, redo logs, archive logs, RMAN backups, Data Pump dumpsets, and flashback logs. Just as with the RAC instance, the ASM instance will fail over to the other nodes in the cluster and continue to manage the disk.

RAC is not necessary for using ASM. In fact, ASM can be installed on a single server as well as used in a RAC environment. However, an ASM instance is needed for each server. In Figure 8-4, you'll see two standalone servers, each with their own ASM instance. Even though each server needs its own ASM instance, one ASM instance can manage the files for more than one database instance on that server. Each of the databases for that ASM instance on that server has access to all of the disk groups, which are the available disks that have been allocated by creating groups.

As you can see in Figure 8-5, the difference with ASM instances in the RAC environment is that they are also instances that are available for failover; this means

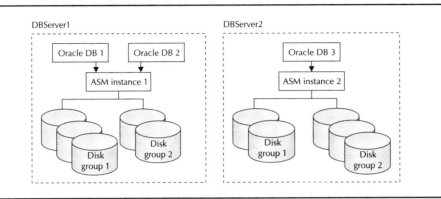

FIGURE 8-4. *ASM instance standalone*

that RAC components need to be available to manage the failover. An ASM instance is still created on each node, but the instances manage the disk groups and files across all of the nodes.

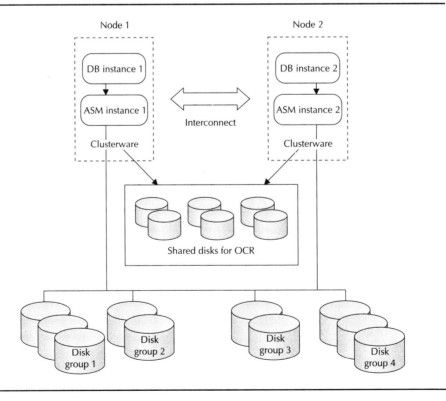

FIGURE 8-5. *ASM instance RAC*

An ASM instance is a small database instance because it is basically the memory structures, and this provides the framework for managing disk groups. The disk groups contain several physical disks and can be from different disk formats. The formats can be a raw disk partition, LUNS (hardware RAID), LVM (redundant functionality), or NFS (can load balance over NFS system and doesn't depend on the OS to support NFS). However, the advantage of ASM is using raw devices which bypass any OS buffering.

The ASM instance can be created on installation of the Oracle software or by using Database Configuration Assistant (dbca). The name of the instance normally starts with +ASM, and then the Oracle Cluster Synchronization Server (CSS) must be configured. This service is added with the localconfig script, which will add the OCR repository that is necessary for ASM. Also, there is a new role to log in as administrator of the ASM instance, SYSASM. The OS group of OSASM goes along with this new role.

The following are screenshots from creating the ASM instance using the Database Configuration Assistant or dbca. In walking through the configuration of a database, you have a choice to create a regular database or to configure Automatic Storage Management. If you want to create a database using ASM, the ASM instance needs to be created first. However, you can also migrate an existing database to ASM, allowing the instance to be created for that migration as well. Either way, the dbca (see Figure 8-6) provides an easy way to get the ASM instance created.

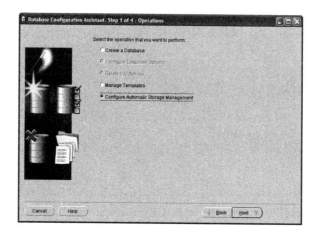

FIGURE 8-6. *Creating ASM instance in dbca*

If the Oracle Cluster Synchronization Server (CSS) has not yet been started, a message will come up that says it needs to be running in order to configure ASM. Another window can be opened to start this; the command is provided in the pop-up window as shown in Figure 8-7.

Now the ASM instance is ready to be created, so a click on OK, as shown in Figure 8-8, will create the ASM instance. Now you'll just need to configure the parameters for finding the available disks and the disk groups.

In order for the ASM instance to discover the available disks, an initialization parameter is used: ASM_DISKSTRING. Other parameters include ASM_DISKGROUPS, which specifics which files are managed by ASM, and ASM_POWER_LIMIT, which is the default value for disk rebalancing. INSTANCE_TYPE is set to indicate that the instance is an ASM instance and not a database:

```
Parameters:
ASM_DISKGROUPS = CONTROLFILE, DATAFILE, LOGFILE
ASM_DISKSTRING = /dev/rdsk/*
ASM_POWER_LIMIT = 0  /* 0 to 11 0 disables and 11 to enable
rebalancing more quickly */
INSTANCE_TYPE = ASM
```

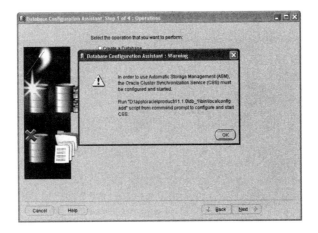

FIGURE 8-7. *Creating ASM instance (CSS)*

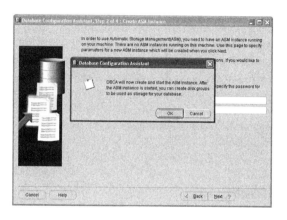

FIGURE 8-8.   *Creating ASM instance (Completion)*

Disk groups can be created during instance creation. After the instance is created, sqlplus is used to start up ASM.

Project 8-1   Install ASMLib

For Linux, there is an option for using raw devices or ASMLib to manage the available disks for Automatic Storage Management. ASMLib is a tool that will need to be installed as a Linux operating system package.

Step by Step

1. After installing the packages as the root user, the Linux software, and the Oracle software, the following packages are needed for the ASMLib:

```
# rpm -Uvh oracleasm-support-2.0.1.-1.i386.rpm
# rpm -Uvh oracleasmlib-2.0.1.-1.i386.rpm
# rpm -Uvh oracleasm-2.6.9-34.ELsmp-2.0.1-1.i686.rpm
```

2. Verify that the package is installed:

```
#  rpm -q oracleasm*
```

(continued)

3. The previous step installed the ASMLib software. Now, to configure, run the following:

```
# /etc/init.d/oracleasm configure
```

4. With the ASMLib software installed, the available partitions can be used to create ASM disks:

```
# /etc/init.d/oracleasm createdisk VOL1 /dev/disk1
# /etc/init.d/oracleasm createdisk VOL2 /dev/disk2
```

5. To view the disks from the OS level that were just created:

```
# /etc/init.d/oracleasm listdisks
VOL1
VOL2
```

Project Summary

This project has taken you through the steps to install the package needed for the ASMLib utility, as well as demonstrated some of the tasks that can be completed using this command-line utility. Having ASMLib configured will be useful for managing ASM disks and files.

CRITICAL SKILL 8.6

Create ASM Disk Groups

Starting up the ASM instance is very similar to a database instance. Instead of connecting as SYSDBA, SYASM should be used:

```
ORACLE_SID=+ASM
SQLPLUS /NOLOG
SQL> connect SYS as SYSASM
Enter password: sys_password
Connected to an idle instance.
SQL> STARTUP
ASM instance started
```

Shutdown is also similar to database instances, but the IMMEDIATE clause checks for databases that are still connected to the ASM instance and returns an error if this is the case. Any databases connected to the ASM instance during a shutdown abort will also abort:

```
SQL> SHUTDOWN NORMAL\IMMEDIATE\ABORT
```

The redundancy type for a DISKGROUP is specified when the group is created and cannot be changed. However new groups can be created with different redundancy types and then migrated to. There are three types of redundancy: EXTERNAL, NORMAL, and HIGH. With EXTERNAL, ASM is not providing any redundancy, and is assuming that an outside source is such as the storage array is providing fault tolerance. NORMAL requires two groups for failover and will handle the failure of one group. HIGH redundancy provides three-way failover and needs three groups. The NORMAL and HIGH redundancies also eliminate the single point of failure for the ASM disk. A small number of disk groups can normally be used even for a large database.

Project 8-2   Create Disk Groups

The next steps will give the commands for creating disk groups with external redundancy or normal redundancy. Once the groups are created they are available to create tablespaces.

Step by Step

1. Create disk groups by using the following:

```
SQL> create diskgroup DGEXT1 external redundancy disk '/dev/rdsk1/disk1';
SQL> create diskgroup DGNORM1 normal redundancy disk
FAILGROUP controller1 DISK
'/dev/rdsk/disk1' name disk1,
'/dev/rdsk/disk2' name disk2
FAILGROUP controller2 DISK
'/dev/rdsk/disk3' name disk3,
'/dev/rdsk/disk4' name disk4;
```

2. Now that you've created the disk groups, validate them by looking at the views that give you information about disks and disk groups:

- **V$ASM_DISKS**   Available disks reflect values in the parameter ASM_DISKSTRING:

  ```
  select * from v$asm_disks;
  ```

- **V$ASM_DISKGROUPS**   Available disk groups and details on redundancy type:

  ```
  select name, state from v$asm_diskgroups;
  NAME              STATE
  --------------------     ------------------DGEXT1      MOUNTED
  DGNORM1           MOUNTED
  ```

3. Adding disks to the disk groups can be done as needed to be able to grow space for the databases:

```
alter DISKGROUP DGNORM1 add DISK
'/dev/rdsk/disk5' name disk5,
'/dev/rdsk/disk6' name disk6;
```

(continued)

4. After ASM is started and disk groups are created it is as simple as saying CREATE TABLESPACE ts_data1, or the disk group name can be used in place of the data file name as used in a non-ASM database:

```
Create tablespace DATATBS1 datafile '+DGNORM1' size 1024M;
```

Project Summary

This project walked through how to create and alter disk groups. After the creation of the disk groups, steps were taken to verify the disk groups were created or altered as expected.

Progress Check

1. What is a typical name for an ASM instance?

2. What does ASM stand for?

3. What are the three types of redundancy for disk groups?

4. What is the initialization parameter for ASM to discover the available disks?

5. How is the ASM Instance created?

CRITICAL SKILL 8.7

Use ASMCMD and ASMLIB

Managing ASM instances can be done through Oracle Enterprise Manager, as well as using the command line in sqlplus and ASMCMD, which is the ASM command-line utility. Oracle 11*g* ASMCMD has new commands to copy files, back up and restore metadata, and list and remap ASM files.

There are several new commands for the ASMCMD with Oracle 11*g*. The new commands are listed next:

- **cp** This copies files between ASM disk groups and copies files from disk groups to the operating system, for example:

```
ASMCMD >cp +DISKGRP1/MMDB.CTF1 /backups
```

Progress Check Answers

1. +ASM

2. Automatic Storage Management

3. NORMAL, HIGH, and EXTERNAL

4. ASM_DISKSTRING

5. Using the Database Configuration Assistant (dbca)

- **Lsdsk** This lists disk information, which is good for creating a list of disks an ASM instance uses.

- **md_backup** This creates a backup file containing the metadata for one or more disk groups to enable you to re-create the disk groups in the future.

- **md_restore** This restores a disk group using the backup from md_backup.

- **remap** This recovers bad blocks on a disk by moving a good copy to a different location on disk.

Next are other commands; this is not a complete list and you will start to see these are similar to linux/unix commands:

- **cd** This changes the directory.

- **du** This displays the total disk space.

- **exit** This exits out of ASMCMD command line.

- **find** This lists occurrences for the specified name.

- **ls** This lists the contents of the ASM directory (when logging into ASM, it starts in the / root directory).

- **mkdir** This creates ASM directories.

- **pwd** This displays the path of the current directory.

- **lsct** This lists information about current ASM clients.

Along with managing the ASM instances, there are performance improvements with Oracle 11*g* ASM, such as the Fast Mirror Resync. The time to recover from a failure is reduced because of improvements here. There are attributes for disk groups for these settings. DISK_REPAIR_TIME has a default of 3.6 hours, with the value determining how much faster the recovery time of the disks is. Faster rebalancing is also possible using RESTRICTED mode for the disk groups. ASM can be configured to read from a preferred mirror copy, which in a RAC environment means that nodes can read from their local storage mirrors instead of possibly having to go through a network with higher latencies.

As mentioned earlier, the rolling patching can be applied to the ASM instances as well as database instances when clustering ASM instances. Since ASM is dependent on the Oracle Clusterware, the clusterware must first be upgraded on all nodes before upgrading ASM. During the patching, normal database functions are possible, but changes to the disk group configurations are limited:

To start patching:
```
SQLPLUS> ALTER SYSTEM START ROLLING MIGRATION TO 11.1.2;
```

```
/*Then each ASM instance can be taken down and upgraded. After all the
upgrades have been completed the migration just needs to be stopped.*/
SQLPLUS> ALTER SYSTEM STOP ROLLING MIGRATION;
```

CRITICAL SKILL 8.8
Convert an Existing Database to ASM

Taking an instance from regular storage to ASM is actually a simple task, but this is making the assumption that the ASM instance has already been created. Using Oracle Enterprise Manager is probably the most straightforward way to do this.

Start by opening up Oracle Enterprise Manager and choosing the option to migrate to ASM. The screen shown in the following illustration is what comes up after you select to migrate to ASM. Migration requires to you to first choose the files to be migrated, which of course include database files, but can also include recovery type files, such as archive logs, backup, and control file copies. If not chosen, the log files and control files will remain on the current disk.

The next screen has options for choosing the disk groups that this database should migrate to.

The job can be scheduled to run as needed with the settings in the following screen. This does require some downtime of the database to run the migration.

The next step summarizes the selections, and then the final step is to submit the job, as shown next. The migration job can be monitored in OEM.

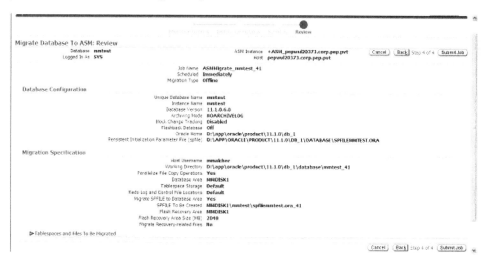

CRITICAL SKILL 8.9

Understand Data Guard

Providing highly available, recoverable, and secure stable environments is definitely a goal that needs several components for handling different areas. We have already discussed RAC and ASM; the Oracle Data Guard environment offers an additional piece to this architecture. Cluster servers normally reside in the same data center because of the requirements for the interconnect and clusters share disk. Because of this, there is potential for failure of this environment. Also, what about restores and disaster recovery sites? Data Guard can provide solutions in this area, as well as help offload some of the intense resource consumers such as hot backups, exports, and reporting. With Data Guard 11*g*, the standby server can be an active server that can be used to offload reporting and backups, as well as continue to operate in its standard role for failover and provide a disaster recovery server. Using Data Guard, one or more standby servers could be at different locations to allow for failover to a different site. So, for high availability, Data Guard provides solutions on both fronts of failover and recovery.

Data Guard has been available in some form since Oracle 8*i*; however, with 11*g* the secondary database can recover while it is open for reading. This means that ad hoc queries (ones that probably haven't been tuned and are resource hogs), reports, backups, and exports can be off-loaded to this system. Being able to use the failover hardware for useful business purposes makes it a cost-effective part of a disaster recovery plan.

The Data Guard manager provides a practical way to manage the primary and secondary servers. It can allow for manual failover, set up the automatic failover, and place the secondary in snapshot mode. The snapshot mode actually puts the database in read and write mode so that testing can be done against a current set of production data. More on this snapshot mode in a little bit, but first let's walk through some of the architecture and setup for Data Guard.

CRITICAL SKILL 8.10
Explain Data Guard Protection Modes

The different modes of setup for Data Guard allow for different configurations that are adaptive and that are dependent on available hardware, processes, and ultimately business needs.

The modes for the Data Guard configuration include maximum protection, maximum availability, and maximum performance. The Data Guard configuration can also have more than one standby database. Having multiple standby databases is even recommended in modes like maximum protection, in order to make sure at least one standby is available.

Maximum protection is designed for zero data loss, while the redo transport is synchronous. Synchronous transport means that you're applying the database transactions at the same time on the primary and secondary database servers. The primary waits for a response telling it that the transaction has been applied to the standby database before it commits the transaction. Having two standbys or even a RAC setup on the secondary site would be recommended in this situation, because if the standby fails, the primary will be halted in this mode.

Maximum availability also has the goal for zero data loss (again with the redo transport being synchronous). The difference is that if the standby fails or if there is a connectivity issue, it will allow the primary to continue and the standby to fall slightly behind. It is not as critical to have more than one standby for this mode because of the fault tolerance.

Maximum performance has the possibility of minimal data loss, but the performance is the concern on the primary. This is because the redo transport is done asynchronously and it doesn't have to check back with the primary before the primary does a commit. So, if transport is a concern for slowing down the primary database and the performance risk is higher than any data loss, the maximum performance mode will allow for that.

NOTE
It can be especially hard with discussions regarding costs and business expectations to come to an agreement on which mode to use. It is probably simplest to set the protection mode; the ability to use the standby server in very practical ways should help defray concerns. To set the protection mode for the database, issue the following statement:
ALTER DATABASE SET STANDBY DATABASE TO MAXIMIZE
(PROTECTION | AVAILABILITY | PERFORMANCE);

As discussed earlier, each mode has different services that take care of the transport and application:

- **Transport Services** are the pieces that handle the synchronous and asynchronous transport. These services move the log or transactions to available standby servers and verify that they are being applied to these servers. Synchronous transports validate that transactions have been applied on both primary and standby servers before committing the transactions. The asynchronous transport will validate that transactions have been sent, but transactions will be committed on the primary even if not completed on the standby.

- **Apply Services** take care of the SQL Apply or the Redo Apply. Apply Services take the SQL statements or redo logs and control applying them to the standby databases. SQL Apply takes the redo and transforms it into SQL statements. After running the SQL statements on primary and standby databases, the standby matches the primary database and can be used as a logical standby database. Redo logs are used for keeping the physical standby database consistent with the primary database. Redo information is applied to the standby databases by Redo Apply and controlled by the Apply Services.

- **Role Management Service** is for the switching of the standby to primary. This is used either for a planned switchover or for the failover due to an outage of one of the servers.

Figure 8-9 shows a configuration of the Data Guard environment and how the primary and standby servers do not even need to be in the same location. The servers can be in the same data center, down the street, or cities apart from each other, depending on the purpose and need. Having the servers in a different city provides high availability even in an event of a disaster in the location of the primary database. Also in Figure 8-9, notice the options that are available for uses of the

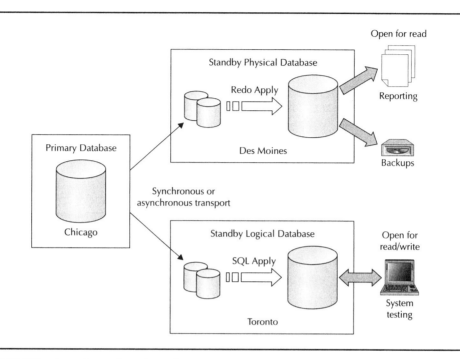

FIGURE 8-9. *Data Guard configuration*

standby server, such as reporting, system testing, or even running backups to take this type of load off of the primary server.

With Redo Apply, the standby database can be opened for read-only queries. The recovery on the standby is canceled and the database is then opened. If you're using the Active Data Guard option, the Redo Apply can be started again to allow the standby to have real-time data while having the database open. This can be done in sqlplus on the standby database:

```
SQLPLUS> ALTER DATABASE RECOVER MANAGED STANDBY DATABASE CANCEL;
SQLPLUS> ALTER DATABASE OPEN READ ONLY; And then to start applying
the redo again:
SQLPLUS> ALTER DATABASE RECOVER MANAGED STANDBY DATABASE
USING CURRENT LOGFILE DISCONNECT;
/* The database is still open for read-only queries and reporting as
the logs are being applied. */
```

Another option for using the standby database is as a snapshot database that can be updated and used for testing. During this time, no logs are applied. After testing, the snapshot database is converted back to standby database by using a restore point with flashback database:

```
Create Snapshot:
SQLPLUS> ALTER DATABASE CONVERT TO SNAPSHOT STANDBY;
Convert back to Standby:
SQLPLUS> ALTER DATABASE CONVERT TO PHYSICAL STANDBY DATABASE;
```

When using a snapshot database with SQL Apply, stopping the apply of the SQL statements is not necessary. This is because the standby is kept synchronized by having the same SQL being applied on the primary applied on the standby as well. So, while the standby is still being synchronized, it is also available for queries, running reports, or backups. The commands for setting up the standby for read access shown here are not necessary, but are done during the initial setup to show that SQL Apply is being used:

```
SQLPLUS> ALTER DATABASE START LOGICAL STANDBY APPLY IMMEDIATE;
```

Progress Check ⊖

1. What service handles the failover from primary to standby?

2. What protection mode will cause the primary to wait on new transactions if it is not able to apply logs to at least one of the standbys?

3. How many protection modes are there?

CRITICAL SKILL 8.11

Create a Physical Standby Server

All of the databases, whether physical or logical, must be created as a physical standby first. The tools used to create the standby are RMAN, Data Guard Broker, or Oracle Grid Control. Steps must be completed on both primary and standby servers. However, the steps on the primary database only need to be done once, no matter how many standby servers are being created. Oracle 11*g* RMAN provides a simple command for creating the standby database and backing up the database at the same time.

Progress Check Answers

1. Role Management Service

2. Maximum protection mode

3. Three: maximum protection, maximum availability, and maximum performance

Project 8-3   Create a Physical Standby Server

Step by Step

1. Complete the following steps on the primary server:

   ```
   select FORCE_LOGGING from v$database;
   alter database force logging;
   -- forces all changes to be logged even if nologging
   might be set on an object
   ```

2. Configure the redo transport authentication; use a remote login password file.

3. Add standby logfiles to the primary. The logs on the standby need to be the same size or larger than on the primary in order for the primary redo to be applied to the standby redo logs.

   ```
   alter database add standby logfile '/u...' size 50M;
   ```

4. Set initialization parameters on the primary server:

   ```
   DB_NAME =
   DB_UNIQUE_NAME   (Doesn't change even if the standby becomes the primary)
   CONTROL_FILES
   LOG_ARCHIVE_CONFIG='dg_config=(DG01,DG02)'
   LOG_ARCHIVE_DEST_1='LOCATION=/u01/oraarch/DG01'  ## local archive directory
   LOG_ARCHIVE_DEST_2='service=DG01 ASYNC
   VALID_FOR=(ONLINE_LOGFILE,PRIMARY_ROLE) db_unique_name=DG01' ## sets the type
   of transport and used for physical standby
   REMOTE_LOGIN_PASSWORDFILE = Exclusive
   LOG_ARCHIVE_DEST_STATE_n
   ```

5. Put the primary server in archive log mode.

6. The network configurations for the standby database need to be configured on both the primary and secondary servers. Using Oracle Net Manager on both servers will help configure this. (Refer to the discussion in Chapter 3.) In configuring a service name, use the unique_db name for the standby server. After setting up the listener and service on both servers, verify that the password file has been copied over and the directories for adump, bdump, flashback, and so on have been created.

7. Creating the standby database over the network, start up the standby database in NOMOUNT mode.

(continued)

8. On the primary server, issue the RMAN command and connect as sysdba:

```
RMAN> connect auxiliary sys/password@DG02
RMAN> run {
allocate channel disk1 type disk;
allocate auxiliary channel stby type disk;
duplicate target database for standby from active database
spfile
parameter_value_convert 'DG01','DG02'
set db_unique_name='DG02'
set db_file_name_convert='/dg01/','/dg02/'
set log_file_name_convert='/dg01/','/dg02/'
set control_files='/u01/app/oradata/controlfiles/dg02.ctl'
set log_archive_max_processes='5'
set fal_client='dg02'   ## FAL (fetch archive log) client and is used if
roles are switched
set fal_server='dg01'
set standby_file_management='AUTO'
set log_archive_config='dg_config=(dg01,dg02)'
set log_archive_dest_1='service=dg01 ASYNC
valid_for=(ONLINE_LOGFILE,PRIMARY_ROLE) db_unique_name=DG01'
;}
```

9. Log into the primary server and switch the logfile:

```
SQLPLUS>alter system switch logfile;
```

10. Start the recovery process on the standby server:

```
SQLPLUS> alter database recover managed standby database
using current logfile disconnect;
```

Primary and standby servers have been created and now should be verified.

Project Summary

In this project, primary and standby databases were created. The configuration of the parameters and starting up the instances all need to be completed before the recovery process on the standby server starts. Following these steps should give you a good idea what it takes to create a standby server.

To manage the Data Guard system, the Data Guard Broker (command line) or Oracle Enterprise Manager Grid Control can be used. In order to use the Data Guard Broker, the parameter DG_BROKER_START needs to be set to TRUE and the listener needs to have the databases with broker services added. DGMRGL is the command to invoke the broker. For Oracle Grid Control, once the database targets are added to the Grid, the Data Guard management is possible. These tools provide a way to failover the database to the standby and back again to primary. They hold the configurations and allow modifications as well as managing and monitoring the Data Guard environment.

Tie It All Together

High availability is an important topic for database systems with the effort to remove all single points of failure in business critical applications. There are several components of Oracle 11*g* which, either standing alone or in combination, provide highly available solutions. Oracle Real Application Clusters (RAC) along with Data Guard provides a very fast failover system with the capabilities of an off-site standby database for disaster recovery. Automatic Storage Management (ASM) offers several advancements for managing the database files and disk in order to provide a stable environment that can minimize maintenance windows and downtime. Planning with your business and reviewing these as well as other database features should assist you in developing and implementing a well-architected, highly available database system.

☑ Chapter 8 Mastery Check

1. Which component is not part of a RAC environment?

   A. Interconnect

   B. Clusterware

   C. DGMGRL

   D. OCR

2. True or false: The Cluster Verification Utility is run after the RAC database is created to verify that the interconnect is running properly.

3. In a RAC environment, OCR stands for

   A. Oracle Cluster Registry

   B. Oracle Connection Repository

   C. Oracle Clusterware Record

   D. Oracle Cluster Recovery

4. In a RAC environment, how many IP addresses are needed for a server?

5. What is the command-line interface that can be used to copy, back up, and list the files in ASM directories?

6. True or false: ASM redundancy types are EXTERNAL, HIGH, and LOW.

7. When shutdown abort is used to shut down the ASM instance, what happens to the database instances connecting to that ASM instance?

8. What is the administrator's login role on the ASM instance?

9. What does the following sqlplus command do? Does it run against the primary or standby server?

   ```
   SQLPLUS> alter database recover managed standby database using current
   logfile disconnect;
   ```

10. True or false: Asynchronous transport of redo logs means that the redo is being written to the primary and standby locations at the same time.

11. Which of the following is not a characteristic of the Data Guard Protection mode of maximum protection?

    A. Synchronous transport

    B. Zero data loss

    C. Standby fails, primary is halted

    D. Performance is the biggest concern

12. Which tools can be used to manage the Data Guard environment?

CHAPTER 9

Large Database Features

CRITICAL SKILLS

9.1 Learn to Identify a Very Large Database

9.2 How and Why to Use Data Partitioning

9.3 Compress Your Data

9.4 Use Parallel Processing to Improve Performance

9.5 Use Materialized Views

9.6 Use SQL Aggregate and Analysis Functions

9.7 Create SQL Models

n this chapter, you will be exploring the topics and features available in Oracle Database 11g that you'll need to be familiar with when working with large databases. These features are among the more advanced that you will encounter, but they're necessary because databases continue to grow larger and larger. When you start working with Oracle, you will find yourself facing the trials and tribulations associated with large databases sooner rather than later. The quicker you understand the features and know where and when to use them, the more effective you will be. Of course, these features are not just valuable for large databases; they provide value to everyone who is looking to optimize their Oracle database environment.

CRITICAL SKILL 9.1

Learn to Identify a Very Large Database

Let's start by describing what we mean by a very large database (VLDB). Large is a relative term that changes over time. What was considered large five or ten years ago is small by today's standards, and what is large today will be peanuts a few years from now. How many people remember buying a computer with 20MB of storage and wondering how they could ever fill it up? Today, personal computers may come with more than a terabyte of storage; with the types of information you store, you know that you will fill these storage systems to capacity sooner or later. Each release of Oracle has included new features and enhancements for addressing the need to store more and more data. For example, Oracle8*i* was released in 1999 and could handle databases with *terabytes* (1024 gigabytes) of data. In 2001, Oracle9*i* was released and could deal with up to 500 *petabytes* (1024 terabytes). Oracle Database 11*g* now offers support for *exabyte* (1024 petabytes) databases. You won't come across too many databases with exabytes of data right now, but in the future at least you know Oracle will support them. In addition, Oracle produces a new high-performance hardware and software solution called "The Database Machine," which will provide speed improvements and large amounts of storage as the importance of large databases continues to expand and evolve over time.

The most obvious examples of large database implementations are data warehouses and decision support systems. These environments usually have tables with millions or billions of rows or wide tables with large numbers of columns and many rows. There are also many OLTP systems that are very large and can benefit from the features you are about to explore. Since you have many topics to get through, let's jump right in and start with data partitioning.

NOTE
Many of the topics discussed in this chapter could take an entire book to cover completely. Since this is an introductory book, specifics for some topics have been omitted. Real-world experiences and additional reading will build on the material presented here.

CRITICAL SKILL 9.2
Why and How to Use Data Partitioning

As user communities require more and more detailed information to remain competitive, it has fallen to database designers and administrators to help ensure that the information is managed effectively and can be retrieved for analysis efficiently. In this section, we will discuss partitioning data and the reasons why it is so important for working with large databases. Afterwards, you'll follow the steps required to make it all work.

Why Use Data Partitioning

Let's start by defining *data partitioning*. In its simplest form, it is a way of breaking up or subsetting data into smaller units that can be managed and accessed separately. It has been around for a long time, both as a design technique and as a technology. Let's look at some of the issues that gave rise to the need for partitioning and the solutions to these issues.

Tables containing very large numbers of rows have always posed problems and challenges for DBAs, application developers, and end users alike. For the DBA, the problems are centered on the maintenance and manageability of the underlying data files that contain the data for these tables. For the application developers and end users, the issues are query performance and data availability.

To mitigate these issues, the standard database design technique was to create physically separate tables, identical in structure (for example, columns), but each containing a subset of the total data (this design technique will be referred to as *non-partitioned* here). These tables could be referred to directly or through a series of views. This technique solved some of the problems, but still meant maintenance for the DBA with regard to creating new tables and/or views as new subsets of data were acquired. In addition, if access to the entire dataset was required, a view was needed to join all subsets together.

Figure 9-1 illustrates a non-partitioned design. In this sample, separate tables with identical structures have been created to hold monthly sales information for 2005. Views have also been defined to group the monthly information into quarters using a union query. The quarterly views themselves are then grouped together into a view that represents the entire year. The same structures would be created for each year of data. In order to obtain data for a particular month or quarter, an end user would have to know which table or view to use.

Similar to the technique illustrated in Figure 9-1, the partitioning technology offered by Oracle Database 11*g* is a method of breaking up large amounts of data into smaller, more manageable chunks, with each of the partitions having their own unique name and their own storage definitions. But, like the non-partitioned technique, it is transparent to the end user, offering improved performance and reduced

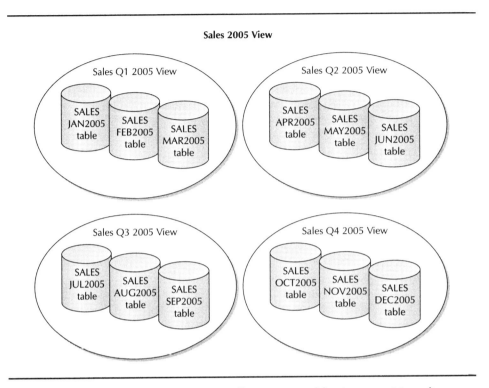

FIGURE 9-1. *Partitioning using physically separate tables (non-partitioned)*

maintenance. Figure 9-2 illustrates the same SALES table, but implemented using Oracle Database 11*g*'s partitioning option. From the end user's perspective, there is only one table called SALES and all that is required to access data from the correct partition is a date (or a month and year).

Oracle partitioning was first introduced in Oracle8, is only available with the Enterprise Edition, and is an additional option to the version. As previously suggested, it is one database option that is a must-have for anyone with a large volume of data that needs to be quickly retrievable or with a need for speedy data archiving. Many improvements have been made since then, and Oracle Database 11*g* contains all of the latest features. The remainder of this section discusses these features in more detail.

Manageability
When administering large databases, DBAs are required to determine the most efficient and effective ways to configure the underlying data files that support the tables in the database. The decisions made at this time will affect your data accessibility and availability as well as backup and recovery.

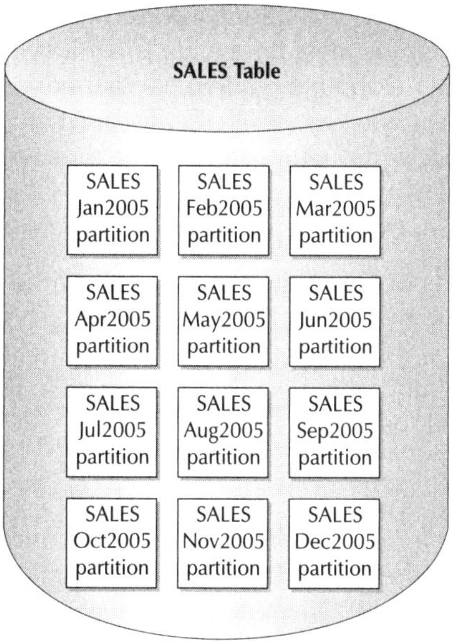

FIGURE 9-2. *Partitioning using Oracle 11g partitioning*

Some of the benefits for database manageability when using partitioned tables include the following:

- The size of each underlying data file is generally smaller for partitioned tables than for non-partitioned tables. This allows for easier and quicker data selections and smaller backups.

- Historical partitions can be made read-only and will not need to be backed up more than once. This also means faster backups. With partitions, you can move data to lower cost storage by either moving the tablespace, sending it to an archive via an export (datapump), or some other method.

- The structure of a partitioned table needs to be defined only once. As new subsets of data are acquired they will be assigned to the correct partition, based on the partitioning method chosen. In addition, with Oracle 11g you now have the ability to define intervals that allow you to define only the partitions that you need. It also allows Oracle to automatically add partitions based on data arriving in the database. This is an important feature for DBAs, who currently spend time manually adding partitions to their tables.

- Individual tablespaces and/or their data files can be taken offline for maintenance or archiving without affecting access to other subsets of data. For example, assuming data for a table is partitioned by month (later in this chapter, you'll learn about the different types of partitioning) and only 13 months of data is to be kept online at any one time, the earliest month is archived and dropped from the table when a new month is acquired. This is accomplished using the command alter table abc drop partition xyz and does not affect access to the remaining 12 months of data.

- Other commands that would normally apply at the table level can also be applied to a particular partition of the table. These include, but are not limited to: delete, insert, select, truncate, and update. You should review the Oracle 11*g* Partitioning Guide for a complete list of the commands that are available with partitions and subpartitions.

Performance

One of the main reasons for partitioning a table is to improve I/O response time when selecting data from the table. Having a table's data partitioned into subsets can yield much faster query results when you are looking for data that is contained within one subset of the total. Let's look at an illustrative example.

Assume the SALES table contains 100 million records representing daily sales revenue for the three years 2005 to 2008 inclusive. You want to know what the total revenue is for February 2008. Your query might look something like this:

```
select sum(amount_sold)
from sales
where time_id between to_date('2008-02-01', 'YYYY-MM-DD')
  and to_date('2008-02-28', 'YYYY-MM-DD');
```

Ask the Expert

Q: Can you use the analyze table command to gather statistics on partitioned tables?

A: No, at least not correctly. The supplied DBMS_STATS package should be used to gather statistics on partitioned tables instead. The analyze table command does not gather all required statistics for partitioned tables (in particular, global statistics). In addition, the analyze command will eventually be phased out (for all types of table and indexes) and only those statistics gathered by the DBMS_STATS package will be used by the cost-based optimizer.

Using a non-partitioned table design, all 100 million rows would need to be scanned to determine if they belong to the date criteria. Using a partitioned table design based on monthly partitions, with about 2.8 million rows for each month, only those rows in the February 2008 partition (and therefore only about 2.8 million rows) would be scanned. The process of eliminating data not belonging to the subset defined by the query criteria is referred to as *partition pruning*.

With the basic concepts of partitioning and why you use it under your belt, you can now learn about the finer details of how to implement partitioning.

Implement Data Partitioning

Implementing data partitioning in Oracle Database 11*g* is a process that requires careful planning to ensure success. You will need to understand your database environment, hardware, structures, and data before you can make the appropriate decisions. The next few sections will outline the steps you will take when partitioning. Let's start by looking at the characteristics of the candidate table.

Analyze the Candidate Table

The first step in the partitioning process is to analyze and understand the candidate table, its environment, and its uses. Following are some criteria to consider.

Table Structure and Data Contents   You will need to look at the attributes that are available and the distribution of the data within each attribute. You must consider currently available data as well as projected future data. The distribution of data over each attribute is important because you want to ensure that the resulting data subsets are evenly distributed across the defined partitions.

Consider a table called PHONE_USAGE that contains detailed mobile phone call records with over 300 million records per month. It has many attributes, including the toll type (toll_type_cd) and the date of call (call_date). Table 9-1 shows a sample row count for a month by toll_type_cd. As you can see, using this attribute would probably not be an ideal choice for creating subsets because the distribution is heavily skewed toward LOCAL calls.

toll_type_cd	Record Count (Sample Month)
INTNL	27,296,802
CONTNL US	52,227,998
LOCAL	189,554,584
NRTH AMRCA	36,367,841

TABLE 9-1.   *Toll Type and Record Counts*

Table 9-2 looks at the distribution of the same data by the day of the week (for example, Sunday to Saturday based on call_date).

You can see that the day of the week provides a relatively even distribution that is more suitable for partitioning. Having a relatively equal data distribution of your data across the partitions will result in better performance during queries, as processing can be spread equally across the partitions. When a table is skewed to one partition, this can result in a very large data set within your table, which would defeat the purpose of partitioning the table in the first place.

How the Data Will Be Accessed   To access the data, you will need to know what the commonest data selection criteria are. This is perhaps the most important part of the analysis because, as stated earlier, query performance is the most noticeable gain of data partitioning. In order for this to be realized, your data subsets need to be defined according to the commonest selection criteria so that unnecessary partitions can be pruned from the result set. The selection criteria will be determined largely by your user community and can be determined using historical query patterns (if available) or consulting business requirements.

Referring to the SALES table example, your analysis of query patterns for a three-month period (averaging 400 queries per month) yields the results shown in Table 9-3.

The analysis tells you that time_id and promo_id are both frequently used as query predicates. You could use this information along with the corresponding row distribution to determine which attribute would result in the better partitioning strategy.

Hardware Configuration   Factors such as the number of physical disks and disk controllers will contribute to the effectiveness of your partitioning strategy. Generally, the greater the number of disks and/or controllers, the better—you can spread the partitions over more hardware to improve I/O performance.

Day of the Week (Based on call_date)	Record Count (Sample Month)
SUN	41,635,356
MON	44,235,019
TUE	42,875,502
WED	43,235,721
THU	43,922,997
FRI	45,005,293
SAT	44,537,337

TABLE 9-2.   *Counts Based on Day of the Week*

Attribute	Times Used in Query Selection Criteria (Average/Month)
prod_id	33
cust_id	40
time_id	355
channel_id	55
promo_id	298
quantity_sold	25
amount_sold	20

TABLE 9-3.   *Query Counts Based on Data Attributes*

Identify the Partition Key

Once you understand the characteristics of your candidate table, the next step in the partitioning process is to select the attribute(s) of the candidate table that will define the partition subsets and how the subsets will be defined. The selected attributes will form the *partition key*. Only one set of attributes can be chosen to partition the data. This is an important decision, since it will affect the manageability and usability of the table.

The results of your analysis of the candidate table should provide you with a good idea of the attributes to use. The best attributes will be those that satisfy the most criteria. Keep in mind, though, that the adage "you can satisfy some of the criteria some of the time, but you can't satisfy all of the criteria all of the time" applies here. Despite your best efforts and planning, there will still be situations when the table will be treated as if it were non-partitioned. Take, for example, a perfectly valid query submitted by the user community that does not include the attributes of the partition key as part of the selection criteria or groups by the partition key. In this case, data from the entire table (that is, all partitions) would be scanned in order to satisfy the request.

Select the Type of Partitioning

After you have selected the partition key, the next step in the partitioning process is to decide which type of partitioning you want to implement on the candidate table. Oracle Database 11g provides seven ways to partition data:

- ■ Range partitioning
- ■ List partitioning
- ■ Hash partitioning

- Composite partitioning

- Reference partitioning

- Virtual column-based partitioning

- Interval partitioning

The type of partitioning you choose will depend on the results of your analysis of the candidate table. The commonest type of partitioning is range partitioning and this will be covered in the most detail. Let's look at the characteristics of each type of partitioning.

Range Partitioning   *Range partitioning* has been around the longest of all partitioning types and is the one implemented most often. In most cases, the ranges are based on some date column, such as quarters, months or, in the case of very large data volumes, days. (Theoretically, you can go down to any level of time—hours, minutes, and so on—assuming you have a time component. But the maintenance implications of defining this many partitions make it unrealistic.) The ranges selected will again be based on the results of your analysis of the table, using dates, numeric values, or character values. Following is an example based on the SALES table you saw earlier in the chapter.

NOTE
The partitioning examples presented in this chapter do not address all of the command options available. They are meant to give you a taste of what is available.

To create your SALES table as non-partitioned, you would use the standard create table statement as shown in this listing:

```
create table sales (
   prod_id        number        not null,
   cust_id        number        not null,
   time_id        date          not null,
   channel_id     number        not null,
   promo_id       number        not null,
   quantity_sold  number (10,2) not null,
   amount_sold    number (10,2) not null)
tablespace example_tblspc_1;
```

Based on the analysis of the usage patterns and row distribution, you have decided that the optimal partition strategy for this table is based on sales month. You will now redefine the SALES table using time_id as your partition key to create monthly partitions for January 2007 to December 2009, inclusive. Creation of data partitions is accomplished using extensions of the create table statement. The following listing shows the creation of the table with range partitions. Explanations of the important lines are given in Table 9-4.

```
 1 create table sales (
 2  prod_id        number        not null,
 3  cust_id        number        not null,
 4  time_id        date          not null,
 5  channel_id     number        not null,
 6  promo_id       number        not null,
 7  quantity_sold  number (10,2) not null,
 8  amount_sold    number (10,2) not null)
 9  storage (initial 65536  minextents 1 maxextents 2147483645)
10 partition by range (time_id)
11 (partition sales_200701 values less than
12                   (to_date('2007-02-01','YYYY-MM-DD'))
13                   tablespace sales_ts_200501,
14  partition sales_200702 values less than
15                   (to_date('2007-03-01','YYYY-MM-DD'))
16                   tablespace sales_ts_200502,
17  partition sales_200703 values less than
18                   (to_date('2007-04-01','YYYY-MM-DD'))
19                   tablespace sales_ts_200503,
...
113  partition sales_200811 values less than
114                   (to_date('2008-12-01','YYYY-MM-DD'))
115                   tablespace sales_ts_200711,
116  partition sales_200812 values less than
117                   (to_date('2009-01-01','YYYY-MM-DD'))
118                   tablespace sales_ts_200712,
119 partition sales_max values less than (maxvalue)
120                   tablespace sales_ts_max);
```

Lines	Important Points
9	This defines the default table-level storage parameters that will apply to all partitions. It is possible to override these defaults at the partition level in favor of specific parameters required for a particular partition.
10	This defines the type of partitioning (for example, range) and the partition key (for instance, time_id).
11–118	Define each partition based on the values of time_id (repetitive lines for Apr 2007 to Oct 2009 omitted for brevity's sake). For each partition, the upper boundary of the partition key value is specified (as defined by the values less than clause), as well as the name of the tablespace where the subset is to be stored. Values must be specified in ascending order and cannot overlap. It is good practice to give meaningful names to both the partitions and tablespaces.

TABLE 9-4. *Explanation of Range Partitioning Syntax*

NOTE
Lines 11 to 13 define the first partition to hold data where time_id is less than February 1, 2007. The intention in this example is that this first partition will only hold data for January 2007 (our data analysis tells us that there is no data before this date). However, if there happens to be data prior to January 2007, it will also be placed in this partition and may skew the row distribution by placing many more rows than intended in this partition.

That completes the discussion on range partitioning. Let's now have a look at list and hash partitioning.

List Partitioning   There may be cases when, after your analysis of a candidate table, you decide that range partitioning is not the best fit for your table. Another way to subset your data is to use *list partitioning,* where you group a set of discrete partition key values and assign them to their own tablespace. By using this type of partitioning, you can control the placement of the records in specified partitions, thereby allowing you to group related records together that may not otherwise have a relationship.

As an example, assume you have an INS_COVERAGE table that contains insurance coverages. Your analysis of this table and its usage leads you to decide that you should partition, based on the attribute COV_TYPE_CD, into the buckets shown in Table 9-5.

COV_TYPE_CD	Grouping
TERM 65	Life
UL	Life
ADB	Life
COLA	GIB
GPO	GIB
WP	Disability
DIS	Disability
MF	Investment

TABLE 9-5.   *Insurance Coverage Groupings*

The syntax of the create table statement is similar to that for range partitioning. An explanation is provided in Table 9-6:

```
 1 create table ins_coverage (
 2  plan_id          number        not null,
 3  cust_id          number        not null,
 4  time_id          date          not null,
 5  dist_channel_id number        not null,
 6  cov_type_cd      varchar2(50)  not null,
 7  cov_amt          number (10,2) not null,
 8  prem_amt         number (10,2) not null)
 9  storage (initial 65536  minextents 1 maxextents 2147483645)
10 partition by list (cov_type_cd)
11 (partition cov_life values ('TERM 65', 'UL', 'ADB')
12               tablespace cov_life_ts,
13  partition cov_gib values ('COLA', 'GIB')
14               tablespace cov_gib_ts,
15  partition cov_dis values ('WP', 'DIS')
16               tablespace cov_dis_ts,
17  partition cov_inv values ('MF')
18               tablespace cov_inv_ts
19  partition cov_other values(default));
```

TIP
If you discover missing partition keys values that need to be added to existing partition definitions after the table has been created, you can issue and alter table abc modify partition xyz add values ('value1', …).

Lines	Important Points
10	This defines the type of partitioning (for example, list) and the partition key (cov_type_cd, for instance). Note that with list partitioning, only one attribute from the table can be chosen as the partition key—in other words, multicolumn partition keys are not permitted.
11–18	This defines each partition based on the groups of values of cov_type_cd.

TABLE 9-6. *Explanation of List Partitioning Syntax*

Hash Partitioning   If you determine from your table analysis that neither range nor list partitioning is appropriate for your table, but you still want to reap the benefits offered by partitioning, Oracle Database 11*g* provides a third partitioning option called *hash partitioning*. With hash partitioning, you define up to 16 partition key attributes as well as the number of partitions you want to spread the data across. As long as each partition is on its own physical device and most of the queries use the partition key as a predicate, you should see performance gains. Hash partitioning is useful if the distribution of data is unknown or unpredictable.

The following listing is an example of hash partitioning. Table 9-7 explains the important lines:

```
1 create table sub_activations (
2   sub_id          number        not null,
3   dist_channel_id number        not null,
4   act_date        date          not null,
5   deact_date      date          not null,
6   sales_rep_id    number        not null)

7 partition by hash (sub_id)
8 partitions 4
9 store in (subact_ts1, subact_ts2, subact_ts3, subact_ts4);
```

It is beyond the scope of this book to discuss the hashing algorithm used by Oracle Database 11*g*. However, it is based on the number of attributes in the partition key and the number of partitions selected.

Composite Partitioning   The final method of partitioning that you will read about here is a combination of two of the previous types. Combining two types of partitioning is called *composite partitioning*. There are a few basic combinations: range with hash, range with range, and range with list and others. Using composite partitioning allows you to take advantage of the features of either hash or list partitioning within the higher groupings of ranges.

Lines	Important Points
7	This defines the type of partitioning (for instance, hash) and the partition key (for example, sub_id).
8	This specifies the number of partitions over which to spread the data.
9	This specifies the tablespaces into which the partitions will be placed.

TABLE 9-7.   *Explanation of Hash Partitioning Syntax*

A good example of where this type of partitioning is used would be the PHONE_USAGE table you saw in your candidate table analysis. In this case, you have a table that is being loaded with 300 million records per month. You could choose to implement range partitioning by month and then subdivide the monthly partitions into four hash partitions. The following listing shows the SQL syntax that accomplishes this, and Table 9-8 provides the explanation of the important lines:

```
 1 create table phone_usage
 2 (sub_id              number,
 3  call_date           date,
 4  call_type_id        number,
 5  called_location     varchar2(50),
 6  service_carrier_id  number)
 7 storage (initial 65536?  minextents 1 maxextents 2147483645)
 8 partition by range (call_date)
 9 subpartition by hash(sub_id)
10 subpartition template(
11  subpartition sub1 tablespace ph_usg_ts1,
12  subpartition sub2 tablespace ph_usg_ts2,
13  subpartition sub3 tablespace ph_usg_ts3,
14  subpartition sub4 tablespace ph_usg_ts4)
15 (partition phoneusg_200601 values less than
16                  (to_date('2006-02-01','YYYY-MM-DD')),
17  partition phoneusg_200602 values less than
18                  (to_date('2006-03-01','YYYY-MM-DD')),
19  partition phoneusg_200603 values less than
20                  (to_date('2006-04-01','YYYY-MM-DD')),
21  partition phoneusg_200604 values less than
22                  (to_date('2006-05-01','YYYY-MM-DD')),
23  partition phoneusg_200605 values less than
24                  (to_date('2006-06-01','YYYY-MM-DD')),
25  partition phoneusg_200606 values less than
26                  (to_date('2006-07-01','YYYY-MM-DD')),
27  partition phoneusg_max values less than (maxvalue));
```

Ask the Expert

Q: If the partition key of record in a partitioned table is updated and the new value means that the data belongs to a different partition, does Oracle Database 11g automatically move the record to the appropriate partition?

A: Yes, but the table must have the enable row movement option before the update is made. This option is invoked as either part of the create table statement or using an alter table statement. Otherwise, the update statement will generate an Oracle error.

Lines	Important Points
8	This defines the higher-level partitioning type (for example, range) and its partition key (for instance, call_date).
9	This specifies the secondary partitioning type (in this case, hash) and its partition key (here, sub_id).
10–14	This specifies a template that will be used to define the tablespace names for each subpartition, as well as the tablespace names. The name of each subpartition will be composed of the higher-level partition name concatenated with an underscore, then the subpartition name specified in the template. For example, data for January 2006 will be placed in tablespace ph_usg_ts1 and divided into four subpartitions called PHONEUSG_200601_SUB1, PHONEUSG_200601_SUB2, PHONEUSG_200601_SUB3, and PHONEUSG_200601_SUB4.
15–27	This specifies the ranges for the higher-level partition based on the call_date partition key.

TABLE 9-8.   *Explanation of Composite Partitioning Syntax*

Reference Partitioning   *Reference partitioning* is one of the latest methods that Oracle has provided you for partitioning your data in Oracle 11*g*. The method used by reference partitioning allows you to partition data based upon referential constraints. As previously discussed, referential integrity in a database allows data to be correct and to be consistent. The idea is that you would not have any order line items without an order. RI is implemented to ensure data is correct, complete, and consistent. This leads you to the challenge of partitioning data in a productive manner, such that you may have consistent partitioning between parent and child tables. So, if you partition ORDERS by date range, you want the ORDER_ITEMS to follow the same method. Before its introduction in Oracle 11*g*, you could achieve this in a manual way, which may include adding additional attributes to child records (ORDER_ITEMS) to allow you to provide the same partition keys. With reference partitioning, you can now equipartition parent and child tables without the need to duplicate keys. In addition, partition maintenance tasks will cascade from parent to child to reduce errors or omissions in the two tables.

Let's look at an example of how you could set up a reference partitioned table. First, you should define the parent table:

```
CREATE TABLE orders
    ( order_id         NUMBER(12),
```

```
        order_date          DATE,
        order_meth          VARCHAR2(8),
        customer_id         NUMBER(6),
        order_status        NUMBER(2),
        order_tot           NUMBER(8,2),
        sales_rep_id        NUMBER(6),
        campaign_id         NUMBER(6),
        CONSTRAINT orders_pk PRIMARY KEY(order_id)
    )
  PARTITION BY RANGE(order_date)
    ( PARTITION Q1_2008 VALUES
                  LESS THAN (TO_DATE('01-APR-2008','DD-MON-YYYY')),
      PARTITION Q2_2008 VALUES
                  LESS THAN (TO_DATE('01-JUL-2008','DD-MON-YYYY')),
      PARTITION Q3_2008 VALUES
                  LESS THAN (TO_DATE('01-OCT-2008','DD-MON-YYYY')),
      PARTITION Q4_2008 VALUES
                  LESS THAN (TO_DATE('01-JAN-2009','DD-MON-YYYY')),
      PARTITION UNCLASSIFIED_ORDER VALUES (DEFAULT)     )
/
```

Now that you have the parent ORDERS table defined, you should take the time to notice that you defined a primary key constraint within the table definition. This is a requirement for the next step. Oracle reference partitioning depends solely on the definition of this integrity between entities, so consider this when deciding to utilize this method of partitioning. Now you can move on to the child table definition. In this case, you will define the table and then reference back to the parent table so that the partitioning is now based upon the parent's partitioning methods, ultimately leveraging the database's defined referential integrity:

```
CREATE TABLE order_items
    ( order_id            NUMBER(12) NOT NULL,
      line_item_id        NUMBER(3)  NOT NULL,
      product_id          NUMBER(6)  NOT NULL,
      unit_price          NUMBER(8,2),
      quantity            NUMBER(8),
      CONSTRAINT order_items_fk
      FOREIGN KEY(order_id) REFERENCES orders(order_id)
    )
   PARTITION BY REFERENCE(order_items_fk)
/
```

As can see in the previous listing, this is a powerful method for partitioning data in a manner that logically follows the way that you store and read your data in a parent-child type relationship. Although you define only one partitioning method, this will reduce your workload because it really defines the method used by two or more tables, ultimately reducing the maintenance of your database. This method should be considered in operational and more relationship-oriented data sets.

Virtual Column-based Partitioning   Earlier in the book we discussed the theory of virtual columns. *Virtual columns* are columns that are defined in metadata and are provided with the ability to create in-table derivations. This is valuable to many applications. To extend the virtual column idea to partitioning is the next logical extension of this functionality. Beginning in the Oracle 11*g* version of the database Oracle provides us with *virtual column-based partitioning*. By implementing this method of partitioning you can now use value derivations.

Before we discuss this method, we need to discuss the concept of the *INTERVAL* clause. The INTERVAL clause is used by Oracle to calculate the range of partitions. In our example we will use a one-month interval, but this range can be set to other values. Let's look at an example of how a table is partitioned using this method:

```
CREATE TABLE sales
    ( prod_id       NUMBER(6) NOT NULL
    , cust_id       NUMBER NOT NULL
    , time_id       DATE NOT NULL
    , channel_id    CHAR(1) NOT NULL
    , promo_id      NUMBER(6) NOT NULL
    , quantity_sold NUMBER(3) NOT NULL
    , amount_sold   NUMBER(10,2) NOT NULL
    , total_amount AS (quantity_sold * amount_sold)

    )
PARTITION BY RANGE (time_id) INTERVAL (NUMTOYMINTERVAL(1,'MONTH'))
SUBPARTITION BY RANGE (total_amount)
SUBPARTITION TEMPLATE
    ( SUBPARTITION p_small VALUES LESS THAN (1000)
    , SUBPARTITION p_medium VALUES LESS THAN (5000)
    , SUBPARTITION p_large VALUES LESS THAN (10000)
    , SUBPARTITION p_extreme VALUES LESS THAN (MAXVALUE)
    )
(PARTITION sales_before_2007 VALUES LESS THAN
        (TO_DATE('01-JAN-2007','dd-MON-yyyy')))
ENABLE ROW MOVEMENT
PARALLEL NOLOGGING;
```

The previous example provides you with a few partitioning features. The first is the use of the virtual column partitioning. As you can see, the virtual column *total amount* is the column that will be used in the subpartitions. Subpartitions are used in secondary partitioning. This is known as *composite partitioning,* or the combining of two types of partitioning providing two layers of partitioned data. In this example you are combining range on date and range on the virtual column. The power of virtual columns is focused on providing a complete control over how and where data is stored to optimize performance.

Define the Partitioned Indexing Strategy

Okay, so now you have decided how you are going to partition your data. To really get the most out of partitioning, you will need to look at some indexing strategies. There are two types of indexes applicable to partitioned tables: local and global. Let's take a brief look at each.

Local Partitioned Indexes   *Local partitioned indexes* are indexes that are partitioned in the exact same manner as the data in their associated table—that is, they have a direct one-to-one relationship with the data partitions and use the same partition key. This association is illustrated in Figure 9-3; as you can see, each partition has its own associated "local" index. This drawing is based on Figure 9-2, which you saw at the beginning of the chapter. It shows how the data and indexes for each monthly subset are related and then joins it with the concept of the local index.

Because of this relationship, the following points apply to local indexes:

■ You cannot explicitly add or drop a partition to/from a local index. Oracle Database 11*g* automatically adds or drops index partitions when related data partitions are added or dropped. Looking at Figure 9-3, if you dropped

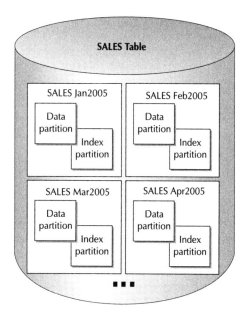

FIGURE 9-3.   *Local partitioned indexes*

the data partition for January 2005, the corresponding index partition would automatically be dropped as well. Likewise, if you added a new data partition for January 2006, a new index partition would automatically be created.

■ One of the advantages of partitioning data is to allow access to other subsets while maintenance is being carried out on another partition. Since local index partitions are in line with the data partitions, this advantage still exists.

■ Local partitioned indexes require less maintenance than global indexes as you will see later in this chapter.

The SQL syntax for creating a local index is presented in the next listing, which refers to the SALES table you created in the "Range Partitioning" section. Table 9-9 contains an explanation of the syntax:

```
 1 create index sales_idx_l1 on sales (time_id)
 2 local
 3 (partition sales_idx_200501  tablespace sales_ts_idx_200501,
 4  partition sales_idx_200502  tablespace sales_ts_idx_200502,
 5  partition sales_idx_200503  tablespace sales_ts_idx_200503,
...
37  partition sales_idx_200711  tablespace sales_ts_idx_200711,
38  partition sales_idx_200712  tablespace sales_ts_idx_200712,
39  partition sales_idx_max  tablespace sales_ts_idx_max);
```

Lines	Important Points
2	This specifies that the index is to be local. This line alone tells Oracle Database 11*g* that the index is to be partitioned along the same ranges as the data.
3–39	This defines the partition names and tablespaces for each partition. These lines are optional, but without them, Oracle Database 11*g* would use the same partition names as the data and would also place the index in the same tablespaces as the data—a situation that is less than ideal for performance!

TABLE 9-9. *Syntax Highlights*

Ask the Expert

Q: After a table and its local indexes have been defined using range partitioning with a default maxvalue partition, how can you add more partitions as new subsets of data are received?

A: Use an alter table statement to split the default data partitions, adding your new partition ranges. For example, to add a data partition for January 2008 data in the SALES table in the previous listing, issue the following command:

```
alter table sales
split partition sales_max at (to_date('2008-02-01','YYYY-MM-DD'))
into (partition sales_200801 tablespace sales_ts_200801,
      partition sales_max tablespace sales_ts_max);
```

This alter table command will split the default index partition for sales_idx_l1. However, it will use the data partition names (for example, sales_200801) and tablespaces (sales_ts_200801, for instance); remember in the local index example you explicitly specified the partition names and tablespaces for the index. Therefore, the partition names and tablespaces will need to be adjusted using alter index commands, as follows:

```
alter index sales_idx_l1
rename partition sales_200801 to sales_idx_200801;

alter index sales_idx_l1
rebuild partition sales_idx_200801 tablespace sales_ts_idx_200801;

alter index sales_idx_l1
rebuild partition sales_idx_max tablespace sales_ts_idx_max;
```

Some other points about local partitioned indexes:

- They can be unique, but only if the data partition key is part of the index key attributes.
- Bitmap indexes on partitioned tables must be local.
- Subpartitioned indexes are always local.
- They are best suited for data warehouses and decision support systems.
- Local unique indexes also work well in OLTP environments.

Global Partitioned Indexes *Global partitioned indexes* are indexes that are not directly associated with the data partitions. Instead, their partitions are defined independently, with the partition key sometimes different from the data partition key. This association is illustrated in Figure 9-4. (This figure is again based on Figure 9-2, seen at the beginning of the chapter.) It shows that the data is partitioned by monthly ranges, with a global index partitioned by product.

One advantage of global indexes is that if partition pruning cannot occur for the data partitions due to the predicates of a query, index partition pruning may still be possible with the global partition index. Global partitioned indexes are available as either range-based or hash-based. When using range-based global indexes, you must specify a default partition with maxvalue. Let's look at an example for creating a global partitioned index and then discuss how it would be used.

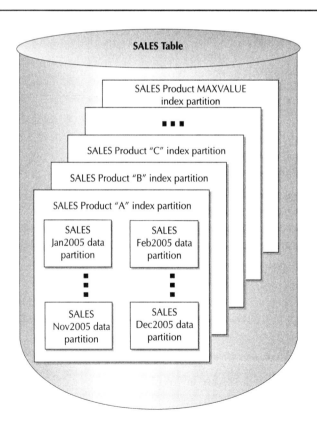

FIGURE 9-4. *Global partitioned indexes*

Referring again to the PHONE_USAGE table you created in the Composite Partitioning section, you should now create a global index on the call_type_id. The following listing is the SQL for this, with the explanation presented in Table 9-10:

```
1 create index phone_usg_idx_g1 on phone_usage (call_type_id)
 2 global
 3 partition by range (call_type_id)
 4 (partition ph_usg_idx_g1 values less than (2)
 5                    tablespace ph_usg_ts_idx_1,
 6  partition ph_usg_idx_g2 values less than (3)
 7                    tablespace ph_usg_ts_idx_2,
 8  partition ph_usg_idx_g3 values less than (4)
 9                    tablespace ph_usg_ts_idx_3,
10  partition ph_usg_idx_g4 values less than (5)
11                    tablespace ph_usg_ts_idx_4,
12  partition ph_usg_idx_gmax values less than (maxvalue)
13                    tablespace ph_usg_ts_idx_max);
```

Now, assume the following query is executed against the PHONE_USAGE table:

```
select count(*)
from phone_usage
where call_type_id = 3;
```

Without the global index you just defined, no partition pruning would occur since the query predicate does not refer to the data partition key call_date. But, with the global index, only the index entries from the partition ph_usg_idx_g3 would be scanned and therefore only data records related to those entries would be used in the result set.

Some other points on global partitioned indexes:

- They require more maintenance than local indexes, especially when you drop data partitions because the indexes become invalid and will require rebuilding before they are available for use.

- They can be unique.

Lines	Important Points
2	This specifies that the index is to be global.
3	This defines the type of partitioning (here, range) for this index and the partition key (call_type_id, in this case).
4–13	This defines the partition names and tablespaces for each partition.

TABLE 9-10. *Explanation for Global Partitioned Index Syntax*

- They cannot be bitmap indexes.

- They are best suited for OLTP systems for direct access to specific records.

Prefixed and Nonprefixed Partition Indexes   In your travels through the world of partitioning, you will hear the terms *prefixed* and *nonprefixed* partition indexes. These terms apply to both local and global indexes. An index is prefixed when the leftmost column of the index key is the same as the leftmost column of the index partition key. If the columns are not the same, the index is nonprefixed. That's all well and good, but what effect does it have?

It is a matter of performance: nonprefixed indexes cost more, from a query perspective, than prefixed indexes. When a query is submitted against a partitioned table and the predicate(s) of the query include the index keys of a prefixed index, pruning of the index partition can occur. If the same index is nonprefixed instead, all index partitions may need to be scanned. (Scanning of all index partitions will depend on the predicate in the query and the type of index: global or local. If the data partition key is included as a predicate and the index is local, then the index partitions to be scanned will be based on pruned data partitions.)

Project 9-1   Create a Range-Partitioned Table and a Local-Partitioned Index

Data and index partitioning are an important part in maintaining large databases. We have discussed the reasons for partitioning and shown the steps to implement it. In this project, you will create a range-partitioned table and a related local-partitioned index.

Step by Step

1. Create two tablespaces called inv_ts_2007q1 and inv_2007q2 using the following SQL statements. These will be used to store data partitions:

```
create tablespace inv_ts_2007q1
   datafile 'inv_ts_2007q1_1.dat' size 10m;

create tablespace inv_ts_2007q2
   datafile 'inv_ts_2007q2_1.dat' size 10m;
```

2. Create two tablespaces called inv_idx_ts_2007q1 and inv_idx_2007q2 using the following SQL statements. These will be used to store index partitions:

```
create tablespace inv_idx_ts_2007q1
   datafile 'inv_idx_ts_2007q1_f1.dat' size 10m;
```

```
create tablespace inv_idx_ts_2007q2
    datafile 'inv_idx_ts_2007q2_f1.dat' size 10m;
```

3. Create a partitioned table called INVOICE using the following listing, based on the following information:

   a. Define the table with the columns identified in Table 9-11.

   b. Use order_date as the partition key and then subset the data into the first and second calendar quarters 2007.

   c. Define the table with the data partitions and tablespaces identified in Table 9-12.

   d. Use the enable row movement option:

```
create table invoice (
  invoice_id   number,
  customer_id  number,
  order_date   date,
  ship_date    date)
partition by range (order_date)
(partition INV_2007Q1 values less than
                    (to_date(2007-04-01','YYYY-MM-DD'))
                  tablespace inv_ts_2007Q1,
 partition INV_2007Q2 values less than
                    (to_date('2007-07-01','YYYY-MM-DD'))
                  tablespace inv_ts_2007Q2,
 partition inv_max values less than (maxvalue)
                  tablespace inv_ts_max)
enable row movement;
```

Column Name	Data Type
INVOICE_ID	NUMBER
CUSTOMER_ID	NUMBER
ORDER_DATE	DATE
SHIP_DATE	DATE

TABLE 9-11. *INVOICE Table Columns*

(continued)

	Partition Name	**Tablespace Name**	**Upper Range Limit**
Data Partitions	INV_2007Q1	INV_TS_2007Q1	Apr 1, 2007
	INV_2007Q2	INV_TS_2007Q2	July 1, 2007
	INV_MAX	INV_TS_MAX	MAXVALUE
Index Partitions	INV_IDX_2007Q1	INV_IDX_TS_2007Q1	Apr 1, 2007
	INV_IDX_2007Q2	INV_IDX_TS_2007Q2	July 1, 2007
	INV_IDX_MAX	INV_IDX_TS_MAX	MAXVALUE

TABLE 9-12.   *INVOICE Table Data and Index Partitions*

4. Create a local partitioned index called inv_order_dt_idx on call_date using the following listing as well as the index partitions and tablespaces identified in Table 9-12.

```
create index inv_order_dt_idx on invoice(order_date)
local
(partition inv_idx_2007q1  tablespace inv_idx_ts_2007q1,
 partition inv_idx_2007q2  tablespace inv_idx_ts_2007q2,
 partition inv_idx_max  tablespace inv_idx_ts_max);
```

Project Summary

The steps in this project reinforce some of the more common scenarios you will encounter: range-based partitioning and prefixed local partitioned indexes. Separate tablespaces were used for data and indexes, quarterly partitions were defined, a local index was defined, and the enable row movement was used to allow the database to automatically redistribute rows to their related partitions in the event of an update to the partition key.

Well, you have certainly covered a lot in this section. Having the background information on these topics will serve you well when maintaining and tuning large databases. Before you move on to the next section, let's take a quick progress check to make sure it all sank in.

Progress Check

1. List at least three DML commands that can be applied to partitions as well as tables.

2. What does partition pruning mean?

3. How many table attributes can be used to define the partition key in list partitioning?

4. Which type of partitioning is most commonly used with a date-based partition key?

5. Which partitioning types cannot be combined together for composite partitioning?

6. How many partition keys can be defined for a partitioned table?

7. Which type of partitioned index has a one-to-one relationship between the data and index partitions?

8. What is meant by a prefixed partitioned index?

Progress Check Answers

1. The following DML commands can be applied to partitions as well as tables: delete, insert, select, truncate, and update.

2. Partition pruning is the process of eliminating data not belonging to the subset defined by the criteria of a query.

3. Only one table attribute can be used to define the partition key in list partitioning.

4. Range partitioning is most commonly used with a date-based partition key.

5. List and hash partitioning cannot be combined for composite partitioning.

6. Only one partition key may be defined.

7. Local partitioned indexes have a one-to-one relationship between data and index partitions.

8. A partitioned index is prefixed when the leftmost column of the index key is the same as the leftmost column of the index partition key.

Compress Your Data

As you load more and more data into your database, performance and storage maintenance can quickly become concerns. Usually at the start of an implementation of a database, data volumes are estimated and projected a year or two ahead. However, oftentimes these estimates turn out to be on the low side and you find yourself scrambling for more space in order to load new data. In addition to the partitioning abilities discussed in the previous section, Oracle Database 11*g* has the ability to compress your data and indexes to further address the concerns of performance and maintenance.

Compression can be performed at the data or index levels. In this section, you'll learn about the options available with Oracle Database 11*g* and the impacts these options have on your database.

Data Compression

With *data compression,* duplicate values in a database block are removed, leaving only a reference to the removed value, which is placed at the beginning of the block. All of the information required to rebuild the data in a block is contained within the block.

By compressing data, physical disk space required is reduced; disk I/O and memory usage are also reduced, thereby improving performance. However, there are some cases when data compression is not appropriate. The following should be considered when looking at whether or not to compress data:

- Does the table exist in an OLTP or data warehousing environment? Data compression is best suited for data that is updated infrequently or, better yet, is read-only. Since most data in a data warehouse is considered read-only, data compression is more compatible with this type of environment.

- Does the table have many foreign keys? Foreign keys result in a lot of duplicate values in data. Tables with these structures are ideal candidates for data compression.

- How will data be loaded into the table? Even when compression is enabled, data is only compressed during bulk loading (for example, SQL*Loader). If data is loaded using a standard insert into statement, the data will not be compressed.

Compression can be specified for various data-related objects using the create or alter object commands. Table 9-13 identifies these objects and their first-level parent object, from which default compression properties are inherited if not specified for the base object. For example, if no compression property is specified for a table, it

Object Type	Compression Property Inheritance Parent
Table	Tablespace
Materialized View	Tablespace
Partition	Table

TABLE 9-13. *Compression Property Inheritance*

will inherit the property from its tablespace. The same applies to a data partition—if not specified at the partition level, the default property from the table will be used.

The following listing demonstrates the creation of a table with compression enabled. Line 7 contains the keyword compress to tell Oracle that data compression is to be enabled:

```
1 create table commission (
2  sales_rep_id     number,
3  prod_id          number,
4  comm_date        date,
5  comm_amt         number(10,2))
6 tablespace comm_ts pctfree 5 initrans 1 maxtrans 255
7 compress;
```

Because compression can be enabled or disabled at different points in an object's lifetime (say, by using an alter command), and because the compression action only occurs on new data being loaded, it is possible for an object to contain both compressed and uncompressed data at the same time.

Ask the Expert

Q: Can existing data in a table be compressed and uncompressed?

A: Yes. There are two methods. The first is by using an alter table statement such as

```
alter table sales
move compress;
```

The second method is by using the utilities contained in the dbms_redefinition package.

Index Key Compression

Index key compression works in a similar manner to data compression in that duplicated values are removed from the index entries. It's a little more complicated, however, because it has more restrictions and considerations than data compression, partly due to the way indexes are structured. Since the details of these structures are beyond the scope of this book, you will focus on the benefits of, and the mechanisms for, defining index compression.

Compressing indexes offers the same benefits as data compression—that is, reduced storage and improved (usually) performance. However, performance may suffer during index scans as the burden on the CPU is increased in order to rebuild the key values. One restriction we should mention is that index compression cannot be used on a unique index that has only one attribute.

Enabling index compression is done using the create index statement. If you need to compress or uncompress an existing index, you must drop the index first and then re-create it with or without the compression option enabled. The following listing illustrates the syntax for creating a compressed index. Table 9-14 provides an explanation of the syntax:

```
1 create index comm_sr_prod_idx
2  on commission (sales_rep_id, prod_id)
3  compress 1;
```

Using data and index compression can provide substantial benefits in the areas of storage and performance. In the next section, you will see how to improve query performance using Oracle Database 11*g*'s parallel processing options.

Lines	Important Points
1–2	This specifies that the index is to be created on columns sales_rep_id and prod_id.
3	This specifies that the index is to be compressed, with the number of prefixing (leading) columns to compress. In this case, you used a value of 1 to indicate that duplicate values of the first column, sales_rep_id, are to be removed.

TABLE 9-14.   *Explanation of Index Compression Syntax*

CRITICAL SKILL 9.4

Use Parallel Processing to Improve Performance

Improving performance (and by this we usually mean query performance) is always a hot item with database administrators and users. One of the best and easiest ways to boost performance is to take advantage of the parallel processing option offered by Oracle Database 11*g* (Enterprise Edition only).

Using normal (that is, serial) processing, the data involved in a single request (for example, user query) is handled by one database process. Using *parallel processing,* the request is broken down into multiple units to be worked on by multiple database processes. Each process looks at only a portion of the total data for the request. Serial and parallel processing are illustrated in Figures 9-5 and 9-6, respectively.

Parallel processing can help improve performance in situations where large amounts of data need to be examined or processed, such as scanning large tables, joining large tables, creating large indexes, and scanning partitioned indexes. In order to realize the benefits of parallel processing, your database environment should not already be running at, or near, capacity. Parallel processing requires more processing, memory, and I/O resources than serial processing. Before implementing parallel processing, you may need to add hardware resources. Let's forge ahead by looking at the Oracle Database 11*g* components involved in parallel processing.

Parallel Processing Database Components

Oracle Database 11*g*'s parallel processing components are the *parallel execution coordinator* and the *parallel execution servers.* The parallel execution coordinator is responsible for breaking down the request into as many processes as specified by the request. Each process is passed to a parallel execution server for execution during which only a portion of the total data is worked on. The coordinator then assembles the results from each server and presents the complete results to the requester.

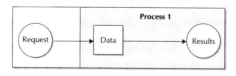

FIGURE 9-5. *Oracle serial processing*

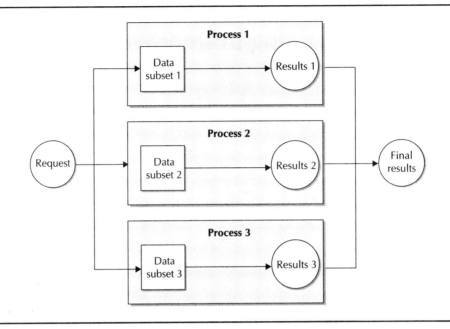

FIGURE 9-6. *Oracle parallel processing*

Parallel Processing Configuration

Generally, not much configuration is required for Oracle Database 11*g* to perform parallel processing. There are, however, a number of configuration options that are required and will affect the effectiveness of parallelism.

To begin with, parallel processing is enabled by default for DDL (for example, create and alter) and query (for example, select) commands, but disabled for DML (say, insert, update, delete, merge) commands. If you wish to execute a DML command in parallel mode, you must first issue the following command for the session in which the command is to be executed, as in the following:

```
alter session enable parallel dml;
```

Several database initialization parameters affect parallel processing. These are shown next. When an Oracle instance starts, the parameters in the initialization file are used to define or specify the settings for the instance. Table 9-15 identifies the initialization parameters that affect parallel processing. In many cases, the default values will provide adequate results for your large database. Specifics of your own environment will influence your decisions on the best values to use.

Parameter	Default Setting	Comment
PARALLEL_ADAPTIVE_MULTI_USER	True	When set to True, this enables an adaptive algorithm designed to improve performance in multiuser environments that use parallel processing.
PARALLEL_AUTOMATIC_TUNING	False	This is no longer used. Exists for backward compatibility only.
PARALLEL_EXECUTION_MESSAGE_SIZE	Installation Dependent	This specifies the byte size of messages for parallel processing.
PARALLEL_INSTANCE_GROUP	Installation Dependent	This is used in Real Application Cluster environments to restrict parallel query operations to a limited number of database instances.
PARALLEL_MAX_SERVERS	# of CPUs available to the database instance	This specifies maximum number of parallel processes for the database instance.
PARALLEL_MIN_PERCENT	0	This specifies minimum percentage of parallel processes required for parallel processing. Value is a percentage of PARALLEL_MAX_SERVERS.
PARALLEL_MIN_SERVERS	0	This specifies minimum number of parallel processes for the database instance. Cannot be greater than value of PARALLEL_MAX_SERVERS.
PARALLEL_THREADS_PER_CPU	Usually set to 2, depending on operating system	This specifies the number of parallel processes per CPU.

TABLE 9-15. *Initialization Parameters Affecting Parallel Processing*

As you can see from Table 9-15, there are dependencies between parameters. Modifying one may necessitate modifying others. If you modify any of the parallel processing parameters, you may also have to modify the following database/instance parameters:

- INSTANCE GROUPS
- PROCESSES

- SESSIONS

- TRANSACTIONS

Invoke Parallel Execution

Parallel execution can be applied to tables, views, and materialized views. Assuming all necessary configurations have been made, there are several ways to invoke parallel execution. The first way is during table creation (including materialized views), using the parallel clause. If the table is being created using the results of a subquery, the loading of the table will be parallelized. In addition, by default, all queries that are executed against the table will be parallelized to the same extent. The next listing shows an example of specifying the parallel option for a table creation:

```
1 create table commission (
2  sales_rep_id    number,
3  prod_id         number,
4  comm_date       date,
5  comm_amt        number(10,2))
6 tablespace comm_ts
7 parallel;
```

The important line here is Line 7, specifying the parallel clause. This line could also have included an integer to specify the *degree of parallelism*—that is, the number of processes that are to be used to execute the parallel process. As the degree of parallelism is omitted in this example, the number of processes used will be calculated as the number of CPUs × the value of the PARALLEL_THREADS_PER_CPU initialization parameter. The degree of parallelism for a table or materialized view can be changed using an alter statement.

Parallel processing can also be invoked when the parallel hint is used in a select statement. This hint will override any default parallel processing options specified during table creation. The following listing illustrates the use of the parallel hint. Line 1 contains the parallel hint, specifying the table to be parallelized (commission) and the degree of parallelism (4):

```
1 select /*+ parallel (commission, 4) */
2   prod_id, sum(comm_amt), count(*)
3 from commission
4 group by prod_id;
```

In some cases, Oracle Database 11*g* will alter how, or if, parallel processing is executed. Examples of these include the following:

- Parallel processing will be disabled for DML commands (for example, insert, update, delete, and merge) on tables with triggers or referential integrity constraints.

- If a table has a bitmap index, DML commands are always executed using serial processing if the table is non-partitioned. If the table is partitioned, parallel processing will occur, but Oracle will limit the degree of parallelism to the number of partitions affected by the command.

Parallel processing can have a significant positive impact on performance. Impacts on performance are even greater when you combine range- or hash-based partitioning with parallel processing. With this configuration, each parallel process can act on a particular partition. For example, if you had a table partitioned by month, the parallel execution coordinator could divide the work up according to those partitions. This way, partitioning and parallelism work together to provide results even faster.

CRITICAL SKILL 9.5
Use Materialized Views

So far, you have reviewed several features and techniques at your disposal for improving performance in large databases. In this section, we will discuss another feature of Oracle Database 11g that you can include in your arsenal: materialized views.

Originally called snapshots, *materialized views* were introduced in Oracle8 and are only available in the Enterprise Edition. Like a regular view, the data in a materialized view are the results of a query. However, the results of a regular view are transitory—they are lost once the query is complete and if needed again, the query must be re-executed. In contrast, the results from a materialized view are kept and physically stored in a database object that resembles a table. This feature means that the underlying query only needs to be executed once and then the results are available to all who need them.

From a database perspective, materialized views are treated like tables:

- You can perform most DML and query commands such as insert, delete, update and select.

- They can be partitioned.

- They can be compressed.

- They can be parallelized.

- You can create indexes on them.

Materialized views are different in other ways and have some interesting features associated with them. Before we talk about those, let's look at some ways to use materialized views.

Uses for Materialized Views

Materialized views are used as a performance enhancing technique. Following are some usage examples. In this section, you will learn about the first four uses, as they are applicable to the topic of large databases.

- Performing data summarization (for example, sums, averages)
- Prejoining tables
- Performing CPU-intensive calculations
- Replicating and distributing data

In large databases, particularly data warehousing environments, there is always a need to summarize, join, perform calculations, or do all three at once on large numbers of records for the purposes of reporting and analysis. To improve performance in the past, a combination of views and physical tables were usually implemented that contained the results of these operations. The summary tables would require some type of extraction, transformation, and load (ETL) process to populate and refresh them. In addition to the base tables containing the detailed data, the users would need to know which combinations of the views and/or summary tables to use. These structures are illustrated in Figure 9-7.

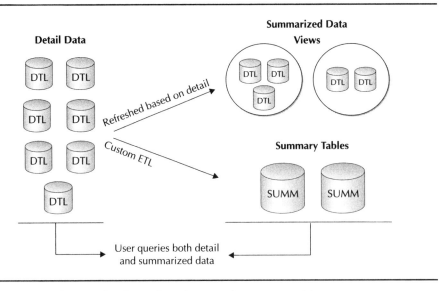

FIGURE 9-7. *Summarization using views and summary tables*

Using materialized views has several advantages over more traditional methods. These include the following:

- Materialized views have a built-in data refresh process, which can provide an automatic update or repopulation of a materialized view without any programming on the part of the DBA.

- As mentioned earlier, the data in materialized views can be partitioned, using the same techniques that apply to tables.

- Materialized views are transparent to the users. This is probably the most attractive feature of using materialized views, and we will expand more on this in the next section when we discuss automatic query rewriting.

Figure 9-8 illustrates summarization using materialized views.

Query Rewrite

Earlier, you learned that one of the benefits of using materialized views was that they are transparent to the users. But what exactly does that mean and how can they be used if the users can't see them? In fact, because materialized views are so much like tables, you can give the users access to materialized views, though generally this is not done.

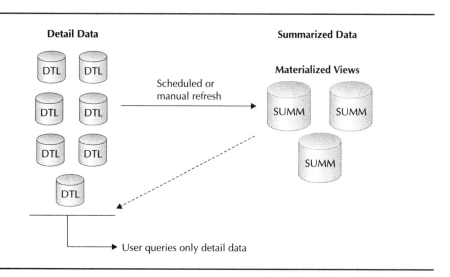

FIGURE 9-8. *Summarization using materialized views*

Instead, as indicated in Figure 9-8, the users always query the tables with the detail data—they don't usually query the materialized views directly. This is because the query optimizer in Oracle Database 11*g* knows about the materialized views and their relationships to the detail tables and can rewrite the query on the fly to access the materialized views instead. This results in huge performance gains without the user having to do anything special—just query the detail data. There is a maintenance benefit of this feature for the user as well: the queries do not have to change to point to different summary tables, as is the case with the more traditional summarization approach.

In order for the query to be rewritten, the structure of the materialized view must satisfy the criteria of the query. The following two listings demonstrate the query rewrite process. Let's assume you need to summarize the COMMISSION table you saw in the data compression section using the following query:

```
select prod_id, to_char(comm_date, 'YYYY-MM'), count(*), sum(comm_amt)
from commission
group by prod_id, to_char(comm_date, 'YYYY-MM');
```

Assume further that a materialized view (called comm_prod_mv) exists that contains summarized commission data by sales_rep_id, prod_id, and comm_date (full date). In this case, the query would be automatically rewritten as follows:

```
select prod_id, to_char(comm_date, 'YYYY-MM'), count(*), sum(comm_amt)
from comm_prod_mv
group by prod_id, to_char(comm_date, 'YYYY-MM');
```

By rewriting the query to use the materialized view instead, a large amount of data-crunching has been saved and the results will return much more quickly. Now turn your attention to determining what materialized views should be created.

When to Create Materialized Views

At this point, you may be asking yourself: "How do I determine what materialized views to create and at what level of summarization?" Oracle Database 11*g* has some utilities to help. These utilities are collectively called the SQLAccess Advisor and will recommend materialized views based on historical queries, or based on theoretical scenarios. They can be run from the Oracle Enterprise Manager Grid Control (OEM) or by calling the dbms_advisor package.

Create Materialized Views

Materialized views are created using a create materialized view statement, which is similar to a create table statement. This can be performed using SQL Developer, SQL*Plus, or OEM. The following listing shows a simple example of how to create the comm_prod_mv materialized view mentioned earlier and Table 9-16 provides an explanation of the syntax:

```
1 create materialized view comm_prod_mv
2    tablespace comm_prod_mv_ts
3    storage (initial 50k next 50k)
4    refresh complete  next sysdate + 7
5    enable query rewrite
6 as select sales_rep_id, prod_id, comm_date, count(*), sum(comm_amt)
7    from commission
8    group by sales_rep_id, prod_id, comm_date;
```

In the next three sections, you will learn about some higher-level concepts: Real Application Clusters, Automatic Storage Management, and Grid Computing. But first, complete this progress check.

Lines	Important Points
2–3	This specifies the tablespace and storage parameters.
4	This specifies how and when to refresh the data. In this case, the materialized view will be populated immediately and be completely refreshed every seven days thereafter.
5	This specifies that query rewrite is to be enabled.
6–8	This specifies the query that will act as the source of the data.

TABLE 9-16.   *Explanation of Materialized View Creation Syntax*

Progress Check

1. True or False: Tables with many foreign keys are good candidates for compression.

2. Name the two processing components involved in Oracle Database 11*g*'s parallel processing.

3. What is the function of the SQLAccess Advisor?

4. True or False: In order to access the data in a materialized view, a user or application must query the materialized view directly?

5. List the ways in which parallel processing can be invoked.

6. In what situation can index key compression *not* be used on a unique index?

CRITICAL SKILL 9.6

Use SQL Aggregate and Analysis Functions

Once your database has been loaded with data, your users or applications will, of course, want to use that data to run queries, perform analysis, produce reports, extract data, and so forth. Oracle Database 11*g* provides many sophisticated aggregation and analysis functions that can help ease the pain sometimes associated with analyzing data in large databases.

Aggregation Functions

Oracle Database 11*g* provides extensions to the standard SQL group by clause of the select statement that generate other totals as part of the result set that previously required multiple queries, nested subqueries, or importing into spreadsheet type applications. These extensions are rollup and cube.

Progress Check Answers

1. True.

2. The parallel execution coordinator and the parallel execution servers.

3. The SQLAccess Advisor recommends potential materialized views based on historical or theoretical scenarios.

4. False. While the end user or application can query the materialized view directly, usually the target of a query is the detail data and Oracle's query rewrite capabilities will automatically return the results from the materialized view instead of the detail table (assuming the materialized view meets the query criteria).

5. Parallel processing can be invoked based on the parallelism specified for a table at the time of its creation, or by providing the parallel hint in a select query.

6. If the unique index has only one attribute, key compression cannot be used.

rollup

The rollup extension generates subtotals for attributes specified in the group by clause, plus another row representing the grand total. The following is an example of the rollup extension, using the SALES table you have seen throughout this chapter:

```
select c.cust_gender gender,
       b.channel_class channel_class,
       to_char(a.time_id, 'yyyy-mm') month,
       count(*) unit_count,
       sum(a.amount_sold) amount_sold
from sales a, channels b, customers c
where a.channel_id = b.channel_id
and   a.cust_id = c.cust_id
and   to_char(a.time_id, 'yyyy-mm') between '2001-01' and '2001-02'
group by rollup(c.cust_gender,
                b.channel_class,
                to_char(a.time_id, 'yyyy-mm'));
```

GENDER	CHANNEL_CLASS	MONTH	UNIT_COUNT	AMOUNT_SOLD
F	Direct	2001-01	4001	387000.9
F	Direct	2001-02	3208	365860.13
F	Direct		7209	752861.03
F	Others	2001-01	2486	242615.9
F	Others	2001-02	2056	229633.52
F	Others		4542	472249.42
F	Indirect	2001-01	1053	138395.21
F	Indirect	2001-02	1470	189425.88
F	Indirect		2523	327821.09
F			14274	1552931.54
M	Direct	2001-01	7038	719146.28
M	Direct	2001-02	6180	641192.61
M	Direct		13218	1360338.89
M	Others	2001-01	4310	414603.03
M	Others	2001-02	3751	391792.61
M	Others		8061	806395.64
M	Indirect	2001-01	1851	211947.81
M	Indirect	2001-02	2520	285219.79
M	Indirect		4371	497167.6
M			25650	2663902.13
			39924	4216833.67

In the results, we can see that counts and sums of amount_sold are returned at the following levels:

- By GENDER, CHANNEL_CLASS, and MONTH
- Subtotals by CHANNEL_CLASS within GENDER

- Subtotals by GENDER
- Grand total

cube

The cube extension takes rollup a step further by generating subtotals for each combination of the group by attributes, totals by attribute, and the grand total. The following is an example of the cube extension, using the same query you used for rollup:

```
select c.cust_gender gender,
       b.channel_class channel_class,
       to_char(a.time_id, 'yyyy-mm') month,
       count(*) unit_count,
       sum(a.amount_sold) amount_sold
from sales a, channels b, customers c
where a.channel_id = b.channel_id
and    a.cust_id = c.cust_id
and    to_char(a.time_id, 'yyyy-mm') between '2001-01' and '2001-02'
group by cube(c.cust_gender,
              b.channel_class,
              to_char(a.time_id, 'yyyy-mm'));
```

GENDER	CHANNEL_CLASS	MONTH	UNIT_COUNT	AMOUNT_SOLD
			39924	4216833.67
		2001-01	20739	2113709.13
		2001-02	19185	2103124.54
	Direct		20427	2113199.92
	Direct	2001-01	11039	1106147.18
	Direct	2001-02	9388	1007052.74
	Others		12603	1278645.06
	Others	2001-01	6796	657218.93
	Others	2001-02	5807	621426.13
	Indirect		6894	824988.69
	Indirect	2001-01	2904	350343.02
	Indirect	2001-02	3990	474645.67
F			14274	1552931.54
F		2001-01	7540	768012.01
F		2001-02	6734	784919.53
F	Direct		7209	752861.03
F	Direct	2001-01	4001	387000.9
F	Direct	2001-02	3208	365860.13
F	Others		4542	472249.42
F	Others	2001-01	2486	242615.9
F	Others	2001-02	2056	229633.52
F	Indirect		2523	327821.09

```
F       Indirect              2001-01      1053     138395.21
F       Indirect              2001-02      1470     189425.88
M                                         25650    2663902.13
M                             2001-01     13199    1345697.12
M                             2001-02     12451    1318205.01
M       Direct                           13218    1360338.89
M       Direct                2001-01      7038     719146.28
M       Direct                2001-02      6180     641192.61
M       Others                            8061     806395.64
M       Others                2001-01      4310     414603.03
M       Others                2001-02      3751     391792.61
M       Indirect                          4371      497167.6
M       Indirect              2001-01      1851     211947.81
M       Indirect              2001-02      2520     285219.79
```

In the results, you can see that counts and sums of amount_sold are returned at the following levels:

- By GENDER, CHANNEL_CLASS, and MONTH

- Subtotals by MONTH within CHANNEL_CLASS

- Subtotals by MONTH within GENDER

- Subtotals by CHANNEL_CLASS within GENDER

- Subtotals by MONTH

- Subtotals by CHANNEL_CLASS

- Subtotals by GENDER

- Grand total

Analysis Functions

Oracle Database 11*g* provides a number of ranking and statistical functions that previously would have required some pretty heavy SQL to perform or an extract to a third-party application. In this section, you will look at the analysis function available and examine examples of their use where appropriate.

NOTE
Some of the functions in this section are based on complex statistical calculations. Don't be worried if you are unfamiliar with these concepts. It is more important for you to know that these functions exist than it is to understand the theory behind them.

Ranking Functions

Ranking functions provide the ability to rank a row of a query result relative to the other rows in the result set. Common examples of uses for these functions include identifying the top ten selling products for a period, or classifying or grouping a salesperson's commissions into one of four buckets. The ranking functions included in Oracle Database 11*g* are

- rank
- dense_rank
- cume_dist
- percent_rank
- ntile
- row_number

rank and dense_rank Functions　The simplest ranking functions are rank and dense_rank. These functions are very similar and determine the ordinal position of each row within the query result set. The difference between these two functions is that rank will leave a gap in the sequence when there is a tie for position, whereas dense_rank does not leave a gap. The results of the following listing illustrate the difference between the two:

```
select prod_id,
       sum(quantity_sold),
       rank () over (order by sum(quantity_sold) desc) as rank,
       dense_rank () over (order by sum(quantity_sold) desc) as dense_rank
from sales
where to_char(time_id, 'yyyy-mm') = '2001-06'
group by prod_id;
```

```
   PROD_ID SUM(QUANTITY_SOLD)       RANK DENSE_RANK
---------- ------------------ ---------- ----------
        24                762          1          1
        30                627          2          2
       147                578          3          3
        33                552          4          4
        40                550          5          5
       133                550          5          5
        48                541          7          6
       120                538          8          7
        23                535          9          8
       119                512         10          9
       124                503         11         10
       140                484         12         11
       148                472         13         12
       139                464         14         13
```

123	459	15	14
131	447	16	15
25	420	17	16
135	415	18	17
137	407	19	18
146	401	20	19

As you can see, the ordinal position 6 does not exist as a value for rank, but it does for dense_rank. If from this result set you wanted to see the top ten listings for prod_id, you would use the original query as a subquery, as in the following listing:

```
select * from
  (select prod_id,
         sum(quantity_sold),
         rank () over (order by sum(quantity_sold) desc) as rank,
         dense_rank () over (order by sum(quantity_sold) desc) as dense_rank
  from sales
  where to_char(time_id, 'yyyy-mm') = '2001-06'
  group by prod_id)
where rank < 11;
```

To see the bottom ten prod_ids, use the same query, but change the order by option from descending (desc) to ascending (asc). The next two functions, cume_dist and percent_rank, are statistical in nature but still part of the family of ranking functions, so the important feature is that these functions properly handle ties in the rankings.

cume_dist and percent_rank Functions   The cume_dist function calculates the cumulative distribution of a value in a group of values. Since this is not a statistics beginner's guide, we will not attempt to provide the theoretical background on cumulative distribution. However, we can offer these points:

- The range of values returned by cume_dist is always between 0 and 1.

- The value returned by cume_dist is always the same in the case of tie values in the group.

- The formula for cumulative distribution is

$$\frac{\text{\# of rows with values} <= \text{value of row being evaluated}}{\text{\# of rows being evaluated}}$$

Looking at the query y used when discussing rank, the following listing calculates the cumulative distribution for quantity_sold. The results immediately follow the listing:

```
select prod_id,
    sum(quantity_sold),
    cume_dist () over (order by sum(quantity_sold) asc) as cume_dist
```

```
from sales
where to_char(time_id, 'yyyy-mm') = '2001-06'
group by prod_id
order by sum(quantity_sold) desc;

   PROD_ID SUM(QUANTITY_SOLD)  CUME_DIST
---------- ------------------ ----------
        24                762          1
        30                627 .985915493
       147                578 .971830986
        33                552 .957746479
        40                550 .943661972
       133                550 .943661972
        48                541 .915492958
       120                538 .901408451
        23                535 .887323944
       119                512 .873239437
       124                503 .85915493
       140                484 .845070423
       148                472 .830985915
       139                464 .816901408
       123                459 .802816901
       131                447 .788732394
        25                420 .774647887
       135                415 .76056338
       137                407 .746478873
       146                401 .732394366
```

The percent_rank function is similar to the cume_dist function, but calculates a percentage ranking of a value relative to its group. Again, without getting into the theory, we can make some points about percent_rank:

- The range of values returned by the function is always between 0 and 1.

- The row with a rank of 1 will have a percent rank of 0.

- The formula for calculating percent rank is
$$\frac{\text{rank of row within its group} - 1}{\text{\# of rows in the group} - 1}$$

The next listing and its results demonstrate the percent_rank function using the base query you have been using in this section:

```
select prod_id,
       sum(quantity_sold),
       rank () over (order by sum(quantity_sold) desc) as rank,
       percent_rank ()
               over (order by sum(quantity_sold) asc) as percent_rank
```

```
from sales
where to_char(time_id, 'yyyy-mm') = '2001-06'
group by prod_id
order by sum(quantity_sold) desc;
```

PROD_ID	SUM(QUANTITY_SOLD)	RANK	PERCENT_RANK
24	762	1	1
30	627	2	.985714286
147	578	3	.971428571
33	552	4	.957142857
40	550	5	.928571429
133	550	5	.928571429
48	541	7	.914285714
120	538	8	.9
23	535	9	.885714286
119	512	10	.871428571
124	503	11	.857142857
140	484	12	.842857143
148	472	13	.828571429
139	464	14	.814285714
123	459	15	.8
131	447	16	.785714286
25	420	17	.771428571
135	415	18	.757142857
137	407	19	.742857143
146	401	20	.728571429

The ntile Function The ntile function divides a result set into a number of buckets specified at query time by the user, and then assigns each row in the result set a bucket number. The most common number of buckets used are 3 (tertiles), 4 (quartiles), and 10 (deciles). Each bucket will have the same number of rows, except in the case when the number of rows does not divide evenly by the number of buckets. In this case, each of the leftover rows will be assigned to buckets with the lowest bucket numbers until all leftover rows are assigned. For example, if four buckets were specified and the number of rows in the result set was 98, buckets 1 and 2 would have 25 rows each and buckets 3 and 4 would have 24 rows each.

Let's look at an example. Using your base query of amount_sold in the SALES table, you want to look at amount_sold by product subcategory and rank the amounts into four buckets. Here's the SQL:

```
select b.prod_subcategory,
       sum(a.quantity_sold),
       ntile(4) over (ORDER BY SUM(a.quantity_sold) desc) as quartile
from sales a, products b
where a.prod_id = b.prod_id
and to_char(a.time_id, 'yyyy-mm') = '2001-06'
group by b.prod_subcategory;
```

As you can see in the following results, the number of product subcategories was not evenly divisible by the number of buckets specified (in this case, 4). Therefore, six subcategories were assigned to the first quartile (bucket 1) and five subcategories were assigned to the second, third, and fourth quartiles.

PROD_SUBCATEGORY	COUNT(*)	SUM(A.QUANTITY_SOLD)	QUARTILE
Accessories	3230	3230	1
Y Box Games	2572	2572	1
Recordable CDs	2278	2278	1
Camera Batteries	2192	2192	1
Recordable DVD Discs	2115	2115	1
Documentation	1931	1931	1
Modems/Fax	1314	1314	2
CD-ROM	1076	1076	2
Y Box Accessories	1050	1050	2
Printer Supplies	956	956	2
Memory	748	748	2
Camera Media	664	664	3
Home Audio	370	370	3
Game Consoles	352	352	3
Operating Systems	343	343	3
Bulk Pack Diskettes	270	270	3
Portable PCs	215	215	4
Desktop PCs	214	214	4
Camcorders	196	196	4
Monitors	178	178	4
Cameras	173	173	4

row_number Function   The row_number function is a simple function that assigns a unique number to each row in a result set. The numbers are sequential, starting at 1, and are based on the order by clause of the query.

You will again use your SALES table query as an example. Using the query from your ntile example and adding a new column using row_count, you get

```
select b.prod_subcategory,
       sum(a.quantity_sold),
       ntile(4) over (ORDER BY SUM(a.quantity_sold) desc) as quartile,
       row_number () over (order by sum(quantity_sold) desc) as rownumber
       from sales a, products b
where a.prod_id = b.prod_id
and to_char(a.time_id, 'yyyy-mm') = '2001-06'
group by b.prod_subcategory;
```

In the following results, each row is assigned a number, depending on its position defined by the order by clause. As you can observe, the ROWNUMBER is simply the row position in the list without any intelligence, whereas quartile is a calculated field and could have repeating values:

PROD_SUBCATEGORY	SUM(A.QUANTITY_SOLD)	QUARTILE	ROWNUMBER
Accessories	3230	1	1
Y Box Games	2572	1	2
Recordable CDs	2278	1	3
Camera Batteries	2192	1	4
Recordable DVD Discs	2115	1	5
Documentation	1931	1	6
Modems/Fax	1314	2	7
CD-ROM	1076	2	8
Y Box Accessories	1050	2	9
Printer Supplies	956	2	10
Memory	748	2	11
Camera Media	664	3	12
Home Audio	370	3	13
Game Consoles	352	3	14
Operating Systems	343	3	15
Bulk Pack Diskettes	270	3	16
Portable PCs	215	4	17
Desktop PCs	214	4	18
Camcorders	196	4	19
Monitors	178	4	20
Cameras	173	4	21

Windowing Functions

Before you get into the details, you need to learn a couple of terms: analytic partitioning and analytic window.

- *Analytic partitioning* is the division of the results of an analytic function into groups within which the analytic function operates. This is accomplished using the partition by clause of the analytic function. Do not confuse this partitioning with data partitioning discussed earlier in this chapter. Analytic partitioning can be used with any of the analytic functions we have discussed so far.

- An *analytic window* is a subset of an analytic partition in which the values of each row depend on the values of other rows in the window. There are two types of windows: physical and logical. A physical window is defined by a specified number of rows. A logical window is defined by the order by values.

Windowing functions can only be used in the select and order by clauses. They can be used to calculate the following:

- Moving sum
- Moving average

- Moving min/max

- Cumulative sum

- Statistical functions

Now look at an example of a moving sum function. The following shows the listing and results for calculating the moving sum from the SALES table by product category for a six-month period:

```
select b.prod_category,
       to_char(a.time_id, 'yyyy-mm'),
       sum(a.quantity_sold),
       sum(sum(a.quantity_sold)) over (partition by b.prod_category
                              order by to_char(a.time_id, 'yyyy-mm')
                              rows unbounded preceding) as cume_sum
from sales a, products b
where a.prod_id = b.prod_id
and b.prod_category_id between 202 and 204
and to_char(a.time_id, 'yyyy-mm') between '2001-01' and '2001-06'
group by b.prod_category, to_char(a.time_id, 'yyyy-mm')
order by b.prod_category, to_char(a.time_id, 'yyyy-mm');
```

PROD_CATEGORY	TO_CHAR	SUM(A.QUANTITY_SOLD)	CUME_SUM
Hardware	2001-01	281	281
Hardware	2001-02	306	587
Hardware	2001-03	442	1029
Hardware	2001-04	439	1468
Hardware	2001-05	413	1881
Hardware	2001-06	429	2310
Peripherals and Accessories	2001-01	5439	5439
Peripherals and Accessories	2001-02	5984	11423
Peripherals and Accessories	2001-03	5104	16527
Peripherals and Accessories	2001-04	5619	22146
Peripherals and Accessories	2001-05	4955	27101
Peripherals and Accessories	2001-06	5486	32587
Photo	2001-01	2802	2802
Photo	2001-02	2220	5022
Photo	2001-03	2982	8004
Photo	2001-04	2824	10828
Photo	2001-05	2359	13187
Photo	2001-06	3225	16412

As you can see in the results, the moving sum is contained within each product category and resets when a new product category starts. In the past, windowing analysis used to require third-party products such as spreadsheet applications. Having the capabilities to perform these functions right in the database can streamline analysis and report generation efforts.

Other Functions

There are many other functions included with Oracle Database 11*g* that can be used to analyze data in large databases. While we will not be going into any detail for these, they are listed here for completeness:

- Statistical functions, including:
  - Linear regression functions
  - Descriptive statistics functions
  - Hypothetical testing and crosstab statistics functions (contained a new PL/SQL package called dbms_statistics)
- first/last functions
- lag/lead functions
- Reporting aggregate functions
- Inverse percentile functions
- Hypothetical rank and distribution functions

As was stated earlier, database administrators do not have to know the theory behind the functions provided by Oracle Database 11*g* or even how to use their results. However, you should be able to let your users know what capabilities are available. Knowing this, your users will be able to take advantage of these functions and construct efficient queries. In the next section, you'll learn about a new feature in Oracle Database 11*g*—SQL models.

CRITICAL SKILL 9.7

Create SQL Models

One of the more powerful data analysis features introduced in Oracle Database 11*g* is *SQL models*. SQL models allow a user to create multidimensional arrays from query results. Formulas, both simple and complex, can then be applied to the arrays to generate results in which the user is interested. SQL models allow inter-row calculations to be applied without doing expensive self-joins.

SQL models are similar to other multidimensional structures used in business intelligence applications. However, because they are part of the database, they can take advantage of Oracle Database 11*g*'s built-in features of scalability, manageability security, and so on. In addition, using SQL models, there is no need to transfer large amounts of data to external business intelligence applications.

A SQL model is defined by the model extension of the select statement. Columns of a query result are classified into one of three groups:

- **Partitioning** This is the same as the analytic partitioning defined in the Windowing Functions section.

- **Dimensions** These are the attributes used to describe or fully qualify a measure within a partition. Examples could include product, sales rep id, and phone call type.

- **Measures** These are the numeric (usually) values to which calculations are applied. Examples could include quantity sold, commission amount, and call duration.

One of the main applications of SQL models is projecting or forecasting measures based on existing measures. Let's look at an example of the model clause to illustrate. The listing and its results show an aggregate query using the SALES table:

```
select c.channel_desc, p.prod_category, t.calendar_year year,
       sum(s.quantity_sold) quantity_sold
from sales s, products p, channels c, times t
where s.prod_id = p.prod_id
and    s.channel_id = c.channel_id
and    s.time_id = t.time_id
and    c.channel_desc = 'Direct Sales'
group by c.channel_desc, p.prod_category, t.calendar_year
order by c.channel_desc, p.prod_category, t.calendar_year;


CHANNEL_DESC      PROD_CATEGORY                     YEAR QUANTITY_SOLD
----------------  --------------------------------  ---- -------------
Direct Sales      Electronics                       1998          7758
Direct Sales      Electronics                       1999         15007
...
Direct Sales      Hardware                          2000          1970
Direct Sales      Hardware                          2001          2399
Direct Sales      Peripherals and Accessories       1998         44258
...
Direct Sales      Software/Other                    2000         64483
Direct Sales      Software/Other                    2001         49146
```

In the results, you can see the historical aggregate quantity_sold for each year by product category for the Direct Sales channel. You can use the model clause to project the quantity_sold. In the following listing, you'll project values for 2002 for the product category Hardware in the channel. The quantity_sold will be based on the previous year's value (2001), plus 10 percent. Table 9-17 explains the syntax of the listing:

```
 1 select channel_desc, prod_category, year, quantity_sold
 2 from
 3 (select c.channel_desc, p.prod_category, t.calendar_year year,
 4         sum(s.quantity_sold) quantity_sold
 5  from sales s, products p, channels c, times t
 6  where s.prod_id = p.prod_id
 7  and   s.channel_id = c.channel_id
 8  and   s.time_id = t.time_id
 9  group by c.channel_desc, p.prod_category, t.calendar_year) sales
10 where channel_desc = 'Direct Sales'
11 model
12    partition by (channel_desc)
13    dimension by (prod_category, year)
14    measures (quantity_sold)
15    rules (quantity_sold['Hardware', 2002]
16              = quantity_sold['Hardware', 2001] * 1.10)
17 order by channel_desc, prod_category, year;
```

Lines	Important Points
3–9	This defines an in-line select that will be the source for the query. It is basically the same query you started with before the model clause.
10	This specifies that you are only going to look at Direct Sales channels.
11	This specifies the model clause.
12	This specifies the partition by clause (in this case, channel_desc).
13	This specifies the dimension by clause (here, prod_category and year). These elements will fully qualify the measure within the channel_desc partition.
14	This specifies the measures clause (quantity_sold).
15–16	This specifies the rules clause—that is, calculations you want to perform on the measure. In this example, we are referring to a specific cell of quantity_sold, described by the dimensions prod_category (Hardware) and year (2002).

TABLE 9-17. *Explanation of Model Clause Syntax*

Following are the results of the previous query. Notice that a new row has been added for Hardware in 2002. Its quantity_sold is 2638.9, which is the previous year's value (2399) plus 10 percent:

CHANNEL_DESC	PROD_CATEGORY	YEAR	QUANTITY_SOLD
Direct Sales	Electronics	1998	7758
Direct Sales	Electronics	1999	15007
...			
Direct Sales	Hardware	2000	1970
Direct Sales	Hardware	2001	2399
Direct Sales	Hardware	2002	2638.9
Direct Sales	Peripherals and Accessories	1998	44258
...			
Direct Sales	Software/Other	2000	64483
Direct Sales	Software/Other	2001	49146

The model clause has many variations and allows for very powerful calculations. Let's point out some of the characteristics and/or features you should be aware of. Supported functionalities include the following:

- Looping (for example, FOR loops)

- Recursive calculations

- Regression calculations

- Nested cell references

- Dimension wildcards and ranges

- The model clause does not update any base table, although in theory you could create a table or materialized view from the results of the query using the model clause.

Restrictions include the following:

- The rules clause cannot include any analytic SQL or windowing functions.

- A maximum of 20,000 rules may be specified. This may seem like plenty, but a FOR loop is expanded into many single-cell rules at execution time.

Project 9-2   Use Analytic SQL Functions and Models

Once all the database structures have been put in place and data has been loaded, the users will want to analyze it. Knowing what functions are available is important, and so is their use as well, at least to some extent. So, in this project you will walk through a more complex analytical example that includes using the lag function and creating a SQL model.

Step by Step

1. Create a view of the SALES table using the following listing. (The SALES table should have been created during your Oracle installation process.) This view will calculate the percentage change (called percent_chng) of quantity_sold from one year to the next using the lag function, summarized by prod_category, channel_desc, and calendar_year:

```
create or replace view sales_trends
as
select p.prod_category, c.channel_desc, t.calendar_year year,
       sum(s.quantity_sold) quantity_sold,
       round((sum(s.quantity_sold) -
             lag(sum(s.quantity_sold),1)
                 over (partition by p.prod_category, c.channel_desc
                   order by t.calendar_year)) /
             lag(sum(s.quantity_sold),1)
                 over (partition by p.prod_category, c.channel_desc
                   order by t.calendar_year) *
             100 ,2) as percent_chng
from sales s, products p, channels c, times t
where s.prod_id = p.prod_id
and   s.channel_id = c.channel_id
and   s.time_id = t.time_id
group by p.prod_category, c.channel_desc, t.calendar_year;
```

2. Select from the sales_trends view using the following listing. Notice that quantity_sold and percent_chng reset after each channel_desc. This is a result of the lag function's partition by clauses in the view definition:

```
select prod_category, channel_desc, year, quantity_sold,
percent_chng
from sales_trends
where prod_category = 'Electronics'
order by prod_category, channel_desc, year;
```

3. Select from the sales_trends view using the following listing that contains a model clause. In this query, you are projecting quantity_sold and percent_chng according to the following rules:

   a. Filter the prod_category to only select Electronics.

   b. Project for years 2002 to 2006 inclusive.

   c. The projected quantity_sold is calculated as the previous year's value plus the average percent_chng over the previous three years.

(continued)

d. The projected percent_chng is the average percent_chng over the previous three years:

```
select prod_category, channel_desc, year, quantity_sold, percent_chng
from sales_trends
where prod_category = 'Electronics'
model
   partition by (prod_category, channel_desc)
   dimension by (year)
   measures (quantity_sold, percent_chng)
   rules (
     percent_chng[for year from 2002 to 2006 increment 1] =
       round(avg(percent_chng)[year between currentv()-3 and
                                       currentv()-1], 2),
     quantity_sold[for year from 2002 to 2006 increment 1] =
       round(quantity_sold[currentv()-1] *
         (1 + (round(avg(percent_chng)[year between currentv()-3 and
                                       currentv()-1] ,2) / 100))))
order by prod_category, channel_desc, year;
```

4. Notice the projected values for 2002 to 2006 for each channel_desc.

Project Summary

The steps in this project build on the discussions you've had on Oracle Database 11*g*'s analytic capabilities. You used the lag function to calculate percentage change and used the model clause of the select statement to project sales five years into the future based on past trends. By going to the next level of examples, you can start to appreciate the significance of these functions and how they can be used.

Oracle Database 11*g*'s analytic functions provide powerful and efficient analysis capabilities that would otherwise require complex SQL and/or third-party tools. All of these functions are part of the core database—ready and waiting to be exploited by your users.

So, now you have come to the end of your exploration of large database features. A great deal of material has been presented in this chapter and you have really only seen the tip of the iceberg! However, you can feel confident that with this background information, you are primed to tackle almost any large database environment out there.

☑ Chapter 9 Mastery Check

1. What data population methods can be used on a compressed table that results in the data being compressed?

2. What are the three basic types of partitioning?

3. _____ partitioned indexes are defined independently of the data partitions, and _____ partitioned indexes have a one-to-one relationship with the data partitions.

4. Explain the functions of the parallel execution coordinator in parallel processing.

5. For which of the following SQL commands is parallel processing *not* enabled by default?

   A. select

   B. insert

   C. create

   D. alter

6. What is meant by "degree of parallelism"?

7. What analytic feature can be used to forecast values based on existing measures?

8. What two methods can be used to run the SQLAccess Advisor utilities for materialized views?

9. _____ partitioning allows you to control the placement of records in specified partitions based on sets of partition key values.

10. What analytic function would you use to assign each row from a query to one of five buckets?

11. What are the two types of windows that can be used in analytic functions?

12. The _____ automatically collects workload and performance statistics used for database self-management activities.

13. When creating partitioned tables, what option should you use to ensure that rows are redistributed to their correct partition if their partition key is updated?

APPENDIX

Mastery Check Answers

Chapter 1: Database Fundamentals

1. **The _____ background process is primarily responsible for writing information to the Oracle Database 11*g* files.**

   The database writer, or dbw0, background process is primarily responsible for writing information to the Oracle Database 11*g* files.

2. **How many online redo log groups are required to start an Oracle Database 11*g*?**

   A. 3

   B. 2

   C. 4

   D. 1

   B.

   Explanation   The minimum number of redo log groups required to start an Oracle Database 11*g* is two, though many DBAs add more groups than that. This increases the fault tolerance of the database.

3. **Of the following four items of information, which one is not stored in Oracle Database 11*g*'s control files?**

   A. The name of the database files

   B. The creator of the database

   C. The location of the database files

   D. The sizes of the database files

   B.

   Explanation   The creator of the database is not stored anywhere in the assortment of Oracle Database 11*g* support files.

4. **What is the function of a default temporary tablespace in the support of Oracle Database 11*g*?**

   The default temporary tablespace is the location where sessions build intermediary objects to satisfy queries and perform sort operations.

5. **Differentiate between an Oracle Database 11*g* and an instance.**

The database is a collection of files, whereas an instance is a handful of processes working in conjunction with a computer's memory to support access to those files.

6. **Activities such as allocating space in the database and user management are commonly performed by the DBA. What feature in Oracle Database 11g allows some of these secure operations to be carried out by non-DBA users? How are these rights given out?**

System privileges allow the DBA to give out rights for performing selected secure operations to other Oracle Database 11g users. These privileges are given out with a grant statement.

7. **As a user of Oracle Database 11g is created, you often specify a default tablespace. In this context, what does *default tablespace* mean?**

   A. The system tablespace

   B. A tablespace that the user can occupy space in, without a private or public synonym

   C. The tablespace that objects are created in if a location (tablespace) is not explicitly mentioned as a table is created

   C.

   Explanation   Often, when one creates a table, the tablespace that the table resides in is not mentioned. The default tablespace feature ensures that tables created in this way always end up in the correct location.

8. **The _____ GUI interface is used to create a new database.**

The Database Configuration Assistant (or dbca) GUI interface is used to create a new database.

9. **What happens when one tries to store the text "Madagascar" in a field with a specification of varchar2(8)?**

An Oracle error is returned and processing of the offending SQL statement terminates.

10. **What is the most common way one uses triggers in Oracle Database 11g? Give an example of this activity.**

Triggers are most commonly used to perform auditing operations. When an employee's salary is changed, a trigger could record the time, date, and name of the operator who performed the changes.

11. **What programming language, native to Oracle Database 11*g*, is used to create stored objects such as triggers and functions?**

    A. SQL*Plus

    B. OEM Grid Control

    C. Basic

    D. PL/SQL

    D.

    Explanation   PL/SQL, the Oracle Database 11*g* procedural programming language, is what you use to code items such as triggers and stored procedures.

12. **What is the role of the sysaux tablespace in Oracle Database 11*g*?**

    The sysaux tablespace is a mandatory container holding an assortment of tables that support some of the administrative tasks related to Oracle Database 11*g*.

13. **The clob and blob data types differ in all but one of the following three ways. Which one *does not* apply to the differences between the two data types?**

    A. The clob holds standard alphanumeric data, whereas the blob may store binary information.

    B. The blob contains a time (hour/minute) component, but the clob does not.

    C. The blob contains unstructured freeform data, whereas the rules governing the type of information that can be stored in the clob are more stringent.

    C.

    Explanation   As much as possible, system architects stick with the clob data type. It is much easier to work with than its close relative—the blob data type.

14. **There are many ways to replicate data from one node to another. What main feature does Oracle Streams provide that is missing from many other methods?**

    Oracle Streams can keep one node's data in sync with another, which is an almost insurmountable chore in many do-it-yourself solutions.

15. **What does the acronym SQL stand for?**

    A. Structured Query Language

    B. Simple Query Language

    C. Straightforward Question-based Learning

A.

Explanation   SQL is the industry standard for many relational database systems. Interestingly enough, as you become more familiar with its syntax, it reads very much like plain and simple English. This makes it even more attractive as a data retrieval language.

Chapter 2: Installing Oracle

1. **How much disk space is needed for installing Oracle software on Linux?**

   The software requires between 3.5 to 5GB, just for the binaries. You also need to add space for your data needs.

2. **What users and groups are used for installing the Oracle software?**

   The user that is needed is the *oracle* user. The groups that are needed include *oinstall* and *dba*.

3. **True or false: Installing Oracle software will automatically install an Oracle database.**

   False.

   Explanation   This is an option and is not automatic.

4. **What are the prerequisites for installing Oracle software?**

   You need to review OS requirements, hardware requirements (1GB RAM), disk space, kernel parameters, and needed OS packages before installing the Oracle software and database.

5. **What are the types of installation options for the Oracle software?**

   Standard, Enterprise, and Custom

6. **What is the Oracle home directory? Can there be more than one?**

   The Oracle home directory is where the Oracle software is installed. Yes, there could be a different Oracle Home for each version of the Oracle software or different options that are installed in each Oracle Home.

7. **Besides the database, what are some of the other products that are installed by default?**

   SQL Developer, Database Vault, Configuration Manager, Application Express, and Warehouse Builder are installed during the standard installation of the Oracle database.

8. **What is the tool for creating a database, after the Oracle software install?**

   The tool that is provided to create a database is named the Database Configuration Assistant (dbca).

9. **What is the default password for SYS and SYSTEM users in the database?**

   Whatever password is chosen for the database during creation will be the password for these accounts; the passwords can all be set the same or they can be each be different and may be changed after logging into the database.

10. **Which scripts need to be run by root (system administrator) after the install of the software?**

    The scripts that need to be run after installing the Oracle software on Linux or UNIX are named: root.sh and orainstRoot.sh.

Chapter 3: Connecting to Oracle

1. **The _____ background process registers the service information to the listener.**

   The PMON background process registers the service information to the listener.

2. **True or false: The LOCAL_LISTENER parameter should be set to work with port 1521.**

   False.

   Explanation   The LOCAL_LISTENER parameter is defined when port 1521 is not used.

3. **The _____ is used during installation to configure Oracle Net Services.**

   The Oracle Net Configuration Assistant is used during installation to configure Oracle Net Services.

4. **The _____ file can be used to define grant or deny access to the Oracle database server.**

   The sqlnet.ora file can be used to define, grant, or deny access to the Oracle database server.

5. **The _____ utility can also be used to test a service.**

   The tnsping utility can also be used to test a service.

6. **A _____ contains a set of parameters that define Oracle Net options on the remote or database server.**

A profile contains a set of parameters that define Oracle Net options on the remote or database server.

7. **The ldap.ora file location can be manually specified with the _____ or TNS_ADMIN environmental variables.**

   The ldap.ora file location can be manually specified with the LDAP_ADMIN or TNS_ADMIN environmental variables.

8. **True or false: The easy naming method is a valid naming method.**

   True.

   Explanation   The easy naming method is a valid naming method.

9. **The Oracle LDAP directory is called the _____.**

   The Oracle LDAP directory is called the Oracle Internet Directory.

10. **True or false: The Oracle Management Service is a repository of information generated by the Management Agent.**

    False.

    Explanation   The Oracle Management Service interfaces with the management agents to process and monitor information. It is not the repository.

Chapter 4: SQL: Structured Query Language

1. **DDL and DML translate to _____ and _____, respectively.**

   DDL stands for Data Definition Language. DML stands for Data Manipulation Language.

2. **Which of the following descriptions is true about insert statements?**

   A. Insert statements must always have a where clause.

   B. Insert statements can never have a where clause.

   C. Insert statements can optionally include a where clause.

   B.

   Explanation   Insert statements can *never* have a where clause. Every insert will create a row, providing it doesn't violate any constraints.

3. In addition to the two mandatory keywords required to retrieve data from the database, there are three optional keywords. Name them.

The optional parts of a select statement are the where clause, an order by clause, and a group by clause.

4. Write a SQL statement to select the customer last name, city, state, and amount sold for the customer represented by customer ID 100895.

Possible solutions include any of the Oracle and ANSI join options. The following SQL statement joins the CUSTOMERS and SALES tables using a simple Oracle join:

```
SQL> select cust_last_name, cust_city, cust_state_province,
  2            amount_sold
  3  from    customers c, sales s
  4  where   c.cust_id = s.cust_id
  5  and     c.cust_id = 100895;
```

5. Retrieve a list of all product categories, subcategories, names, and list prices where the list price is greater than $100 while displaying the results for the product category all in uppercase.

The following statement returns a list of all product categories, subcategories, and names for products with list prices greater than $100. The product categories are also all output in uppercase:

```
SQL> select UPPER(prod_category),
  2            prod_subcategory,
  3            prod_name,
  4            prod_list_price
  5  from    products
  6  where   prod_list_price > 100;
```

6. Rewrite the query from the previous question and round the amount sold so that there are no cents in the display of the list prices.

The following SQL statement alters the previous answer to return the list price without cents:

```
SQL> select UPPER(prod_category),
  2            prod_subcategory,
  3            prod_name,
  4            round(prod_list_price,0)
  5  from    products
  6  where   prod_list_price > 100;
```

7. Retrieve a list of all customer IDs and last names where the customer has more than 200 entries in the SALES table.

The list of all customer IDs and last names for customers that had more than 200 sales is returned by the following SQL statement:

```
SQL> select c.cust_id, cust_last_name, count(*)
  2  from    customers c, sales s
  3  where   c.cust_id = s.cust_id
  4  group by c.cust_id, cust_last_name
  5  having count(*) > 200;
```

8. **Display the product name of all products that have the lowest list price.**

   To display all the product names that have the lowest list price, the following SQL statement would be used:

```
SQL> select prod_name
  2  from    products
  3  where   prod_list_price = (select min(prod_list_price)
  4                             from    products);
```

9. **Create a view that contains all products in the Electronics category.**

   The DDL to create a view with only Electronics products could be created this way:

```
SQL> create view electronics_products
  2  as
  3  select prod_name
  4  from    products
  5  where   prod_category = 'Electronics';
```

10. **Sequences provide _____ generated integers.**

    Sequences provide sequentially generated integers. Without this valuable object, sequentially generated numbers could only be produced programmatically.

11. **This referential integrity constraint defines the relationship between two tables. Name it.**

    A foreign key is the referential integrity constraint that relates two tables to each other.

12. **Check constraints enable users to define and enforce rules for:**

    A. One or more tables

    B. No more than one column

    C. One or more columns

    D. Only one table

    C.

    Explanation   Check constraints enable users to define and enforce rules individually for one or more columns within a table.

13. **Deferred constraints are not checked until the _____ statement is issued.**

Deferred constraints are not checked until the commit keyword statement is executed.

Chapter 5: PL/SQL

1. **Where is PL/SQL executed?**

   PL/SQL is executed within the confines of the database. It will receive parameters and return data, but all program execution is performed in the database.

2. **Which type of PL/SQL statement would you use to increase the price values by 15 percent for items with more than 1500 in stock and by 20 percent for items with fewer than 500 in stock?**

   A. A cursor FOR loop

   B. An **IF/THEN/ELSE** command

   C. An insert statement

   D. An update statement

   B.

   Explanation   To be able to perform a validation of your data and then perform one task if the condition is met and another when the condition is not met, you must use the IF/THEN/ELSE construct.

3. **What is the fetch command used for?**

   The fetch command is used to retrieve data from an open cursor that had been opened previously.

4. **What will the following command do?**

   ```
   V_PRICE_TOLERANCE := 500;
   ```

   It will set the value of the variable to 500.

5. **What is wrong with this function definition?**

   ```
   CREATE OR REPLACE FUNCTION raise_price
       (original_price IN NUMBER)
   RETURN number
   IS
   BEGIN
       RETURN (original_price * 1.25);
   END lower_price;
   ```

   The END clause needs to have the same name as the name of the procedure. This value should be raise_price, not lower_price.

6. **What is the advantage of using the %TYPE attribute when defining PL/SQL variables?**

   The advantage of using the %TYPE attribute when defining PL/SQL variables is that it links the definition of the variable to the database definition. It also allows a program to adjust for changes to database structures while impacting the execution of the PL/SQL program.

7. **What Oracle Database 11g facility, besides PL/SQL, supports exception handling based on error numbers?**

   No other Oracle Database 11g facility besides PL/SQL supports exception handling based on error numbers.

8. **A commit that is issued in a PL/SQL program will commit what?**

   All transactions that are currently pending will be committed, unless the commit is issued within an autonomous transaction.

Chapter 6: The Database Administrator

1. **What is the benefit of a role?**

   A *role* is used to group privileges together so that the group (called a role) can be granted to Oracle. Beyond the management savings, think about the savings that are achieved in the catalog. If we give the same 2000 grants to 3000 users, we would have 6,000,000 grants stored in the database. If they were put into a single role, however, there would be only 3000 grants. An extreme example perhaps, but it illustrates the point.

2. **Should a table that is in tens or hundreds of extents be reorganized?**

   No.

   Explanation   Do not reorganize (reorg) tables unless you need to. The tables' extents are a contiguous set of blocks and if these are large enough, having many extents will not impact performance. You only need to reorg a table when there are a large number of chained rows. You can also consider reorging once your table is in thousands of extents.

3. **What is the preferred method for collecting object statistics?**

   In Oracle Database 11g, use an automatic statistics collection whenever possible.

   Explanation   Setting the Oracle Database 11g initialization parameter statistics_level to typical (the default) allows Oracle to automatically update statistics as a background task. In pre–Oracle Database 10g releases, the DBMS_STATS package should be run manually.

4. **What is a segment?**

   Each segment is a single instance of a table, partition, cluster, or index or a temporary or undo segment. A segment is broken down further into extents.

5. **What is an extent?**

   An extent is a collection of contiguous data blocks that all belong to the same segment. One or more extents can exist for a single segment. New extents can be added to the segment as long as space allows.

6. **Name two reasons for implementing an index.**

   Indexes are optional objects built on tables to improve performance and/or to help implement integrity constraints such as primary keys and uniqueness.

7. **How can you place a database in maintenance mode without first shutting it down?**

   SYS and SYSTEM users can query the database without stopping the database and performing a subsequent startup restrict using the command alter session quiesce restrict when the Database Resource Manager option has been set up. The activities of other users continue until they become inactive.

8. **How can you limit the resources that a particular user can consume and how does this work?**

   You can use the Profile feature to do some of this, but profiles are now being used more to manage password policies than system resources. The preferred approach is to use the Database_Resource_Manager package to limit system resources such as CPU, parallelism, undo pool space, execution time limits, and the number of sessions that can be active for a group.

   A resource plan schedule can be used to schedule when groups will be enabled and disabled. Group switching can move a user to another group once a specified threshold has been met.

9. **When managing undo segments, what are the things that you need to think about?**

   You need to first determine the length of time that undo will need to be retained for. Once you have decided this, you'll need to calculate the undo tablespace size based on system activity.

10. **What is likely to happen if you turn on the autoextend property for undo and temporary tablespaces with a maxsize set to unlimited?**

    They will continue to grow indefinitely until they eventually use up all of the space in the directory.

11. **What is special about the SYS user account and how does it differ from SYSTEM?**

The SYS account is used as the schema to store the Oracle catalog. This has the DBA role as well as the SYSDBA privilege. The SYSTEM account also has the DBA role but not the SYSDBA privilege.

12. What are temporary tablespaces used for?

They store internal data used by Oracle while queries are running. Sort operations make use of the temporary tablespace if there is not enough room in the SGA to perform the sort operation. Data in temporary tablespaces is transient and not persistent. As soon as a transaction has completed, the data in the temporary tablespace can no longer be used. It can be thought of as a scratch pad area for Oracle.

13. What are the two aspects of security that are covered in Oracle's implementation?

Two key security aspects that must be implemented are authentication and authorization. Creating a distinct user in Oracle accomplishes authentication in that the user must be authenticated when they enter the database and we must know who they are. Once in the database, they still need to be authorized to access objects and resources. This is accomplished by granting privileges to the user.

14. Name and describe the types of privileges that can be granted to a user.

Two types of privileges can be given to a user: system and object. System privileges are used to give authority to overall system objects rather than individual ones. The ability to perform a create tablespace is an example of this. Object privileges are a lower-level authority where a named object is granted to a user. Granting select on an individual table is an example of an object privilege.

15. How would you implement your corporate password policy in Oracle?

A profile can be used to implement a password management policy as well as to limit resources for a user. You can specify the number of days after which a user must change their password. You can also establish a policy where a password cannot be used again before a specified number of days has elapsed, and/or the new password must differ from the old by a certain number of changes. A function can also be used to ensure that the user will create a complex password.

Chapter 7: Backup and Recovery

1. What are some advantages of cold backups, and when would you use them?

Cold backups are consistent and very simple to implement. They are useful in situations where the database can be brought down to perform a backup.

No recovery is required after a restore from a cold backup, if you choose not to perform one. You can also perform a cold backup of a database in archivelog mode and perform a recovery of that database. These deliver simplicity and flexibility in cases where you can take a database down to back it up.

2. **What is a disadvantage of cold backups?**

The database is not available during the backup.

3. **Describe the difference between a logical and a physical backup.**

A physical backup is performed by utilities such as RMAN or by a hot or cold backup and operates on the underlying database data files. A logical backup, on the other hand, is performed by utilities such as Data Pump Export or Import and allows for a backup or restore to be performed on logical database structures such as tables or indexes.

4. **Name three different types of backups.**

Three different types of backups are physical, hot and cold backups; logical backups as implemented by Data Pump Export/Import; and RMAN backups.

5. **What is the difference between an RMAN backup and an RMAN image copy?**

Image copies are complete copies of binary data files as they exist in the database. They can be created through a hot or cold backup or by RMAN. Backups are created by RMAN and can only be used by RMAN since they are in a proprietary format. Backups compress unused data blocks, while image copies do not.

6. **Under what situations should redo logs be restored in a recovery situation?**

Redo logs can be restored where a cold backup of a database without archive logging was performed; otherwise, they should not be restored.

7. **Name three interfaces that can be used to perform a Data Pump Export and Import.**

The three interfaces that can be used to perform Data Pump Exports and Imports are the command-line interface, a command-line interface that uses a parameter file called parfile, and an interactive interface.

8. **List some advantages of using RMAN.**

RMAN has many advantages, including the following:

- The ability to perform incremental backups.
- The ability to create backup scripts.
- The ability to compress backups so that only blocks that were written to are backed up.

■ Its tablespaces are not put into backup mode, so no extra redo is generated.

■ Simplified scripting and management of both files and archive logs.

9. Why would RMAN's recovery catalog be used to implement the repository rather than a control file?

RMAN's recovery catalog has many advantages over using a control file. Some of these are:

■ Scripts of common tasks can be created and stored.

■ All backup information, including file names, is stored in the catalog for a longer period of time if needed.

■ Complete reporting capabilities.

■ The ability to recover a control file if it has been lost.

■ Multiple databases can be managed from one backup location.

10. Are there any disadvantages to an RMAN recovery catalog?

One disadvantage to the recovery catalog is that it must be backed up itself. This is simple since it is a very small schema.

11. How can default settings be set up by you for future runs of RMAN?

Default settings can be set up by you with the RMAN configure command. Channels can be configured to achieve optimal performance and other backup configurations can be created to simplify backup and recovery scripts.

12. What is an RMAN backup set, and how does it relate to a backup piece?

A backup set is made up of one or more backup pieces and constitutes a full or incremental backup. A backup piece is a file that is managed by RMAN.

13. Describe the ways in which corrupt blocks can be detected and recovered.

Individual data blocks can be recovered while the database is online and available to users. You need to specify which block can be recovered, which can be found in the alert log or the v$backup_corruption or v$copy_corruption views. Block media recovery is only available with RMAN.

14. What are some advantages to incremental image copies?

Incremental image copies save disk space and network resources since the backup files are smaller. They can also speed up recovery when compared to applying archive logs.

15. **When performing a recovery from a hot backup, do all files and tablespaces need to be brought forward to the same point in time?**

   All files and tablespaces (except for files in read-only tablespaces) need to be brought forward to the same point in time.

Chapter 8: High Availability: RAC, ASM, and Data Guard

1. **Which component is not part of a RAC environment?**

   A. Interconnect

   B. Clusterware

   C. DGMGRL

   D. OCR

   C.

   Explanation   DGMGRL is the command for accessing the Data Guard Broker.

2. **True or false: The Cluster Verification Utility is run after the RAC database is created to verify that the interconnect is running properly.**

   False.

   Explanation   Cluster Verification Utility is run before the install of the Clusterware. This verifies that the environment is configured to have Clusterware installed.

3. **In a RAC environment, OCR stands for**

   A. Oracle Cluster Registry

   B. Oracle Connection Repository

   C. Oracle Clusterware Record

   D. Oracle Cluster Recovery

   A.

4. **In a RAC environment, how many IP addresses are needed for a server?**

   Three. One for each of the following networks: Public, Private, and Virtual.

5. **What is the command-line interface that can be used to copy, back up, and list the files in ASM directories?**

   ASMCMD

6. **True or false: ASM redundancy types are EXTERNAL, HIGH, and LOW.**

   False.

   Explanation   EXTERNAL, HIGH, and NORMAL

7. **When shutdown abort is used to shut down the ASM instance, what happens to the database instances connecting to that ASM instance?**

   They will also shutdown abort.

8. **What is the administrator's login role on the ASM instance?**

   SYSASM

9. **What does the following sqlplus command do? Does it run against the primary or standby server?**

   ```
   SQLPLUS> alter database recover managed standby database using
   current logfile disconnect;
   ```

10. **True or false: Asynchronous transport of redo logs means that the redo is being written to the primary and standby locations at the same time.**

    False. That is true for synchronous transport.

11. **Which of the following is not a characteristic of the Data Guard Protection mode of maximum protection?**

    A. Synchronous transport

    B. Zero data loss

    C. Standby fails, primary is halted

    D. Performance is the biggest concern

    D.

    Explanation   The biggest concern is the data and changes.

12. **Which tools can be used to manage the Data Guard environment?**

    OEM Grid Control or DGMGRL (Data Guard Broker)

Chapter 9: Large Database Features

1. **What data population methods can be used on a compressed table that results in the data being compressed?**

   For data to be compressed, you must either bulk load it into the table or issue an alter table statement to compress existing data.

2. **What are the three basic types of partitioning?**

   RANGE, HASH, and LIST

3. **_____ partitioned indexes are defined independently of the data partitions, and _____ partitioned indexes have a one-to-one relationship with the data partitions.**

   Global partitioned indexes are defined independently of data partitions, and local partitioned indexes have a one-to-one relationship with the data partitions.

4. **Explain the functions of the parallel execution coordinator in parallel processing.**

   The parallel execution coordinator is responsible for breaking down a request into as many processes as specified by the request. After the processes are complete, it then assembles all of the results and presents the complete data set to the requester.

5. **For which of the following SQL commands is parallel processing *not* enabled by default?**

   A. select

   B. insert

   C. create

   D. alter

   B.

   Explanation   Parallel processing is not enabled by default for insert.

6. **What is meant by "degree of parallelism"?**

   "Degree of parallelism" refers to the number of processes that are to be used to execute a parallel process.

7. **What analytic feature can be used to forecast values based on existing measures?**

   The SQL model clause in a select statement can be used to forecast values based on existing measures.

8. **What two methods can be used to run the SQLAccess Advisor utilities for materialized views?**

   OEM or dbms_advisor package can be used to run the SQLAccess Advisor utilities for materialized views.

9. _____ partitioning allows you to control the placement of records in specified partitions based on sets of partition key values.

   List partitioning allows you to control the placement of records in specified partitions based on sets of partition key values.

10. **What analytic function would you use to assign each row from a query to one of five buckets?**

   ntile is used to assign each row from a query to one of five buckets.

11. **What are the two types of windows that can be used in analytic functions?**

   Physical and logical windows are the two types of windows that can be used in analytic functions.

12. **The _____ automatically collects workload and performance statistics used for database self-management activities.**

   The Automatic Workload Repository automatically collects workload and performance statistics used for database self-management activities.

13. **When creating partitioned tables, what option should you use to ensure that rows are redistributed to their correct partition if their partition key is updated?**

   Use enable row movement in the create table or alter table statements to ensure that rows are redistributed to their correct partition if their partition key is updated.

Index